the
CANADA
CHRONICLES

A Four-year
Hitchhiking Odyssey

Text and Photographs by
Matt Jackson
Summit Studios

National Library of Canada Cataloguing in Publication

Jackson, Matt
      The Canada chronicles : a four-year hitchhiking odyssey / text and photographs by Matt Jackson.

Includes bibliographical references.
ISBN 0-9734671-0-X (bound).-ISBN 0-9734671-2-6 (pbk.)

      1. Jackson, Matt--Travel--Canada. 2. Hitchhiking--Canada.
3. Canada--Description and travel. I. Title.

FC76.J32 2004   917.104'648   C2004-900853-6

Principal Editing by Curtis Foreman
Designed by Kirk Seton, Signet Design Solutions
Map by Roberta Voteary
Printed and bound in Canada

Summit Studios
#105, 2572 Birch St.
Vancouver, BC V6H 2T4
www.summitstudios.biz

This book is lovingly dedicated to my parents, Bud and Sandy Jackson, who've been there for me along every road that I've travelled.

"To look at a thing is very different than seeing a thing. One does not see anything until one sees its beauty."
- Oscar Wilde

Table of Contents

Foreword

By Pat Morrow

Canada is a panoramic nation whose sparse multicultural population is unified by a vast network of roads stretching from sea to sea to sea. And as an adventure journalist, I've travelled my share of roads, both physical and metaphorical.

I've hitched rides on donkey carts at the edge of the Taklamakan Desert in western China, army trucks on Russia's Kamchatka Peninsula, battered taxis that ran on gasoline fumes in the sub-Saharan region of Ghana, twin otters aiming for windswept ice runways in Antarctica and on the back of a float festooned with scantily-clad mulatto women in a samba parade in Rio de Janeiro. Perhaps the most hair-raising ride of all was courtesy of an Alaska-bound motor home on the Trans-Canada Highway, driven by a morose drunk who had left his wife in Texas and needed someone to spill his guts to.

All these adventures were launched under the thinly veiled guise of trying to make a living with a camera and notepad. But in reality, my motivation was curiosity, which often led me into richly rewarding moments of self-discovery.

Every once in a while, my wife and I receive an enquiry from a keen young writer/photographer intent on learning the dubious secret of how we make a living as freelancers. In the early 1990s we received one such letter with an Ontario postmark. It read something like this:

"Dear Mr. Morrow,

I've just read one of your books and want to let you know how much I admire you and your wife for your magazine articles and books about adventure around the world. I myself am interested in developing photography and writing skills, and I hope to carve out a lifestyle like you and your wife have done. Could we meet someday to discuss what it would take for me to follow a similar career path?"

I responded with my standard off-putting and pragmatic reply that it's really hard to survive in the financially insecure world of adventure journalism. However, in the next sentence I admitted that I couldn't think of a more exciting and rewarding way to make a living while seeing the world at the same time. I suggested that if he was ever near our home in the Rockies, he stop by for a "brewski" (if we weren't off on an assignment that is, which is the case for about six months of every year). If he did, we would give him some firsthand pointers on how to become independently poor.

It's rare that these enquiries lead to forming an acquaintance, so it was a pleasant surprise when our scruffy pen pal actually turned up a few months later. We got a call from a noisy phone booth on the outskirts of town. It was Matt Jackson.

The man appeared at our door with a big smile and even bigger backpack. After lubricating him with several tumblers of cheap red wine he told us he would have been there sooner, but since school had finished he had hitchhiked across Canada. "You save a lot of money and it's a great way to meet people," he confided. And it occurs to me as I write this, it was hitchhiking that brought Matt Jackson to us.

By the time we had unscrewed the cap on the second jug, Matt expounded on his plans to write a travel book with photographs based on his preferred method of travel.

In the novel *Even Cowgirls get the Blues* Tom Robbins invents the ultimate hitchhiker, Sissy Hankshaw. Sissy is born with oversized thumbs, and is so effective with these dexterous appendages that she can even "hitchhike wallpaper".

With his tall, lanky frame, I can imagine the eye-catching figure that Matt strikes as he wields his own thumbs like an Eastern Township's gunslinger. With his leading arm cocked in the direction he's headed and the other resting on his hip, I can see his big smile beaming a message to his would-be chauffeurs that he will accept any ride without prejudice. Almost.

Matt persevered with his dream, and continued his countrywide perambulations for several years. In the end he has gathered enough material for a whole library of road warrior's tales. Lucky for my wife and I he settled in our area, and we've spent many a joyous evening looking at his growing slide collection and hearing his many stories in various stages of development.

Now it's time that he shared those stories and photos with a much larger audience. For any of you who have ever wondered what it would be like to pick up a hitchhiker and to see our country through his eyes, here is your big chance!

Enjoy!

Pat Morrow, Canmore, Alberta

Map of Canada

author's route ━

0   500 Miles

0   500   1000 kilometres

HUDSON BAY

LABRADOR

QUEBEC

NEWFOUNDLAND

Gros Morne National Park

St. John's

Deer Lake

Corner Brook

Port-aux-Basques

ONTARIO

St. Lawrence River

Gulf of St. Lawrence

Douglastown

Caraquet

Cheticamp

Breton Cove

Cambellton

Chicoutimi

Lac-Saint-Jean

Roberval

Burnt Church

P.E.I.

Charlottetown

Borden

Quebec City

Moncton

Pictou

Hwy 11

Fredericton

N.B.

Halifax

pigon

Marathon

Pukaskwa National Park

Thunder Bay

Trans-Canada Hwy

Sudbury

Pembroke

Gatineau

Montreal

Sherbrooke

Saint-Benoit-du-Lac

Bay of Fundy

Yarmouth

Pubnico

NOVA SCOTIA

Lake Superior

Little Current

Algonquin Provincial Park

Ottawa

Manitoulin Island

Peterborough

Lake Huron

Hwy 401

Orangeville

Toronto

Lake Ontario

London

Waterloo

Lake Michigan

Hwy 401

Lake Erie

ATLANTIC OCEAN

New Beginnings

"If you don't know where you're going, how will you know when you get there?"
- Unknown

Chapter 1

Magic Shadows

October 1993 - Calgary, Alberta

The Toyota hatchback didn't look like much from a distance, but when it rattled onto the road shoulder beside me, I could see that it was actually much less. Large flecks of yellow paint were peeling from its rusted exterior, and the guttural reverberations from its muffler would have likely killed any bird or small mammal chancing to stray within a few metres. Still, I wasn't about to refuse the ride. The night before I had been stranded near Calgary's outskirts, and only the kindness of a donut shop employee had spared me the fate of having to sleep in a ditch. I was now feeling grubby and more than a little bleary-eyed. In short, I was itching to get back for some shut-eye at the Lake Louise hotel where I had been working for the last few months. By this time, I would have accepted a ride from pretty much anybody.

Groggy preoccupation with sleep is rarely a good thing—mostly because it tends to lead you into making decisions you wouldn't necessarily make with greater soundness of mind. I paid little attention, for example, to the gaping hole in the floor as I climbed into the vehicle, even though it was large enough that I could have dangled a foot through and touched the pavement. Nor did it alarm me particularly when Jed, the friendly but somewhat scruffy-looking guy behind the wheel, started whizzing at 150 km/hour through a cavalcade of traffic on the Trans-Canada Highway, while dragging at an endless line of cigarettes. Indeed, it was only after an RCMP cruiser pulled us over near Banff—causing Jed to jump from the car with his hands flailing wildly in the air—that I started questioning the wisdom of having accepted a ride from him.

By then, of course, it was too late.

Jed disappeared inside the squad car a few seconds later, and for twenty minutes I sat in his Toyota with all kinds of desperate thoughts running amok through my head. While Jed had climbed into the police vehicle quite willingly, his response to being pulled over for speeding wasn't exactly what you would call "textbook." Was he in trouble with the law? A convict fleeing from his parole officer? As Jed's willing (though entirely ignorant) accomplice, would I eat my next meal behind bars? I had been in his car for only a short time, but aside from his habit of speeding, Jed hardly seemed like a criminal. Indeed, he was on his way to Kamloops to visit family, including a young niece who he had described with great candour and affection.

Eventually the police officer climbed from his car and strolled toward my open window. "Howdy," he said, tilting his brimmed cap back with one hand. "Son, do you realize that you're riding in a stolen vehicle?"

"Uh ... really?" I replied in as stupefied a voice as I could muster. "This is a stolen car?"

The police officer nodded.

"The one I'm sitting in?" I wanted to make sure I had heard him right.

"Yes, the one you're sitting in," the officer said flatly.

In all the time I had been driving with Jed, it hadn't occurred to me once that he might be inclined towards car thievery. He seemed too pleasant for that sort of thing—and really, what sort of crook would get caught stealing a car like this? The answer: one whose keenly honed instincts told him that gunning through a national park at sixty kilometres over the speed limit was a sure way to avoid detection.

Alas, some thieves aren't very good at what they do. Whether Jed had stolen the car himself or bought it from somebody else who had stolen it, I never did find out. At least he had the decency to inform the police officer that I was a simple hitchhiker with no knowledge of the car's, er ... special status. It meant that after answering a couple of questions, I was free to be on my way.

And so there I found myself, standing on the road shoulder yet again, feeling far less tired than I had before, surrounded by nothing more than trees, mountains, a sorry-looking Toyota and the whirring lights of a police cruiser. Still, I couldn't help but laugh at my predicament. The absurdity of the situation was almost too much to bear. I had met some offbeat and interesting characters on the road, no question about it, but Jed took the cake. Here was a guy who was obviously dealing with his own issues, yet he had still found the time to stop for somebody who needed a ride. Is it any wonder that I fell in love with hitchhiking?

May 1993 - Leaving Waterloo, Ontario for the Canadian Rockies

A wise man once said that it's the journey through life that matters, not the destination. If that's true, hitchhiking should be considered a path to enlightenment rather than a semi-deviant activity. And although I'm not sure what sort of wisdom can be gained from sleeping with your head propped up against a toilet roll dispenser at a 24-hour donut shop, it remains clear to me that the wise man was on to something. Whatever the case, hitchhiking sure beats wearing sandals and sitting cross-legged at the top of a mountain, philosophizing with goats and growing a beard that could double as sailboat rigging.

Jokes aside, it was actually mountains that first led me to the road, in a roundabout sort of way. The year that would change my life began in May 1993 following my sophomore year at university, when for the second summer in a row my friend Jason Hoerle and I packed our belongings into a deplorably small hatchback and set out across the rolling pastureland of southern Ontario. We had just finished three weeks of gruelling exams at Wilfrid Laurier University, and had set our sights once again on the snow-capped Canadian Rockies more than 3,500 kilometres (2,000 miles) to the west. Spending four months there the previous summer had left us with but a taste, a fleeting glimpse of something bigger. It had also imprinted a mark on our young psyches that would ultimately derail our carefully laid career plans.

These career plans of ours, I should briefly explain, had us moving in the direction of Bay Street, the Holy Grail of success that every aspiring business student in Canada dreams about. I had put in excruciating hours during high school to qualify for one of the best business schools in the country, where I would have the option of applying for a prestigious business co-op program. After that, I planned to follow through with a chartered accountant's designation. Jason was an economics student who had applied for an accounting diploma program, a stepping stone that he hoped would also lead him into professional accounting and, eventually, to a high-paying job in corporate Toronto. But somewhere between that first summer in the mountains and our return to school in southern Ontario, something had snapped. In short, the seeds had been planted for a change of dramatic proportions.

Jason and I arrived in Lake Louise four days after leaving southern Ontario that second summer, exhausted yet giddy from our first glimpses of glacier-fed rivers rushing through valleys, jagged peaks rearing thousands of feet in the air. The sights brought back vivid memories of 1992, even though we had spent little time exploring those lofty peaks, choosing instead to fund our university education by working long hours. I had been particularly guilty of this, and I swore that I wouldn't make the same mistake two years in a row.

It wasn't long before Jason and I settled into a familiar routine. We found work at Deer Lodge, a quaint old hotel that was originally built in 1921. Jason worked the graveyard shift; I joined the hotel's housekeeping department. While my university colleagues earned big bucks pushing papers in Toronto office buildings, I was cleaning the hotel's hallways, lobby and public washrooms. It was a glamorous job dubbed "pube patrol" by those of us who appreciated its more subtle nuances. The greatest benefits the position offered were three-day weekends and a favourable thirty- to thirty-five-hour work week. Fewer hours meant more freedom, and I had soon traded in my dreams of a suit and tie for Gore-Tex hiking boots, a collapsible one-burner camping stove and a large expedition backpack.

The crowd that Jason and I met at Deer Lodge that summer couldn't have fit more perfectly with our newfound spirit of adventure. Along with two dozen other employees, we formed a loose-knit group of vagabonds, not only hailing from other parts of Canada, but from exotic lands as far away as Europe, Japan and Australia. There was even somebody from Newfoundland. Without a care in the world, we revelled in loud music and excessive drinking, even as we developed a love for adrenaline sports. Apart from hiking and scrambling (moderate climbing without ropes), we soon discovered the thrill of technical rock climbing, whitewater rafting and skydiving.

It was during those long summer days that I met another friend who would greatly impact my life. Cam "Wildcat" Owens was a breakfast waiter and guitar player who was an unofficial leader when it came to jam sessions and partying. More to the point, he was also an avid outdoorsman. It was surely the inspired cockiness we felt when together that led to us into a foolhardy plan one evening. Against the sound advice of both friends and common sense, Cam and I threw a few sandwiches into our backpacks and set out to climb a route on the southwest ridge of

3,540-metre (11,600-foot) Mount Temple at night. Temple was the highest peak within a hundred kilometres, and our plan was to reach the top before sunrise so that we could watch dawn's first rays lick distant peaks. It was marginally comforting to know that our route of choice was deemed "easy," even though we had little hope of finding it in the dark.

Shortly after midnight, a friend dropped us at a parking lot near Moraine Lake where we began our long trudge up through shadowy forest into Larch Valley. Against the star-flecked night sky we could see Temple's summit rising an incredible two thousand metres above the valley floor; precious time was lost when we reached the base of the mountain to find increasingly steep cliffs instead of the easy ridge walk the guidebook had promised. Leading the way over loose, rotten rock, I soon found it necessary to clench a flashlight between my teeth so that my hands would be free for climbing. It was a desperate plan that actually worked quite well—at least until the looming bands of rock had turned to snow and ice. After an hour, we found ourselves trapped beneath a cliff that was too steep, too slippery and too difficult for us to climb in the dark. Stuck on a narrow ledge high on the mountain, Cam and I huddled together, trying to stay warm until the sun came up.

When the first rays of dawn started slicing across a flawless morning sky, we shook ice from our frozen joints and continued climbing. We could see that we had wandered dangerously off route, and that it would be necessary to traverse far to our left to regain the gently sweeping southwest ridge. We started climbing diagonally across the snow, firmly planting our ice axes as we went. We gained elevation rapidly until we had reached a steep snow slope that was as hard as granite.

As we kicked steps across the icy crust a loud *whumping!* noise suddenly reverberated under our feet. A crevasse opened in front of me, fracturing the slope all the way to the summit ridge before grinding to a sudden halt. We knew that we were in over our heads, but as novice alpinists, we had no idea what to do. So, after a few moments of erratic breathing, we settled on what in hindsight was probably the best of the really dumb options. We cautiously backtracked, then down-climbed two hundred metres before finishing our traverse on slopes that were far less intimidating. Once we were on safe terrain, what followed was one of those ecstatic, sick-to-your-stomach moments that I'm sure follows any near-death experience. We hugged each other and quite literally kissed the frozen ground we were kneeling on.

After reaching Temple's summit, Cam and I safely made our descent and returned to the staff residence at Deer Lodge, where we were greeted as heroes. Excited that we had made it to the top and lived to tell the tale, everyone gathered in a circle to listen while Cam and I embellished our grand adventure. In reality, we were lucky to be alive. After talking to a professional mountain guide later that week, I realized how foolish we had been and how close we had come to being avalanched off the mountain. Yet that night on Temple convinced me that life was so precious it should never be wasted—by either brashness or boredom. It was a lesson I would carry with me as I began to make life-altering decisions in the weeks and months that followed.

Chapter 2

Life is a Highway

July 1993 - Lake Louise, Alberta

Standing at the side of a highway with your thumb sticking out is something, quite frankly, that takes some getting used to. This is especially true if you were raised in a family that tends to lump hitchhikers in with dodgy characters like Jed. During my childhood, for as long as I can remember, I learned to associate hitchhiking with the down-on-your-luck crowd. As a kid, the only hitchhiker I can remember seeing was a dirty, mop-haired man near Saskatoon who tried—quite unsuccessfully, I might add—to grab the side of a passing truck.

After my family moved to southern Ontario in 1987, I don't remember seeing any hitchhikers at all. My only exposure to the art of travelling by thumb, in fact, was a movie I watched as a teenager. It was called The Hitcher. Basically, it's about a dark, brooding guy who hitchhikes around murdering people and causing mayhem. One critic called it a "hair-raising, gut-wrenching, heart-stopping journey into hell that combines every terrifying tale about evil hitchhikers in one dark and diabolically unnerving adventure." The same critic also said that "it will leave you so frightened you won't want to stop for the next red light." With crap like that out there, is it any wonder hitchhiking has fallen out of favour with the general public?

It wasn't until Jason and I travelled to Banff that I started seeing a few authentic hitchhikers. Actually, they were everywhere. In the national parks it was not uncommon to see two or three hitchhikers (or groups of hitchhikers) crowding the off-ramps near Banff or Lake Louise.

One sunny afternoon in May, eager to save a few bucks on bus fare, I decided to try thumbing into Banff to buy some groceries. I wasn't robbed or murdered, and the driver didn't play any Chris de Burgh albums, so I considered the short jaunt a great success. It went so well, in fact, that one day late in the summer when I needed to run some errands in Calgary, I decided on a whim to try thumbing instead of buying a bus ticket.

That first trip into Calgary is one I will never forget. My first ride was in a white van with a trio of construction workers wearing muscle shirts and tool belts. They were only headed as far as Cochrane, though, so they had to drop me at a highway exit near the edge of the mountains. Standing there with the breeze in my face, I noticed for the first time the road peeling back toward the edge of a boundless horizon. And I swear there was pure, unadulterated freedom on that wind, the kind that only comes from not knowing where the day will lead you. How was I going to get to Calgary? Who would I meet next? It was all a great mystery.

Then there was the scene unravelling before me. There was the smell of asphalt steaming under the sun after a passing thundershower, the arc of a double rainbow in the distance, the peaks dipping down to kiss the great sprawling plains. It was pure magic! Twenty minutes later, there was also the smiling face of a driver who pulled over and beckoned me into his car. His name was André, and he was the manager of a hotel at the Sunshine Village ski area. For the entire trip he waxed about the coming ski season in the Rockies, to the point where I don't know what enthralled me more: my luck at catching a ride so quickly, or Andre's stories about skiing powder so deep you practically needed a snorkel. When we finally arrived in Calgary, André even drove fifteen minutes out of his way to drop me exactly where I needed to go. I don't think I need to mention that Greyhound doesn't do that.

So it was that I caught my first glimpse of hitchhiking. And what a beautiful glimpse it was: the short but privileged windows into the lives of others, the unsolicited generosity of strangers, the spontaneity. As a young business student I had valued the precision of balance sheets, the concise nature of business correspondence and the assurance of deadlines. Why was I suddenly so infatuated with the utter unpredictability of the road?

September 1993 - Lake Louise, Alberta

As summer melted into autumn, the tourists and seasonal hotel staff all started leaving. It was around this time that Jason and I announced to everybody that we had decided to drop out of school for a year and be ski bums. Our parents, thinking we had tripped off the deep end, did their best to talk us out of it. But we had already made up our minds; nothing they could say was going to deter us. You see, neither of us had a clue what we wanted to do with our lives—all we knew was that the words "corporate business" and "Bay Street" had ceased to be part of our vocabulary. The ski season, we hoped, would offer some much-needed perspective.

After confirming a position at the hotel's front office for the winter (where I was promised form-fitting dress clothes and a tie instead of the ridiculous, neon-green capri pants I had been wearing all summer), I quit my job in the housekeeping department. My plan was to focus on hiking and climbing for several weeks before the really cold weather arrived. But the Rockies had other plans. The stormy weather that had been prevalent for much of the summer suddenly got worse, and I grew increasingly frustrated as rain turned to snow and the high mountain slopes were buried under a blanket of white.

A week after I had quit my job, I woke on the floor of Jason's bedroom to the sound of wind hammering against the window. Outside, snow was whirling across the road in vicious gusts. I had been planning to start a multi-day hike along the continental divide, but I knew that to venture out in weather like this would be little fun, and could possibly even be dangerous. "That's it," I told Jason, rolling up my sleeping bag and stuffing it into my backpack. "If the weather's not going to improve, I'm hitchhiking back to Ontario." My younger brother Rick would soon be leaving for college in the United States, and I hadn't seen any of my other friends and family since April.

Jason sat up in bed, rubbed the sleep from his eyes, and looked at me as if I were talking through a beer bottle. "You're kidding, right?"

Jason had hitchhiked between Lake Louise and Banff a few times himself, but it wasn't until that moment of boredom and impoverished desperation that either of us had considered going much beyond the national park boundary. Perhaps our parents' generation had hitchhiked across entire continents during the sixties, but that was, well … that was decades ago, when society wasn't filled with every stripe of wacko, crackpot and lunatic imaginable.

Still, for some reason I was skeptical of this narrow take on reality. My few recent hitchhiking forays had convinced me that the open road was not such a dangerous place. There was kindness, generosity and compassion everywhere, and people were more or less what you made them out to be. If you expected to end up in a vehicle with a chainsaw slasher, sliced and diced and thrown into a ditch somewhere, well, perhaps you were right. If you thought you might get picked up and assaulted by a tattooed truck driver named Bunny, maybe you would be. On the other hand, I had a feeling that if you practiced seeing the goodness in people, the road would accommodate those views as well, and reward openly that which was perceived.

"When are you going to leave?" asked Jason.

"Right after lunch," I said.

Two hours later, Jason dropped me at the edge of the Trans-Canada. All I had with me was a small daypack stuffed with bread, a jar of peanut butter, a wool sweater and my rain jacket. Five minutes later, a car pulled over and I was on my way to Calgary with an insurance salesman.

The journey back to southern Ontario was an eye-opener, no question about it. For one thing, I managed the trip in only three rides, standing at the side of the road for a grand total of twenty-five minutes … which is respectably faster than a Greyhound bus trip if you take into account all the detours and parcel stops. My most interesting ride was with two guys who I will refer to as John and Bernie, pulling a trailer across the country with an old Cadillac. John and Bernie were on their way to Thunder Bay after a summer of picking fruit and practicing meditation in BC's southern Kootenays. Both men were friendly and laid-back, probably due (at least in part) to the fact that they smoked marijuana the entire trip. They let me spell them off at the wheel whenever they got tired, which seemed to be quite often.

Like me, John and Bernie were also at a crossroads in life, which is probably one of the reasons we hit it off so quickly. They would spontaneously break into spells of shouting, "Hoo-wah! Hoo-wah!" whenever they got excited. "It's something we came up with this summer," Bernie explained. "We got sick of using tired, worn-out phrases like yahoo! and yee-haw!"

The highlight of the trip was undoubtedly in northern Ontario, when I woke from a nap to find the car pulled over onto the shoulder. "Wanna join us?" Bernie asked. He looked back at me with mischief scrolling across his face.

"We're going for a swim," said John.

The next thing I knew, my pot-smoking chauffeurs were running across the Trans-Canada buck naked, headed straight for a small lake. I heard a car horn toot with either indignation or approval before two loud splashes sounded from across the road. John and Bernie waded further into the water, where they swam in circles for several minutes, retreating only after a small fishing boat with four American tourists motored across the lake, wanting to see what all the commotion was about. The boys weren't the least bit bashful, though, and they generously allowed two American ladies to take full advantage of the view.

"Hoo-wah!" said Bernie when he got back to the car. "As soon as life starts to get mundane, you have to shake things up a bit."

Chapter 3

Crossroads

Winter 1994 - Lake Louise, Alberta

The following year turned out to be the sweetest, hardest, most profound, most fascinating, most difficult, most enjoyable year of my life. Jason and I put in more than sixty ski days, and although we didn't learn anything about tax laws or general accounting principles, by April we had learned how to drop a ten-foot cliff onto a thirty-five-degree snow slope, then seamlessly crank turns through an obstacle course of refrigerator-sized boulders. We tried ice climbing, heli-skiing and backcountry ski touring, and with raccoon eyes and black ski tans we laughed and felt genuinely sorry for our university friends who were locked away in study cubicles, buried in textbooks and assignments. We felt like the luckiest guys on earth.

During those winter months, I also started reading like never before. It was something I had never liked in university because of the mandatory nature of most assignments. At school I read to get decent grades, not for enjoyment. Now I was finding books that spoke to me in marvellous ways, daring me to change my thoughts and my life. One of my favourites was Patrick Morrow's *Beyond Everest: Quest for the Seven Summits*, a book about his now-famous journey to climb the highest peak on each of the seven continents. I found Morrow's personal adventure incredibly compelling, and his photography second to none.

Morrow's writing spoke strongly to me: his determination to forge a career from his passions, his desire to live honestly with himself and his insatiable curiosity that swept across a broad spectrum of places and cultures. When he quoted Aldous Huxley, it felt like he was talking directly to that that small rebel voice that lives inside all of us: "For every traveller who has any taste of his own, the only useful guidebook will be the one which he himself has written." Still, sixteen months of reckless fun in the Rockies had done nothing to straighten my faltering career path.

When I returned for my third year of university in September of 1994, I still had no clue what I wanted to do with my life.

That's when I met Ingrid Nielsen, editor of the student newspaper at Wilfrid Laurier. Somehow we got chatting about my year in Banff, and after hearing a few tales and leafing through some of my pictures, she turned to me with a story idea. If I could put on paper what my time in the Rockies had meant to me—and what lessons I had learned from it—she would publish it in the newspaper. I was unsure that anyone other than friends and family would want to hear my stories, but I agreed to give it a try. A month later, my article came out under the banner "Is it Time for a Break?" It was accompanied by one of my pictures from an ice-climbing foray into Johnston Canyon. Thus started my affiliation with the student newspaper, giving me a forum to develop some much-needed journalistic skills.

Around the same time, I discovered that the best way to tame the mental anguish of finance class was to avoid it altogether, so I purchased an old manual camera and began frequenting a nearby park. My newfound passion for photography caused me to miss more than a few classes. During those warm autumn days in late September and October, I shot roll after roll of film, exposing countless frames of people, sunsets and autumn foliage. Slowly, I learned how to use my camera, and just before Christmas I signed up for a Nikon photography workshop in Toronto, hoping to develop my skills even further.

My final two years at university passed in a mind-numbing blur. As I worked toward finishing my academic obligations, I started sending off query letters and photo submissions, attempting to establish myself as a freelance writer and photojournalist in the competitive national magazine marketplace. I also worked three nights a week at a burger joint, managing just barely to keep my bank account on life support.

I graduated later that spring and bought a new camera, two lenses and a tripod with my last few hundred dollars. Armed with a coil-bound notepad and several rolls of Kodachrome, I spent the next few weeks hiking and paddling throughout northern Ontario. During my downtime, I worked at writing travel stories for several newspapers and magazines, which I would send off to travel editors in both Canada and the United States with great anticipation. Invariably, I would get the stories back a few weeks later, accompanied by curt rejection letters.

It wasn't until early in 1996, after sending out countless story proposals and photo submissions, that I finally made my first sales. In February, I was contacted by Mountain Equipment Co-op for the use of two images in their spring catalogue. Even more exciting was when Marion Harrison, then editor at *Explore* magazine, hired me to write an article and supply photos for a short story about hiking on Manitoulin Island. By the end of the year I had sold two more short pieces, which, when combined, added up to a paltry $475. Hardly a respectable income, but I became enamoured nonetheless with the challenge and fulfillment this line of work offered. I made a commitment to live by my pen and camera as much as possible.

When I graduated in April of 1996, I was free to pursue writing and photography full-time, though my meagre budget permitted only baby steps in those early days. As Mark Twain would have said, I had "a troublesome superabundance of that sort of time which is *not* money." Indeed, to survive my first summer as a freelancer I lived out of a closet in Jason's apartment in Lake Louise. It was not a comfortable existence by any means, but Jason's charity allowed me to focus on what I most needed at the time: developing skills that would eventually allow me to make a reasonable living from my freelance work. If I had realized then how long it would take, perhaps I would not have continued.

To pay for food I ended up working part-time at a camera store in Lake Louise, where I met Steve Agar, my employer and another mentor who would leave a distinct imprint on my life. An impassioned photographer himself, Steve proved to be one of my most steadfast supporters, encouraging my dream in ways both spoken and unspoken. In addition to letting me set my own hours, he gave me discounts on film and photo supplies, and let me use his home computer to write story proposals—often at great inconvenience to both him and his wife Karen. We bounced countless project ideas off one another, and he proved to be one of the few who believed in me and my oddball dreams. When I came up with the idea to publish a photo book about hitchhiking across Canada—even though I had not yet secured a publishing deal—he was behind me one hundred percent.

Which brings us to the whys and wherefores of hitchhiking. Specifically, why would a young photojournalist choose to hitchhike across Canada rather than drive his own car? Let me assure you: there is no short answer to that question. I do know that when a person drives, they are travelling inside a protective shell that largely shuts out the world;

when a person hitchhikes, the driver and passenger must engage one another and in doing so make themselves vulnerable. They know nothing about each other and must therefore demonstrate trust and a willingness to accept one another on terms that have yet to be negotiated. Above all else, personal differences must evaporate.

With this in mind, one can begin to understand the appeal of hitching. If I was going to travel across Canada, I wanted to see more than just the trees and mountains, rocks and lakes that comprise this boundless and beautiful land. I didn't want simply to meet people at restaurants and service stations, I yearned to meet them on their own terms, to visit them in their homes, to hear yarns and stories about life from distant corners of the country. Hitchhiking would force me to do that.

So it was in the spring of 1997 that I sat down with a roadmap of Canada and started drawing bold lines with a red felt marker. Where would I go? What would I see? How long would this trip take? The smorgasbord of options in front of me was both exciting and mind-boggling. Of course, choices would sometimes be made for me—such is the nature of travelling by thumb. As a rule I decided to put my newfound "Zen navigation" principles to the test. I would decide on a general direction and let serendipity lead me from there.

I decided first to thumb west to the Pacific Ocean, then hitchhike and ride north using British Columbia's ferry system and a scattering of northern roads. Then I would continue to the Arctic Ocean, and finally trend my way south and east until I had reached St. John's, Newfoundland. I felt there was something romantic about linking all three oceans, or maybe it was just an excuse to visit exotic corners of the country that I had never seen: the Yukon, the Northwest Territories, Quebec and the Atlantic provinces. Yes, there would be plenty of new territory on this trip. On my map every vein of red branching off in this direction or that represented a different possibility, every place where those lines intersected a different choice.

In many ways, I suppose, hitchhiking is not unlike life in this respect, and along the way I would learn to think of the road as a metaphor. We all face detours and shortcuts, scenic routes and wrong turns (and usually plenty of construction), and for this reason I wanted to simply revel in the journey, wherever it was going to lead me. As it turned out, I would have plenty of opportunity to practice this philosophy. A trip that was supposed to take me five months over one summer ended up taking nearly twelve months spread across four years. People sometimes ask why it took me so long. Generally, I tell them it's because I kept meeting people and seeing sights that gave me no inclination to move faster—though in fact it's just that I'm really bad at reading maps, and ended up criss-crossing Saskatchewan fourteen times. (Just kidding.)

Anyway, my plan was to travel for the sake of travelling, and to make decisions based largely on instinct. I hoped to learn things from countless people, and to learn a few things about myself as well. At times, I would relish the road for its good humour and simplicity; at other times, I would get drawn into discussions about the state of our country. Every corner I visited was distinct: distinct from other parts of Canada, but particularly (and often proudly) distinct from Ontario. This was even true of some parts of Ontario itself—primarily the northern regions that seem so far removed from the bustling pace of the south. The point is that everywhere I went, under the thin veneer of everyday life were the rumblings of a nation in flux, and at times I found it impossible to avoid some of these issues. There was the Quebec question, the dawn of Nunavut, multiculturalism and what one cynical man referred to as "the birth of Canada as the fifty-first state."

But let's not lose perspective. This is a story about a road trip, and I'm not sure what (if anything) a young hitchhiking journalist can say about Canada that hasn't already been said a thousand times by more highly qualified people. All I know is that when I unfolded my roadmap of Canada, I saw and felt freedom—not questions that have weighed heavily on our national psyche for decades. Although it would be impossible to travel across Canada without hearing about (and at times debating) some of these issues, they were never intended to be the primary focus of my trip. If I had to face these questions on the road, I certainly didn't want them to weigh me down or, worse yet, stop me dead in my tracks.

Ultimately, my decision to follow an unlikely dream has resulted in this book, eight years after the idea was first conceived. My primary hope is that it may restore some of that essential faith we seem to have lost in humanity, something we are in great need of right now, especially as the world's media seems bent on dissecting only the details of tragedy. Moreover, I hope that you will enjoy the book for its stories about Canadians, as well as for its humour, adventure and candour, and that it may inspire some of you to pursue your own passions.

Dare to dream big. Dare to laugh hard. At some point in life we, like Robert Frost, must all face a path diverging at the edge of a wood. May you choose your path wisely and may it make all the difference in your own life.

Summit to Seacoast

*"Two roads diverged in a wood and I took
the one less traveled by, and that has
made all the difference."*
- Robert Frost

Chapter 4

The National Dream

April 17, 1997 - Revelstoke, British Columbia

The grind and clatter of a freight train rattling window panes woke me early that first morning on the road, causing me to sit bolt upright and nearly topple from somebody's couch. I was no longer at home, no question about it—but where? I yawned and stretched, running fingers through matted hair as I squinted around a dark room—a room lit only by the incandescent glow of street lamps burning through flimsy curtains. I could taste the rain that had been falling all night, hanging in the air like a damp rag, and it was only then that I remembered where I was. I had holed up for the night at my friend Jacquie's apartment in Revelstoke, a small lumber and railroad town in BC's Selkirk Mountains. As I rubbed sleep from my eyes, I laughed at how the mind can play tricks on itself at the beginning of a long journey.

Lying there half awake, I let my thoughts drift back to the Canadian Rockies and a lifestyle I had just traded in for God only knew what. For the greater part of the last five years—whenever I had not been at school in southern Ontario—my life had revolved around the simple adrenaline rhythms of skiing and climbing. Still, I knew I couldn't do that forever. The ebb and flow of life's tides are constantly shaping, changing, providing opportunities for those who care to look for them. But was this an opportunity ... or just madness? Hitchhiking across Canada had seemed like a grand idea when I was sitting at my kitchen table drawing red lines across a map, but this country was vast enough to swallow a small city without the slightest hint of indigestion. What would happen to a solitary hitchhiker with nothing more than a backpack and a few dollars in savings? In the creeping void of a dark, rainy morning, it felt like my confidence was coming undone.

To be honest, it was the thought of thumbing rides along Canada's remote back roads that concerned me most. In places like rural Saskatchewan, motorists are about as accustomed to seeing hitchhikers as they are to seeing astronauts; in the Far North, there are roads where you're as likely to see a grizzly staring hungrily at you from the roadside shrubbery as a car approaching. Most of my thumbing had been done either in the national parks or along the Trans-Canada Highway corridor, and I now wondered if it would even be possible to hitchhike once I had left the thin ribbon of bitumen that is our country's "Main Street." Clearly, my fate would be in the hands of the loggers, truckers and farm hands that drive these little-travelled roads.

But allowing myself to get discouraged so early would defeat the whole purpose of my trip, an adventure originally fueled by optimism and curiosity. While the 1990s were no longer the days of Canada's "freedom culture"—no longer the country Pierre Trudeau had envisioned when he was elected prime minister in 1968—an essential ingredient of hitchhiking is faith: faith in the road, faith in your instincts and faith in your fellow man. Ever the visionary, there was a time when Trudeau himself had faith. He had faith that the road could educate a young generation of Canadian leaders, a conviction that inspired him to create a national network of government-funded hostels across the country, catering specifically, if not exclusively, to the hitchhiking crowd. He urged young Canadians to take to the road, declaring that there was no better way to see Canada. And for many years they did, as can be seen from a *National Geographic* photograph published in 1980, showing a long line of hitchhikers queuing up for rides along an Alberta highway.

As I lay in the dark room, my thoughts eventually drifted back to the events of the previous day, which made me feel marginally better. It was comforting to remember that I had flagged down a quick succession of rides between the Rockies and Revelstoke. I had been lucky, especially as I hadn't left Lake Louise until after four in the afternoon. As it turned out, my first ride couldn't have been more fitting either, considering it was the Canadian Pacific Railway that first carved a route across this vast land, providing hobos and drifters at the turn of the century with a steel highway to ride. Darcy was a track maintenance worker for the CPR, and as we dropped down the far side of Kicking Horse Pass toward the town of Field, he had explained how this pass was responsible for its fair share of disasters after the railway was first constructed.

The steep pitch on the west side of Kicking Horse Pass, apparently, had a habit of causing trains to run away on conductors. When this happened, a conductor was obliged to signal a switchman so that the train could be diverted onto a side spur, where it would crash and erupt into a ball of flames, typically killing everybody on board. One conductor, understandably reluctant to end his own life, is famous for *not* signalling the switchman. Instead, he ran the Big Hill's gauntlet with a runaway locomotive, thus becoming the first and only man to get his train under control before reaching Field. For his heroics, Canadian Pacific promptly fired him.

Of course, the Trans-Canada Highway is something less of an adventure today, and as Darcy navigated the serpentine road down to the valley bottom, he had casually stroked his goatee the entire time.

Next was Jacques, the Québécois tree planter who had dropped me at Golden. Jacques told me that he hated politics in general, but particularly Quebec politics. His goal was to plant trees in BC and forget about names like Bouchard and Landry.

My last ride had been with Greg, a congenial health-food entrepreneur whose company had recently graced the pages of *Success* magazine, where it was named one of Canada's top fifty growing firms. We got into such a rousing conversation that Greg ended up with a speeding ticket as we burned across Rogers Pass from the Columbia Valley. I took his picture as he sat in the driver's seat—half smile, half scowl—juxtaposed with the RCMP's flashing cherry. Thirty minutes later, he dropped me in the pouring rain near Jacquie's home in Revelstoke.

I have to admit that getting dropped in Revelstoke wouldn't have been my first choice—the town, for me, has never brought to mind postcard paradise. It is surrounded by mountains, certainly, but most of them bear the ugly scars of clear-cutting across their flanks. Revelstoke also seems to be blessed with a perpetual rain cloud hanging over it. If it were sunny across the rest of southern BC, Revelstoke would probably still have rain. I had been through the town on several occasions and had never once seen the sun shining. What I *had* seen were restaurant signs advertising what types of patrons were welcome: some establishments preferred loggers, while others liked the New Age crowd. To me, Revelstoke had always seemed a dreary industry town simmering along its seams, drenched in bad feelings and merciless, penetrating rain. Having said that, others have assured me that there is another side to this community. I have friends who love Revelstoke for its charming old homes, diverse shops and beautiful gardens, and for the fact that two national parks sit in its spacious back yard.

In my case, Revelstoke's most appealing feature was the opportunity to see Jacquie and to take advantage of a warm couch to sleep on. Jason and I had first met Jacquie in 1993 while working in Lake Louise, and she had endeared herself to us immediately because of her warmth and cheer, plus the fact that she laughed at even our worst jokes. There were many times, in fact, after spending a day skiing or hiking with Jason, that I would come up with an excuse to part ways with him shortly after arriving home—laundry, fatigue, that sort of thing. What I really wanted to do, of course, was steal my way over to the clothing store where Jacquie worked so that I could flirt with her. Invariably, I would arrive to find Jason already there, elbow propped strategically on the counter, in the process of charming her with his effortless wit. Such was our relationship with Jacquie.

At 8:30 I could still hear the rain crashing down outside, and I felt very much like rolling over and forgetting that I would soon be standing at the roadside, getting sprayed with truck backwash. But it was time to get moving. Reluctantly, I rolled up my sleeping bag and headed for the shower. Thirty minutes later I was sitting with Jacquie at her kitchen table, eating sliced fruit and oatmeal while sipping at a mug of hot peppermint tea. I was doing my best to stall for time, so you can imagine my gratitude when Jacquie did the stalling for me. She had been hired as a Parks Canada interpreter a few months earlier, which meant that she had been gathering material about Canada's railroad history. Now she needed somebody to practice her spiel on.

"Revelstoke is here because of the railroad," she began, reminding me that my lack of sleep the previous night had been courtesy of one of Canada's most revered national icons. Somehow that didn't make me feel any better. She carried on to tell me about the communities of immigrant labourers that started springing up in the Selkirks during the early 1880s. Willing, able-bodied Europeans had been hard to find, so the federal government imported more than 17,000 Chinese (and paid them half the wage of white labourers) to help with the overwhelming task of carving a railroad through the western mountains. "Of course, it would have been much easier to build the railway through Yellowhead Pass in Jasper," Jacquie explained, "but MacDonald's government was afraid that Canada would sacrifice sovereignty to the Americans if it was built further north."

That meant the railroad had to be pushed through Kicking Horse and Rogers passes, both of which presented the engineers and labourers with some monumental challenges. If the Big Hill near Field caused its fair share of train wrecks, Rogers Pass (which receives enough snow every year to bury a four-storey office building) was famous for burying trains under massive snow slides. At great expense, the CPR built more than six kilometres of snow sheds that were supposed to protect trains, tracks and workmen. Yet avalanches continued tumbling off these precipitous peaks, causing great inconvenience and loss of life. The largest slide in Rogers Pass claimed sixty-two victims in 1910, prompting the construction of the eight-kilometre Connaught Tunnel, which was pushed through the Selkirks at the base of the pass in 1916.

Despite its imperfections, the railroad provided Canada with a much-needed link when it was finally finished at Craigellachie, a few dozen kilometres west of Revelstoke. It was here that CPR president Donald Smith hammered the Last Spike in 1885, officially completing Canada's first national dream. Not surprisingly, the story of the Last Spike (like so many events in Canadian history), has managed to develop more than one version over the years. Smith believed the event symbolic of Canada's birth as a great nation, and his patriotic words have been used for generations to conjure up nationalistic sentiment, reminding Canadians of the impassioned, visionary stock from which we descend. Of course, the immigrant rail workers whose backs the whole thing was built on called it something entirely different. All they saw was a stuffed shirt strutting around in a wool suit, banging at a nail with the well-oiled precision of a blind man trimming nose hairs with a weed-whacker.

Chapter 5

Okanagan Country

April 18, 1997 - Vernon, British Columbia

The road south of Vernon cuts above the waters of Lake Kalamalka, dancing beside a kaleidoscope of greens and blues before winding down through a long row of arid hills to the shore of Okanagan Lake. The lake is reputedly home to Ogo Pogo, a Canadian version of the more infamous Loch Ness monster of Scotland, though the slinky leviathan was nowhere in sight as I skirted the shoreline with my first ride of the day.

His name was Randy, an aboriginal fellow with a long ponytail and black bushy eyebrows that knitted together as he talked. We chatted easily about the weather, politics and Native issues—but it was his stories that proved most entertaining. The best one was about his friend Star Blanket, an unlucky hitchhiker with a knack for getting stranded in the middle of nowhere. This meant he often had to sleep in the ditch or curl up in a highway culvert. It all sounded very amusing until I realized the same thing could (and probably would) happen to me at some point during my trip.

Randy dropped me in Kelowna shortly before eleven, and it wasn't long before I had found a place to stash my backpack, which was so heavy that I felt like an inebriated moose stumbling around under its capacious girth. Over the preceding months I had obviously forgotten how to pack frugally, and I was now suffering the consequences. Desperate for a few hours' relief, I somehow convinced the secretary at Kelowna's municipal building to stow it in her office for the afternoon, which meant I would be free to walk around unhindered for a few hours. "Make sure you're back by five," she warned. "If you're not, you won't be able to get it back until Monday morning."

I soon found a park where a couple of guys in bare feet invited me to join them for a few rounds of hacky sack on the warm grass. The rain had finally abated, and the change in weather after leaving the Selkirk

Mountains had been nothing short of incredible. On the waterfront, a man was slapping a fresh coat of paint on the *Fintry Queen*, the old paddlewheeler that once served as a ferry between the east and west shores of Okanagan Lake. The trees were greening up nicely and the bustling sidewalks indicated that a few office workers were playing hooky, though I was certainly not one to advise them otherwise. It was one of those days when the white-collar crowd stares lustily at landscapers contentedly running their hands through dirt, or garbage truck drivers on their trash-collecting rounds.

For lunch, I wound up at a downtown eatery called Sturgeon Hall, decorated with Canadian memorabilia of all kinds: photographs of Anne Murray, Ben Johnson and even Ron MacLean's old CBC *Hockey Night in Canada* jacket. As I wandered into the dark bar I was greeted by Bernie, one of the owners, who had a pencil stuffed behind his right ear. He was busy pouring beers and taking orders for the lunchtime crowd. I wasn't in the mood for anything heavy, so I ordered a Lorne Greene salad and a chocolate milkshake, then sat down on a barstool beside a window streaming with sunlight. When Bernie came to drop off my milkshake, I told him a bit about my trip and complimented him on his restaurant's decor. He explained that he had recently moved from Sudbury, Ontario, and that the restaurant's Canadian focus was to wage war on the American marketing machine. "They can't be so eager to rewrite Canadian history," he told me, "or to have us believe that we're the equivalent of a fifty-first state."

"Yeah, and he's hoping to get his western Canadian passport any day now," said a silver-haired man, taunting him from across the bar.

Bernie laughed. "That's Bruce," he told me. "He's the big man in town. He owns the Kelowna Rockets, our city's Junior A hockey team."

Bruce had overheard me telling Bernie about my trip, so after Bernie left to fill more lunch orders he invited me to sit at his table. He was busy polishing off some vegetable soup and a Shania burger, but he had time to chat. "You look at southern Ontario and it's already so Americanized," he sighed. "I'm glad there are guys like Bernie around to remind us that we're different than the Yanks."

Bruce was a contradiction of sorts, no question about it. In many ways he came across as a laid-back character, the kind of guy who walks around with the top of his shirt undone on a hot day and who has ample time to open doors for little old ladies. Yet he wasn't afraid to shoot from the hip either, particularly when it came to issues of national importance. For example, when our talk turned to the sacred topic of hockey—a sport that is arguably more vital to our national well-being than clean drinking water—it was understandable that Bruce felt scandalized by the current version of the game. "Hockey is all about money now," Bruce complained as we discussed Canada's financially beleaguered NHL franchises. "How are we supposed to maintain the purity of our sport when we can't afford to play anymore?"

And so our conversation evolved, Bruce explaining his version of how hockey symbolizes Canadian-American relations. He told me that although most Canucks appreciate the close kinship we share with our American brothers, giving the Yanks a good bodycheck into the boards every now and again is rather gratifying. He was speaking metaphorically, of course, not literally.

And who was I to argue? One adhesive that seems to hold Canadians together better than our flag, our national anthem or even a Tim Horton's double-double is our common desire *not* to be American. Why this is so, I can't say, but I guess when you live beside the wealthiest, most powerful nation in the world, the mouse has to defend itself aggressively to make sure the elephant pays attention to where it's walking. If this involves scurrying up its leg and biting at its kneecap, so be it.

The afternoon passed too quickly as I walked around in the sunshine, chatting with strangers. Not needing to be anywhere in particular felt wonderful. In some ways it felt like the day could stretch on forever, yet when the afternoon dissolved into evening there was that strong urge to hit the road again. So I joined the rush-hour traffic in a mad romp across the floating bridge to Westbank, trudging through heat and humidity that had me practicing French swear words under my breath. The bridge was much longer than it had looked from shore, and the steep hill I would have to climb on the far side looked less and less appealing the closer I got to it. I had no idea how far the highway was from the bottom of the hill, but I had a bad feeling that I would be hauling my backpack for some distance yet.

By the time I reached Westbank, a sizable knot had lodged itself between my shoulder blades. Rather than continue my death march up the hill, I changed tactics and stood at the far end of the bridge to thumb a ride. Considering the speed of the traffic and the lack of a shoulder, it was about as bad a place to hitchhike as any. Still, I had one advantage in the form of a cardboard sign that read: TRAVELLING JOURNALIST: BE IN MY STORY. All I could do was hope that it would pique someone's curiosity, leaving them with no option but to stop or turn around and come back for me. Or maybe a passing police cruiser, seeing that I was standing in a "No Hitchhiking" zone, would double back, fine me and ferry me out to the highway. Either way, I was betting my ploy would spare me a hell-bound slog in the heat.

My saviour arrived in the form of a spindly fellow named Mike, a multilingual translator whose non-stop one-liners reminded me of another Mike—specifically, Toronto talk-show host Mike Bullard. I was soon laughing hysterically at his scheme to build pedestrian walkways with padded railings. "That way, foot commuters will be able to read while walking home," he chortled.

His funniest stories were about hitchhiking around Japan, a country where he had worked as a disc jockey for three years. Nobody hitchhikes in Japan, he told me, though as a foreigner he was able to get away with it because motorists were often so curious that they would pull over to ask what he was doing. "If you look friendly, it's easy to get a ride," he admitted. But there was still one major drawback. Although he spoke Japanese fluently, the people who picked him up always brought him to the nearest train station, refusing to believe that he knew where he was going. "You tell them to drop you at a certain place, and then all of a sudden you find yourself at the train station," he said, rolling his eyes. "It's kind of counterproductive."

Mike dropped me at the edge of town, and while nibbling at a granola bar I decided that there was just enough daylight to get me as far as Penticton, which was still over an hour away. Thumbing in the dark as huge transport trucks blast by is not likely to prolong a hitchhiker's life. Nor is it very productive. When you're standing on the road after nightfall, motorists tend to assume that you're up to some mischief.

When I was picked up twenty minutes later, I had to laugh at the irony: the driver was a Chinese businessman named Chris who had recently moved from Hong Kong to manage a chain of Edo Japan restaurants. He explained to me that in Asian countries, it's not common to pick up hitchhikers because of crime. Mike could have told him that. Chris had made an exception for me because he had seen me the previous night at a Tim Horton's in Vernon and thought I looked like "a nice guy." He also told me in an odd, motherly sort of way that he had been worried about me carrying such a large backpack around. "How do you do that?" he asked, scratching his head and giving me a puzzled look. "You must be a strong guy."

"You get used to it after a while," I lied.

It was only after we had reached Penticton forty minutes later that I realized Chris had driven a good hour out of his way. He was actually driving to Merritt, which meant he would have to backtrack thirty minutes north to the turnoff. What a thoughtful fellow. How often in this frantic world does somebody—a stranger, at that—give you an extra hour of their time? I shook his hand and thanked him profusely. When he asked me where I wanted to go, I told him to drop me anywhere but the train station.

SHORTLY AFTER I arrived in Penticton, the clear sky started fading behind a veil of storm clouds scudding in from the west. I wanted to watch the last vestiges of sunlight drop over the water, so I walked down to the Clarion Lakeside Resort—Penticton's fanciest hotel—and found a chair on the patio. Under the flickering light of torch lanterns, I watched the sun drop behind a row of blue-green hills, the *thud thud thud* of nightclub music pounding just a few metres away.

I was jolted back to reality as a short, stocky fellow appeared from nowhere, offering a handshake at the end of his outstretched arm. "So you finally made it," he said. "I saw you standing on the highway outside of Westbank, but when I turned around to come back for you, somebody else had already picked you up."

How about that: motorists fighting over hitchhikers. Maybe the world did have its priorities straight.

And that was only the beginning. Without hesitation Tim invited me into the nightclub, the Barking Parrot, where he worked every weekend as a disc jockey. After he'd bought me a Coke, we chatted casually as he thumbed through his collection of classic rock and modern techno discs, trying to figure out what to play next. "You should see this place in the summer," he told me. "It just rocks!" Then a few seconds later: "Say, where are you staying tonight anyway?"

"I'm not sure," I replied. I hadn't figured that out yet, although a nice slice of beach or a city park where I could pitch my tent would suit me just fine.

"Good, you can stay with me," he said, handing me a room key. "I have a room at the hotel here. Go take a shower, then come back down and enjoy the party."

I was stunned. The road always held a few surprises, but an invitation to stay at Penticton's fanciest hotel? What an incredible opportunity! I definitely wasn't about to turn him down. With gratitude, I accepted his key, then skirted through the hotel lobby with my backpack, fetching suspicious stares from a pair of prim-looking front desk clerks. It took me twenty minutes to shower and change, and when I reappeared back at the nightclub I felt like a new man. I even anted up for a game of pool, though for the most part I was content to sit, watch, listen and contemplate the sometimes surprising generosity of complete strangers.

April 19, 1997 - Penticton, British Columbia

The next morning, I treated Tim to coffee and a pair of Egg McSomethings at the local Golden Arches. I figured it was the least I could do for a guy who had kept me dry and entertained the previous night. When I thanked him, though, he immediately deflected the praise. "I know what it's like to travel," he said in a merry tone, then related how he had met his wife while working at Club Med. "I've always believed that travellers have to look out for one another."

After Tim dropped me at the south end of town, I pulled out my map to check coordinates. I was venturing into unknown (to me) territory: the Crow's Nest Pass route along the southern boundary of BC. The map showed a highway cutting a precarious swath through the southern Kootenays and eventually into the Coast Mountains. I soon realized the fastest way for me to access the highway would be to follow a side road that extends south from Penticton to a town called Keremeos. From there, the Crow's Nest Pass route would lead me through the peaks of Manning Provincial Park, down to the town of Hope, and finally along the Fraser River Valley all the way to Vancouver.

As it turned out, I didn't have to wait long for my first ride. A retired couple picked me up on their way home from church, and their timely arrival saved me from the second deluge to hit Penticton since the previous night. The rain clouds had been silently regrouping for another onslaught, and seconds after I climbed in loonie-sized raindrops started hammering their car.

Unfortunately, the kudos I offered them for perfect timing turned out to be somewhat premature. The couple, long on generosity but perhaps a little short on planning, changed their minds and decided to turn south for

Osoyoos a few minutes after picking me up. They dropped me halfway between Penticton and Keremeos, a long way from any kind of shelter. It was the kind of place where a hitchhiker could get stranded for hours, which inspired a plausible front-page headline to flash through my head: HITCHHIKER FOUND DROWNED AT ROADSIDE: SOAKED THROUGH LIKE A SPONGE. But it wasn't to be, at least not on this particular day. Fifteen minutes later, the first driver I saw pulled onto the gravel shoulder with an abrupt jerk of his steering wheel. His car was a beat-up old hatchback of some description, though its current state of disrepair made it nearly impossible to identify.

When I approached an open window, the fellow inside seemed to be in a similar state of disrepair, with wild hair and a beard tangled like dwarf willow. His clothes were torn and stained, and like Jed's car, his also had a hole in the floorboard on the passenger's side. The grim expression on his face did nothing to reassure me that this man was not the second coming of Charles Manson. But beggars can't be choosers, so with the rain starting to fall around my ears again, I threw my backpack onto his rear seat and climbed inside.

Almost as soon as I had settled into the passenger's seat, I realized my error in judgment. "It's interesting that I've just let you into my car," the man said, spitting the words from a creased corner in his lower lip. He tapped loudly on my cardboard sign with his index finger. "Hitchhiking as a journalist is a bizarre concept."

I asked him a few harmless questions like "What's your name?" but our discussion quickly degenerated, and my nameless chauffeur became more and more agitated as he careened around hairpin turns. "I become increasingly jaded as life goes on," he growled through clenched teeth, ignoring the less confrontational direction I had been trying to steer our conversation. "Nobody hires me. Everyone is rush, rush, rush. WHY ARE PEOPLE IN SUCH A HURRY?"

I tried to calm him down, but this only angered him more. So I asked him to drop me at the next town, not knowing where that was, but wanting desperately to be out of his car. I was extremely grateful when he heard my request and eased his foot off the gas pedal. A few seconds later I even started to breathe again.

But I was not out of trouble yet. As we drove through the centre of Keremeos fifteen minutes later, I had assumed I was home free, but I couldn't have been more wrong. When a pickup truck pulled suddenly from a side street and narrowly missed a pedestrian crossing in front of us, the man erupted again. "Did you see that?" he shouted. "DID YOU SEE THAT?"

"Yeah," I squeaked.

"Well, 'yeah' what? You're a pedestrian! YOU'RE SUPPOSED TO BE FIGHTING AGAINST STUFF LIKE THAT!" I sat there speechless. In all my hitchhiking exploits I had never encountered anger like this. Any response seemed destined to set him off like fireworks. "No one wants to wait for pedestrians anymore!" he barked, his eyes and nostrils flaring. "That guy in the truck should be killed!"

As you might imagine, I was most grateful when he finally pulled the car up to a curb and let me out, without first forcing me to hurl obscenities at the careless truck driver to prove myself a responsible pedestrian. Still, the man had obviously lived a hard life, and as I walked away I couldn't help but feel a touch of sympathy for him.

Despite the distressing ride and less-than-perfect weather, I ended up feeling quite pleased that he had dropped me in the centre of Keremeos, a town that I might otherwise have passed by. It immediately struck me as one of those little back-road gems that most travellers would never think to visit. The town had mostly avoided the plague of sprawling vacation homes and seasonal mansions that wealthy bankers and doctors like to build on quiet country roads so they can squirrel themselves away from city life for several weeks every year. Yes, Keremeos was definitely authentic rural BC. Although there wasn't any fruit in season just yet, one could easily gauge its importance to the local economy. Walking the main strip, I passed a cluster of fresh fruit stands with large, colourful signs displayed prominently along the road to draw in passing motorists. Between the stands were orchards specked white with apple blossoms, stretching across the valley bottoms, hazy blue mountains towering over them on every side.

As I walked past one of the fruit markets, I spotted a loaded-down Jeep that looked like it was heading west. I walked over to see who the owner might be, and found myself face to face with a young kid of about nineteen who had a short, circular mop of blonde hair sprouting from the top of his head. He was wearing a brown Aussie outback jacket and stood there dragging on a cigarette while making small talk with an older man who was tending the market. "I don't suppose you have room for a hitchhiker?" I asked him, still drenched from the storm.

He hesitated at first, then nodded. "I'm headed to Langley," he told me. "That's the direction I'm going."

"Well, no promises, but we'll see if I can fit you in." After five minutes of wrangling with my backpack, we finally managed to stuff it in through the one door that opened on the back (the other door was welded shut), stacking it precariously on top of a collection of boxes, suitcases and various other assorted items.

"Are you moving?" I asked.

"Yup," he said. "My uncle called me two days ago and told me I had a job in Vancouver. So here I am, the country bumpkin heading for the big city."

As we rolled onto the highway, he introduced himself as "Johnny from Rossland." He told me that Rossland was home to the infamously steep Red Mountain ski resort (as if I didn't know), and as the miles whizzed by, he entertained me with stories of life growing up in the remote BC interior: hunting and fishing misadventures, skiing almost every weekend. He was going to miss small-town life, I could tell, but with a new job and his girlfriend following him to Vancouver the next month, he also seemed excited that his life was starting to come into focus.

We cruised past the lumberyards and belching smokestacks of Princeton, then up onto Manning's mountain plateau, where we cut through a series of narrow, steep-walled valleys. The top of Johnny's Jeep had been fastened down with duct tape, and as we drove, its canvas edges started flapping loudly, pinging against the metal frame. Every once in a while he would punch the windshield with a loose fist to jump-start the wiper blades. All this while the nauseating road twisted and turned, eventually dropping us down toward Hope. I suspected the town's name was rooted in pleas of "I *hope* this crazy road ends soon."

Fifteen minutes west of Hope, the Fraser Valley spread wide like the business end of a male peacock, a sure sign that we would soon be in the suburbs of Vancouver. Heavy clouds like swabs of cotton shrouded the sides of dark green mountains, the only visible sign of snow at the very tops of the loftiest peaks.

It started to rain again as Johnny dropped me at a bus stop in Langley, a few suburbs east of Vancouver proper. We shook hands and wished each other luck, in the tradition of travellers who meet for short intervals but will likely never see one another again. The last I saw of Johnny from Rossland was the back of his wild blonde hair as he raced off to meet his uncle, full of boundless enthusiasm to start planning his life.

Chapter 6

West Coast Mecca

April 19, 1997 - Vancouver, British Columbia

Living as I had for several months in Lake Louise, where time and the pace of life are pacifists, arriving in Vancouver proved to be a wee bit of sensory overload. Despite the calming effect of the natural elements that preside over this West Coast mecca—the forested mountains and valleys, the beaches and ocean and smell of salt air—it was the constant drum of traffic and wail of sirens that hit me like a five-ton truck. I felt painfully out of place, like an Inuit hunter plucked from an Arctic ice floe and dropped into the middle of a Toronto freeway.

As with most seaport towns, Vancouver also has a certain rough-hewn character about it, and over the years I had heard plenty of ominous stories about rampant crime, prostitution and the city's drug trade. Almost every friend of mine living in Vancouver has either had their car stolen or their apartment burglarized. It didn't help to realize that with my backpack and hitchhiking sign, I would be sticking out like a logger at a tea party. Still, I knew which parts of the city to avoid—and of all the places you don't want to end up in Vancouver, the red-light district near East Hastings Street has to rank near the top. This is where much of the city's illicit drug trade and prostitution occurs, and where overworked police officers keep tabs on drug dealers while social workers try to keep young working girls off the street. Such a despondent atmosphere has led to a ghetto of sorts, to a slum with dozens of broken, forgotten souls who have no home and nowhere left to run.

It was with this measured pessimism that I greeted Vancouver—induced in part by the dreary weather. At least I knew better than to stay at the Ivanhoe, a hostel where I had spent a night when passing through three years earlier. It's located not far from East Hastings, and while walking around trying to find it on my previous trip, a car full of angry teenagers had sped past, its occupants shouting profanities and hurling beer bottles out the window at me. Their gesture had truly hurt my feelings. If I wanted to get treated like that, I would walk into an Alberta truck stop wearing a LIBERAL PARTY OF CANADA T-shirt.

My experience with the hostel had been no better. While it was certainly cheap, it also came with several loudly snoring drunks, blankets matted with hair from previous guests and linen with the overpowering ambiance of stale cigarettes and urine. I think it's fair to say that the Ivanhoe is not what Pierre Trudeau envisioned for his network of hitchhiking hostels.

This time, at least, I had possessed the foresight to call my friend Corina before I arrived in town, and although she was going to be away for the weekend, she had invited me to use her apartment. This not only meant a safe port of call with laundry facilities (and no snoring drunks), but a convenient base from which to further explore Vancouver. "I'll leave a spare key buried beside the stop sign on the corner of my block," she had told me. All I would have to do was feed her cat and slide the key under the front door when I was finished.

Even with a warm, dry place to stay, I was on edge as I stood at that crowded bus stop in Langley. I don't know why. I certainly didn't feel like much of an explorer. In fact, as I squeezed through the folding doors of the city bus—nodding faintly at a flock of stone-faced commuters—this edginess only increased. Self-consciously, I hunched down on one of the seats near the driver (two seats, actually, one of which was claimed by my huge pack) and tried to disappear. What was wrong with me? The whole purpose of my trip was to meet people, and after three days on the road I was already trying to avoid eye contact. Was it the weather? Was it the transition from my old life into something entirely new? Or was it the sudden sensory overload of a big city? I folded my cardboard sign toward the floor and turned to stare out the front window through squeaking windshield wipers. Please, no questions. Please!

"Where ya headed dude?" I heard somebody call from near the back of the bus.

I turned around to see a pleasant-looking fellow with sand-coloured hair and glasses staring at me. "Heading into Vancouver," I said, trying to brush away a conversation before it started.

"Oh yeah? What does your sign say?"

Damn! No such luck. By this time everybody on the bus was looking squarely at me, so to appease them all, I reluctantly showed the man my sign. "A journalist!" he exclaimed. "What are you writing about?" I mumbled something about my cross-Canada road trip, my intentions to meet Canadians and to see the country. Nothing particularly special about my journey, I explained, just a good excuse to travel and see more of Canada. He seemed satisfied with this, as did everyone else on the bus, and by this time most of them had resumed ignoring me.

That's when a large, stocky man sitting directly behind me interrupted. "Speaking of stories, have I got one for you." He pulled a wad of pictures from his front pocket, waved them in front of my face and started narrating. Most of them were of animals. One picture showed him pressed head to head with a huge steer. "Guess who always wins?" he said with a grin.

"Are you a farmer then?" I asked hopefully.

"Oh no, they all belong to the zoo," he said. "I go out there a lot since my wife died." He flashed another photo in front of my face, this one of two Siamese cats. "My wife talks to me through these nice puddy cats."

A lady sitting next to the man shifted uncomfortably. I smiled and said, "That's nice," the only thing I could really think of saying. Then I returned my gaze to the front of the bus, all the while wishing I could shrink into the seat and disappear.

I was soon sitting on Vancouver's Skytrain, bound for the city centre, but as darkness fell I had further trouble finding Corina's apartment. Or, more specifically, finding her key. It was pitch black by the time I stumbled onto her street, and the rain, curse it, was still crashing down. Shoving two fingers into the wet grass beside the stop sign, I probed for her apartment key. Nothing. I dropped my backpack and squatted on all fours, sliding an entire hand into the muck. Quite unintentionally, I located and squished a pair of earthworms, but I found nothing even remotely resembling a key. I loped across the street to the only other stop sign on the corner, hoping that she might have hidden it there. Again, there was nothing.

By this time I was drenched and feeling more than a little stupid saying hello to the groin area of every passing pedestrian. I slumped onto the wet grass and stared up at the street sign. Had she forgotten to hide the key?

"Idiot!" I suddenly groaned, smacking my forehead with a muddied palm. "Her apartment is the next block over."

April 20, 1997 - Vancouver, British Columbia

The next day was Sunday, and it dawned bright and blue. I woke to Corina's cat Sushi padding around the apartment, leaping from window to window in the morning light. Sushi had been suspicious of this tall, soppy stranger when I arrived the previous evening, especially when I started hanging wet clothes all over the bathroom and hallway. After I walked to the kitchen and poured him some breakfast vittles, however—making sure to give him an extra shot as a peace offering—he predictably became more affectionate.

My sombre mood from the previous night had improved dramatically with the dawn of a new day. As I straddled Corina's bicycle and cycled down Cambie Street toward False Creek Inlet, the edgy sense of foreboding dissolved with my memories of the previous night's storm. There was no longer a feeling of doom and gloom hanging over me. I guess sunshine does that to a person, particularly in a place like Vancouver where it so rarely shines.

I spent a good half-hour riding across the Cambie Street Bridge, stopping often to watch a procession of sea kayaks and dragon boats gliding across the water. Sunshine glinted off the domed Science Centre and the glass towers of Vancouver's downtown core, even as the steep-walled mountains of the Coast Range reared up from behind. Vancouver boasts a sharp contrast of rainforest and Plexiglas that no other city in Canada enjoys to this degree, and the proximity of untamed mountains to hordes of city dwellers is both a blessing and a curse. While people from Vancouver revel in Nature's bounty, hardly a year goes by without several unlucky or unprepared city folk getting lost, injured or killed within spitting distance of Vancouver's skyline.

I pedalled off the Cambie Street Bridge and into the bustling activity of Granville and Robson streets, a mosaic of business suits, rollerblades and strumming guitars. One man stood with four chessboards assembled in front of him, taking on two challengers at once, while at the same time calling for a third and fourth. Another chap, African-Canadian and wearing a colourful vest, used two sticks to juggle and whirl a third stick in the air. "I originally made these to keep myself busy while selling T-shirts," he admitted with a laugh, "but people kept wanting to buy them, so I decided to get out of T-shirts and into this business."

I continued through Chinatown, which was packed curb-to-curb with Asian people shopping for fresh vegetables and seafood: shellfish, mussels, crab, shrimp and countless varieties of fish. The seafood and fresh produce were being hawked from sidewalk stands, and the scent of fish proved overpowering in the heat of midday. Mandarin symbols checkered the front of every market, and on one corner a Chinese lady worked through a sequence of Tai Chi moves, oblivious to the chaos around her.

Wading through the melee brought home that Vancouver has the second-largest Chinatown in North America (after San Francisco). It has become a veritable haven for Asian immigrants flocking to Canada from Hong Kong, Singapore and other Pacific Rim nations. Thirty percent of Vancouver homes now boast either Mandarin or Cantonese as their first language, and there are several Chinese-language theatres in the city, at least two Chinese television stations and three multicultural radio programs that feature mostly Chinese airtime. As these immigrants arrive, many of them are also bringing money with them, which has meant prices along Canada's West Coast have escalated to match a rising demand for real estate. Some people in Vancouver fear this transition, and during my travels I heard strong opinions from a few of them. "We call it "Hongcouver" these days," said one lady, speaking with more than a touch of distaste. "These people are coming here because they have money and they want to spend it in Canada—which makes it tough for us shmoes to afford it."

Fortunately, it's not all tension, as I soon realized while pedalling around the seawall that rings the outer rim of Stanley Park. The cloudless weekend weather had brought out a variety of sun-seekers, and I took great pleasure in watching a medley of pedestrians, cyclists, rollerbladers and joggers sharing the same pathway, often exchanging courteous words. Laughing children played on swings and in sandboxes, as innocent and unaware of differences as they were of similarities.

There were East Indians, Sikhs with turbans, Latinos and Asians walking hand in hand with their children; there were black people and white people and a Native Canadian man with an eagle feather dangling from his hair. During my ride, in fact, I spotted just about every nationality this side of Martian, largely a result of our country's liberal immigration policies. In fact, no other country in the world integrates such a varied cross-section of ethnic groups into its culture. About twenty-five percent of Canada's immigrants come from East Asia, twenty-five percent from South and Southeast Asia, ten percent from the Middle East, ten percent from Africa and the Caribbean, ten percent from Latin America and about twenty percent from Europe and the United States. *Canadian Geographic* magazine has noted that this mix roughly matches the overall distribution of the world's major ethnic groups. It's a mix that has benefited our country immeasurably when one considers the skills, education and international business contacts Canada has gained as a result.

This mixing can also be viewed as a remarkable achievement, particularly when one considers that it has been accomplished with very little disruption or bloodshed. But then, I'm part of a generation already converted, someone who is impressed by these sorts of things. I'm one of those proud Canadians who is comfortable with diversity because I have grown up with it. When I read of Canada's mosaic on Molson T-shirts or hear about it in the news, I tend to puff out my chest, sniff loudly and proclaim: "Now *that's* my country! That's what it means to be Canadian!"

Perhaps some of those reluctant Canadians then, rather than getting flustered about our perceived lack of identity, should consider the advantages to being so diverse. We are not just one thing, but many things. "Canadians could be people who recognize that our country is a state in process," argues Toronto author Bruce Powe, "rather than a nation with one absolute goal." We are a nation without limits, if you will, and the first one to truly embrace this kind of fence-sitting posture.

But enough about the politics of multiculturalism. As I coasted to the end of the Stanley Park seawall, the sun was dropping fast behind the treed slopes of Vancouver Island, which was my cue to turn back toward Corina's apartment. What I experienced that day, as I see it, is what most Canadians envision when they talk about our country's multicultural mosaic. It's the freedom for a person of any colour, race or religion to get out and enjoy some sunshine and a chocolate chip ice cream cone while walking along the beach, without fear of being targeted by piercing stares or racist remarks. As a warm glow rippled through me, it became apparent that when I first arrived, I had been seeing Vancouver in entirely the wrong light.

Chapter 7

Island Beat

May 8, 1997 - Vancouver, British Columbia

The day I left Vancouver, I gave my backpack a nickname. I decided to call it "the piano," which as you can probably tell is somewhat less than affectionate.

While I could put up with the piano under most circumstances—mainly because it deftly carried food and clothing for me—riding Vancouver's transit system together proved to be more than we could handle. For one, the buses are ill-equipped to serve travellers carrying anything larger than a small handbag. For another, the bus drivers (demonic creatures every one) are exceptionally skilled in the art of accelerating then braking, accelerating then braking. They do it with such catastrophic precision that even the most sure-footed person can't help but whirl like a prairie twister from the front of the bus to the back in a matter of seconds. Considering this, it doesn't take much to imagine the effect on somebody hefting around a sixty-five-pound backpack. On one crowded bus, if it hadn't been for fast reflexes and a thick metal bar positioned conveniently at fist level, I would have ended up in the lap of a woman who vaguely resembled my grandmother. She had a cane, and if her persnickety expression was anything to go by, she knew how to use it on deviants like me.

The most deplorable buses are those ones with an obtrusive bar separating the front folding doors into two. How this aids commuter efficiency is beyond me, because even those people without a piano seem irritated by this bar. As for me, well, all it took was getting stuck once to turn me off the design entirely. Somehow I managed to wedge myself between the bar and the front folding doors at rush hour, where a gaggle of unimpressed-looking commuters were forced to glare at me as I vainly struggled to free myself. After I had writhed about for what seemed a short eternity, the driver shook his head, planted his foot on my chest and gave me a powerful kick. "Wait for the next bus," he said gruffly, then shut the door.

Riding the ferry between Horseshoe Bay and Nanaimo was, by comparison, the antidote to cure me of all transit woes: the salt breeze on my face, the liquid blue of sky reflecting off the water, the wide corridors and generously padded seats. I stacked my feet on a cushioned armrest and passed the time writing in my journal. Little did I know that serendipity was already arranging for my next ride.

As I walked off the ferry in Nanaimo, down the metal plank and into the parking lot with swarms of other foot passengers, I pondered the best way to reach the outskirts of the small city. Although it was late afternoon, there was still enough daylight to press north, and I hoped to reach the small town of Parksville, where a care package from home was waiting for me at the post office.

Suddenly, a young couple approached me. The fellow wore tan shorts and sandals, and had a tidy black goatee. His companion was a tall and attractive woman with short, dirty-blonde hair pinned back on both sides. They were roughly my age, and looked like they were marching to the relaxed beat of island life.

"We saw your sign on the ferry," said the man, speaking with an accent I couldn't quite place, "and we were wondering where you're planning to go next."

"Well, I'm trying to get to Parksville," I replied, "but even if you can give me a lift up to the highway, that would be helpful."

"We're actually driving right through Parksville," replied the woman, "so why don't you tag along with us?" Although my astonished expression might have suggested otherwise, I didn't need further convincing. It was as if fate had sent them to make up for all the headaches of that afternoon.

As we drove out of the terminal, the couple introduced themselves as Stephen and Heather. Stephen was a law school grad and South African expatriate who had met this tall, cool Canadian girl in Australia and then proposed to her several years later during a reunion of sorts. The defining moment, he explained, had occurred when he nursed her back to health after a bus accident down under—it just took her a few years to realize it. "She had to love me after that," he said slyly, a comment designed to elicit a faint chuckle and a slight rolling of eyes from her.

After Stephen finished, Heather continued with her version of the story. For most of her adult life, she had been working as a cook at remote tree-planting camps, primarily in northern BC. She explained that, contrary to Stephen's point of view, it was really his deep love for her that had caused him to give up practicing law in South Africa, move to Canada, and agree to work as a dishwasher at her tree-planting camp that summer.

"I'm going to be a dish pig," he laughed, "but at least I'll get paid to wash dishes for my wife now." She reached over and patted his bare leg affectionately. I asked him, tongue in cheek, whether he considered this slight change in career plans a step backwards. "Nah!" he said. "I'm a very adaptable person—I think this kind of experience brings us all down to earth." Besides, he added, it's only for one summer.

As we continued north through a smattering of quiet coastal communities, it struck me how the three of us were chatting like old friends rather than people who had been strangers fifteen minutes earlier. As if reading my mind, Heather blurted a sudden invitation to stay with them at her mother's house, where they had been crashing for the past few weeks since arriving from South Africa. "We're sleeping on the pull-out sofa in the living room," she said, "but I think there's room for you on a foam mattress at the foot of our bed."

Of course, there was the slight problem of having to explain to Jill, her mother, who I was and where I had come from. I was a tall, unshaven stranger carrying a large backpack—would she really want me staying in her home? Heather decided to risk it. "Not to worry," she told me. "If my mother doesn't want you there, she won't be shy about telling you."

Who was worried?

As we rolled into Qualicum Beach we spotted Heather's mom a couple of blocks from her house, a smart-looking British lady with white hair and large round spectacles. "This is Matt," explained Heather, rolling down the passenger window to greet her mother. "He's a hitchhiker we picked up in Nanaimo. Would it be okay if he stayed with us tonight?" I said hello and pasted the most convincing Boy Scout smile I could muster across my face.

"Not at all," Jill said without hesitating. "I'll see you at home shortly. We can all sit down and have some tea together."

As we drove off, Heather rolled up her window, then turned around and grinned at me. "Isn't my mom the coolest?" she said.

May 9, 1997 - Qualicum Beach, British Columbia

I woke at the foot of Stephen and Heather's bed to the smell of coffee brewing in the kitchen. Jill was up setting the table for breakfast while her husband Dave lounged in a burgundy housecoat, reading the morning paper. Dave, a tall man with gentle quips, greeted the three of us with a singular nod when we entered the kitchen. I thanked the family yet again for their unexpected hospitality, a comment that encouraged Dave to turn to me and say: "You know, Matt, this household is well known for taking in strays, which surely explains why I'm here."

Over breakfast, Dave entertained us with stories about growing up on a Saskatchewan wheat farm, which he claimed had put soil in his blood. He had married Jill a little over twelve years earlier and, although he now favoured the more temperate coastal climate, he also had many fond memories of the prairies. He told us stories about walking to school in bare feet, about using the Eaton's catalogue in the outhouse for more than just reading, and of course, how he had witnessed the founding of the New Democrat Party by political activist Tommy Douglas.

He recalled one visit to his small town by the now-famous politician, who gave a speech at a nearby farmyard because the Liberal candidate had already booked the town hall. "Douglas climbed to the top of a big pile of manure so that everyone could hear him," Dave told me with a wink. "Then he said: 'Pardon me ladies and gentlemen, but you'll have to bear with me because this is the first time I've had to speak from the Liberal platform.'"

A couple of hours later, Stephen and Heather drove me to the Parksville post office. As Stephen unlocked the trunk to remove my backpack—carefully lifting my belongings from their trunk—something made him stop. He looked up at Heather, then glanced over at me, his eyebrows furrowed into a tight knot. "You can't leave us yet," he suddenly announced. "We're just getting to know you."

Heather and I stared blankly at each other for a moment, not sure whether we had heard him right.

"I think we have room for all his stuff, plus our bikes," he said to Heather. "Why doesn't he come down to Jim and Libby's with us?" Jim and Libby were old friends of Heather's, he explained, and tonight they were throwing a backyard barbecue and mountain-biking party at their home in Crofton.

By this time we were all chortling uncontrollably, no doubt because Stephen's offer sounded so comical. It was like inviting a panhandler into your home and not allowing him to leave until he had showered, enjoyed three square meals and sat down for some quality conversation. Nevertheless, the proposition sounded like a good one. "Jim and Libby are travellers too," Heather told me, "so I'm sure they won't mind." The couple looked expectantly at me. I nodded assent, and within minutes we had packed their car and were burning south on the island highway toward Crofton.

JIM AND LIBBY Connor met while hiking the West Coast Trail in the late 1980s. Now, almost a decade later, they were living in an idyllic little house in an idyllic little town overlooking an idyllic vista of the Coast Mountains, the Gulf Islands and the Strait of Georgia. They had two handsome young boys, who were as blonde and blue-eyed as their father—boys that had already developed an addiction for bicycles. Luke, a curious four-year-old, already looked like a pro as he steered his tiny BMX down the sloping street in front of their home. And judging by several enthusiastic attempts to mount his father's bike, two-year-old Zachary would not be far behind.

When Jim arrived home from work, Stephen and I helped him unload several sheets of drywall into the garage. Jim sported a mop of wild blonde hair and the lean, rugged appearance of a man who loved anything to do with the outdoors. Yet he also came across as incredibly humble and soft-spoken, a paradox of sorts. It was obvious that he and Libby were not rich, but whatever they had, they seemed willing to share with others—even with an equally not-rich hitchhiker they had met earlier that evening. I liked them immediately.

Heather and Libby busied themselves in the kitchen, making salads and vegetable wraps, while Jim, Stephen and I migrated to the back yard with cold drinks and the boys. Other guests started arriving soon thereafter: two brothers named Tim and Mike with Tim's pregnant wife Grace, as well as another couple, Colin and Marie, with their two young sons in tow. Both of their youngsters quickly joined Luke and Zachary in the back yard.

At most backyard barbecues food is of primary importance, but at this particular gathering it soon became evident that mountain biking ruled the roost. The girls, with the exception of Grace, donned spandex shorts and bike helmets just before dinner and disappeared like quicksilver down the lane. They returned an hour later, basking in the radiant glow of mud that covered them from top to bottom. It was the boys' turn next, and thanks to Marie, who loaned me her bike and helmet, I was able to join in the fun.

Fun, of course, is a relative thing. While living in the mountains, I had discovered early on that barrelling down steep forest trails while perched on a mountain bike—trails typically cluttered with rocks and trees, I might add—rather terrifies me. Whenever a friend had managed to talk me into a bike trip, I had invariably ended up walking my bicycle up and down long sections of trail. The thought of catapulting headfirst over my handlebars into a tree (and most mountain bikers seem to have stories about such incidents) has for some reason never appealed to me.

Considering this, you can probably imagine the mixed resolve with which I joined this group of bona fide mud hounds. As Jim led us confidently through the forest on an old cart track, I could feel the anxiety building with every stroke of my pedals, though to be fair, the first thirty minutes were actually quite pleasant. It was hard work, but as we slogged steadily uphill along a trail festooned with puddles and mudholes, a forest of stately old trees enveloped us in a soothing calm. And there's no question I quite preferred this to screaming downhill, except for the grim realization that what goes up must also come down.

Eventually the incline steepened, which proved to be less of a problem for Jim, Stephen and Colin, who were used to this sort of thing. For Tim, Mike and me, however, it was like trying to climb a greased cookie sheet with curling shoes.

"The sad thing is that this is probably their easy trail," Tim choked, wiping sweat from his brow. Mike and I just shook our heads, sucked hard for oxygen, and felt grateful that there were three of us to share in the suffering.

"Well, we're at the top," Jim finally announced.

"Oh, here we go with that 'We're at the top' speech," griped Colin, probably doubting the top would ever appear. All of us, with the exception of Jim, were by this time wheezing desperately, and we appreciated the few seconds he gave us to catch our breath. It didn't last long. The next thing we knew, Jim was leading us down a short, narrow trail to a rocky bluff and a view that proved to be well worth our efforts. The sky, which had been hidden above the forest canopy, was now a soft peach colour, bathing the green hills, rich pastureland and scattering of country bungalows with warm evening light. Jim stood at the end of the point with his bike, a perfect silhouette, surveying his kingdom like ... well, like somebody who had been up there before. For long moments we sat in awe, the silence cleansing us in a way that no words could have.

"We'd better get going," Jim finally said, breaking the forest's hush. "It's going to get dark in about a half-hour." Reluctantly we left our perch, mounted our bikes and, noticing the long shadows starting to creep across the forest floor, followed blindly after Jim as he disappeared down a narrow side trail.

The next half-hour encapsulated my worst mountain-biking fears in all too vivid detail: pitching violently through mud, zinging under tree limbs, crashing through dense foliage. I wasn't sure what frightened me more: taking a nasty spill or losing everyone in the shadows, taking a wrong turn and missing dinner. Regardless, Mike and I decided to walk a couple of sections for fear of decapitating ourselves, and it was only once we had reached a flat section crossing a field that I was truly able to relax. As the last rays of light faded from the forest, frog-song erupted from swamps along the fringe of the trail, and I felt a pleasant and at once singular peace wash over me. The next instant I hit a tree stump at the edge of the trail and pitched violently over my handlebars.

Arriving back at the house, we were greeted with news that dinner was almost ready. After spraying ourselves off with a garden hose and licking our war wounds, we changed into fresh clothing for what was, in my mind, the most important part of the festivities. It was nearly nine and all of us were famished. Much to my delight, we were soon sitting around the kitchen table laughing loudly, sharing stories from the trail and digging into steaming hot quiche, Chinese noodles, vegetables and fresh French pastry.

As we ate, the grand coincidence of the whole experience dawned on me in a way that it never had before. What if I had never met Stephen and Heather on the ferry, never stayed with them in Qualicum Beach, never joined them on their trip down to Crofton? Of course, if I hadn't met Stephen and Heather, I never would have met Jim and Libby and their circle of friends, nor would I have seen the perfect, breathtaking vista Jim had shared with us earlier that evening. Strangely, I felt sad for the opportunity I might have missed, even though I hadn't.

These thoughts led me to ponder what other grand adventures had passed by without me even realizing it. An infinite number of roads lead to an infinite number of possibilities. Suddenly, Canada seemed much larger than it ever had before.

Chapter 8

Quart-a-Whiskey Cove

May 14, 1997 - Quadra Island, British Columbia

After spending three days touring the southern part of Vancouver Island with Stephen, Heather and their entourage of friends, my primary goal was simply to hitchhike north on the Island highway without getting further sidetracked. I was already more than two weeks behind schedule, and I realized that my money was running out. If I wanted to make it even halfway across Canada by summer's end, I would have to move faster and find a way to magically stretch my bank account.

The trouble with thumbing through paradise, of course, is that getting sidetracked seems to be more of a rule than an exception. And the nice weather wasn't helping much. Every bend in the road seemed to be enticing me into rudderless abandon. Perhaps that's why I listened when a high school teacher named Trevor told me that I would always regret leaving the West Coast without first visiting the Gulf Islands. "If you pass by without seeing them," he had warned me, "you'll miss a part of Canada that exists only here."

That was how I ended up on Quadra Island.

It didn't take me long to figure out that the Gulf Islands, as he had promised, truly are a world apart. Novelist Fred Bodsworth described this part of the coast as an "invisible cage," its separateness illustrated as much by what it keeps out as by what it prevents from leaving. The Gulf Islands are famous for their eclectic blend of artists, environmentalists, musicians and hippies ... not to mention a pace of life that can fairly be described as lax. In the past, particularly before real estate skyrocketed, these islands were havens where people came to escape the crushing drive of what most of us call progress. They formed a society where value was placed on how little you worked and what gadgets you *didn't* own, as opposed to the yardsticks of status and money used everywhere else.

Living in a land of plenty, people from the Gulf Islands have for years enjoyed boundless opportunity for creative pursuits. And it should come as no surprise that artistic people often arrive at creative solutions to the most basic problems of subsistence. It was on Quadra that I heard a story—true or false, I will never know—about a community of hippies who for several years "shared" a child, mainly so that several families could claim child welfare benefits. The charade apparently lasted for quite some time, and may have carried on indefinitely had it not been for a hawk-eyed child welfare worker. Realizing that she had seen the same child at another home, she called for an investigation and put an end to benefit payments. Much to their dismay, the hippies were forced to get jobs.

Before crossing Johnstone Strait on the ferry, I was lucky enough to meet two people who were still living this lifestyle (without the welfare fraud, of course). Not unlike a Shire hobbit, Zack was short and stocky, with curly brown hair that sprouted from underneath a straw hat. His girlfriend Stephanie wore a colourful dress patterned like a rainbow, and from her hair dangled an eagle feather. She also walked around in bare feet, which seemed strangely out of place on the concrete sidewalks of downtown Campbell River. "It's so I can feel the vibrations of Mother Earth," she told me.

While different, these people were certainly not lazy castaways running from real life. They had jobs, and they came across as vibrant and absolutely brimming with positive energy. Stephanie's smile blended with the afternoon sunshine, and was so radiant that she actually made me blush. It was like being a high-school freshman all over again. Half of me wanted to stare at her, while the other half wanted to look the other way. I felt more the fool knowing that Zack was standing right beside her. This odd feeling, which I chalked up to copious quantities of sun, fortunately started fading as they told me about their lives. They had met while travelling around Australia several years back, and their mutual love of music had eventually brought them to Quadra Island, where they started building drums out of windfall logs. "We wouldn't think of cutting down trees to build our instruments," Stephanie assured me.

I listened with interest as the pair described how they constructed the drums by cutting logs into hoops, then stretching cut goatskin over the top and tying it in place with brass rings and rope. When they weren't working, they played and composed music—not only using drums, but with piano, flute, saxophone, harmonica and didgeridoo. "I enjoy spreading life and love through my music," Stephanie explained. "I think you can use it to reach people and help them." As an afterthought, she added: "That's why we're here, isn't it? To make a difference in the world with our own unique gifts?"

I couldn't have agreed more. My unique gift, of course, was bumming rides off people, then finding a way to get invited home with them so that I could feed my face. To be fair, I always offered stories and insights from my travels in return—and, not infrequently, my skills as a dishwasher. It was a fact: more than once I had told people I was crossing Canada on a dishwashing tour, a pronouncement that was always greeted with heartfelt cheer. "More clean dishes across Canada than any man who's gone before," I would boast. I didn't have a guitar, as a young Stompin' Tom Connors had when he hitchhiked all over Canada, so I had to offer something else. Some gifts, you have to realize, are not for the faint of heart.

AS AFTERNOON TURNED to evening, I found myself on Quadra, sitting on some grass at the edge of a steep embankment overlooking Quathiaski Cove. My gas stove was hissing, and in the bubbling pot were pasta noodles for dinner. Again.

Directly below, a collection of tugs, barges, sloops and fishing boats lay nestled in the protected waters of a marina. As I surveyed the scene, I found myself falling into a silent reverie, a lull, a meditative trance. And how couldn't one, really, faced with the spectacle of bright streaks of mustard and crimson blending with the dark green of forest on water. The scene felt like serenity manifest. No, the scene *was* serenity manifest. The only thing cutting through the mirror calm was a small skiff floating silently offshore, from which two fishermen were casting for rock cod.

That was when I met the burly fellow. Before I saw him, I heard the *crunch, crunch, crunch* of padded feet walking along the road behind me.

"Once you've been here, you never stop comin' back," said a gruff voice, piercing the evening's calm like an arrow. He appeared with two friends, his face streaked with soot and grime, and as he passed he tilted his grease-stained ball cap with blue-collar hands. The man was broad-shouldered and walked with a tough swagger, yet his coy smile was definitely not that of a thug.

"I'm sure most people never want to leave," I replied, my annoyance at being disturbed quickly evaporating.

"Yep, Quadra Island is a world unto itself," he admitted. "But if you're looking for the real world, you won't find it here." Seconds later, he and his friends descended to the pier and disappeared behind some boats.

About an hour later, I wandered to the end of the dock with my camera, just as the sun dipped behind the eagle-talon spires of Vancouver Island. I found the burly chap and his mates sprawled across the wharf talking shop, discussing in painful detail the miserable state of the West Coast fishery. When I first arrived, their banter stopped, regaining its momentum only after they saw it was me. I overheard the big fellow talking about trade connections with California, and listened as a fellow with a French-Canadian accent discussed British Columbia's sovereignty movement. (Apparently the French are separatists on both sides of the country.) Curious, I snapped a few photos, then wandered over and sat on the dock beside them. I no longer felt awkward wandering up to complete strangers and striking up a conversation. Rather, three weeks into my hitchhiking trip, it felt abnormal not to. One of the greatest gifts that hitchhiking bestows on its practitioners is the ability to connect quickly with people, to charge into the unknown with the expectation of success, and to do so on a shoestring budget.

If the fishermen were offended by my brashness, they didn't show it, and soon I was listening to them talk in heated tones about what the federal government should do with its fishing policies. It was similar to what Heather's stepfather Dave had done with the Eaton's catalogue in his prairie outhouse.

"Dere aren't any fish left," the French guy complained. "What do dey expect us to do out 'ere? Learn 'ow to knit?" The comment was aimed at me more than anyone.

"We have more in common with California than Ontario," said the burly fellow. He looked over at me and introduced himself as Victor. "Trade has always been north-south on the West Coast. As far as I'm concerned, Canada can stop at the Rockies."

And so the conversation went for quite some time, everyone taking turns voicing disgust with Ottawa's political elite. It was like a Jerry Springer special for disenfranchised fishermen—or perhaps a net-and-tackle hospice group—and for several minutes I wondered if I might bear witness to a sudden and bloody uprising. Then again, this was Canada, and the men's angry words soon faded with a call to drink beer rather than a call to arms.

Thirty minutes later Victor and I ended up at the Landing Pub, grubbing for last call. The atmosphere was definitely lively when we arrived, and I saw Victor scan the bar and offer subtle nods to a few people before we found a table. The place had the earthy feel of a greasy spoon mixed with the homey ambiance of a grandmother's kitchen, except for the dull roar of rock music blending with laughter in the background.

A working man to the core, Victor had obviously lived a hard life. For the most part, he had fished when the catch was good and hauled timber when it wasn't. Yet belying his rugged appearance was a jovial, almost gentle wisdom in his eyes that was hard to ignore. And there was no doubt that my youth and naivety amused him: "So how big is an average fishing boat? What do you guys catch out here? Can you make a lot of money in the fishing industry?"

But he didn't make fun of me. Instead he pointed up at the wall where a photo of the famous *BC Packers 45* was displayed. Beside it was a copy of the old Canadian five-dollar bill. "The first million-dollar sockeye catch was made on that boat," he told me. "Fishing can be pretty lucrative when there's fish in the water and the market prices are up."

Part of the reason for recent quotas and restrictions, he admitted, was that fishing in the old days had been based on a "gold rush" mentality. "The longer you stayed awake, the more fish you caught, and the more fish you caught, the more money you made." He described how a fishing crew would literally carry on for several days without sleep, grabbing twenty minutes here and there when they really needed it. "Any gillnetter'll tell ya that when you return from a three- or four-day opening, you can't walk on the wharf because it's not moving. And when you wake up, you have no idea where you are."

This gold rush mentality actually had its beginnings with the trade in sea otter pelts. British sailors nearly wiped out the entire population of sea otters between the years 1785 and 1825. The chinook and sockeye salmon were next, followed by the pink, coho and chum. There are countless stories of coastal rivers so thick with fish during the spawning frenzy that a grown man could have practically walked from one bank to the other on their backs. Then, in the 1990s, everything collapsed. Dozens of salmon runs were suddenly in danger of disappearing altogether, and rivers that had once hosted millions of spawning fish every fall were reduced to a trickle of a few hundred. "What happened?" I asked Victor.

Like many fishermen, he was reluctant to talk, but in the end he explained how the collapse of the fishery was related to several factors, most of which had to do with poor planning and greed. As logging companies stripped the land of timber (often wiping out salmon spawning grounds in the process), modern fishing technology had allowed boats to become too efficient for their own good. Couple these factors with poor management of the fishery, and the Pacific's bounty—which had once seemed limitless—could no longer support itself.

The pub closed around one, about the time my eyelids started feeling like bricks of mortar. Seeing that I was falling asleep, Victor invited me to crash for the night on his boat, an invitation that I was not about to turn down. I had always wanted to try sleeping on the water for a night. "We'll soon see if you have a liking for it," Victor chuckled. "Some people never get used to the rocking."

Once outside, we walked for a few moments in silence, a pale moon casting an eerie glow across the water. Suddenly Victor stopped, lit a cigarette and looked at me with a furrowed brow. That's when the fisherman-philosopher came pouring to the surface. "You know, when I was your age I remember an old feller comin' up to me and sayin': 'All the world needs to get rid of is hate, greed and envy.'" Victor paused for a moment, as if to contemplate his own words. "I've thought a lot about that statement all through my life."

"That's a nice idea," I replied. "Making it stick is the hard part."

He nodded as though my statement were inconsequential. "It's a nice thought anyway."

We walked down to his boat, and in the process of trying to load my piano on board I managed to bruise and scrape pretty much every exposed part of my body. Once we were inside, Victor pointed at a short plywood bench, which he cleared to make room for me. Below deck was a slightly larger cabin where he slept. "Sorry it's not fixed up right now," he offered apologetically, "but I've been working on a few things." By this time I was feeling absolutely exhausted, and would have been quite satisfied sleeping on the dock. So I unpacked my sleeping bag, unrolled my foam mattress along the bench and crawled in for a good night's kip.

From below deck, Victor continued with more of his stories, and as a result I drifted in and out of sleep for some time. I did catch a few of the tales, even though most of the meaning and details were lost; the last thing I remember hearing was a story about picking mushrooms on Vancouver

Island. Victor was walking through the forest when he stumbled onto a log with a huge mushroom growing at the far end—"the largest mushroom I'd ever seen," he raved. Delighted, he carried on picking the smaller ones until he had worked his way to the far end of the log. The surprise came when he reached the mushroom and discovered that it wasn't a mushroom at all. "Somehow, that mushroom had turned into a cougar," he said. Regrettably, I didn't get to hear what happened next, as that's precisely when I drifted off to sleep.

May 15, 1997 - Quadra Island, British Columbia

Slipping discreetly from Victor's boat early the next morning, I wandered up the hill to a small lodge where I found public showers and a laundromat. I was ecstatic! It had been five days since I had showered and washed my clothes. It was to the point where my odour was starting to offend even me. Once I was squeaky clean, I sat in the sun and spent over an hour penning notes in my journal, listening to birds singing and watching squirrels cartwheel through the treetops. *Choices bring chance encounters*, I wrote, *and these chance encounters can teach us valuable lessons.* That's how I felt about meeting Zack, Stephanie and Victor—not to mention Stephen, Heather and the assortment of other characters across southern BC. Choice had led me to this unexpected part of the coast, where by chance I had met each of them. The rewards for my efforts, I realized, were the ideas my new friends had shared with me.

I bumped into Victor at the Landing Pub shortly after twelve. He was sitting at the bar with a cup of coffee, rolling a cigarette, not in any particular rush to get on with his day. "How did you enjoy sleeping on the water?" he asked.

"Fine," I replied. "Actually, I think I could get quite used to it."

He smiled a mischievous smile. "When you're out fishing, sometimes you'll come down off a wave and hit the ceiling," he told me. "That's when going for a pee in the middle of the night gets pretty interesting."

The Landing Pub is one of those places where everybody of importance within twenty kilometres gathers for gossip at appropriate hours of the day. So after roaming the island for several hours that afternoon, I returned there for dinner, just in time to join the boisterous reverie of happy hour. I didn't see Victor, so I sat in a corner by myself and ordered some food, anticipating an evening of drinking coffee and writing in my journal.

I couldn't have been more wrong. Before I had written two sentences, a gregarious waitress named Beverley had pried information from me, and without even asking, dragged me to a table where several blokes sat laughing and telling stories at a mile a minute. The loudest character of them all was a fellow named Bill O'Connor, logging pioneer and one of the "founding fathers" of Quadra.

"Welcome to Quart-a-Whiskey Cove!" Bill roared, crushing my pinky finger in his vice-like grip. "Nobody here can even spell Quathiaski."

Bill was a grey-haired, barrel-chested man with a laugh that was something beyond contagious. He had everyone within earshot in stitches, relating stories about debauchery in Uranium City from his time there during the early 1950s. Uranium City is a now-abandoned mining town in the bush country of northern Saskatchewan, but when he worked there, it was prosperous by regional standards. He had worked hauling ore from the Eldorado mines across Lake Athabasca; that was before he got a more lucrative job driving taxi. "I swear, there was no more than ten miles of road," he laughed, "but there were twenty-one cabs." Apparently, all the taxi drivers were into bootlegging, until an undercover cop busted the ring and brought them all to justice. They were given a choice: pay a thousand-dollar fine or spend two months in jail.

"The feds thought they were gonna get this big pile o' cash," chortled Bill, "but all the boys stuck together and chose the jail term." As a result, the government had to fly a big plane all the way in to get them—at great expense—and then fly them back out once they had served their time. "After that, they didn't worry about bootlegging anymore."

After I had wolfed my dinner down, Bill drained the last of his beer and invited me back to his acreage, a short drive up the road. "I've got something you'll probably want to see," he told me with a grin. By this time I was well used to island life, and didn't think twice about leaving my backpack unattended in the restaurant for a few hours.

Now, I've never been much of a car fanatic, but what I saw when Bill opened the large sliding door on his shed impressed even me. From one end to the other, the shed was filled with nothing but antique cars—some covered, most dusty, all parked in hodgepodge fashion. Bill pointed to a 1931 Model A, "just like the one Bonnie and Clyde were driving when they got all shot up," a 1918 Chevy truck (the first year the company made trucks) and a 1962 Lincoln convertible, "exactly like the one JFK was assassinated in." He tapped the Lincoln's rear bumper, almost affectionately. "I've been collecting cars for thirty-five years," he told me. "The only thing I don't have is the Batmobile."

We continued across his yard, walking past several antique logging trucks parked in front of a long row of trees. They were painted with crisp yellow and green markings, the trademark O'Connor shamrock displayed prominently on all sides. The biggest treat, however, was waiting for us in his driveway. It was a spindly-looking two-seater with an open-air cockpit, two seats and spokes across the wheels. Tied to the back was a large, weathered tree stump. Whatever it was, it was obviously old.

"What is it?" I asked.

"This here is a 1912 Atterbury logging truck," he grinned. "It was built in Buffalo, New York and has a top speed of sixteen miles per hour. Wanna go for a ride?"

"Absolutely."

When Bill fired the truck's cylinders, I could feel the thing vibrate before it jumped suddenly to life. He stepped on the gas and we lurched forward, almost giving me whiplash in the process. It wasn't long before we were sputtering along the highway in front of Quadra's strip mall, attracting the attention of children playing softball in the warm evening light. They waved at Bill enthusiastically, stopping their game to watch us drive by. "I'm just a crazy old collector," Bill laughed, waving back at his adoring fans.

This crazy old collector also had a devilish streak, which became apparent when I looked back over my shoulder and noticed a plastic replica of a spotted owl perched on the tree stump. The spotted owl, of course, is the bird most revered by environmentalists for helping them stop the logging of old-growth forests on the west coast of the United States; loggers, not surprisingly, despise the bird for the same reason.

"We got some interesting reactions from people when we drove it down to a show in Spokane," Bill told me with a chuckle, changing gears and turning back toward his house. "When we go back this year, I think we're gonna put an arrow through the sucker."

Chapter 9

Flying Poodles

IMAGINE, IF YOU will, planning a dream vacation across Canada. You and your wife are from the southern United States and have slipped comfortably into the golden years of retirement. Now that you are financially secure and have plenty of time on your hands, you can afford to fulfill one of your great lifelong ambitions. You plan to venture north to see some of western Canada's awe-inspiring wilderness—its rugged mountains, ancient forests and abundant wildlife—everything from grizzly bears to humpback whales. So you purchase a top-of-the-line RV, fill it with creature comforts, and set off with your wife and little dog Fifi in search of adventure.

Now imagine travelling to the Queen Charlotte Islands, where it's been promised you will find an abundance of all this. You locate a quaint bed and breakfast, settle in, then head out for a walk along one of the sweeping beaches on Graham Island's east side, sauntering peacefully through the dune grass in bare feet. There are Sitka black-tailed deer tracks criss-crossing the sand, flocks of plovers and other shorebirds pecking at flotsam, the sound of surf lapping at the shoreline. You are holding hands with your wife, smiling contentedly, and watching Fifi as she roars across the dunes in search of seagulls to chase.

And look at all those bald eagles! You have never seen so many in one place all at the same time. There have got to be at least two dozen of them—perched in the trees, nibbling at crabs and fish scraps washed up along the high-tide mark. What an idyllic, postcard-perfect scene. This, you realize, is what it feels like to be at one with nature. Ahhhhhh! The gritty feeling of sand between your toes, the majesty of towering Douglas fir, the perfect arc of a bald eagle's wings as it dips toward the ground and ... Oh my God! Oh my God!!! Fifi? Fifi!

Now imagine getting back into your RV—without Fifi—and driving to the ferry dock, vowing never to visit the Queen Charlotte Islands again. If you can imagine all this, you'll get a pretty good picture of how an retired couple from Texas must have felt when this very thing happened to their pet poodle while walking along Tlell Beach.

May 20, 1997 – Queen Charlotte Islands, British Columbia

The conflict between man and nature has a long history in Canada, but the region just north of Tlell on the Queen Charlotte Islands is particularly well known for it. This is where the Canadian government started an agricultural program around the turn of the nineteenth century, offering free land to homesteaders willing to take a gamble. The region surrounding Tlell is one of the few places on the Charlottes flat enough for agriculture, although the thick forest and low-lying bog proved as difficult for settlers to deal with as the mountains. Eventually the island's wild, remorseless elements and poor drainage chased homesteaders back to the mainland, and many of them abandoned farm fields and livestock in the process.

Today, these islands are still populated with rugged individualists not unlike those who inhabit the Gulf Islands: Haida artists, loggers, fishermen and modern-day homesteaders who thrive in a remote and difficult environment. The people who disappear into these far-flung places often do so because society proves too stressful, too complicated or too fast-paced for them. Nature can certainly be unpredictable, but in a nonjudgmental sort of way. It treats everyone and everything equally— with kindness or severity, depending on its mood. It doesn't apologize. It simply is what it is, and there is a soothing reassurance to that.

Although I was received warmly wherever I travelled, I couldn't help but marvel at the love-hate relationship some islanders have with terrorists (also known as tourists). More than once I was cornered by an islander with glazed-over eyes, babbling on about ferry-induced claustrophobia during the height of the summer tourist rush. Apparently this sort of thing can invoke nightmares—the kind that involve waking up behind a gridlock of RVs coming off the ferry, or perhaps serving tourists who ask questions like: "Is this fish fresh?" Many people who live on the Charlottes were born and raised with island blood, and for the turncoat mainlanders who ended up here, they came to escape the throngs of civilization. Fortunately, islanders seem to place hitchhikers in a different sort of category. Although there was little traffic on the roads, I rarely had to wait more than a few minutes to catch a ride.

Such was the case one afternoon when I was thumbing towards Tlell from just outside of Skidegate. It wasn't long before a family sedan zoomed past me, hit the brakes, and cranked a hard U-turn before roaring back in my direction. The driver was a middle-aged lady, and beside her in the passenger's seat sat a teenage girl. "My daughter Sarah saw your sign and wants to be in your story," the lady told me. "My name's Joan Anderson. Jump in—we'll take you home and feed you."

Twenty minutes later, we pulled into an open farmyard, a slice of paradise tucked away from the rat race of mainland BC. When the Andersons and their three children sold their house and moved from Kamloops to the Charlottes five years ago, they went through some big changes. "Basically, we had to start from scratch," said Joan. They cut a road in to their property, dug a well and built their house and barn from the ground up. The acreage was now a hobby farm by choice, complete with ducks, pheasants, geese and chickens two-stepping around the yard.

For the kids, adjusting hadn't been easy. "For three years we didn't even have a television," lamented Sarah, "so we did a lot of camping and walking along the beach to make up for it." Joan and her daughters learned how to collect spruce and pine cones, selling them to a local dealer who would in turn sell them to a seedling warehouse in BC's interior. The cones were then distributed across the province for replanting. "We got good at chasing little squirrels around and ripping off their caches," Joan chuckled. "They learned to fear all of us."

Joan's husband Bruce, a heating and plumbing contractor, drove into the yard a few minutes after we did. He was a slender man with a fiery red beard and lucid catchlight in his eyes. He spoke with both kindness and authority, and when he shook my hand, the down-to-earth gesture made me feel right at home. It wasn't long before I joined him for his daily rounds feeding the animals, listening intently as he talked to his birds. "Hello ducks!" he chirped, scattering alfalfa pellets across the lawn. "Hey there little fellers," was his greeting to a pen of juvenile turkeys. He turned to me and explained. "When I talk to the animals, they relax a little bit."

On our way through the chicken pen, Bruce collected a handful of fresh eggs and handed them to me for safekeeping. It was then that we stumbled across Mother Goose, the queen of the barnyard. "How are ya Mother Goose?" Bruce cajoled. Mother Goose always deserved some extra TLC, Bruce explained, so he picked her up, tucked her webbed feet in one palm and snuggled her close to his chest. He stroked her feathers gently, and for his efforts received a sharp beak tearing at his whiskers.

Dinner was well underway by the time we made it into the house, and the kitchen was filled with the kind of mouth-watering aroma that makes you want to start chewing on your arm. "What are you cooking?" I asked Joan, salivating heavily.

"Island special," she replied. "Fresh halibut and North Beach crab."

"Sounds delicious."

"Wait'll you taste it," said Bruce. "The halibut melts in your mouth like a marshmallow." He pursed his lips for visual effect, smacking them loudly. "You can pretty much live off the ocean here. And there aren't many places in the world where you can still do that."

"You don't even need to be a fisherman," added Joan.

As if to reinforce Joan's point, Bruce pulled out a picture of a middle-aged lady standing beside a gargantuan fish. "This here is a 225-pound halibut," he told me, emphasizing the weight with words just so it would sink in. "I was helping a friend of mine on a fishing charter, and I told this lady I'd kiss her bait for luck."

"Did you actually kiss it?"

"Of course I did," he said. "How do you think she caught this thing?" Then he added, almost thoughtfully: "Murphy's Law, I tell ya. She was visiting from Toronto. The beginner always gets the big one."

Sarah joined us in the kitchen, along with her sister Valerie, and the five of us were soon feasting. The Andersons continued talking about how the Charlottes are a land of plenty, a place where most people still rely heavily on what they shoot in the woods and what they collect from the ocean. The forests are full of black-tailed deer, and despite the decline of the commercial fishery, the ocean and rivers are still teeming with salmon and halibut, rock cod and steelhead. Wild blueberries and salmonberries can be picked in the lowlands; razor clams and king crab are collected along the beaches. Even kelp loaded with herring spawn is harvested for those brave individuals who appreciate this salty delicacy.

"It turns my stomach to watch kids gnawing away at the stuff," admitted Joan. "But some of them eat it like candy." I had already seen long strips of kelp hanging from several island porches, but until then had no idea what it was.

But enough about kelp and herring spawn. We were in the middle of feasting on fresh halibut—which, as Bruce had promised, was like nothing I had ever tasted. Grilled to perfection, it melted in my mouth as fast as I stuffed it in. This was accompanied by crab, which we extracted with nutcrackers and forks, pulling the tender white flesh from spindly legs and dipping it into hot garlic butter. I was in heaven. I came back for seconds, then thirds.

"Enjoy it," said Bruce. "These crabs are a pain in the ass to catch all right." He went on to describe the technique, making the pursuit sound like a Charlie Chaplin slapstick comedy. "Mostly, it involves a lot of shuffling back and forth through knee-deep water," he explained, "trying to scoop them out of the drink with a pitchfork covered in chicken wire." His words were riddled with the kind of nostalgia only a veteran crab chaser would understand. "I can tell you this," he added. "You haven't lived until you've tried to outrun a crab in half a metre of water." If nods were anything to go by, the girls and Joan heartily agreed.

The more the Andersons talked, the more I became enthralled with island life. They talked about it like it was normal, but with a colourful spin that made it anything but normal. This was especially true when they described the strange ritual known as Hospital Day, an annual day of special events organized to raise money for island hospitals. The most famous event is the cow pie lottery, which is eagerly anticipated for several weeks prior to the carnival. A baseball diamond is marked off in a grid, with squares that are numbered to correspond with lottery tickets. On the day of the actual event, an oblivious cow is set loose in the field, no doubt wondering why huge crowds of people have gathered to cheer loudly as it ambles from square to square. As might be expected, whichever square the cow desecrates first wins the corresponding ticket holder a vacation. You might say the event has given new meaning to the term "shitty luck."

Before I retired to their living-room couch for the night, Bruce had one more surprise in store for me. I was organizing my belongings when he walked across the kitchen, opened the freezer and grabbed a plastic bag with a ten-inch frozen crab inside. He walked to the kitchen table and dropped it in front of me with a loud *thunk!* I had been so impressed with the evening meal, he wanted to give me something for the road—a token to remember the Andersons by.

"Take this with you," he told me, grinning at my shocked expression. "It'll be ready to eat about noon tomorrow."

June 1, 1997 – Queen Charlotte Islands, British Columbia

During my last day on the Queen Charlottes, I was lucky enough to meet Nelson Cross, one of the renowned Haida carvers who worked with Bill Reid on the large cedar canoe displayed at the Canadian embassy in Washington, DC. I first bumped into Nelson at an art gallery in Queen Charlotte City, and after talking to him for a few minutes he invited me back to his carving shack to see some of his work. It was there that I watched him put the finishing touches on a four-foot yellow-cedar totem, listening intently as he talked about Haida legends and the potlatch custom—the gift-giving ceremonies held by chieftains to validate status and rank in their clan.

The stories were nice, but it was Nelson's carving that held my attention, and I marveled at the incredible cartoonish faces taking shape under his knife. "Where did you learn to carve like that?" I asked.

"All my uncles were good with knives," he explained, "I told them from day one that I was going to be a carver, so they were always showing me things."

The Haida have always been exceptional artists. Unlike many other Native groups in Canada, they had plenty of time for cultural pursuits—the favourable climate and rich bounty of the West Coast ensured that much. According to Pierre Berton in his book *Seacoasts*, Natives with fully stocked larders would take to the woods for the ceremonial season, which happened during the winter months. Nearly everything was endowed with the carver's signature: huge dugout canoes, longhouses with cedar planks, totem poles and elaborate masks carved to mourn the passing of relatives.

When Captain James Cook first landed off the BC coast in 1778, he was shocked to find these master woodworkers already using complex tools—everything from knives, jade chisels and drills with stone bits, to precision tools constructed from the teeth of large rodents. And as trade between white explorers and West Coast Natives progressed, the Haida distinguished themselves as master tradesmen. It was not the cheap plastic beads and trinkets they demanded, but rather the more sophisticated iron tools that would become so important to their woodworking culture—tools that carvers like Nelson are still using today.

"How long did it take you to carve this?" I asked, admiring the totem.

"Let's see," Nelson said, hemming and hawing. "Maybe two months." This was longer than normal, he added, because he had worked on it piecemeal. And how much would he get for it? The four-foot pole would probably fetch upwards of ten thousand dollars at a specialty art shop in Vancouver. "There's a big demand for the smaller house poles these days," he told me. "A lot of people are willing to pay seven to ten thousand for them."

Nelson finished up for the evening, and as he did, he pointed to the faces taking shape in the wood—the wolf, the raven and the eagle. All of these animals are important to Haida mythology, he explained, because each one represents a different Haida clan. Of all the creatures, I liked the eagle best, positioned near the top of the pole with a fish dangling from its outstretched talons. As we closed the door behind us, I couldn't help but wonder what an eagle might look like clutching a poodle, and whether Haida mythology had a legend for that one.

Chapter 10

Alberta Bound

June 5, 1997 – Prince Rupert, British Columbia

It was the second week in June when I finally left the Queen Charlotte Islands to the crabs, carvers and plethora of colourful characters. Although I had intended to catch the ferry from Prince Rupert to Alaska, my travel plans changed once I reached the mainland. For one thing, the American ferry that sails to Skagway proved to cost almost four times what I had paid to travel from Vancouver Island to Prince Rupert. It was an expense that my rapidly shrinking bank account couldn't handle. For another thing, an unexpected opportunity presented itself when I picked up a phone at the ferry terminal and called my grandmother in Edmonton. She told me that she and my step-grandfather Bob were leaving for Alberta's Peace River country in a few days, and that they were hoping to find somebody to drive their motorhome.

"Would you like to come along?" my grandmother asked hopefully, aware that my plans for the summer would likely interfere.

I pondered. It was a last-minute decision, but one that might work for everyone involved. I had never met my uncles, aunts and cousins from the Peace—hospitable country folk who live in the farming belt just north of Grande Prairie. Over the years I had heard plenty of stories about them, particularly stories about my grandmother's eldest sister Toots. My father fondly remembers her dino-sized steaks and the fact that she used to hide him under the porch so that my grandfather couldn't spank him. He was also fond of her command of the English language, which he claimed would have made a sailor blush.

Yes, my father had always regretted not taking our family up to the Peace, but after moving away from Alberta, we never seemed to have the time or money to make it back for family gatherings. And now here it was—the golden opportunity I had been waiting for, a chance to meet everybody for the first time. Considering the litany of family histories I had listened to over the last few weeks, I couldn't pass up the chance to learn more about my own.

I told Gram that I would be there in two days. Three days, tops.

June 12, 1997 – Edmonton, Alberta

The Yellowhead highway was easier to travel than I had expected, and I managed to cover the distance between Prince Rupert and Edmonton in only four rides. It felt odd to leave behind the quiet fishing villages of the West Coast, only to be swallowed up two days later in the utter pandemonium of traffic jams and the West Edmonton Mall. I had grown accustomed to the lush forests and the savoury scent of salt water, and now I was swimming through urban congestion and arid heat. I couldn't wait to get back to the laid-back ways of rural life.

In its own way, the rolling agricultural land that surrounds Edmonton is as picturesque as any place in Canada, although people who look at it with "tourist's eyes" might disagree. The people who most appreciate this landscape tend to be those born unto it. In the absence of rushing rivers, mountain spires and cathedral forests, prairie people are content to look elsewhere for inspiration. Where visitors see an endless patchwork quilt of farm fields, interrupted only by occasional pincushions of scrub brush (in short, nothing of much scenic value), those who live here see fertility, bountiful harvest, human history and an endless, dancing sky.

One of the most interesting features of the Peace River Valley is the fact that it is safely hidden from those who lack modern road maps. It lies beyond a wide swath of boreal forest in a place where you wouldn't expect to find rich soil and prime pastureland. Driving north on Route 43 motorists leave behind the arable farmland west of Edmonton, and—just beyond Whitecourt—are suddenly swallowed by shadowy forests. Then, just when they think civilization has disappeared entirely, the highway cuts back onto the fringe of farmland near Valleyview. That crops can flourish this far north—further north than some polar bears living along the coast of Hudson's Bay—is testament to the fertile effect of the extra-long daylight hours.

As the three of us chugged north, the scenery brought back many fond memories of my own childhood; I had grown up on an acreage just north of Saskatoon, where my family had moved when I turned seven. As I gazed at bulrushes and reeds sprouting from marshes in the ditch, it made me think of a harvest moon in September and the sweet scent of clover drifting on prairie winds. I remembered how my brother and I had chased grasshoppers and frogs, built tree forts and hiked along the endless kilometres of abandoned railway tracks that sprawled across the countryside. We had also played soccer, football and hockey, inventing curious versions of these games that generally involved using my sister's Barbie Powder Puff accessories as goalposts (at least until they had been smashed to smithereens).

The journey called up even more powerful memories for my grandmother and Bob. As we drove, they pointed to important features of the landscape, and sometimes to dying towns that had once been bustling communities. The funny thing about this pair was that during the Great Depression their families had known each other quite well. The two had even spent time at each other's homes, yet they couldn't remember one another. For all they knew, they had never met ... until friends introduced them in 1992, after they had both been widowed. It was only then that my grandmother and Bob realized their connection—that they had literally grown up in each other's back yard—a fact that made a second marriage a much easier pill to swallow.

It wasn't until late afternoon that we finally reached my uncle Lawerence and aunt Dorothy's farm near Spirit River. As we eased up the gravel lane, we were greeted by two large dogs barking and racing after the motorhome. We pulled into an open farmyard with two houses, a large silver Quonset, plus a collection of storage bins, shacks and other buildings scattered about. Beside the larger, more modern home was a dugout surrounded by poplar seedlings.

Still, it was the vast assortment of farming equipment that most caught my attention. If the size and quantity were anything to go by, these people were serious about farming. As I looked out the motorhome's window, I was tempted to think John Deere was my cousin rather than a brand of tractor.

Toots's daughter Dorothy (who my grandmother calls Dot) came running from the house and threw her arms around each of us in turn. Dot looked to be in her mid-fifties and sported jet-black hair, curly and slightly pouffed up on top. Healthy after years of working on the farm, this woman was no Minnie Mouse, and she greeted us all with down-home country fervour. Rumours of a warm reception had not been exaggerated.

We followed Dot into the house, where the savoury smell of roast beef and garden-fresh turnips wafted from the stove. The entrance opened into a spacious kitchen with vinyl floors, dark oak cupboards and a table with seating room for twelve. This was a country kitchen all right, simple and functional, ready to serve a house full of starving farmhands in a pinch. "I hope you guys are hungry," said Dot, "because I've been cooking all afternoon."

Twenty minutes later, my uncle Lawrence walked through the door, grumbling about the weather. He was wearing work jeans and cowboy boots, and his thick silvery hair was hidden beneath a baseball cap. When we shook hands, his vice-like grip reminded me of Bill O'Connor's (the logger I had met on Quadra Island) because he nearly crushed my knuckles to dust. "God, I haven't seeded this late in a long time," he said, obviously worried about what looked like rain moving in from the west. "The stuff that's in is good, but an inch of rain would probably finish us for the season."

After hanging his jean jacket in the hall closet, Lawrence gestured for me and Bob to follow him into the living room. On the way, he pointed out the back door to his father's old farmhouse, which sat directly across the road from his own. This was where Lawrence's eldest son Kelly was living with his family, while Kelly's brother Trevor and his clan were living in the farmhouse where Lawrence and Dot had raised them, a few dozen metres across the farmyard. Both sons worked as farm hands.

"We're gambling like hell on frost," sighed Lawrence, easing back into a plush sofa chair. "Whatever we plant now might get hit before we can get it out of the ground. I tell you, I'm sixty-two and I'm starting to get tired of this game. I mean, I still love the land and all, but I've driven enough tractors. Dorothy wants me to cut back or quit. The only problem is, I don't know how much money you need to retire these days." Lawrence paused for a second, lost in thought. "Last year I ran a tractor for sixty-seven hours non-stop ... it's definitely time to retire."

"How many acres are you running now?" asked Bob.

"Thirty-six hundred," Lawrence replied. "We've already got three thousand acres planted, but the six hundred around the house haven't been done yet."

"How long will it take to seed that?" I asked.

"We should be done by the end of the week, if the weather holds."

Farming is not unlike gambling. And a person really can't know the meaning of the word risk until they have thrown tens of thousands of dollars into the ground, hoping and praying that there will be plenty of sunshine, rain when it's needed and no hail or frost to kill the crops before they're taken off the fields. The story about the farmer who won a $10 million lottery jackpot is charmingly cynical and slightly absurd, but it makes its point. When asked what he would do with his winnings, the farmer smiled and replied that he would probably keep farming until the money was all gone.

That's probably how Lawrence and his father felt after purchasing their first farm, after which they faced five years of one disaster after another. "I thought I'd made the biggest goddamn mistake of my life," he told me. The only way that he and Dorothy had survived was by opening a confectionery in Spirit River—a venture, he recalled, that was saved by hordes of children who came in with fists full of change to buy penny candies.

"Thank God those kids used to kick and scream," Lawrence laughed. "It was them getting their parents to come in that gave us our first real start."

I was also surprised to learn that Lawrence's parents (my relatives, no less) were originally from Quebec, part of a large flock of French-speaking settlers who purchased one-way train tickets to Alberta during the early 1900s. Many of them wanted to farm on a larger scale, and by that time the heavily populated St. Lawrence river valley no longer gave them that option. "When we talked to Dad, he always spoke to us in French," Lawrence recalled. "I used to be able to read, write and speak French fluently, and my grandmother never did learn to speak English. She would go to church, but other than that she never really left the farm."

It wasn't long before Dot called us for dinner. As we got up, I gave Lawrence a pat on the back and asked him the most pointed question yet: "If there's so much hardship involved with farming, why get into the business at all?"

He paused for a moment, obviously taken off guard. "It's kind of hard to explain," he replied, scratching his chin. "I like being my own boss, of course, but it's more than that." Another pause. More chin scratching.

By this time I was feeling kind of uncomfortable, figuring that I had put poor Lawrence on the spot by calling into question his decision to start farming. Not exactly protocol for the first time you meet your uncle.

We Canadians thought we were free from the deadly livestock plagues of Great Britain, yet here I was displaying acute symptoms of Foot-in-the-Mouth disease.

There was a mad stampede for the food, and it wasn't until we were comfortably seated with roast beef and all the other fixings on our plates that Lawrence finally answered my question. "I guess I got into farming because of my connection to the land," he told me. "You can pick up a pile of dirt and run it through your fingers ... and it's your dirt. Plus, I kind of like that I can walk from here all the way to the golf course on my own property."

June 15, 1997 – Spirit River, Alberta

The weather held for the next three days, and as can be expected, Lawrence, Kelly and Trevor took full advantage of it. Lawrence typically rose before dawn, which arrives unbearably early during the summer months when you're this far north. He would clomp around the house for a few minutes in his cowboy boots while Dot fixed him some coffee, then disappear into the farmyard, where he rendezvoused with his sons and another hired hand named Pete to outline the day's activities.

For those of us who preferred to eat a more leisurely breakfast, we were kept updated on progress and greatly entertained by the many stories and observations filtering in over the kitchen's CB radio: "This soil is too goddamn lumpy," somebody would say. "It's the shits for planting," would answer another. Invariably, Lawrence would chime in with his two cents' worth: "You know, some days I could give this goddamn farm away."

Dot usually just shook her head, mumbling something barely audible and with great exasperation under her breath. "You know, Matthew," she told me at one point, "to be a farmer, you have to learn how to swear first."

Her eldest son Kelly was a prime example. Over dinner one evening, he recalled with a certain misty-eyed fondness a ritual that he and his mother used to have. "When I was a kid, she used to put Tabasco sauce on my tongue whenever I cursed," he told me. He laughed a little, then shrugged his shoulders. "It obviously didn't work. All it did was give me a taste for hot food."

Out in the fields, Lawrence drove the lead tractor, dragging a harrow to loosen the soil while Kelly followed with liquid nitrogen fertilizer. Trevor, a short muscular fellow with shoulder-length brown hair and a grin permanently plastered to his face, spent his time picking up supplies in town or loading the seeder with canola seed for the third and final pass. All this took place with a great deal of efficiency, yet Lawrence rarely took his eyes off the horizon, scanning for thunderstorms that could spell the end of spring planting.

One evening late in the week, I jumped into a tractor with Kelly. Stout and blonde, he was the spitting image of what you might expect a prairie farmer to look like: muscle shirt, nicotine-stained moustache, Cargill cap on backwards. It was a beautiful night, and the summer sun streamed in through the windshield of the tractor, even though it was already nine in the evening. We circled the field again and again, a cloud of dust billowing from the back of Kelly's machine as he dragged off an endless line of cigarettes. "I could sit here and tell you what a perfect guy I am, but why lie?" he said bluntly. "Why try and hide what I am? Some people say I'm obnoxious, and to tell you the honest truth, they're probably right."

There was no question—I liked this guy. He was rough around the edges and shot straight from the hip. There was no mystery. What you saw was what you got, which according to Kelly is an important ingredient for any true friendship to stand the test of time. As we did our rounds, he related with similar brutal honesty his love for working the land, and his strong desire to continue on where his father would soon be leaving off. While his younger brother Trevor planned to move south and open up a gym, Kelly planned to stay in Spirit River permanently with his wife Dallas and stepson Dustin, inheriting part of the farm when Lawrence and Dorothy retired.

"Could anything possibly change that?" I asked him.

He pondered for a moment, almost as if the thought had never occurred to him. "I guess the one thing that might conceivably change that," he told me, a noticeable twinkle in his eye, "is if I won ten million in the goddamn lottery."

Chapter 11

Twenty Days Across Canada

June 17, 1997 – Grimshaw, Alberta

He was a man with a bike. That's all I knew. He was leaving the next day to attempt a cross-Canada bike marathon in twenty days. If he was successful, he would break a world record and return to the small town of Grimshaw, Alberta a hero. If he was unsuccessful, he would still return to Grimshaw a hero. Either way, I was certain he would return to Grimshaw and sleep for a very long time.

I never cease to be amazed by the funny twists and turns the road takes when travellers are open to possibilities. Perhaps that's why hitchhiking was so popular in the sixties—because its compass bearing was oriented toward discovery more than brute functionality. Unlike Generation X—the generation of rudderless cynicism—young people from my parents' generation figured out that even without direction, the road still gave them answers. And the more I travelled, the more I realized that those same rules apply today. If you have faith, the road has a perfect, seamless way of leading you to where you must go next.

It was those strange cosmic laws that surely rescued me from a KFC restaurant in Grimshaw, where I had been sitting since my grandmother and two of my aunts had dropped me off earlier that morning. Staying at Lawrence and Dorothy's farm had been a great opportunity to learn more about my own family's history—and it had been a nice break from the uncertainty of a hobo's life. But I was on a road trip, and comfort is the death of nomadism. I had to push on.

My goal after leaving the farm was to reach Yellowknife for the summer solstice celebrations, which are held every year on the twenty-first of June. The only problem was that riotous thunderstorms had appeared out of nowhere, and now I was trapped inside good ol' Colonel Sanders's chicken barn, waiting for the deluge to stop. The storm was the kind that whips needles of rain at you horizontally from every direction, soaking you through and chilling you to the bone no matter what you're wearing.

There was a lot of nothing between the Peace River and Yellowknife, and the thought of getting stranded, turning blue and hypothermic as eighteen-wheelers doused me with plumes of icy water, didn't appeal much. With each passing hour I grew more certain that I would never make it to Yellowknife in time.

That's when a lady with a thick German accent walked past my table and asked what I was writing. "Are you trying to change the world?" she laughed. Lost in thought and not in the mood to chat, I offered a curt answer, hoping that she would move along quickly. But she didn't. Instead, she grabbed my hand and tugged me toward the door, saying: "Come on, you have to meet my husband." A minute later, I had thrown my backpack into the trunk of her tan Mercedes, only to get pinned to the seat as she burned out of the parking lot.

Her husband, as it turned out, was the man with the bike. The reason I didn't know his name yet (or her name, for that matter) was that she had dropped me at their home and then promptly disappeared again, speeding off to pick her kids up from school. "Make yourself at home," she told me on her way out the door. "I'll be back in twenty minutes."

MY MYSTERIOUS NEW friends, I soon learned, were from South Africa—not Germany as I had initially presumed. Cezanne and her husband Arno had arrived in Canada seven years earlier, with five hundred dollars in their pockets and a baby on the way. Inuvik, a small Native community in the Northwest Territories, was in desperate need of a surgeon, so Arno agreed to spend three years working in the high Arctic in exchange for Canadian citizenship. "I cried when we went there and I cried when we had to leave," Cezanne chuckled. "The sun never set, the mosquitoes never stopped biting and the kids would stay outside until two in the morning."

It didn't take long to build an easy rapport with Cezanne's family. Her daughter Natasha, when she learned I was a writer, fished out some poetry for me to read. And it wasn't long before Cezanne's son, Arno Jr., dragged me to a nearby schoolyard to shoot some hoops. It had stopped raining—indeed, the sun had appeared as though from nowhere—yet I couldn't bring myself to leave without spending at least one night with these people. They were far too eccentric and interesting to pass by at a glance, so I suppressed my urge to set off for Yellowknife. Unforeseeable events would prove my decision to be a sound one.

It wasn't until dinner that I had an opportunity to sit down and visit with Arno, a short, lean man with silver-streaked brown hair and an exceptionally strong South African accent. I had to listen carefully to understand what he was saying. It's an accent that I can't reproduce on paper either, so you'll just have to imagine it for yourself.

"I'm a bit of an obsessive personality," Arno admitted, shovelling food into his mouth. "I was feeling a bit flat last year, so I thought, 'Why not cycle from here to Edmonton in one day?'" So he did—covering more than five hundred kilometres to raise money for a fitness centre at the local hospital. This success is what led him to plan the Extreme Challenge, a coast-to-coast bike marathon from Victoria to St. John's. He would break a world record if he were able to complete it in the twenty days allotted.

As we talked, it became clear that Arno was no stranger to extreme adversity. He had participated in more than forty marathons, not to mention cycling trips across both South Africa and the United States. But why plan something so difficult? As Sir John A. Macdonald duly noted, Canada is a country short on history and long on geography … not the sort of geography one typically tackles on a bike, and certainly not in twenty days. "I don't care about quantity, only quality," Arno explained, easing back in his chair. "A person has to challenge himself every day. I want to raise awareness that people can do this sort of thing their entire lives."

As the next day was the big send-off, friends and well-wishers started dropping by in droves to wish Arno luck. One of the visitors was John Isinger, one of two friends who had volunteered to handle trip logistics for Arno; among other things, he would follow Arno across Canada in a motorhome, cooking meals and stopping whenever Arno needed to stop. I followed the two men outside to where the RV was parked, and after poking around inside to make sure everything was in order, they started discussing the final details of their travel itinerary.

The evening passed with much laughter and merriment, beer and liquor flowing in volumes the equal of the mighty Peace River itself. Arno sat in the living room telling jokes and laughing about how he would have to face the press with a terrible hangover the next day. Cezanne's parrot B.J. fluttered up from the basement, alighting on shoulders at random—first Cezanne's, then Natasha's, then mine. Cezanne and Natasha talked to him in a strange language, clucking and squawking. I assumed that they were using some form of parrot dialect until they informed me that it was actually Afrikaans, an official language of South Africa.

I retired to a spare bed in the basement shortly after two in the morning, unable and unwilling to hold my eyes open any longer. Most of the revellers had departed by this time, but both Arno and Cezanne were still going strong. Nobody was going to put an end to this party—that much was clear. As I listened to their infectious laughter echoing down the staircase (which seemed to thwart even my best attempts at stuffing pillows around my ears) it was hard to believe that this man would be climbing onto a bicycle and leaving on a record-breaking journey in a few days. All I could think as I drifted off to sleep was: better him than me.

June 18, 1997 – Grimshaw, Alberta

When I woke the next morning and made my way upstairs, I found Cezanne surprisingly bright-eyed and in the process of making breakfast. As I pulled back the living room curtains and stared outside, I saw that my greatest fears had been realized. The rain had returned with even greater intensity, and showed no sign of letting up. I was just about to write Yellowknife off for good when Cezanne chimed in with some unexpected news. "One of our Inuvik friends stopped by last night and said that he's driving up to Yellowknife late this afternoon," she told me. "If you ask him nicely, maybe he'll take you along with him."

Fifteen minutes later Robb Stemp walked through the front door, holding a black leather carrying case. He was a middle-aged fellow with a wiry build, short dark hair and facial hair that lined his face not unlike felt trim. It wasn't so much his appearance but his mannerisms that immediately shouted "Salesman!" Not con-artist salesman by any means, but the kind of person who genuinely enjoys the process of bartering and selling. "I'm Robb with two 'b's," he grinned, holding out his hand for the requisite deal-sealing handshake.

"Pleased to meet you," I replied. "I'm Matt with two 't's." I hoped that my firm grip and smart reply would seal a deal for my ride to Yellowknife.

Robb with two 'b's sat down at the kitchen table and opened the snap links on his carrying case with a loud *Click!* His eyes were lit with the bubbly enthusiasm of a five-year-old. He was ready to do business.

"I've got a couple ideas that are going to swamp Canada in the next two months," he bragged to Cezanne, pulling out a package of what looked like small metal clips. On the package was written, "Book Darts." He held them up proudly and beamed from ear to ear. "I've just secured full Canadian distributorship."

More items poured from his leather case. He had an assortment of rocks, beluga whale teeth and a tea-coloured piece of plastic that he identified as nuclear glass. "It's not radioactive because it's seventy-percent lead," he assured us. Then he pulled out two trays of sparkling gemstones, each specimen housed inside a small circular case made of plastic. "These are Australian blue sapphires," he said, unveiling a small capsule of bright blue stones. "And these here are Thai blue-green sapphires. You should see them when they're polished." He bounced his eyebrows for visual effect. "That's when they really sparkle." Nonchalantly, he told us that we just happened to be in the right place at the right time. The Australian blues were on sale for a mere two thousand dollars; the Thai blue-greens he would let go for an easy grand.

We were all quite impressed, not least because the precious stones, knives, textiles, ceramics, incense and toys were all from Southeast Asia. Robb puffed out his chest and told Cezanne that his latest gig involved twenty-five hundred dollars' worth of uncut sapphires—precious gemstones that he had acquired while on business in Thailand. He had talked a fellow living in southern BC into cutting and polishing them, and once that was done, he figured he would be able to sell them on the US market for an easy seventy-five grand.

As for talking him into giving me a lift to Yellowknife? I must not be a bad salesman myself, because I had sold him on the idea even before bringing it up.

IT WASN'T UNTIL after lunch that Arno arrived home from the medical clinic and went running upstairs to change into his track uniform. It was primarily black, with blue and lime markings on the sleeves. On the back it read: CANADA IN TWENTY DAYS. "I'm kind of nervous," Arno admitted as we drove to the airport in his motorhome. Robb and Cezanne were following in her Mercedes, so he could talk freely without having to worry his wife. "Normally when I do things like this, I just do them. I'm not used to all this publicity."

And publicity there was. Oodles of it. By small-town standards, his journey was a breaking news event, and it looked like the entire community (along with a small army of small-town reporters) had come out to see him off. At least forty people were jammed into the lobby of the Peace River's dime-sized airport, along with banners, decorations, kegs of coffee and several trays of Mr. Mugs donuts. Almost immediately, Arno was whisked away by a television reporter, then by another for a newspaper story. When he finally made it to the front to claim his prize— a succulent honey-glazed donut—some wisecracker at the back commented on his healthy diet.

"Fueled by donuts across the country," retorted Arno, his mouth full of dough and sugar. "What could be more Canadian than that?"

The speeches were next. Arno, Cezanne and Robb crowded together and accepted a letter of safe passage presented by an elderly, balding man who was apparently the mayor of Peace River. Already signed by him and the good mayor of Grimshaw, the letter was thereafter to be presented for signatures to the mayors of all major cities along Arno's route.

After a few more speeches and a quick spin on his bicycle around the airport's indoor hangar (for pictures, of course), it was time to go. "I want to thank everybody for sharing my dream," Arno shouted, wheeling his bike out the front doors of the airport and into the pouring rain. "I just want everyone to know that I won't let them down."

Last-minute preparations were unbelievably frenzied back at their house. Arno and Cezanne had made plans to drive to Hinton that night, which was several hours away, and they still had plenty of packing to do. I wasn't surprised, considering that the previous night's festivities had carried on into the wee hours of the morning. Not wanting to be underfoot, Robb and I decided to pack up and leave. He walked me out to his motorhome, opened the door, and showed me where to stash my backpack so that it would be out of the way.

It was here that I first met Jazz, Robb's Japanese Bear dog. At first, I thought Jazz was quite friendly—until I tried re-entering the motorhome when Robb wasn't there. A low, guttural snarl seemed to indicate that I was not yet familiar enough to be walking around untethered. Luckily for me, I beat a hasty retreat. I would learn later that Jazz, if feeling the slightest bit suspicious of somebody, has been known to remove limbs for future DNA identification.

By seven that evening, having wished Arno luck for the thousandth time, Robb, Jazz and I climbed into the RV and pulled away. Before leaving Peace River, we tanked up on gas, then stopped at a Subway for some chicken Caesar sandwiches and cookies. Although Jazz had dibs on riding shotgun—and he suspiciously eyed me as I, in turn, eyed his seat—he relinquished the privileged position at Robb's prompting. "I would have been quite happy to let him sit there," I told Robb, which was quite true. The last thing I wanted to do was perpetuate further bad feelings between myself and Robb's toothy sidekick.

As for Arno's world record, I called Cezanne several months after returning to the Rockies, eager to hear about his cycling trip. She told me that for more than a week it had looked as though Arno might actually pull it off ... until, not unlike Terry Fox, he reached Thunder Bay. It was there that he rounded a hairpin turn and blew his knee out—a great disappointment for a man who expects so much of himself. Not surprisingly, almost immediately after getting back he started planning a second attempt.

Whether Arno ever breaks his world record doesn't matter to anybody else, of course. As far as the good people of Grimshaw are concerned, he's still a hero.

Chapter 12

The Story of Robb

June 19, 1997 – Route 35 near High Level, Alberta

"That's an incredible sunset," I said off-handedly, gazing through the bug-spattered windshield of Robb's RV. The digital clock on his console read just past one in the morning as piercing beams of red, orange and mauve danced across an endless flat expanse of scrubby boreal forest lining both sides of the highway.

"Actually, that's sunrise," Robb corrected me.

"Oh."

Even though we were still several hundred kilometres south of the Arctic Circle, this late in June the night was really just perpetual twilight. The sun would drop below the horizon for perhaps three or four hours, but the sky was never completely dark. As I would soon learn, getting used to this can be quite challenging.

I looked back and watched Jazz snoring softly, stretched out across one of the padded bunks in the back. He was probably counting the sheep he would like to chase down and decapitate. "He's a good friend to have around," Robb said. "When I was up in Whitehorse last summer, I came out from having dinner and found the driver's side window smashed and glass scattered everywhere. When I climbed inside, I saw that my CD case had been moved from under the front seat to the dashboard—and beside that on the floor was a pool of blood. Jazz was lying in the back like nothing had even happened. Nothing else had been touched."

As we drove, Robb entertained me with stories about his life as a swashbuckling salesman and modern-day road warrior. At my prompting, he carried on to relate a good part of his life's story, the tale of a professional free spirit poking around Canada, the United States and Asia. He was seven years old when he first went to a foster home, and for several years he was bounced around from family to family. He hated school and was kicked out in grade eleven because of problems getting along with teachers. During his self-described "rough years," he even landed himself in jail for eighteen months. But he was philosophical about it. "Sometimes you need to see how bad it can get before you can see how good it really is," he told me.

After he got out of jail, his life regained some critical direction. He finished high school and found work as a welder and carpenter, yet he felt there had to be more to life than working for somebody else. So he moved to Inuvik and started a hardware store called Arctic Rim Distributors. It was there that he learned to work harder than he had ever worked—and party harder than he had ever partied. He lived in a flat with plywood floors because it was easier to clean up after an Arctic brouhaha. Sometimes he would wake up completely disoriented, not even knowing what day it was—the combined effect of work, play and odd daylight hours in the far north.

Still, during those surreal years Robb learned to tap into the power of positive thinking. "You have to look at every day as a good day," he explained, "and then sometimes you have a great day, or several great days in a row. You have to love what you do, which in my case is haggling." He explained that he was at his best when buying, selling or trading—and for that reason, he hangs up a sign that advertises free haggling lessons. "Hell, I've sold freezers to Inuit people," he laughs. "If I can do that I can do anything."

We stopped for a pee break at the side of the road, roughly thirty minutes after passing High Level. It was then that I discovered another grim reality of the Far North: mosquitoes. To avoid the little blighters, I found myself two-stepping along the road at high speed while urinating— no doubt a comical sight—while doing my best to miss my shoes. On such short notice, it was the only thing I could think of to protect my privates from the swarms of bloodthirsty insects. Robb apparently felt no need to do the same. In fact, as he ambled back to the RV, he casually plucked several large insects off the front grille. "Great fishing bait," he extolled.

Back in the cab, we discovered to our dismay that Robb had left one of the windows open, and for the next few minutes we were on a seek and destroy mission to kill several dozen "mozzies" that had penetrated our otherwise bug-proof fortress on wheels. Outside, thousands of them were clinging to the windshield like a bad sequel to Hitchcock's classic thriller *The Birds*. "And this isn't the worst I've seen them," Robb told me. When he lived in Inuvik, two youngsters from town had decided to run away from home one night. They were eventually found—one dead from overexposure to insect bites, the other in critical condition from the same. "Mosquitoes are not to be taken lightly up here."

With the RV clear of insects, my attention turned back to the sunrise as it continued to brighten the pastel sky. What had been thunderheads and sooty black clouds hanging over the Peace River valley had cleared entirely once we reached High Level. We rode in quiet contemplation for some time, watching a halo of crimson shimmer across the open road, creating an eerie glow around the hundreds of tiny bug carcasses splattered on the windshield. The surrounding land was pancake-flat with miles of swamp and green muskeg in every direction, except for the occasional homestead chiselled into the land by some determined soul. "Do you want to hear a good story?" Robb finally asked, breaking the silence.

"Sure."

"I remember this day at the Inuvik dump, shortly after they closed down the Canadian Forces base. I was standing there unloading some garbage when a huge military truck pulls up alongside and dumps this huge pile of copper wire right in front of me. The good stuff, you understand. Well, I just about choked. I spent six hours hauling it home and another six hours packing it into canisters. Then I shipped it down to a copper plant in Edmonton." He paused, letting the punchline hang in the air for several seconds. "So what do you think happened next?" he asked. He was grinning from ear to ear.

"You ... got some money?" I suggested.

"I drove down to Edmonton three weeks later and picked up a cheque for twenty-eight thousand dollars," he beamed, laughing out loud. He finished his sentence with a loud *Chi-ching!*

"I'm not sure people will want to hear that story," I chuckled. "Maybe I should write a book about all the ways our government wastes tax dollars."

"That'd be one long book," he said. "Loooooonnnng book!"

To keep his eyes open, Robb continued sharing stories as he drove. He told me about the small golf course that locals from Tuktoyaktuk have made on the barren tundra. He also told me about getting swarmed on the Dempster highway by thousands of migrating caribou, and about sleeping beside Liard Hot Springs in the dead of winter, relying on steam alone to keep him warm. I had always imagined I would treasure my time in the north—but now I knew that I would.

As the glow of the rising sun crept ever closer, our conversation drifted on to more serious topics. "Are there any important lessons about life that you've learned over the years?" I asked Robb. I've always had a passion for these philosophical questions, and I suspected he did as well.

He thought about it for a while, scratching his beard with his thumb and forefinger. "You know, relationships are what life's all about," he finally told me. "You have to try to love people unconditionally. Drugs are temporary, sex is temporary, pretty much everything is temporary. You've gotta feel that peacefulness and bliss inside, because that's what really lasts."

It was nearly four in the morning when we finally pulled over to get some shut-eye. The sky was by then a bright peach and the sun was threatening to leap above the horizon at any moment. Robb pulled some cushions down from the top bunk, which I laid on a flat wooden plywood panel, grateful that Jazz moved onto the floor at Robb's urging. Despite the Arctic day already creeping in through the windows, both of us quickly passed out. Tomorrow was already here, and we both knew that we had better get some sleep while the day was still young.

Chapter 13

Ravin' Mad Days

June 19, 1997 – Yellowknife, Northwest Territories

Suffering the effects of acute sleep deprivation, Robb and I arrived in Yellowknife by mid-afternoon later that same day. I had to rub my eyes in disbelief as the lonely gravel track we were following suddenly turned to pavement, and as the barren rock and dwarf forests of the last several hundred kilometres faded into the multi-storey office buildings of Yellowknife's downtown core. I hadn't been sure what to expect from the capital city of the Northwest Territories; I only knew that I hadn't expected a centre that was so cosmopolitan. I mean, there's certainly no reason northern Canada shouldn't have all the amenities we enjoy in the south— it was just embarrassing to realize that southerners like me knew so little about the place.

The next day—the start of the Ravin' Mad Days solstice celebration— was blistering hot. The midnight sun must have been pushing thirty-five degrees, yet the mood in Yellowknife was anything but lethargic. There was a nervous energy pervading the city in anticipation of the night that never ends. There would be live bands, dancing, pub crawls, a midnight carnival and a golf tournament (which would start at three in the morning). I learned that some people even go water skiing on Great Slave Lake during the wee hours of the morning.

At around five that afternoon, I discovered Robb waiting less than patiently to set up his merchandise along Franklin Avenue, griping that traffic was still clogging the streets in what must be Yellowknife's version of rush hour. "It normally takes me two hours to set up," he groaned. "How do they expect me to get all of this ready for six o'clock?" Things got worse. By the time traffic was finally halted and Robb could finally move his trailer into position, it was actually after six. I offered to give him a hand, knowing how far behind schedule he was. "I really appreciate this," he told me, unlocking the trailer doors. And with that we started hauling boxes full of merchandise and plunking them on the sidewalk, their contents spilling onto the street: incense, sand animals, hats, purses, jewelry and all manner of assorted knick-knacks. Robb even had a rolling rack stacked with clothing for sale.

It was then that another welcome surprise happened along: a friendly girl with curly chestnut-coloured hair. Her name was Jennifer, and as I unpacked she explained that she had met Robb through a mutual friend the previous night, at the same time I had been sitting in an all-night coffee shop writing in my journal and trying to keep my bloodshot eyes open. Anyway, Robb and Jennifer had apparently hit it off, so he had recruited her to help with sales during the festivities. She had a sparkling smile, and I would have stopped to chat with her for longer had we not been so frantically emptying boxes full of goodies onto fold-out tables.

The streets were soon filled with the sound of a carnival in full swing. There were, of course, the usual concession stands serving up the worst in fast food: candy floss, snow cones, hot dogs and French fries. It's the kind of stuff that gives you rotgut, but it tastes so good and is so culturally linked with this type of event that for one night nobody cares about eating huge quantities of food with fourteen-syllable ingredients. There were also teenagers racing through the side streets on their skateboards, dousing each other with cans of Gillette foamy shaving cream, occasionally covering innocent bystanders by mistake.

Halfway down Franklin Avenue, a large, padded gladiator ring had been set up for sparring competitions. I could tell Northern kids were not used to seeing games like these, because they were literally vibrating with excitement as they waited in line. There were oversized boxing gloves and padded poles for jousting, not to mention the funniest sight of all: jumbo-sized sumo suits that children could actually fasten themselves into. Once secure, they were free to run around bouncing off the walls (or each other) with little fear of being hurt. Of course some parents (being parents), had grand notions of letting every child try this wondrous game. Whether this was in the spirit of fairness, or simply in the spirit of ignorance, it was hard to say. The problem was that some children were simply too small to fit the gigantic sumo suits properly, and once fastened inside they just sort of rolled around with a terrified look on their face until somebody decided it wasn't working.

I checked in with Robb several times over the next few hours. Each time I walked back to his display, I found him and Jennifer mobbed by customers pawing through his merchandise. He was raking in a fistful of cash and beaming from ear to ear. "It was definitely worth coming up here," he told me at the end of the night, handing me a leash and asking me to take Jazz for a walk. To my amazement Jazz was quite agreeable, and when we returned to the trailer fifteen minutes later, we found Robb and Jennifer tearing things down and packing up.

Shortly after one in the morning, with twilight lingering in the sky, the three of us joined an old friend of Robb's named Francois at a local tavern, where we enjoyed the fruits of Robb's labour. With his take folded neatly in his hands, Robb thumbed through his cash, his face lit like one of those casino slot machines after hitting the jackpot. The final tally was more than fifteen hundred dollars in less than six hours. "The drinks are on me," he crowed. "It's time to toast the midnight sun."

Tragically, the midnight sun didn't seem to care. The bartender kicked us out at two, telling us that he was scheduled to play in the Midnight Sun golf tournament. Robb and Francois decided to head to the links as spectators, but when they asked Jennifer and me if we wanted to join them, we both hesitated. By this time I was feeling more than a little groggy, which was hardly a surprise considering I hadn't slept more than a few scattered hours since leaving my uncle's farm. How many nights ago was that? I counted four on my fingers. Geez, unless I found a place to sleep soon, this would be night number five without some quality shut-eye.

But, of course, I don't often listen to my own best advice, particularly when there's an interesting, attractive woman to flirt with. "Do you want to grab a coffee?" Jennifer asked. "I'm not really in the mood to go to the golf course." She smiled at me sweetly from across the table.

"Uh, sure," I replied smoothly. I knew that I would regret my decision to stay up, but I figured that the caffeine and sugar would at least help me keep my eyes open. If not, I would probably fall asleep at the table, start drooling profusely from a crease in my mouth, and Jennifer would have a great story to tell her friends about the lamest date she had ever been on.

So we walked to an all-night coffee shop and sat spinning yarns until well after sunrise. Jennifer told me about her plan to attend architecture school in Calgary and, like many young people I had met in Yellowknife, how she was looking forward to working down south. At around 6:30, she yawned and finally said, "I've gotta go and get some sleep." I couldn't have agreed more. Lack of sleep, combined with lethal doses of caffeine and sugar, had me feeling like death warmed up in a microwave, and my ability to fake coherence was fast diminishing. I was beyond tired, my nerves were beyond frayed and my head was pounding like a jackhammer. Somehow, I managed the necessary coordination to give Jennifer a farewell hug, and after wishing her well, I walked around the corner and started searching desperately for the nearest plot of shrubs to pitch my tent and collapse.

That's when it dawned on me: I had left my tent in Robb's RV. Aarrgghh! I couldn't even find some secret little forested nook free from insects where I could curl up for a few hours, some safe haven where I could sleep, sleep, sleep, sleeeeeeeppp!

With grim realization, I realized that my situation was grim. I could no longer think clearly, which was a sure sign that my thinking was no longer clear. But what could I do? Would I have to push through another day? Clearly, my inclination was to hunch down into the fetal position and start weeping, but instead I gathered my wits (there were two missing) and set off in search of a restaurant serving breakfast. My delusional brain told me that if I could at least fill my belly with food, perhaps it would give me enough energy to carry on for a few more hours. Then I could find Robb, reunite with my tent and locate a hidey-hole where I could finally pass out.

After dragging my feet for three or four blocks, I found just the place. I sat myself at a table across from a group of blue-collar workers—cheery, bright-eyed bastards, all of them—no doubt on the way to some choice construction job. What gave them the right to be so chipper? Trying to emulate their upbeat countenance, I ordered a plate of eggs, bacon, and toast—but it was really no use. When my breakfast arrived, I kept doing the head nod, and on several occasions rescued myself a split second before performing a spectacular face plant into my food.

At 7:15, I left the restaurant and set out in a direction that I'm certain made sense to me at the time. That's when something happened that has never happened to me before; nor has it happened since. My body ceased to function. It simply stopped working. My mind told me in no uncertain terms that I was going to lie down right there, at that very moment, no questions asked, thank you very much, goodnight! And so I did, not entirely certain where I was, only that I was falling asleep in the middle of a sidewalk somewhere in downtown Yellowknife.

June 21, 1997 – Yellowknife, Northwest Territories

I woke to the sound of high-heeled shoes clicking along the pavement next to my head. A minute later I heard a car pull into a nearby parking stall, a door open, a short bit of rustling and finally the crunch of metal on metal as a door slammed shut. I pulled up the rim of my ball cap ever so slightly and scanned the world from ground level. As my eyes adjusted to the light, I realized that I was lying in the middle of a sidewalk, my head propped up against my backpack. People were staring at me as they walked past, and although traffic was still relatively light, cars were rumbling along the street a few metres away.

It took a few minutes to coax myself from the ground so that I could check the time, not to mention all of my important bodily functions. It was almost 10:30 in the morning. I felt numb and my head was still pounding, but three hours of sleep had at least brought me back to the land of the living. I could remember listening to stories from others who had experienced the midnight sun and been tricked into not sleeping. Now I understood how such a thing could happen.

That afternoon, I found Robb and Jennifer working under the shade of some trees near one of the city's parks. It was another day of clear blue skies, and the sun was piercing and relentless. Robb told me that business had been much slower because most people were in the park taking part in the solstice festivities. The summer solstice is an important day for First Nations' groups across Canada, which is why the Canadian government has declared June 21st National Aboriginal Day.

I wandered into the park just as a large gathering of Dene were starting a prayer chant, calling on the Great Spirit to bless the food they had prepared. Seven drummers beat animal skin drums and chanted loudly as three band elders danced around a fire pit, offering morsels of food to the flames. As dozens of onlookers watched, the elders took turns crossing their arms and quietly uttering prayers. Then it was time for the feast. A huge line formed to indulge in fresh bannock, Arctic char, dried whitefish and caribou stew. I was so busy taking pictures that by the time my turn came, most of the food had already disappeared.

Shortly after the feast, singer Laura Vinson and her band The Free Spirit made their first appearance. Everybody stopped to watch, standing under the shade of trees or sprawling out on the warm grass in front of the stage. Laura belted out song after song as if she were oblivious to the heat, and for several numbers she was joined on stage by a young Native girl with eagle feathers braided into her hair, wearing beaded moccasins and a bright red dress with elaborate aboriginal motifs. On several occasions, Laura even managed to get people dancing, and it was then that I noticed the hand-stitched moccasins many of the Native ladies were wearing, laced across the top with hundreds of colourful beads.

After the first set, I walked over to talk with Laura and her band members. I was impressed not only with their musical talent, but by Laura's lyrics, which addressed Native themes even though the music was non-traditional in style. One song called *Roots That Go Deep* was about how music will help Native people hang on to their culture, even as globalization bears down on all of us. Another song called *Let It Go* discussed the historic confrontation between Natives and white people, with a message that Native people must let go of resentment, justified or not, before healing can take place.

"I wasn't always aware of the spiritual side of my heritage," Laura told me, explaining that she was Metis. "I was paying my way through university by singing at bars and dance clubs, and then one day I decided there were better ways to use my gifts than to sell booze." So she started writing songs about Native heritage, brought together The Free Spirit and eventually hired Native dancers to perform at some of the venues where the band played. Songwriting and music became a way for her to share ideas while bringing Native heritage and culture to the general public. And Laura and her band were obviously enjoying some success: they had released eight albums and were planning to tour Europe and Australia with their record label in the fall.

People started trickling out of the park by late afternoon. Robb's sales had been dismal compared to the previous night's figures, and at five he gave the word to start packing his trailer. Dawson City was the next town he planned to visit, and that wasn't until the middle of July, so we had to pack carefully and strap everything down so that it would survive the many potholed northern highways he would be driving. Packing finally accomplished, Jennifer invited the two of us to her place for dinner.

There was a dull roar coming from Jennifer's home when we pulled up, and inside we found her house full of people—in the full swing of summer activity. After a few quick introductions, I found myself standing in front of their barbecue flipping burgers while Jennifer and her mother Wilma boiled fresh corn and tossed a salad. In the meantime, Robb—ever the centre of attention—kept everybody entertained with stories from the road. Francois was there too, as were several of the family's relatives.

Later that evening, as Robb and Francois prepared to leave, Robb mentioned to everybody that he was planning to head south the next morning. He didn't ask if I wanted to travel with him, though, which made me wonder if something was wrong. Did he want to be alone? Had he presumed that I wanted to stay in Yellowknife? Before he left, I grabbed my backpack from his RV, and found myself saying an awkward farewell to both him and Jazz. "Stay out of trouble," was the last thing he said to me. He winked a knowing sort of wink and glanced over at Jennifer. Then he was gone.

Back inside, Jennifer and I washed the dishes together, laughing heartily as we flicked soapsuds at each other. It felt good to be in her company, yet a part of me felt strangely blue for having parted with Robb in such an abrupt manner. Had I said or done something to offend him? It's not like three or four days turns people into best friends—but I had sensed that as fellow travelers we had shared a certain kinship, a fascination for the open road and what there was to learn from it. We were headed in different directions now that Ravin' Mad Days had ended, but I had been looking forward to riding south with Robb, at least as far as Fort Providence.

After the dishes were washed, dried and put away, I took a long, hot shower. While I cleaned myself up, Jennifer and her mother drove to the video store to rent a movie. Soon we had poured some iced tea and settled down on the couch to watch it together, though I started nodding in and out of consciousness almost as soon as she had popped it into the VCR. Eventually I fell asleep, and the next thing I knew, Jennifer was tapping me on the shoulder as the final credits were rolling.

Eagerly anticipating a full night of slumber, I organized my sleeping bag on the carpeted floor, only to realize that Jennifer was wide awake and feeling eager to visit. It wasn't that I didn't want to talk to her—believe me—it was just that fatigue was tugging at my mind with the subtlety of a screaming toddler. Nevertheless, I tried my best to stay awake, to be a respectful guest, and for a short while managed to do so. But in the end it was no use. At some point during the wee hours of the morning I fell asleep on the couch, talking softly and holding Jennifer's hand.

June 23, 1997 – Yellowknife, Northwest Territories

The telephone rang at 9:30 the next morning. It was Robb. He wanted to know if I needed a ride. "If you want to come along," he said, "be ready in an hour." That was all the incentive I needed. I was out of my sleeping bag in a flash, rolling it up and stuffing it into my backpack practically before he had hung up the phone.

After another shower, I sat and talked with Jennifer and her mother while shovelling back a bowl of Corn Flakes. When I told them my next planned stop was Wood Buffalo National Park (provided I could find a ride), Wilma chimed in with a thoughtful motherly warning. "Now don't be going there without a bug jacket," she told me. "That's one of the worst places for mosquitoes. This time of year, you'll get eaten alive." She looked serious, and where mosquitoes were concerned, I already knew that chances were not to be taken. I was a hitchhiker, damn it, not some walking insect smorgasbord.

So for that very reason, after Robb and I had said farewell to the charming Jennifer and her equally charming mother, I asked him to stop at a hardware store on the way out of town. I felt certain that a five-dollar head-net would be one of the wisest investments I ever made in the Far North. It would save my hide while tramping through the woods and pitching my tent, or on those rare occasions when I got stranded on the side of some remote northern road for more than a couple of hours. It was definitely money well spent.

Soon enough we were on the road again, enjoying another perfect day. Robb and I were treated to a solid sheet of blue stretching across the sky, rolling off into the forbidding emptiness of the Territories for what seemed like an eternity. After a few days in Yellowknife, I had almost forgotten how much empty space there is up there. My first clue was the road sign at the edge of the city: EDMONTON—1500 kilometres.

"So when are you planning to retire?" I asked Robb as Bob Seger wailed about the open road from speakers overhead. Robb hadn't said anything about his abrupt departure the previous night, so I decided not to bring it up.

He gave me a surprised look. "What do you mean retire? I am retired. I'm just travelling around doing what I want to do." I considered this for a moment and quite liked his answer. "You never know when the man upstairs is going to pull your string," he continued. "I came to the conclusion a few years back that there's no time to waste. You have to work on who you are and what you want out of life right now."

Was that why I was out here too? I couldn't help but wonder. Life on the road was not always easy, but it was exactly where I wanted to be ... at least most of the time. Yet the answers to the big questions still eluded me: what exactly was I searching for in the bright, bug-infested swamp-forest of the Territories? What had I learned on the West Coast? Was this trip about me, or was it about other people? One thing was certain: I had learned how to dispose of buzzing pests a lot more quickly. Maybe I would write a second book to accompany my hitchhiking chronicle: *A Thousand Ways to Mercilessly Torture Mosquitoes before Squeezing the Last Breath out of Their Worthless, Feeble Little Bodies*. I had a feeling it would be a big seller in the NWT.

When we reached Fort Providence three hours later, I had Robb drop me at a roadhouse beside the highway—a multi-purpose service centre with a gas station, restaurant, bar and motel all crammed into one. He and Jazz planned to drive a few kilometres further south and then turn east onto the Liard Highway, which would eventually spit them out onto the Alaska Highway after four hundred kilometres of the worst potholed gravel track that exists anywhere on the planet. I would have to deal with the Liard in a few days, but I had long ago promised myself that I would hitchhike to Wood Buffalo National Park to see the world's largest bison herd. Although that meant taking a five-hundred-kilometre detour east, I wanted to give it a try.

I spent the rest of the evening sitting at a cramped table, scribbling away in my journal and drinking cup after cup of coffee. The restaurant staff were friendly, and they didn't seem to mind that I went through almost a full pot at one sitting. As an added bonus, I was able to eavesdrop on some of the conversations between staff and customers. "How are the bugs?" was how most conversations started, because small talk up there (if you haven't already guessed) seems to revolve more or less around the intensity of the insects at any given hour of the day.

"There's still one or two out there," a truck driver sighed at one point. He grunted loudly and anted up for the gas.

"The damn thing is you kill one and ten friends show up for the funeral," remarked the attendant, a choice one-liner that solicited laughter from everybody sitting within earshot. I laughed too, which seemed to catch his attention. "I mean, they're not that bad," he told me point-blank, guessing that I was from the south. "At least they don't carry guns and knives, so how bad can they be?"

The cafe closed at midnight, and when I strolled outside I discovered a soft sky the colour of apricot, with millions of tiny black specks swarming beneath it. When the gas station attendant saw me leaving, he quickly stopped me. "You'd better pitch your tent beside the motel," he warned, pointing in the direction of a large building next to the restaurant. "There are a lot of bears around here."

Oh, lovely. Should I really thank him for that information? Mind you, I was still feeling desperately tired. Any bear serious about intruding would probably have to slash through the side of my tent, climb into my sleeping bag and start spooning with me before I so much as stirred. So I thanked the attendant for his information, found a suitable spot, brushed away a few stones and proceeded to pitch my tent even as clouds of mosquitoes swarmed me from every direction, their droning horribly audible even through my protective screen.

Bears and bugs aside, I really couldn't have been happier. In fact, I laughed and laughed, louder and louder, until people inside the motel must have thought the Royal Canadian Air Farce was in town giving an unscheduled comedy performance. But my laughter had nothing to do with Canada's Air Farce, and rather everything to do with my bug-proof head-net. It worked like a charm, and I was merely revelling in the fact that those million billion trillion mosquitoes could kiss my lily-white backside.

Chapter 14

A Tale of Two Vikings

June 24, 1997 - Wood Buffalo National Park, Alberta

A pair of large bison bulls were sprawled ten metres from the car, woofing and snorting and rolling on the ground, with no wind to whisk the dust away. This was their way of dealing with oppressive heat and mosquitoes, but it was a comical sight to behold: massive shoulder blades rubbing into the parched earth while spindly legs pumped at dry air. Their legs were completely out of proportion to the rest of their bodies.

"I only see two of them," said Nils, scanning the low-lying birch and tamarack forest with binoculars. Nils was a Danish traveller I had met in Fort Smith two days earlier, tall and strapping with a full head of blonde hair and a beard that looked like a rhododendron thicket. Give him a white robe and some sandals, I had thought when we first met, and he could have pulled off Jesus in some Hollywood flick.

In the sweltering heat of midday, biting insects weren't a problem— even in Wood Buffalo—so Nils rolled down his window for an unobstructed view of the bulls wallowing in their own private dust clouds. This was not exactly a herd of epic proportions, and I doubted the ground would shake even if we somehow managed to get the two of them running side by side, but then again, these animals represented something special. They were part of the largest free-roaming bison herd in the world—which is exactly what Nils and I had travelled so far to see.

Growing up on the prairies, I had always dreamed of the gigantic herds of bison that had once thundered across the Great Plains. I had even imagined myself as Kevin Costner in *Dances With Wolves*, wakened by the distant roar of a million hooves beating hard against the prairie earth, the ground literally shaking underfoot. Alas, Wood Buffalo National Park was about the closest thing I would get to that in this day and age. The park was home to roughly 4,000 bison—a respectable number if you could gather them in one location—yet finding them in a park that was 44,840 square kilometres in size seemed like wishful thinking. Getting to Fort

Smith (a small town inside the park) was one thing. Finding the bison herd, I realized, would be quite another.

"It looks like they're just hanging out," I said off-handedly. "I guess it's too hot for them to do anything very active right now."

"Can you blame them?" replied Nils.

He touched the gas pedal ever so slightly, which caused a high-pitched whining to erupt from under the hood. The bulls stood up and glared at us, annoyed at having their afternoon rest disturbed. Unfortunately, this was no fancy set of wheels Nils was driving. It was an old chocolate-brown Ford station wagon: 1970s-era, seen-better-days, mind-of-its-own sort of thing. He had bought it in Edmonton for the bargain price of five hundred dollars, and it rattled and hummed and was prone to disturbing the peace of both animals and humans whenever it passed within a few hundred metres. I could think of no worse vehicle to use for a wildlife safari.

Apart from displaying a brash temperament, the car also lacked air conditioning and sported a thick layer of dust across the dashboard and within the upholstery. Then there was the body, which looked as though it was being held together with pure willpower. I recalled a story I heard in Fort Smith about a territorial bison bull that had developed a strange fetish for ramming vehicles; I tried not to think about how we would fare in such a confrontation. But the bulls didn't charge, perhaps deciding that we weren't worth the effort, and we continued to follow the winding gravel road south across the border and into northern Alberta.

All along the road we spotted bison—mostly single or in pairs—grazing on shrubbery or lounging in the shade, not doing much of anything. We eventually reached some decrepit-looking shacks and sheds not far from the silty banks of the Peace River, where our map indicated we had reached the end of the line. "In the winter there's an ice road that cuts down across the delta to Fort McMurray from here," I told Nils, feeling like the official tour guide in a park that I hardly knew. By the delta, of course, I was referring to the huge Peace-Athabasca River Delta that covers much of the southern third of the park. One of the largest in North America, it acts as a vital nesting and staging area for nearly half a million waterfowl.

Nils already knew about the ice road. "Some people I met in Fort Smith, they've already told me so much about this area," he said as we stepped out of the car. Sitting down on a rock, he unpacked a loaf of bread and a jar of chocolate hazelnut spread, with which he covered a slice from corner to corner. He saw my eyes brighten when the spread appeared, so he handed it to me without even asking.

"Yeah, it's definitely one of the friendliest towns I've visited," I told him. A fellow I had met in southern Ontario a few years earlier lived in Fort Smith; when I called him from Fort Providence to let him know that I was coming to town, he invited me to stay with his family for as long as I wanted.

"It's strange, isn't it?" said Nils, taking a bite from his sandwich. "I'm used to being anonymous when I travel, but here everybody wants to talk to you." He explained that on the previous night he had been walking down the sidewalk, lost in his own thoughts, when he passed an elderly couple eating caribou salad on their porch. Apparently, they had already heard about him through the grapevine, so they invited him in for dinner and to stay for the night.

Of course, the speed with which news spreads in a small town can also be a little disconcerting. I had been in town for less than an hour before I met Nils, yet two locals had already told me about him. And not just his name: they knew where he was from, where he had travelled before coming to Canada and where he was planning to go next. In fact, when I first spotted Nils in the town grocery store, my mischievous side had taken over. I walked up to him and said, "Hey man, it's been a while since I saw you in Thailand."

He had glared at me, mildly perturbed. "You saw my shirt," he said flatly, annoyed that I would even attempt to deceive him.

"No seriously," I said, putting on my most sincerely injured expression. "Your name is Nils, right? You're from Denmark."

Suddenly he wasn't so sure anymore. "How did you know where I'm from?" he had said, both surprised and irritated. I couldn't keep the charade going any longer and broke down laughing. Fortunately, he saw the humour in it all, and after we had eaten lunch together he invited me to explore the park with him. We later found out that a few people had seen us eating together and had started a rumour that two Vikings had been seen walking around Fort Smith.

It was late afternoon by the time Nils and I headed back toward town. The sun was still high in the sky, but for some reason the wildlife was more energetic, possibly having finished their afternoon siestas. Soon we spotted a half-dozen bison on the road, but in no time at all they had bolted into the trees and out of sight. Not wanting to miss an opportunity, Nils and I parked the car and launched ourselves into hot pursuit. Alarm bells went off in my head, suggesting that chasing a fifteen-hundred-pound animal through country that he knew a lot better than I did might not be the smartest decision I had ever made. Regardless, I sprinted on, justifying the chase with thoughts of missed photographs.

Once we were in the forest, Nils and I found and followed a well-used game trail. Just ahead of us we could hear the crashing of foliage as the animals tried to make a run for it. It wasn't long before we broke into a grassy clearing, where we noticed that all but one of the bison had successfully made their escape. We listened for crashing noises in the forest, but all we could hear was the faint rustle of wind on birch leaves.

The last bison stood his ground. He glared at us from fifty feet away, almost as if he were daring us to come closer. I gingerly plucked my camera from my fanny pack, snapped on a telephoto lens and inched closer. I was trying to get myself into the perfect position for a full-frame portrait—and was just about to ask him to say "Cheese!"—when the bison (I'll call him Crusty) started trotting along the edge of the meadow. Without even thinking, I trotted after him, not moving any closer but keeping pace as Crusty looked for an escape route.

Considering all the room he had to wander freely across the clearing, to this day I can't understand how Crusty might have felt cornered. Perhaps he was simply feeling a little camera-shy that afternoon, and after a day spent lounging in the shade, I guess I can't really blame him. All I know is that within a matter of about two seconds, Crusty decided that the best route of escape was directly over my soft, flimsy body. Perhaps the way my hair was parted faintly resembled a game trail. Whatever the case, through my camera's viewfinder Crusty was suddenly getting very big, very quickly.

My immediate response was to acknowledge that I had made a slight error in judgment getting this close to a territorial bison bull, and then trying to run after him as he fled into the woods. My second response (quite contrary to sound logic) was to stand my ground. Not that I had much choice. By the time Crusty had galloped across the clearing, there was really nowhere else for me to go. At the last possible instant—and I do mean *last*—Crusty veered to one side and off into the forest, missing me by what must have been less than three metres.

"I think I'm ready to go back to the car now," I told Nils, who had watched my little drama unfold with a combination of horror and amusement. And going back to the car is exactly what we did, being ever so careful not to surprise any other bison bulls that might have been lurking in the trees. At least Crusty had granted my wish, the wish I had cherished long before coming to Wood Buffalo. I had come here to feel the ground vibrate with the thunder of stampeding bison hooves, and there's no denying that's exactly what I had felt.

Chapter 15

Stranded

June 29, 1997 – The Liard Highway near Fort Providence, Northwest Territories

I woke with a holy-terror scream to the sound of highway thunder: broken glass and fingernails against chalkboard. Two eighteen-wheelers roared past me from the direction of Fort Smith, and I'm certain they didn't even slow down. Probably sped up, actually, when they saw me curled up on the road shoulder sleeping like a little baby. Truckers' entertainment: let's scare the hell out of the poor stranded hitchhiker. So much for compassion.

I dozed fitfully for another couple of hours, then got up, stretched sluggish muscles and slowly packed everything back into its proper place. It was six in the morning, which meant that I had been stranded on the Liard Highway at the junction south of Fort Providence for fifteen hours. For breakfast, I drank some water and liberally spread peanut butter on a few stale Oreos, the last of my food.

I watched another transport truck pass on the long haul, its driver putty-faced and determined. Forty-five minutes later, a car screamed by with several Native passengers crammed inside. With an average of one vehicle passing every hour, I wondered whether I might have to backtrack all the way south into Peace River country before cutting across to the Alaska Highway.

I had pretty much given up hope of reaching the Alaska Highway via the Liard when, shortly after nine, a small pickup truck with a canopy approached from the direction of Fort Providence, then rounded the corner toward me. I quickly plucked three twenty-dollar bills from my wallet and waved them in the air as if my very life depended on getting this ride. The driver pulled over.

"Thank you so much for stopping," I beamed. "I was beginning to think I'd never get picked up."

As it turned out, Mac was only on his way to Fort Simpson—a small Native community about halfway between the Alaska Highway and Fort Providence. He was a large, jovial fellow with a thick moustache and glasses, on his way to visit his wife for the weekend. He told me that he would drop me at Checkpoint Junction—a gas station, restaurant and service centre a few kilometres outside Fort Simpson—where I would be able to buy food and get stranded in somewhat more pleasant surroundings while I waited for a ride to the Alaska Highway.

"And put that money away," he laughed. "You're going to get yourself into trouble waving that stuff around."

Inside the truck I met Foxy, Mac's dog, best friend and hunting partner. As we drove, Mac entertained me with stories of bird hunting along the Liard. During the summer, he explained, tanker trucks water the gravel highways to keep the dust down, and the runoff attracts birds. "Ol' Foxy thinks we're out on a big hunting trip right now," he said, patting his dog on the head, "so he's a wee bit cranked up." Foxy was indeed cranked up—a nervous ball of energy, in fact, just itching to mangle some poor bird. Or my face. Whichever happened to be nearest. His eyes, I noted gratefully, were fixed on the passing scenery for the most part, though his tail thrashed wildly against my chin whenever we rounded a sharp curve.

At one point, Mac had to stop and let Foxy out to run beside the truck. He was getting much too anxious and had started crawling and drooling all over me. We drove along slowly, watching the hyperactive dog bound through the broad ditch, his head occasionally appearing through the brush at the side of the road. It wasn't long before we heard a splash resonate from a short distance away. "Ooh, I think ol' Foxy's found some water," Mac said sheepishly. "He'll be a little wet when he gets back in the truck."

That was an understatement if ever one was made. When Mac called Foxy back, he was not just wet, he was drenched, and I was certain that I saw a big doggy grin stretched across his face. He must have realized that he could dry himself off against my T-shirt. Mac graciously fetched a towel to place between us, but this did little to insulate me from Foxy's wet fur and the horrible, all-embracing stench of doggy odour. Every time we hit a large pothole—which was often on this godforsaken stretch of road— the undeniably cheerful Foxy would end up sprawled across my lap.

WHEN I FIRST walked into the restaurant at Checkpoint Junction, I wasn't much impressed with what I saw. The lighting was dim and the wooden tables and chairs, although clean and respectable enough, looked old and profoundly uncomfortable. The decor spoke of brute functionality rather than anything designed to particularly please the senses. It was the kind of hard-knuckled northern way station where Steven Seagal might appear in his ponytailed perfection to start throwing furniture at people, emerging from the brawl a few minutes later as the only man standing, not a single hair out of place.

Still, it was a veritable oasis for someone who had been stranded in the middle of nowhere since early the previous afternoon. After eating, my next goal was to reach the Alaska Highway, and by way of that, the Yukon. That was assuming my credit card company didn't cut me off first. I sat down and ordered a large burger, fries and a Coke, noticing as I did that the sugar shakers were nearly empty. This was probably a result of the relaxed, devil-may-care attitude that rules this part of the country (if you don't like the service, where else are you going to go?), or perhaps because, like everything else in the Northwest Territories, even the most basic conveniences are not always available on short order.

To my surprise, Gerry and Susan, the hospitable live-in operators of the joint, had me developing a sort of detached fondness for the place in relatively short order, despite the lack of a non-smoking section. Gerry had a mop of long, curly grey hair, glasses, and a perpetual chain of cigarettes hanging from the corner of his mouth. Despite my travel-worn appearance, he served me like he would any other customer. That is, in a friendly and courteous manner ... but without filling up the sugar shaker on my table. Around mid-afternoon, Gerry turned on the television and flipped through the channels to find the all-star baseball game. I've never been much of a baseball fan, so I knew nothing about the teams or players, but Gerry seemed to enjoy it and offered to educate me. Over coffee and small talk, I learned that he and Susan had recently moved north from Ottawa, primed for a fresh start. "We wanted to give the restaurant business a whack," he told me. "Plus my buddy needed help in a bad way."

"Bit of a change up here, don't you think?"

"Sure," he said, hauling on his cigarette. He blew the smoke halfway across the empty restaurant. "But the North has always appealed to me because of the pioneering attitude, which is something you don't find in a government town like Ottawa. Everyone wants a nice cushy job with a big pension. It made me sick to my stomach."

And so I waited at Checkpoint, hour after hour as it turned out, listening to Gerry or listening to the television, or listening to Gerry and the television at the same time. Meanwhile I hoped and prayed for a ride: *any* vehicle headed south for the Alaska Highway. I could have done without the cigarette smoke, of course, but I liked Gerry. I had long since grown sick of talking to myself at the side of the road, or throwing pebbles at anthills in the ditch, or listening to the drone of mosquitoes through my head-net, or playing the dozen or so other games you play with yourself to pass the empty hours.

With Gerry's permission, I even altered my hitchhiking strategy. I sat at a table in the corner of the restaurant working on my journal, my cardboard sign propped up at my feet so that patrons entering the restaurant would see that I was not merely a hitchhiker, but in fact a roving journalist, a respectable person who worked and paid taxes just like they did. Of course, I didn't look like much of a journalist, but my mind was made up: today I would wait for the rides to come to me. I told Gerry to make up some story about me being stranded there for a week.

The hours passed, and before long it was dinnertime. A few people came and went, but few even glanced sideways. At one point, a young couple asked where I was going, but they were travelling in the wrong direction. At about nine, I started to feel nauseous from drinking too much coffee, so I asked for water instead. Eventually Gerry told me that they would be closing up shop, but pointed to a plot of grass near the side of the building where he told me I could pitch my tent. "See ya in the morning," he said.

I rapped on the front door first thing and greeted a half-asleep Gerry, who was walking around in his stocking feet, getting the restaurant ready for breakfast. He gingerly opened the door and let me in, asking how I had slept before coming over to pour me a cup of coffee. I wondered if this man might be sick of seeing me in his restaurant yet, but if he was he gave me no reason to think so at this point.

"What do you want for breakfast?" he asked. I rummaged through my wallet and found it despairingly short on cash and other valuable commodities, so I meekly asked how much an order of toast would be.

"Do you want some eggs, too?" he asked with a lopsided grin. "Hitchhiker's special—I'll only charge you three dollars."

I picked through the folds of my wallet and found three loonies. "It's a deal. Thanks."

After breakfast, I continued to write in my journal, hitchhiking the lazy man's way. Every time I saw a vehicle pull into the gas station, I went out to ask which way the people were travelling, and whether they might have room for a stranded journalist. "Journalist" sounded much better than "hitchhiker," but it was difficult to appear non-threatening when it looked as though I had just crawled from a dumpster. From the general tone of the responses I received, this distinction was not lost on the people I was trying to convince. As the rejections stacked up, I began to contemplate my predicament. Under the circumstances, would even I pick myself up?

At lunchtime, a convoy of pickup trucks pulled into the parking lot, and soon fourteen or fifteen hungry Native travellers had stormed the place looking for some grub. From my seat, I watched Gerry and Susan running around in the back trying to prepare an avalanche of orders, so I strolled over to the kitchen door and asked if they needed help. Gerry looked surprised, and mildly touched, but declined my offer. Two hours later he sheepishly approached me, and in a tone that suggested he felt like a first-class Scrooge, asked if I would mind leaving after I had eaten supper. I couldn't blame him. I had been in his restaurant for more than a day and I was getting nowhere. I could tell that he felt bad about asking me to go, but he knew that I could be stranded there for a week if I didn't get a little more aggressive with my tactics. I suspected that he was secretly worried about his supply of coffee as well.

Jokes aside, as I dropped my backpack onto the road shoulder, I found myself feeling lonely and desperately forlorn. No doubt about it, I was feeling sorry for myself, and with every passing vehicle I sank further into self-pity. Why was I feeling like this? Would I be stranded there for days? I thought of Robb and Jennifer and my friends from Lake Louise, which cheered me marginally. Yet there was not a single vehicle in sight, which meant the Alaska Highway might as well have been on the moon.

I had been standing there for about two hours when a pickup truck finally appeared on the horizon, wheeled around the corner from the direction of Fort Providence, and blasted by me. I choked momentarily on its dust cloud . . . and was shocked when it braked hard a few hundred metres down the road and started backing up. Through the rear window I could see two men, and when they stopped beside me the driver rolled down his window. "We saw your sign and thought you looked kind of interesting," he said. "Where are you headed?"

Praise the sign!

"Fort Nelson," I told him. "Or even down to the Alaska Highway." The town of Fort Nelson was a few kilometres from where the Liard joins the Alaska Highway, and I figured that I might as well get into town if I could.

"We're only going to Fort Liard," the man replied, "but you're welcome to ride that far with us if you like." Fort Liard was the halfway point between Checkpoint and Fort Nelson. I thought for a second and decided that although Fort Liard wasn't quite the Alaska Highway, it was at least mileage in the right direction. Perhaps if I got that far, I would be able snag another ride the following day. I threw my gear into the back of the truck and climbed into the cab behind the front seat. To my surprise, my spirits lifted immediately, almost as if nothing had ever been wrong.

The driver's name was Ron, and his passenger was a soft-spoken fellow named Darcy. Both were in the prime of life and looked clean-cut and responsible. As we talked, though, I occasionally caught sight of a fire that danced in Ron's eyes. The fire, it turned out, was the result (or perhaps the cause) of a recent divorce. Maybe it wasn't fire after all, but the catchlight of newfound freedom.

Ron did most of the talking, reminiscing about life as a kid living up and down the Mackenzie Valley with his game-warden father. "You learn to appreciate the outdoors pretty quickly up here," he told me. "Freeze-up and break-up are the only times I don't like being in the Northwest Territories, and that's because you can't go anywhere." He had spent most of his adult life in Yellowknife working in the cable television industry. He and Darcy were actually on a business trip, heading down to Fort Liard to hook up a cable connection for one of the town elders. It seemed amazing to me, even with all the road-tripping I had done, that they would drive for sixteen hours for a single cable customer. It was never more obvious that people from the Northwest Territories are of a different breed.

We continued to bounce along the highway at a remarkably good clip (considering the serpentine road and minefield of potholes) until we got stuck behind the dust cloud of a transport truck. Ron tailed the truck for a few minutes—brief glimpses of it appearing through the plume of smoke—before he suddenly pulled into the far lane to pass. This surprised me, considering we were driving blind and had no way of knowing what was on the other side of the dust cloud. A large buffalo? Another truck?

A sudden bend in the road? Fortunately, I was wrong on all counts, and a few tense seconds later we shot out the far side. I guess what I had taken for freedom in Ron's eyes was actually the dance of fire after all.

We weren't far from Fort Liard when Ron asked where I was heading next. When I mentioned Whitehorse, he started listing the names of people I should phone when I arrived in town. I wrote a few of them down, as I always did when people were kind enough to offer friendly contacts, but I did it more out of courtesy than because I planned to phone anyone. I preferred to meet people along the way, letting serendipity work its magic. After all, that's what my trip was all about.

Suddenly Ron got the faintest of twinkles in his eye. "You know, we should almost drive this guy to Whitehorse," he told Darcy. Darcy didn't say anything. He just sat there, stiff as a board, quite aware that Ron was probably not joking.

"Whaddaya say, Darce?" Ron continued. "We could be in Whitehorse before noon tomorrow. It's only twelve hours from Liard."

Darcy mumbled something under his breath and tried to avoid Ron's contagious grin and piercing stare. The fire in Ron's eyes was flashing again—the kind of intense enthusiasm you see in the eyes of rock stars on stage, or Olympic athletes who have just won a gold medal. I sat there wondering who to defend, quite amused by the mere suggestion that anybody would drive twelve hours out of their way (twenty-four hours if you count both directions) to drop me off.

A few miles of uncomfortable silence passed. Finally Ron leaned close to Darcy's ear and whispered, "Or we could do the circle route down to Vancouver." Ron straightened, still grinning, and continued talking in his normal voice. "C'mon, Darce! You can buy a toothbrush, you can buy a T-shirt, you can buy a pair of pants. What else do you really need?"

Darcy chuckled grimly, the sound of a death-row inmate the night before his execution. "I don't know," he said, pausing. "My wife is expecting me..."

Ron turned to me and abruptly changed the subject, pretending not to hear Darcy's feeble rebuttal. "You see, I don't want to be chained to a desk somewhere. If everything works out the way I want, I'll have my job in Ottawa, my family in Edmonton, my boat in Vancouver and my investments in Yellowknife."

There were a few more minutes of awkward silence before we arrived in Fort Liard, only to discover that the man Ron and Darcy had travelled eight hours to see had decided to go fishing instead. I was completely and utterly shocked. "It happens," Ron told me, shrugging it off. He didn't seem the least bit bothered.

I looked over at Darcy, and to my surprise he didn't seem bothered either. "This guy is an important man in the village," he explained. "There's no reason he should be kept waiting for the likes of us." It made no sense to me, but I supposed it had its subtle northern logic, the kind of logic that southerners aren't apt to understand.

Before leaving town, we visited a convenience store bustling with restless teens. I bought some crackers and iced tea, figuring that if I was going to be stranded on the road for another night I might as well have some food. Out of the corner of my eye, I could see Ron chipping away at poor Darcy, but I figured common sense would eventually prevail.

As we walked back to the truck, I looked over to find a huge grin plastered across Ron's face. I immediately knew that something was up. When Darcy walked out of the store, however, he only looked calm, like a man who by this time had accepted his fate. "We're driving to Fort Nelson tonight," Ron announced, after we had climbed into the truck. "And tomorrow we might even drive you to Whitehorse."

June 30, 1997 - Fort Nelson, British Columbia

The absence of charm is awesomely evident along the main drag of Fort Nelson. A typical rough-and-tumble resource community catering to seasonal labourers—men working on the oil rigs or in the forests—Fort Nelson boasts a main street lined with motels, car lots, fast food outlets, a bus depot and a couple of seventies-era strip malls. Even more primary to the town's business district, however, are the hunting and tackle shops, an all-terrain vehicle outlet and two strip joints that face one another from opposite sides of the highway.

We arrived there just before ten that night, and after Ron checked us into a motel, we opted for a late dinner of beer and buffalo burgers, the latter of which I happily imagined to be kin of Crusty's. When we returned to the motel, Darcy called his wife to explain the circumstances. Ron and I could tell from his tone of voice and facial expressions that she was not happy. Despite Darcy's best efforts, his wife couldn't seem to understand the pressing need to drop a hitchhiker in Whitehorse before coming home.

Darcy shrugged, stared at the floor, talked in monosyllables and eventually hung up the phone. He didn't say much to either of us after that.

Ron and Darcy never did drive me to Whitehorse, and in fact, I didn't make it there myself until the following summer. Over breakfast the next morning, Ron announced that they were heading back to Yellowknife. Perhaps he was feeling guilty for pressuring Darcy and didn't want to take responsibility for his friend's marital woes. It was also over breakfast that my credit card indicated its unwillingness to go any further, making it abundantly clear that my summer of travel had come to an abrupt end. With less than five hundred dollars to my name, I needed to get back to the Calgary area to look for work as soon as possible.

The Yukon would have to wait.

Above The Arctic Circle

Photo by Pat Morrow

"Not everything that counts can be counted, and not everything that can be counted counts."
- Albert Einstein

Chapter 16

Potholes to Progress

July 22, 1998 - Fort Nelson, British Columbia

There are easier things in life than trying to hitchhike out of Fort Nelson, let me assure you. Some of these include hanging from a tree branch by your teeth, withstanding Chinese water torture, or trying to sell the Pope on the benefits of birth control. Whatever the appropriate metaphor, trying to leave Fort Nelson most reminded me of a movie I had seen as a child; it starred Steve McQueen and James Garner trying to escape from a German POW camp during World War II. Still, after two days of fruitless thumbing, I didn't feel half as resourceful as they had looked on the silver screen.

It was the middle of July 1998 and I had arrived in town two days earlier by way of the Greyhound bus. I had decided to start my summer exploits in Fort Nelson primarily because that was where my money had run out the previous year. I was still eager to see the Yukon and to hitchhike to the Arctic Ocean, and now that my bank account was somewhat replenished, I could do that without worrying that I might become a permanent fixture on the Arctic landscape.

When I had returned to Alberta in July of 1997, I had been practically destitute, and it was thanks only to the goodwill of friends and relatives that I managed not to starve. Over the winter, I found work as a night auditor at a hotel in Calgary, and spent my days writing and trying to sell magazine articles. When the magazine work was slow—which at this stage of my career was still most of the time—I began to doubt that my finances would ever recover enough to continue my trip. It eventually did happen, marginally and in degrees, and my savings grew until I was finally able to start planning the second phase of my Canadian hitchhiking odyssey.

Now that I had returned to Fort Nelson, the immediate challenge appeared to be simply getting out of town. One of the first stories I heard after arriving involved two hitchhikers from Massachusetts who had been stranded there for a week. Apparently, they had thumbed with relative ease all the way from Boston, then came to a sudden grinding halt in what locals have termed "the black hole of hitchhiking." Out of money and out of food, they waited with increasing desperation until several townspeople eventually bought them groceries and bus tickets to Whitehorse. And it was precisely this story that convinced me, after an entire day without catching a ride, to change my tactics lest the same thing happen to me. Standing at the roadside had started to feel pointless. Feeling grumpy and resentful, I walked into the visitor reception centre, sat down and spent the morning sprawled at a small wooden table, writing in my journal.

The biggest problem seemed to be the type of traffic that was passing me. Most vehicles were either long-distance rigs—which rarely stop for hitchhikers—or RVs filled with pasty-faced tourists, good-naturedly tooting their horns as they passed. I already knew that tourists of the RV variety tend to lump hitchhikers into the same category as drug dealers, pedophiles and axe murderers, so my hope was to spot a likely driver at the visitor centre, strike up casual conversation and then determine where they were headed and whether they might have room for me. Although this tactic had failed me on the Liard Highway the previous summer, I was getting desperate.

It wasn't long before I met an elderly couple from Montana, driving north on a rambling vacation. The lady cooed over my hitchhiking sign and asked all kinds of questions about my travels across Canada. It had just started to feel like I was getting somewhere when she interjected with her own sales pitch. "Since you're carrying that big backpack around," she told me, "I've got just the thing for you." She rummaged through her purse for a few seconds and then, with a kind of grand and sweeping gesture, produced a small plastic vial filled with green-coloured tablets. I smiled warmly (still hoping to sell her on the merits of giving me a ride) and listened to why her vegetable vitamin pills would make such a *huge* difference in my life.

"Here, try a couple," she said. Reluctantly, I opened my palm and allowed her to shake what looked like three or four alfalfa tablets into my hand. They were the sort of thing, say, a rabbit would quite enjoy, but I had doubts about their mass-market appeal for humans. Nevertheless, I popped them into my mouth and was immediately sorry I had done so. They tasted terrible. Imagine what a bowl full of glue and sawdust tastes like and you'll get the general drift. In order to secure my ride, though, I pursed my lips, swallowed the blighters and politely accepted the remainder of the bottle for later.

"They're delicious, aren't they?" she said. Her eyes sparkled with enthusiasm.

"Oh, they're quite something," I replied, putting on my best Boy Scout smile.

"Say, what direction are you guys trave..."

"I knew you'd like them," she continued. "*Everybody* who tries them does! Which is why I'm thinking you'd be the perfect person to sell and distribute these."

"Well, actually..."

"Think about it!" She was beaming, her fingers rummaging for more tablets. "Look, I have to go out to the RV for a second. Wait here. There are a few things I want to give you."

This was no understatement. She had more than a few things to give me. There were multicoloured vitamin capsules, plastic bags with a rainbow assortment of samples, pamphlets with detailed information about the benefits of vitamins, information on where to sign up to become a distributor, and her own business card, presumably so that we could stay in touch and synchronize our vitamin-selling strategies along the road. It was an impressive business operation, really, and she had somehow pegged me as the perfect person for the job. Or perhaps the only person willing to listen to her.

The strange thing was that I not only found myself accepting everything that she gave me, but listening intently as she continued her sales pitch. I guess it's one thing to tell off some slick, vacuum cleaner salesman with a receding hairline—it's quite another to tell off somebody's grandmother.

Twenty minutes later, she and her husband left me sitting at the table, my backpack filled with vitamin tablets and a stack of brochures several centimetres thick. Apparently we were business partners now, yet not once did she ask if I needed a ride.

BY EARLY AFTERNOON I was getting bored, so I decided to give the highway another try. I marched out to the road and plunked my backpack down on the gravel shoulder. Within five minutes an old rusted Taurus pulled to the side, already riding low because of its heavy cargo. Inside, I could see two adults and a young child crammed together, mountains of clothes and other belongings stacked everywhere. They obviously didn't have room for me, so why had they stopped? Maybe they wanted to buy some vitamins.

The man behind the steering wheel opened his door and climbed out. He had thick locks of dark curly hair and a broad, friendly smile. "My name is Michael," he told me. "I'm sorry we don't have room for you, but we wanted to at least give you this." He handed me a crisp twenty-dollar bill, folded neatly into quarters. I must have looked stunned, because after standing there speechless for several moments he decided to explain. He, his wife Lisa and their two-year-old daughter Gabriel were from North Carolina and they had received word from God in April that they should pack up all their belongings and move to Fairbanks, Alaska to become missionaries. He described the clear compulsion he felt that Fairbanks was where they needed to be, and when he had called ahead to look for work, there happened to be two jobs waiting for them.

"My boss has a sick sense of humour," Michael told me with a wink. "Two years ago I moved from Connecticut to North Carolina to get away from the cold." We laughed, shook hands and he was quickly on his way again. I liked the guy, and was truly touched by his gesture. He offered no sermon, no conditions—there was just a pure willingness to help others. And judging by the look of the family car, they didn't have much to give. Everywhere you go, there are lessons to learn.

The afternoon didn't bring any rides my way, but it did offer more entertainment, this time from several children (and a short blonde lady) standing beside the road waving at truck drivers as they passed. Whenever a trucker approached, the children would pump their fists up and down in a series of swift jerking motions, indicating that the driver should toot his horn. Practically every passing truck let loose with a long refrain of horn blasts. This is apparently what kids do during the summer months in Fort Nelson.

Their game was cut short when a thunderstorm appeared from out of nowhere, causing all of us to bolt for the visitor's centre. As I sprinted across the grass with my large pack tilting me off balance, I was intercepted by several boys between the ages of about six and eight. They proceeded to inundate me with questions: "Are you really a hitchhiker? Where are you going? Do you ever get lonely?"

One of them saw my sign, and when I told them about the book I was writing, they started hopping up and down like midget grasshoppers, chanting in unison that they wanted to be in my story. I jollied them along until I was grabbed by the lady who had been with them at the roadside. I half expected her to give me a hawkish look (or even to tell me to leave), but instead she introduced herself as Linda, director of the town's summer recreation program. "The kids would love to meet a real hitchhiker," she told me. "Would you mind coming up to the recreation room and telling them a few stories?"

For the third time that day, I was bowled over. I could only imagine the response if a hitchhiker were invited into a classroom in any major city in southern Canada. He would probably need a psychological evaluation, a criminal record check and two armed escorts before anybody would let him near a school. "No problem," I told her. "I would love to."

Upstairs, I was swarmed by excited children who fired off a barrage of questions in rapid-fire sequence. I shook hands with the other group leaders and told the kids to line up so that they could try lifting my backpack. This, I snickered to myself, would quickly steal a bit of wind from their sails. And it did. It was a comical sight: one by one the children wrapped their tiny arms around the huge pack, grinding their teeth as they tried with all their might to heave it into the air. The backpack weighed more than fifty pounds, so only a few managed to lift it off the ground. For me and the group leaders, it was all incredibly entertaining.

Somewhere in the confusion, a youngster named Seth—probably about six years old—started crying when he thought he had missed his turn. He was pleased when I knelt down on the floor and personally showed him how to do it. After he had tried, without luck, he turned to me with an exasperated look and asked, "You've gotta lug that thing with you everywhere?"

"Yup, everywhere I go," I told him, patting him on the back.

He seemed despondent. He threw his arms up in the air and sighed heavily. "I guess I'll never be a hitchhiker then."

When the children found out that I was also a photographer, they wanted to see my camera. I removed the film and let them take turns slinging it around their necks and clicking the shutter, pretending they were vagabond photojournalists. Next, I showed them how to assemble my camp stove and how to (hypothetically, of course) cook food if they were hungry. The last thing I had them practice was standing with my cardboard sign, their thumbs in the air so that passing cars would be able to see them. Coordinating all of these things is no easy task when you're only six years old.

Before I realized it, the afternoon had slipped away and parents began arriving to pick up their children. Everybody seemed rather nonchalant about my presence, almost as if having a hitchhiker in to entertain the class was a routine exercise.

"Have you seen our pet mouse?" asked a little blonde girl named Nadia, after the other children had gone. "He's named Bart Simpson." She took my hand and led me across the room to a small fish tank standing in the corner. Inside, Bart nibbled away at some tiny food pellets. I thought momentarily about leaving him some vitamin tablets, but in the end decided against it. I would have felt terrible if the little guy croaked.

Suddenly Nadia scrunched up her face as if something important had just occurred to her. "Do they like Bart Simpson in Calgary?" she asked me, looking a little concerned. "You know, the Bart Simpson on TV?"

I smiled at that, suddenly glad that I had been stranded in Fort Nelson for the last two days. Maybe the black hole wasn't so bad after all. "Yes they do, Nadia," I told her, grinning from ear to ear. "They most certainly do."

Chapter 17

Gypsy Road

July 24, 1998 - Fort Nelson, British Columbia

The Alaska Highway can be a hard ride even when you manage to get one. So it proved to be on my third morning, the day I finally managed to escape from the black hole.

By a convenient coincidence, I was picked up by a young forestry engineer who recognized me from the Fort Nelson pub, where we had briefly met a couple of nights before. It had been karaoke night, and some locals in various stages of drunkenness had somehow talked me into getting up and singing (perhaps "singing" is too strong a word) a rendition of Robert Palmer's *Addicted to Love*. I'm certain that it was a less-than-memorable performance, even if I did manage to get into the act: rocking my hips back and forth, snapping my fingers and tilting my head back as though to swallow the microphone. It was obviously enough to convince the fellow to offer me a ride, though, which at this point was all that mattered.

"My name's Travis," he said after I had tossed my backpack into the rear of his truck. Then: "That was an interesting version of *Addicted to Love* you sang at the bar the other night." His voice was flat and expressionless, so I wasn't quite sure how to take it.

"Thanks," I said. I was half expecting him to lay down some ground rules for the ride—like no singing in his truck, for example. But not another word was said about Robert Palmer or love addictions, and conversation quickly turned to hunting, fishing and Travis's life as a logging-road surveyor. He was on his way to a job.

As I had suspected, getting out of Fort Nelson was the solution to all my problems. Travis was only able to take me as far as the Steamboat Cafe, a small service centre about an hour west of town, but that was all I needed. Less than two hours after I arrived in Steamboat, another truck pulled over, this one with a middle-aged Native couple inside.

They motioned for me to throw my backpack into the rear of their pickup, which I did eagerly before climbing in.

"We're on our way to Whitehorse for the weekend," the woman told me as I settled into the passenger's seat. I couldn't believe my luck. As I searched for my seatbelt, however, a little alarm bell suddenly started clanging in my head. The man gestured toward the back of the truck. "Before you get in buddy, grab me a beer from the cooler, willya?"

I looked at him, then at the woman, wondering how to respond. "Don't worry," she said, "he's only had a couple of beers. He'll be fine." With a dark cloud of uncertainty hanging over me, I walked to the back and plucked a beer from the cooler, then returned to my seat and handed it across the cab. The driver didn't sound drunk, but I had no way of knowing how many beers he had already had.

Their names were Don and Lenora, and for the next few minutes we chatted with uncomfortable fits and starts, until it was obvious to me that they weren't really looking for conversation. And it was difficult to maintain focus anyway, because Don was gunning down the road at speeds approaching 130 km/hour, the truck practically standing on edge as we rounded corners. The only saving grace was Lenora's biting words. Every time Don tried to speed past 130, she would grab his leg and bark at him to slow down.

Of course, for motorists who are used to driving on highways like the Trans-Canada or Toronto's 401 superhighway, 130 doesn't sound overly impressive. But there are major differences between those roads and the Alaska Highway. Although some sections of the latter have been straightened over the decades, there are still plenty of stretches that resemble a limp spaghetti noodle. When the highway was originally designed during World War II, the American government feared that Japanese fighters might bomb the road, so military engineers were instructed to build as many twists and turns into the highway as they could manage, making it nearly impossible to bomb. The only problem is, it also made the road nearly impossible to drive.

In most parts of Canada, when a road sign tells you to slow down while rounding a corner, you can generally add 20 km/hour to the suggested speed and feel safe. But on the Alaska Highway, adding even five will likely land you and your vehicle in the trees. The road's temperament is best summed up by a poem that was found years ago, scribbled on a napkin somewhere along the route. It has since been reprinted on a postcard and distributed in cafes and souvenir shops along the highway:

Winding in and winding out
Fills my mind with serious doubt
As to whether the lout who built this route
Was going to hell or coming out

As Don continued burning down the highway with blatant disregard for common sense, hell was looking more likely with each passing moment.

Five minutes later, Don rounded a corner at the top of a long hill and—rather than hit the brakes—started accelerating down the far side. The highway was under construction in this section, so it was covered with shards of slippery gravel and monstrous potholes. Thus it was really no surprise when Don lost control of his truck and it started fishtailing wildly from side to side.

All I remember seeing at this point was the angled shoulder approaching in slow motion—no guard rails—and the possibility of a ten- or fifteen-metre plunge down into the forest a real possibility. That's when Lenora grabbed Don's leg and shouted at the top of her lungs, "SLOW DOWN, YOU IDIOT!" Don started pumping the brakes just before the truck reached the edge, and somehow we shuddered to a halt before sailing off the road into oblivion.

"Wha's the problem?" he said, the slur in his speech by this time very evident.

"ARE YOU CRAZY, YOU FREAKIN' IDIOT!" screamed Lenora. "YOU'RE GOING TO KILL ALL OF US!"

If that didn't wake him up, my decision to get out of the truck certainly did. "I've had enough, guys," I said tersely, my head and stomach still spinning. "Good luck getting to Whitehorse in one piece." I wasn't just terse; I was spitting venom.

I already had one foot out the door when Don said something unexpected. "Hey... Hey man, I'm sorry ... I promise buddy ... I'll slow down. Just don't get out, cause you'll be stuck out here for hours dude ... maybe days."

This was true. I didn't have much food with me either, and after my experience on the Liard Highway the previous summer, being stranded out there didn't appeal much. Then again, the idea of being in Don's truck when it bounced off the road and rolled half a dozen times appealed even less. "I'll ride with you to the next service centre on one condition," I said. "If you promise to slow down *considerably*." I stressed the word *considerably* to make my point crystal-clear. I had just stared death in the face, and no ride was worth that price.

Don looked embarrassed. "I'm sorry," he mumbled again. He fidgeted and looked down at his feet. "I promise to take it easy." And for the most part he did, with the occasional reminder from Lenora to "SLOW THE HELL DOWN!"

I have rarely been so happy to climb from somebody's vehicle as I was from Don's. When we reached the roadhouse at Summit Lake half an hour later, one foot was already out the door before he had even stopped. I was in such a rush, in fact, that I left my cardboard hitchhiking sign in his truck, which to this day I've hoped was the lucky charm they needed to get to Whitehorse without killing themselves or anybody else.

THE ROADHOUSE AT Summit Lake looked like most service centres along this serpentine route: spartan and somewhat ramshackle. The broad gravel parking lot swept back from the highway toward the main building—a restaurant and motel office covered with faded murals and peeling paint. Surrounding this were several weather-beaten shacks, some boarded up, others used but obviously in need of maintenance. One of the shacks was covered with license plates, and I later learned that it's called the doghouse because it was used for keeping military dogs around the time of the war.

If the service centre lacked a certain pleasing glow, the mountains surrounding Summit Lake made up for any visual deficiency. They were not particularly lofty, but had a craggy and elegant appearance. The treeless ridges were bordered by lush green meadows, which were in turn carpeted by velvety wildflowers. The air was cool and refreshing, and it made my skin tingle as I walked toward the cafe.

Sauntering inside, I found the atmosphere to be pleasant enough. Several tourists were sitting at sturdy wooden tables eating food that looked and smelled delicious. A moose head was mounted on the wall in the middle of the long, narrow dining room, wearing a baseball cap that read: THE BOSS! At the far end of the dining room was a snarling wolf with another hat that identified him as THE CREDIT MANAGER! I ordered some coffee and asked the waitress if I could work on my journal until dinnertime. "No problem, honey," she said with a down-home twang. "Just so long as you write nice things 'bout us."

That evening, after feasting on a seasoned chicken breast, home fries and fresh bread, I decided to hike up the mountain on the far side of the highway to capture a few photos of the setting sun. My plan was to hike about two thirds of the way to the summit and pitch my tent for the night. Heather, the owner and operator of the cafe, assured me that there was a good trail, even though she thought I was bonkers. "Just so you know, there are grizzly bears up there."

"It's the little critters that I worry about more," I replied. "They're the ones that like to chew holes in your gear and torment you all night long."

"The big ones don't just chew holes in your gear," she said with a slanted look.

In spite of dire predictions that I would become a midnight snack for Boris the wandering grizzly, I was soon following a well-maintained trail that cut north along the edge of a babbling brook. I stopped to fill my water bottle, then crossed the creek and climbed onto a bluff that led along the edge of a long forested slope. It was here that I bumped into a hiker from Quebec, returning from a climb to the top. "Da view is incredible," he assured me, "but it's pretty damn windy on da ridge."

Fortunately, the wind had died by the time I reached the ridge, and true to my absurd plan, I continued climbing up and over the rubble-strewn slope to a place where I found a soft pocket of meadow grass, about two thirds of the way up the mountain. It was a stunning location, with a panoramic view of lakes, wildflower meadows and slotted vales. I saw dark clouds gathering on the western horizon, but didn't think anything of it as I pitched my tent. Camping near the top of a mountain was something I had done many times before in the southern Rockies, and I felt certain that my tent would hold even if the wind picked up again. And if it didn't, well, it would be my first experience hitchhiking the jet stream.

July 25, 1998 - Near the top of Summit Peak, British Columbia

It was shortly after four in the morning when I woke to the sound of wind hissing over the rocky ridge, battering hard against the side of my tent. What stirred me was not so much its intensity—the wind had been building all night—but the ominous sound it was making. It sounded like fire and ice colliding, like a coiled rattlesnake ready to strike at its prey. And my best guess at this point was that the prey happened to be me.

Drifting slowly back to consciousness, I tried to remember how many good peg placements I had made outside. A few seconds later I heard a tent pole snap, and an instant later my tent had flipped upside down and was airborne. The next thing I knew, I had smashed face-first into the ground, my camera, hiking boots and metal tripod raining down around my ears. I lay there for a few seconds, listening to the terrifying sound of wind ripping at tent fabric, then performed a mental inventory of bruises and puncture wounds. I wondered how far I was from the first big drop-off. The ridge where I had camped was fairly wide, but I probably wasn't more than a few metres from taking the express elevator down to the Summit Cafe.

When the wind subsided momentarily, I leapt into action, pulling off my sleeping bag and filling my backpack with gear. Then I heard another gust jump over the ridge. I flattened myself against the ground just before it hit the tent and literally willed it to stay in place. Surprisingly, it did. When the wind passed yet again, I jumped from the tent wearing nothing but underwear which, thinking back, must have been a fairly comical sight. I was a half-naked madman running around at the top of a mountain in the misty pre-dawn light, reaching into his tent to grab assorted items of food and clothing, stashing them behind a big rock, then scurrying back for more. Whenever the wind returned, I had to hold onto my tent with a Vulcan death-grip, and in the process developed goosebumps the size of raisins. Once the tent was free of my sleeping bag and other gear, I cut the damaged pole loose, folded the tent down and packed it away. The pole had snapped in two places, slicing through the tent fabric and fly, but with a liberal application of duct tape I was certain it would be good as new.

To say that Heather and her restaurant staff were surprised to see me before seven that morning is a monumental understatement. The walk down the mountain might have warmed me up, but it did little to improve my bedraggled appearance. "What the hell happened to you?" asked one of the waitresses, not shy about harassing a customer so early in the morning. Subtlety and tact were obviously not her strong points.

"Got caught in a wind storm," I said flatly.

"I should say, honey." She looked at me with a lopsided grin, sizing me up before pouring me a cup of coffee. "It looks like you were humped by a grizzly."

"Thanks."

And so it was that my sorry appearance won me much sympathy at Summit Lake Lodge that morning. They gave me a free breakfast, tools to fix my tent, and some cardboard and a felt marker to make another hitchhiking sign. Perhaps my appearance even helped me nab a ride from an old codger named Al, who was eating lunch as I scribbled a message on my new piece of cardboard. He asked where I was going, and when I mentioned Whitehorse, he told me that he was on his way to Muncho Lake. "It's only an hour up the road," he said. "But you can ride with me that far if you like."

Meeting Al proved fortuitous for another reason as well: I soon learned that he had a unique historical perspective on the Alaska Highway. As a kid growing up in Saskatchewan, he had always dreamed of the Rocky Mountains, so when the US army hired him to help build the road to Alaska, he wasn't about to turn down the job. He moved to Muncho Lake from Regina in 1941.

"It was a dream comin' up here when the land was first bein' discovered," he admitted. "I thought life was so beautiful back then. Still do, as a matter of fact. I always yearned to have a look at them mountains I read about in school."

Al was well into his seventies, but I could tell by looking at his muscular hands and bulky forearms that he had worked hard all his life. Still, his demeanour was gentle, and I thought it was touching the way he stopped to let a herd of mother stone sheep and their lambs cross the road. "Awww, aren't they just the cutest things you ever seen," he cooed, clucking like a mother hen. He pulled a video camera from behind his seat and started filming the sheep parade. "That's why I still come up here, to see the wildlife and virgin country."

Al was an expert at talking and driving at the same time, and soon we had dropped into a narrow gorge surrounded by towering cliffs and a mountain river with a glacial aquamarine blush. "Yessir, it's been a long, hard life for me," he said, referring to his years of near-starvation during the Great Depression. He seemed as proud of his hardships as he was of his accomplishments—not to mention the fact that he had left home when he was only fourteen. "When you're hungry and destitute and have no money, what are you going to do?" His question was rhetorical. "Well, you're going to do the best you can, that's what!"

Eventually, conversation came around to the Yukon, one of Al's favourite places in the world. He had more than a few stories about the early years up there, but one of his favourites involved a successful entrepreneur who had lived during the gold rush era. Rather than dig for gold himself, he would lend people three hundred dollars to start a claim on the condition that if they gave up or died while trying to find gold, ownership of the claim would revert to him. As can be imagined, far more gold claims were abandoned than ever amounted to anything, so this fellow ended up owning a vast expanse of land. He made his mint when the large dredges started appearing in the Yukon, and he was able to sell the claims for big bucks.

The unusual part of his story is that the fellow became a millionaire several times over—yet he lived for years in a cave on a remote part of the Yukon River, a caribou skin stretched across the cave's entrance. He even used to come into Dawson City to search for clothes by picking through trash cans. Al had bumped into the man at a saloon one autumn while on a hunting trip to Dawson City, and watched with great interest as the chap ordered two scotches on the rocks, then sat by himself at a small table. First he sat on one side and drank a toast to the empty chair. Then he took a hefty swig, changed seats and toasted with the other drink. The most entertaining part was when an argument broke out between the man and himself, screaming across the table at the empty seat before changing sides and screaming back at the seat where he had just been sitting. It was never clear who won the argument.

"Boy, the language he was using was sure colourful," chuckled Al. "It was probably a case of gold fever driving him crazy. The more gold he had, the more he wanted."

This was not the last I would hear about gold fever.

Chapter 18

Trail to the Klondike

August 2, 1998 - The Chilkoot Trail, British Columbia

The first highway to cut north across the Yukon's sawtooth border was not one of concrete or asphalt. Rather, it was a footpath pushed through the wilderness by a legion of desperate men chasing dreams of unimaginable wealth. Most of them arrived in the town of Skagway, Alaska during the winter of 1898, their hardened eyes set on staking a claim at the Klondike gold fields near Dawson City. Toiling with the requisite two thousand pounds of food and supplies in tow, these "cheechakos" (Chinook for "tenderfeet") set out onto the Dead Horse Trail, not knowing what to expect. What they found were impossible hardships and the sickly stench of carrion embracing them at nearly every turn. Quite literally, the trail they followed up the Taiya River canyon and over Chilkoot Pass was the closest thing to hell on earth.

Thankfully, the stench of carrion is not so evident these days, presumably overwhelmed by the scent of bacon and eggs frying on a hot skillet. It was this delightful aroma that roused me from my tent at Sheep Camp, the last point of rest before Chilkoot Pass rears like a mad stallion eight hundred metres into rarefied mountain air.

While talking with Al two days earlier, I had realized that in order to truly understand the Yukon, one must walk this foot highway. And walking and paddling the old gold rush trail to Dawson City would be a perfect excuse to "go bush" for a couple of weeks. My mind made up, I hitchhiked south to Skagway where I had lunch at the Red Onion saloon, then departed north on foot for the summit of the infamous pass.

It quickly became clear that I wasn't the only person with this plan. As chance would have it, 1998 happened to be the Klondike's one hundredth anniversary. On my way through Skagway, I met at least a dozen hikers who had come to the Yukon specifically to take part in the centennial. There was a young East German couple, Thorolf and Marion, who between them spoke about seven words of English. Somehow, I managed to discern that Thorolf had dreamed of hiking the Chilkoot Trail ever since he was a boy; had the Berlin Wall not fallen, he would have been prepared to swim the Bering Sea to reach it. I also met two Québécois hitchhikers who had managed to thumb from Winnipeg to Whitehorse in a single ride, and a church group from Smithers, BC who invited me to hike with them. All in all, parks staff told us they were expecting several thousand hikers that summer. Like the thousands of stampeders who had gone before us, we would all start at sea level, wind our way along the fifty-three-kilometre trail to the top of the pass, then drop down to Bennett Lake.

Regrettably, the bacon and eggs were not mine, so I boiled water for oatmeal and a hot cup of cocoa instead, then walked over to greet my new friends. To prepare for the day's gruelling climb, Everett (the group's handsome young minister) gathered everybody together for devotions. Pulling at his thick, sandy-brown moustache, he launched in with a unique blend of motivational pep talk and backwoods preaching. "We might be tempted to view the trail as something to conquer," he told us, glancing around the semicircle at his congregation, all seated comfortably on logs and thick cushions of moss. "But really, it's something inside ourselves that we must conquer. By turning to God, we can overcome our perceived physical and psychological barriers." A minister, apparently, is never on vacation.

Our tents were soon packed, and after a few stretching exercises we set off along the trail through the fading remnants of second-growth forest. In 1898, Sheep Camp was the final place stampeders were able to cut firewood before crossing the pass, so its boundaries stretched to the edge of the tree-line. The camp quickly became so muddled with tents and seedy hovels that men could barely squeeze between them, and it wasn't long before the scene degenerated into utter pandemonium. At its peak, Sheep Camp boasted sixteen hotels, fourteen restaurants, thirteen supply houses, five drug merchants, three saloons, two dance halls, two laundromats, a hospital, a lumberyard and a post office ... and hundreds of dead horses buried beneath the snow. The camp served between six and eight thousand transient residents, although most of them had packed over the pass by May of 1898.

Now it was our turn to pack over the Chilkoot, and the steep switchbacks soon had us gasping for air, even as the last ostrich ferns and devil's club gave way to a barren moonscape. Further up the valley, we spotted a curtain of glacier ice hanging precariously off a mountain to the west, and it wasn't long thereafter that we reached the Scales, the last place of rest before tackling the pass. The area was littered with various gold rush artifacts: pickaxes, shovels, wagon parts and bleached bones that had presumably belonged to a horse at one time. There were also vast quantities of rusted wire cable that had once linked Skagway to Bennett by telephone—nearly two decades before the same service was available anywhere else in North America—as well as thick cable rope, a leftover from the tramway that had carried supplies to the top of the pass for those few who could afford it.

Stopping at the Scales to contemplate Klondike insanity, we looked up at the Chilkoot to where several small ants were struggling against the trail as if climbing a brick wall. They weren't really ants, of course. They were other hikers. But this elongated perspective made it abundantly clear that historians have bandied about the term "mountain pass" rather loosely. Still, we were wearing ergonomically designed, form-fitting backpacks, so I should take a moment to put things into perspective. An average stampeder carried between sixty and eighty pounds of goods over the pass on every trip, shuttling and caching supplies in eight-kilometre increments. Thus each stampeder made roughly thirty round trips along the trail and walked more than four thousand kilometres before reaching Bennett Lake. That's like walking from Vancouver to Toronto.

What went over the pass? Everything from farm plows to pianos to live chickens. A large Native packer reputedly carried a 350-pound barrel to the top of the Chilkoot on a dare. A. J. Goddard, a wiry engineer from the United States, disassembled and carried two sternwheeler vessels across the pass in bits and pieces.

Despite the Chilkoot's steep pitch, we found it littered with large firmly set boulders that actually made climbing relatively easy. We were lucky because the rock was dry, a rare condition in a valley exposed to wind and driving rain whipping off the Gulf of Alaska. Mind you, the direct sun that had dried the rocks also slowed our progress. The cool glacial wind slipping down off the shoulders of the mountains did little to regulate our temperatures—and as two Quebecers passed us halfway up the Golden Stairs, I saw that we were not alone in our discomfort. The fellow in front was in good spirits, but his friend, packing a more generous girth around his waist, looked as though he might flop over and start convulsing violently at any moment. Short on breath and with sweat pouring off his stubbly face, he stopped beside me to suck oxygen and regain some composure. "Right now, I need a Budweiser shower," was all he said before continuing up the hill.

It was early afternoon by the time the church group and I reached the Chilkoot's summit, which is also the international border between Canada and the United States. A small warden's cabin was flying the red Maple Leaf, and was surrounded by the rubble of buildings that had long ago belonged to the North West Mounted Police. It was from here that legendary Mounties like Sam Steele had acted as a barricade to the lawlessness of Skagway, gazing down on the never-ending human cavalcade as it struggled skyward. From their lofty perch, the Mounties enforced the "two thousand pounds of supplies" rule, collected duties and ensured fair conduct among stampeders. The collected money was stuffed into a mattress inside the cramped policeman's quarters.

Happy Camp was visible from the top of the pass, and after a leisurely break we set out across meadows ablaze with wildflowers, intent on pitching camp there for the night. Crater Lake sprawled across the alpine basin directly below the pass, lit by the sun and reflecting a pleasing turquoise hue. It was rather aptly named, I thought, considering it has been chiseled into the bedrock like some gigantic lunar swimming pool. While my friends from Smithers hiked ahead, I decided to cop a short nap in the meadow grass, and an hour later met Thorolf and Marion coming down off the summit, exhausted but beaming with pride. The only part of their story I couldn't understand was the part about startling some "snow chickens."

"Snow chickens?" I asked, a little puzzled. In response, Thorolf started squawking and madly flapping his arms as though possessed by some crazed bird demon.

"Yah, snow chickens," Marion repeated, hardly able to contain herself for her boyfriend's strange behaviour.

It was only after much back and forth that I finally determined a snow chicken was not actually some mountain myth from the German Alps, but rather some type of alpine nesting bird from Canada, possibly a ptarmigan or grouse. Whatever it was, they hadn't been able to kill it with their slingshot, which was really too bad. After reaching Happy Camp, I would have really enjoyed a couple of fried snow chicken legs after my Budweiser shower.

August 3, 1998 - Lindeman Lake, British Columbia

The evening sun slanted hard against the peaks ringing Lindeman Lake, a place of relative tranquility after four days of hard slogging along the Chilkoot Trail. Mostly it was the lake's otherworldly turquoise hue and mirror-like surface that brought to mind feelings of triumph and peace—not a whisper of wind disturbing it—though I also felt a certain jubilance for having hiked such an important piece of Canada's history. It was either this realization, or the fact that Lindeman Lake looked so incredibly pristine, that caused me and Brian (one of the hikers from Smithers) to momentarily lose the better part of judgment. Whatever the case, before we could regain our senses we had stripped down to our boxer shorts and leapt with great abandon into the icy water. We lasted about five seconds. As Yukon-sized ice-cream headaches flooded between our ears, we stumbled back to shore, gasping for breath.

For most stampeders, the sight of Lindeman was pure ecstasy, primarily because they were able to pitch camp here, cut and sling trees together to build rafts—and then wait. Once winter was over, these men shot down a precarious canyon to Bennett Lake and, if successful, joined the Yukon River on its journey toward Dawson. Indeed, when the ice finally broke on May 29, 1898, a flotilla of more than seven thousand boats pushed off from the shores of Lindeman and Bennett, bound for the Klondike gold fields. According to Pierre Berton's book *Klondike*, some men ferried themselves downriver in huge scows designed to transport oxen and horses, while others navigated skiffs constructed from a few hastily bound logs. Some even rode inside boxes that resembled coffins. It would be more than eight hundred kilometres of wilderness and dangerous whitewater before they reached the carnival antics of Dawson City.

After throwing together a dinner of odds and ends—pasta noodles and limp vegetables, tossed helter-skelter into a large silver pot—I ventured to the top of a small hill overlooking Lindeman. Everett and his group followed, and we soon found a large wooden cross and several graves surrounded by rough-hewn picket fences. They lay in the middle of a small clearing, as if resisting the wilderness that was trying so desperately to swallow them up. A weathered plaque nearby told a sad story:

Eleven men lie here conquered by the trail. Scurvy, exhaustion, fragile boats and the Lindeman rapids all contributed. Sympathetic companions, restored to normal humanity by rest at Lindeman, established this cemetery. They built fences around the graves, Yukon-style, in a final attempt to separate man from the indomitable wilderness threatening to obliterate him even in death.

Gratefully, it was not a death-defying decent through Lindeman Canyon that concerned me the following morning, but rather making it to Bennett Lake in time for sourdough pancakes. In honour of the centennial, the Yukon Outdoors Club had posted a nineteenth-century cookhouse at Bennett, where every morning they cooked a special sourdough flapjack breakfast for hungry hikers. It was the reward for participating in the Yukon's centennial. With free food on the line, I was up by six, wandering through eleven kilometres of scrub brush and boreal forest. The trail was dry and easy to follow, and the only thing that occasionally stopped me were the scads of wild blueberry bushes dotting the Trail's fringes. I was picking them for the pancakes, of course, but it was hard not to get a little carried away. By the time I reached Bennett, my hands and tongue were stained dark purple.

"Where did you get those blueberries?" demanded a hawk-eyed warden named Roseanne. She had spotted me handing them across the counter to one of the cooks.

"I picked them along the trail," I said defensively. It had never occurred to me that picking blueberries was an offense, and I was a little put off by her tone.

"You're supposed to leave them for the bears," she lectured. She sounded serious ... yet not serious at the same time. Surely there were enough berries for both hikers and bears. That's when she added: "But I might forget I saw them if you give me a few for my pancakes."

"Roseanne's just pulling your leg," said Pat, a chipper-looking blonde lady inside the cook's tent. "She's just sick of eating plain pancakes." This I could understand, and so it was that I graciously poured some blueberries into Roseanne's outstretched hands.

"I tell you, I've never cooked for such an appreciative crowd," Pat said, shaking her head as she handed me my fourth plate. "Hikers are always hungry, and they're always grateful when somebody cooks real food for them." I couldn't have agreed more. By the time I had finished, there were sixteen fewer pancakes at Bennett Lake than when I first arrived.

I soon learned that Pat was a Chilkoot Trail veteran herself, and probably the only person I met who had walked the trail nearly as often as stampeders from the gold rush era. She worked in Whitehorse as a high school teacher, and had hiked over the Chilkoot Pass seventeen times since 1978, including four times with her children. "When I go with my husband, I have to carry most of the food, because he takes ten pounds of chocolate and twenty pounds of camera gear," she chuckled. "For him, everything else is incidental."

Which led us to ponder why people are still so fascinated by this trail. "It's definitely the history," Pat told me, nodding her head soberly. "Those men were absolutely driven beyond the point of no return, obsessed with becoming instantly rich." She told me about one fellow named John Matthews who packed supplies over the pass, lost everything in the Lindeman Rapids, then went back and packed another two thousand pounds to Lindeman. When he upset in the canyon a second time, Matthews swam to shore, pulled out his revolver and shot himself. "And that, to me, sums up the sorrow and futility of this trail," she said.

Chapter 19

Five Fingers, Four Toes

August 5, 1998 - Whitehorse, Yukon Territory

The highway east of Bennett Lake is accessible by way of a grueling thirteen-kilometre slog along the White Pass railway tracks, and after doing just that, I decided to cheat. Rather than hitchhike, I paid a few dollars and hopped on a shuttle bus bound for Whitehorse.

To celebrate a successful crossing of the Chilkoot, I dropped in at the Gold Pan Saloon to ponder a question I had read on a plaque near the beginning of the trail: *Are you following the gold rush trail for the challenge, the history, or for nature?* It was a good question. They all seemed like valid reasons. It has been said that if a person follows in the footsteps of stampeders from a century ago, they will earn their own place in the history books; perhaps that was my reason for making the journey. Or maybe I have a secret love for self-punishment. Whatever the case, one thing I didn't know was whether crossing the Chilkoot and paddling the Yukon River down to Dawson would qualify me as a bona fide "Yukon sourdough," a much-revered title that every cheechako dreams of earning. I put the question to a silver-haired man sitting at the next table.

"Actually," he said, "to qualify for that you have to stick around long enough to see freeze-up and break-up on the Yukon River."

"Really?"

The old guy had mischief written all over his face, like he was dying to fill me in on some tantalizing little secret. "Well, there's a shortcut if you've got the stomach for it lad," he continued. "Have you ever heard of the sour toe cocktail?"

"Can't say that I have."

The man nodded, then grunted slightly. "Well, you're about to."

Over the next thirty minutes, Jim—an artist and self-appointed collector of northern stories—did just that. And what I heard was surely one of the most bizarre rituals ever concocted in the history of mankind. As the tale goes, there were two brothers from Norway named Otto and

Louie Liken who lived as trappers, miners and occasional rum-runners during the days of prohibition in Alaska. Their cabin lay between Dawson and the US border, at the headwaters of the Sixty Mile River, where they would wait for foul weather so that they could discreetly cross with their cargo of illicit goods.

On one of those trips, with the North West Mounted Police hot on their trail, Louie stepped through a crust of snow into some water, soaking his foot. With no means of stopping to warm it up in the middle of the storm, the brothers kept moving, and by the time they had circled back to their cabin, Louie's foot was a solid block of blue ice. To prevent gangrene, Otto decided on a grisly remedy that involved getting his brother good and drunk on overproof rum, then chopping his big toe off with the quick swing of an axe. They pickled the toe in a jar of alcohol—for sentimental reasons, perhaps, or possibly bragging rights—and years later it was found in their cabin by a riverboat captain named Dick Stevenson.

Now Stevenson himself was a character—a true Yukoner if ever there was one—and while talking with a reporter about his discovery one afternoon, he fell upon a grand idea. The idea involved a decidedly northern elixir, one capable of putting hair on people and in places where hair rightly shouldn't grow. Primarily, the elixir would be part of a ritual designed for those poor sourdough wannabes (sods like me) who had dreams of bonding with the Far North, but didn't have the time (or maybe the backbone) to spend an entire winter in the Yukon.

The rules were simple: fix any drink of your choice, plop the toe into your glass, then swig it back until the toe bumped against your upper lip. Much to Stevenson's surprise, the toe became an overnight sensation at Dawson's Downtown Hotel ... until one fateful evening when it was accidentally swallowed by an overzealous patron. Fortunately, by that time the drink was famous enough that it garnered much sympathy from its adoring fans. Before Stevenson could devise a plan for replacing the toe, several donors stepped forward to contribute their, uh, digits to the cause.

"And the rest is history," said Jim.

History for some, maybe ... but for me? Only time would tell if I had the guts to face Cap'n Dick's toe of blight. It was time to paddle down the Yukon River to the Klondike.

August 7, 1998 - The Yukon River near Carmacks, Yukon Territory

The Yukon River hasn't changed much since the days of the gold rush: it's big and bold and dominates the surrounding landscape for hundreds of square kilometres. In 1898, the river also had its fair share of navigational hazards—most notably the rapids at Miles Canyon, near present-day Whitehorse. These rapids alone, comprised of boat-puncturing rocks and foam that danced four feet off the water, sank a hundred and fifty vessels and drowned five men in the first few days after the floating armada left Bennett. There was also a much-feared whirlpool swirling ominously in the middle of the gorge, so incalculably powerful that when two Swedes were accidentally swept into the canyon, they spent six hours spinning deliriously in circles before reaching shore. One can only imagine what they said to each other after that episode:

"Holy geez, Sven, our compass don't tell us which way is north no more."

"It's dat way, Anders."

"Yer pointin' at da sky, you damn fool."

"Maybe we should wait a few minutes until we get off da ground."

"Kinda feel like we been hit by uncle Otto's tractor, ya?"

The boat-eating rapids at Miles Canyon no longer exist, of course, smoothed out of existence by the large dam just outside Whitehorse. The only sizable rapids are the Five Fingers located just north of Carmacks, and even these narrow chutes are tame by comparison. Still, that doesn't mean navigation is easy on the Yukon. The river is to this day a convoluted maze of channels and islands; for that very reason, a Danish traveller named Bo, who I met in Whitehorse, convinced me that we should spare no expense on the best map money could buy. It cost three dollars. If we were going to paddle a canoe several hundred kilometres to Dawson, a moment's inattention could mean picking the wrong channel and thus, rather than enjoying a leisurely float trip, having to get out and drag our canoe across endless gravel flats in ankle-deep water.

But Bo and I were up for the challenge. On day two in our rented canoe, we successfully navigated the Five Fingers, and on day three, after drifting past massive burn sites all day long, we landed at Fort Selkirk. The interesting thing about Fort Selkirk is that it's one of the only Yukon communities to predate the gold rush. It was used for several thousand years by the northern Tutchone people before a Hudson's Bay trading post was established there in 1848. This is where colourful Yukon characters like Copper Joe and Bishop Isaac Stringer hail from. Copper Joe was an Indian medicine man who, according to legend, once summoned a rainstorm to extinguish a forest fire near the village; Bishop Stringer is most famous for a dogsled trip to Fort McPherson, during which he was forced to eat his own leather boots to survive.

The only resident of Fort Selkirk these days is Native watchman Danny Roberts, a wizened hobbit of a man who walks around tapping his willow cane against the ground. Bo and I watched as he wandered the banks of the Yukon, puzzling over the region's lack of rain. While pitching our tent, I asked him why the fort had been abandoned for so long. "Everybody had to move because the boats stopped comin' through," he said matter-of-factly. "After that, there was nothin' here for the people. I only stay to keep watch over the place." For many years, he also ran a trap line near Fort Selkirk, until fur prices plummeted.

Less than an hour after we arrived, the fort's campground was literally crawling with canoeists and kayakers. Like us, most of them had hiked over Chilkoot Pass and were now paddling to Dawson City for the Discovery Days festival, a yearly event that celebrates the discovery of gold in the Yukon. A large group from BC pitched camp beside us, and it wasn't long before an athletic-looking gentleman in his mid-fifties pulled out an old Hudson's Bay Company flag, which he carefully unfolded and raised to the top of a thick wooden pole. "It's been a while since that was flown here," I heard him remark to a friend. We all stared up at the flag for a moment, silently saluting a company that for so many decades was responsible for opening Canada's frontier.

"I don't like this campground," Bo finally muttered. He was dipping into our nachos and salsa, his voice a combination of good humour and diatribe.

"What's wrong with it?" I asked.

"There are too many middle-aged men and not enough women."

To make matters worse, shortly after dinner a loud, lanky firecracker of a man came loping over from near the old telegraph office and plopped himself down at a picnic table near our campsite. He had a black, bushy moustache and a long ponytail that drooped through the back of his baseball cap, well past his shoulders. He was wearing a red mackinaw and grubby jeans that were not only several centimetres too short but were pulled tightly against his crotch—almost as if he were trying to attract attention for all the wrong reasons. He introduced himself as Jimbo, and Bo and I listened intently as he informed Danny and a few of his Native friends that he had come to the Yukon looking for a claim to stake.

We soon learned that Jimbo was from southern Ontario, although he made no bones about where his true loyalties lay. "Toronto is a big blob of crap," he said bluntly. "They should all be washed away in a flood." I wondered to myself: did he actually feel this way, or was he trying to make friends with the locals by handily bashing Toronto? It was hard to tell, because some Canadians enjoy beating up on big ol' mean Toronto almost as much as digging at the Yanks.

"Canadians are spineless!" Jimbo barked. "We need to start a revolution to get rid of the incompetent politicians running our country." The man was on a rant, and it was painfully clear that nothing was going to stop him. "If we get everyone together, not a shot has to be fired," he assured us, as if trying to recruit us for battle. "We can blockade bridges and roads, and make them do what we elected them to do." Perhaps it was just me, but the thought of a pony-tailed, lumpy-crotched Jimbo leading a national revolution seemed a bit absurd.

"I'm SERIOUS!" Jimbo barked again. He had obviously heard me snicker. He hammered a fist against the picnic table. "Our politicians should be doing what we want them to do, and they're not!"

Much to his dismay, nobody else seemed interested in his revolution either. Indeed, if the blank expressions and polite chortles were anything to go by, he was going to have a hard time finding recruits at Fort Selkirk. Then again, once he had staked his claim and struck pay dirt, he could always fund his own army. And I'm sure it would be a great victory for freedom of expression. Outfitted with suspenders, mackinaws, chewing tobacco and blue jeans three sizes too small, his army would ensure that Canadians everywhere had access to fashion of monumental poor taste.

August 10, 1998 - The Yukon River near Fort Selkirk, Yukon Territory

Down the river from Fort Selkirk, the already stunning scenery only improved: sheer basalt cliffs plunged from great heights into the current, while the first breath of autumn colour whispered through rolling, green-backed mountains. Leaves dangled like thin sheets of gold from birch and poplar trees. By this time the wind had acquired some bite, and the miles passed without much chatter, Bo and I preferring to contemplate the wilderness in silence. The only sound was the slip of our paddle blades into the river, then the brief patter of droplets across the water before our blades slurped back in again.

The river had widened significantly, which meant that Bo and I could relax without paying much attention to navigation. We soon fell into a routine that would have made early stampeders shake their heads with dismay. We would generally rise by nine, eat a leisurely breakfast and hit the river by maybe eleven. Paddle for an hour. Nap in the sun with caps pulled across our faces until lunch. Eat. Continue napping with renewed vigour until late afternoon. Paddle for another hour. Start looking for a campsite so that we could relax after a hard day. "I can't believe the torture those stampeders had to endure," a shirtless Bo liked to say from beneath his ball cap. "Prospecting for gold is nothing but work."

Two days before reaching Dawson, Bo and I passed a small sign in the shape of a coffee mug advertising "Coffee Creek." We beached our canoe and strolled through dense forest, passing wagons and a rusty plow on our way toward a small clearing. In the middle of the clearing was a shack with a rack of moose antlers fastened above the front door. The place looked completely deserted, but we decided to knock anyway.

Without warning, two large dogs burst through a hole in the screen door, and a few seconds later their owner appeared from behind. He was a gaunt looking man with a thick beard, wearing a felt hat and with a tobacco pipe hanging from one corner of his mouth. He was the spitting image of a Yukon prospector. As we soon learned, that was exactly what he was doing there.

"People call me Coffee John," he said, gesturing for us to follow him inside the cabin. We entered a large room with a wood-burning stove pushed against the far wall, used both for central heating and for brewing java. In one corner sat a rectangular bathtub, while another corner housed several large shelves stocked generously with boxed and canned goods. John's bed sat in the middle of the room, prime real estate which was quickly reclaimed by his dogs.

"How long have you been here?" I asked him. By this time, John had fetched us mugs filled with steaming black brew.

"I quit my job in Whitehorse five years ago because I wanted to live in the bush and prospect," he replied. "And there's gold all around here," he assured Bo and me with a wink. He sat down in his rocking chair and pulled at his suspender straps.

"How do you go about finding gold?" I asked him.

He looked at me sharply, as if my question was the most ridiculous thing he had ever heard. "By taking a shovel and digging," he said bluntly. "How do you think you'd find it?"

Obviously, I was not a sourdough just yet.

For more than two hours, Bo and I listened intently as John romanticized the life of a modern prospector. Life in the bush, he told us, was never easy, but it did have its rewards: frequent encounters with wildlife, a feeling of connection to the land ... and during the winter months, a sky that shimmered like celestial rapids. Still, the search for that elusive mother lode was what had brought him there in the first place, and it was what held him there to that day.

"Is there anything you don't like about living in the bush?" Bo asked at one point. We both sensed that something was weighing on John's mind.

"It's hard out here, man," John admitted glumly. "I'd be alright if I had a nice bush bunny, but I haven't found any takers." He told us about a small dugout canoe that he had built with a sail and pontoons two years back, and how he had put a note inside advertising for a woman before setting it loose on the current. "But with my luck, it probably got to the Bering Sea, where some whale swallowed it." Bo and I couldn't help but laugh. "Hey, this is no laughing matter," John said, before breaking into laughter himself. "Seriously, it gets lonely out here, guys. You know you're getting desperate when the bears start looking good."

August 14, 1998 - Dawson City, Yukon Territory

Bo and I knew we had reached the Klondike when we found ourselves clomping along the wooden boardwalks lining Dawson's gravel streets. As we pushed through the swinging doors of Dawson's Downtown Hotel on our first evening in town, I realized that our journey along the Yukon's gold rush trail was almost over. Almost. In order to join the ranks of true Northerners, would we rise to the challenge of the sour toe?

Bo shuffled up to the bar, ordered a rye and ginger and stared long and hard at the petrified toe sitting discreetly in a jar of pickling salt on a bar table. He watched as the bartender dropped the bunioned digit—yellow, wrinkled and nauseating—into his glass. For a few seconds, I thought he might balk. But he didn't. After rubbing his chin with a thumb and forefinger, Bo took on the steely resolve of a sourdough possessed. He hammered his drink back with a powerful flick of his wrist, the toe's chiseled nail bumping his upper lip in the process.

That's when the spotlight turned to me. As I ordered my drink and stared hard at the toe, I suddenly thought of the question that had plagued me at the Gold Pan Saloon in Whitehorse more than a week before: *Are you following the gold rush trail for the challenge, the history, or for nature?* I still hadn't figured that one out. One thing was certain, though: I hadn't done it for this damn toe!

Chapter 20

Eldorado

August 17, 1998 - Dawson City, Yukon Territory

It has been said that in the Yukon Territory there are only three seasons: July, August and winter. And while it's true that Bo and I had arrived in Dawson City near the middle of August, there was no denying the sharp, unmistakable tug of old man winter pulling at the end of the month. A day after we arrived, it started to rain. Not the warm coastal rain of Vancouver Island, but rather a penetrating Arctic deluge that was no more than one or two degrees shy of the white stuff. Winter was moving in fast!

Not surprisingly, with the Discovery Days festival in full swing, there wasn't a vacant room to be had in town—which meant no private shower or warm bed after eight days on the river. We did manage to find a shower at the local laundromat, though we had to join a seemingly perpetual line of cold and equally disheartened travellers waiting to use it. Indeed, there weren't even any sites at the local campground, so Bo and I were relegated to the squatters' campground across the river. And by "squatters' campground" I refer to a narrow thicket of trees lining the edge of the highway, pitched on deceptively sloping ground. No picnic tables, no water, no toilets.

To make matters worse, on the night Bo and I arrived in Dawson we had treated ourselves to a celebratory dinner at a local Chinese food buffet, a sort of après-Yukon-River treat. The food had been good, but I had absent-mindedly left my three-hundred-dollar Gore-Tex jacket hanging over the back of my chair after dinner. When I returned to retrieve it fifteen minutes later, our waitress looked at me blankly and said, "Haven't seen it, champ. Sorry."

Likely story. But what could I do?

It's worth noting that a jacket like this is practically a home away from home for a hitchhiker. Consider all the hours spent huddled on the exposed shoulder of the road, braving the sun, wind and whatever else nature has to throw at you. More to the point, the jacket also represented an

The author thumbs for a ride in Waterloo County, Ontario

Views to inspire: Jason Hoerle at the summit of Dolomite Peak.

The Trans-Canada Highway drops through Kicking Horse Pass: the steep grade on this hill caused many train wrecks during the late 19th century.

Proud Harley owners Bill Murphy and Jim Morris share a few road stories at a Vernon coffee shop. "We consider ourselves philosophers," says Jim. "The road gives you a lot of time for introspection. We let the bikes decide where they'll take us."

Hitchhiker's haven: Corina Rothlisberger and her cat Sushi pose for a picture at her apartment in Vancouver.

Breakfast with the Crofton gang. From left to right: Jim Connor, Heather McPhee with Luke, Stephen McPhee and Libby Connor with Zachary.

Victor Balatti (foreground) leads an informal session for disenfranchised fishermen: "As far as I'm concerned," he told me. "Canada can end at the Rockies."

Hitching a ride with logger Craig Stephens on Quadra Island, BC.

Peace River soil may not be the best in the west, but long daylight hours during the summer months coax crops to grow more quickly.

Arno and Cezanne address dignitaries at Arno's big send-off. Fueled by donuts across the country: what could be more Canadian than that?

King of the Road: Robb Stemp and Jazz cruise north towards Yellowknife, one nervous hitchhiker relegated to the back seat.

Northern ingenuity: floating homes on Great Slave Lake allow some Yellowknifers to avoid paying property tax.

Boreal thunder: the author gets close and personal with Crusty, one of Wood Buffalo's local boys.

Gypsum karst sinkholes at the bottom Pine Lake create a rainbow assortment of blues, Wood Buffalo National Park.

Hitchhiker's daycare: preparing Fort Nelson kids for the rigours of the road.

Who's the boss? The pecking order at Summit Lake Lodge.

Tracy Aven and Teresa Keenan soothe aching muscles at Liard Hot Springs.
The hot springs have been soothing the road weary along
the Alaska Highway for decades.

The Golden Staircase: one tough slog for modern adventurers, but at least we didn't have to make thirty round trips.

Sourdough extraveganza: Pat McKenna of the Yukon Outdoors Club serves pancakes to hungry hikers at Bennett Lake.

Goin' bush: Coffee John Bodnarek at his cabin along the banks of the Yukon River.

Twilight falls along the banks of the mighty Yukon.

RCMP officers gather in Dawson City for the annual Discovery Days parade. Their predecessors collected duties, maintained sovereignty and kept the peace during the lawless era of the Klondike gold rush.

Bo's moment of truth: Cap'n Dick's toe of blight never fails to strike dread into the hearts of sourdough wannabes.

Hitchhiker traffic jam: two Quebecois girls perform the "gumboots dance" while standing at the Dempster Highway junction.

Photo by Pat Morrow

Road of Attrition: the punishing 750-kilometre Dempster Highway as it slices through the Richardson Mountains.

Inuvialuit sprites from Tuktoyaktuk play in a windstorm whipping off the Arctic ice pack. The author was dressed in full winter apparel.

Watch those teeth: Joe Nasogaluak nearly gets his fingers clipped while feeding his sled dogs in Tuktoyaktuk.

Peek-a-boo, I see you: Gwich'in toddler Jayden Greenland contemplates the strange man sitting in the back of his family's pickup truck.

Autumn colours of Kluane National Park: home to Canada's highest peaks.

Assiniboine warrior Conrad Rope at Fort Walsh, Saskatchewan. His ancestors were slaughtered here during the Cypress Hills massacre of 1873.

The Queen's Cowboys: a Manitoba reeanctment group strikes a pose worthy of the North-West Mounted Police.

Home again on the range: the author left Saskatchewan as a teenager, only to return twelve years later for a tour by thumb.

A case of mistaken identity: an orphaned elk calf tries to suckle the Rabut's farm dog, much to the delight of the family canine.

Long, cool woman in a farmhouse: enough to give a hitchhiker a bad case of white picket fence disease. Renee Rabut (centre) models her grandmother's wedding dress at Batoche National Historic Site.

Beer-swilling Herrs and Fleet-footed Fraus: the lively German pavilion at Winnipeg's annual Folklorama festival.

A toddler enjoys sun, sand and scenery at Grand Beach, one of Canada's finest beaches.

Pierre Durette and his kitten hitchhiked the Trans-Canada Highway from Quebec to BC's Okanagan valley and back again.

Superior Vision: the world's largest body of freshwater, as seen from cliffs in Pukaskwa National Park.

The Sweepstakes, an eighteenth-century British-style schooner that sank near Tobermory, is one of ten thousand shipwrecks littering the bottom of the Great Lakes.

Does hitchhiking get any better than this? A prime swimming hole at Baie Fine gave us the perfect setting for barbecued pepper sausages, red wine and star-gazing by the glow of a campfire.

My Canada includes cows: the misty croplands of Waterloo County.

Greyhound bus driver Jeff Glover gave me a lift from Orangeville into downtown Toronto.

Marc Lemay and Kathryn Lawson show several youngsters how it's done at their wedding in downtown Ottawa.

Ode to the Maple Leaf: Gatineau's annual hot air balloon festival.

Our home and boisterous land: when national pride is at stake, run through the streets of Ottawa yelling, chanting and jumping up and down on the bumpers of passing taxi cabs.

Partner in crime: Martin Silverstone repairs a model train set at his father's museum just north of Montreal.

Just for Laughs: street performers at Montreal's annual comedy festival.

Quebec City as seen from the south shore of the St. Lawrence River: British cannons bombarded the city during the summer of 1759.

Sebastien Langevin clowns around at a hostel in Ste-Monique.

Talkative toddlers: Rose (right) and Blanche Gagnon at their home near Jonquiere.

Grande-Vallee at twlight: the Catholic Church once held as much influence over Quebec as the provincial government.

Wildflower meadows at Perce Rock: Jacques Cartier first sighted this bay in 1534.

Carnival antics: the Acadian national holiday in Caraquet.

Hitchhiking through Burnt Church during the Mi'kmaq fisheries blockade.

Pink sky at dawn, fishermen yawn: herring seiners after a long night of working the German Bank.

Island tour guide and potato expert: Al MacDonald checks the harvest with his cell phone surgically grafted to his ear.

The Antigonish Highland Games are the longest running highland games outside of Scotland: competitors have gathered every year since 1863.

The hills are alive with the sound of fiddles: three young girls practice their technique near Breton Cove.

Pumpkins for sale in rural Newfoundland: this province is not just barren rock.

The misty waters of Gros Morne National Park.

investment that I couldn't afford to replace—not if I was going to travel north to the Arctic Ocean and back before winter arrived. So on the last day of the Discovery Days festival—a day of gold-panning in the finest of Klondike traditions—I marched to the local hardware store under a black rain cloud, rifled through some cheap plastic slickers, and bought one for the princely sum of twenty-five dollars. It wouldn't keep me warm, but at least it would keep me dry.

By the time I arrived at Bonanza Creek, the crowd already looked sodden and a little worse for wear, although people were still having fun. I walked along Bonanza Creek, where golden poplar leaves swirled in pools along the edge, to where a half dozen metal wash basins had been filled with creek water. In each basin several gold flakes were keeping tourists busy panning and scooping, scooping and panning, doing their best to mimic the moans and groans of disenfranchised prospectors from a century ago. Some tourists had what I would call the WWE style— shaking the pan like a blender, emptying it of contents in a matter of seconds, then pile-driving it back into the wash basin to scoop another pile of gravel out. Others jiggled their pans so feebly and protectively— worried that they would lose their prized flakes, no doubt—that it took them fifteen minutes to empty a single pan.

One man, dressed in a brown rain slicker and red baseball cap, was starting to get a little discouraged. He had been at it for half an hour and still hadn't found a single flake. The man beside him wasn't having much better luck. A girl in her mid-twenties stood across from the pair, coaching and offering her own brand of frontier encouragement. "C'mon guys, shuffle your pans back and forth like this," she instructed, indicating a sideways motion designed to let the gold sink to the bottom. "George Carmacks had to comb thousands of square kilometres to find gold in the Yukon, and all you have to do is plumb the depths of a wash basin."

Somehow, I don't think that made them feel any better.

Another gentleman dressed in a navy blue rain jacket listened patiently while his granddaughter advised him on the finer points of prospecting. This freckled sprite with pigtails flapping was obviously a sourdough straight from kindergarten. She waddled around the wash basin in pink galoshes, saying things like: "No grampa, NOT that way! You're supposed to shake the pan S-L-O-W-L-Y! You'll lose all the gold!" Fortunately, the man took direction rather well, and when he emerged a few minutes later with five gold flakes in his pan, his granddaughter's eyes inflated to the size of saucers. "Look grampa, you're RICH!" she exclaimed with a high-pitched squeal. Then, after the gears had been turning for a few seconds: "Do you think there's enough gold to buy me a new bike?"

Next up was the gold pouring demonstration, and a large crowd had soon gathered around an open tent to watch a good-natured fellow named Simon at work. Wearing a welder's mask and thick industrial gloves, Simon wielded a pair of long metal pincers, which he used to lift a glowing crucible of liquid gold from a vat. He had been boiling and stirring the mixture with a carbon rod, and now that its colour was even, it was time to pour it into the mold.

Ever so carefully, Simon lifted the crucible and let a fountain of fire pour from its mouth. While waiting for the mold to set, he entertained the crowd with a few gold rush stories, most notably his own. He explained that he was related to a prospector named Charles Turgeon, a Quebecer who came north during the stampede. Turgeon, of course, was partner to the more charismatic Tex Rickard, who left the Klondike with a fortune, travelled home to New York City and built Madison Square Gardens. Turgeon, in contrast, bought a steamboat that eventually sank on the Yukon River.

After the gold had hardened, Simon broke the seal and passed the palm-sized gold brick around the semicircle. This demonstration very nearly resulted in a broken wrist for an elderly woman, who grabbed for it like she would grab for a sandwich. "My goodness, is that heavy," she stammered. "How much is that worth, sonny?"

Simon did a quick calculation in his head, something to do with the number of ounces and purity of the refined gold. "Offhand ma'am, I'd say you're holding about thirty thousand dollars," he said. "So no putting that in your purse while I'm not looking."

The last event of the day was a barbecue: for ten dollars, there was a choice of moose burger or fresh salmon fillet straight from the Yukon River. While standing in line for my burger I struck up conversation with a tourist named Tom, who told me that his family was visiting from California. It quickly became clear that Tom was no ordinary tourist, though, for his grandmother Graphie was the daughter of George Carmacks—the first man to pull gold from Bonanza Creek. Indeed, it was Carmacks' discovery that started a chain of events that would ultimately lead to the Klondike gold rush.

"So what does it feel like to come up here for the centennial?" I asked him.

"Graphie was only three when my parents lived up here," he replied, "so she never remembered much. But meeting some of my Native relatives up here ... my God, it's like seeing my grandmother all over again."

We chatted for a few minutes about what he had expected to find in Dawson, what he had actually found and what it meant to him. Then our moose burgers—looking vaguely like lumps of coal—were dumped onto paper plates and Tom excused himself to return to his waiting family. "So do you have any urge to stake a claim yourself?" I joked just before parting. "Maybe carry on the family tradition for a while?"

Tom chuckled, then admitted, "I'm not sure that I have prospector's blood running through my veins. I prefer to enjoy the Yukon as a tourist."

August 19, 1998 - Dawson City, Yukon Territory

Why some men go bonkers over gold—to the point of practically killing themselves to find it—is not easy to explain. History calls this rare form of dementia "gold fever," a term that refers to the insatiable desire to find gold beyond which rational concern for one's own preservation is compromised. Even before Carmacks made his discovery, hundreds of men had been scouring the Yukon for the mother lode. So it was somewhat ironic then that Carmacks—who had little interest in prospecting—should have been the one to pull a thumb-sized chunk of gold from the creek. Carmacks went on to stake his claim, but unlike thousands of his fellow stampeders (who preferred immediate pleasure to long-term profit), he pulled what he could from the Klondike's bedrock, then retired with his family to Vancouver, where he invested in real estate and died a very wealthy man.

While Carmacks never suffered from gold fever, the majority who descended into the quagmire of Dawson were transfixed by its allure. Making matters worse was the carnival-like atmosphere prevailing in Dawson—surely a symptom of this "gold fever." Most prospectors were torn between their insatiable urge to "strike pay dirt" and the equally irresistible urge to spend whatever they found ... sometimes before they even found it. The fact that Dawson was in the middle of nowhere surely fueled this lunacy. There were stone-faced gamblers like Sam Bonnifield, who lost $72,000 and his gambling establishment in a single game of poker, then won it all back again. And there were boozers like Roddy Conners, who sold his claim for $50,000, then danced and drank his money away one dollar at a time.

Arguably the most flamboyant prospector was a diminutive American named "Swiftwater" Bill Gates. He made his millions by buying shares in several claims and letting others do the work for him, which gave him plenty of time to saunter about town in his fancy coat, top hat and starched shirt. Even before his gold was cut from Eldorado Creek, Gates was borrowing money at ten-percent interest so that he could live the high life. He bathed in champagne and played pool at a hundred dollars a frame. On one occasion, he used several coffee tins full of gold nuggets to buy up every fresh egg in Dawson; he did this to frustrate the cravings and so win the affections of an omelet-eating dance hall girl named Gussie Lamore.

Such were the effects of gold fever.

Ever since Bo and I had met Coffee John on the Yukon River, I had been wondering if gold still holds an irrational sway over some people the way it did during the Klondike era. It was surely my quest to answer this question that led me to a dark, gritty dungeon called The Eldorado a couple of days after the festival. It was a watering hole, I was told, where tough-as-nails miners went to either celebrate or drown their sorrows, depending on the day.

When I walked in at ten in the morning, there were already a few stubbly patrons tipping back pints. I sat on a barstool, ordered a coffee and struck up a conversation with a skinny, mop-haired fellow sitting at the bar. His name was Cecil, and his eyes were already glazed over from the beer he had been drinking since he got out of bed.

"So you want to learn about mining, do ya?" he said, dragging hard off a cigarette. "That ain't news, kid. Everyone comes up here with dreams about finding gold." He waved his hand in the air, dismissing my questions as the naive inquiries of a greenhorn who hadn't walked a metre in miner's boots, much less a mile. "And you know what? Then the reality of all the work sets in, and all the money you have to spend…" His slurred speech tapered off into a shoulder shrug. "…and then no one finds gold anyway."

Cecil smiled a horrible smile and pointed at a short, intense-looking man behind the bar. "Dominik and I have been mining partners since the mid-eighties. We were using up all our money digging for gold, so I started buying real estate to pay the bills. I wanted to keep on mining, but I had to sink my money into something more reliable than the ground."

"So is there still gold out there?" I asked him.

"Sure," he replied. "I have some friends who are mining the tailings off an old claim as we speak, and with the latest equipment, I think they're doing alright." Cecil also told me about another friend who had recently pulled a four-thousand-dollar nugget from one of the creeks. "It's still out there, but you might as well be playing the lottery trying to find it."

"What's the largest piece you've ever found?" I asked.

"Well, we found a twenty-five-hundred-dollar nugget back in the eighties." Cecil chuckled, reminiscing about the old days when the mining game was still new and exciting. "The only problem was, we came into town to celebrate, got really drunk, and when we woke up the gold was missing." It turned out that an observant bartender had merely slipped it away for safekeeping; nevertheless, the incident had given Cecil and Dominik a few grey hairs.

Cecil soon wandered off to find the men's room, which gave me the opportunity to ask Dominik about his role in their partnership.

"Partners?" Dominik retorted. "Antagonists is more like it. I'm black and he's white—or is it the other way around?"

"So I guess 'partners' is a delicate word?"

"Oh, there's nothing delicate about it," he said, raising his fists into a fighting stance. "Ol' Cecil and I have gone a few rounds."

When Cecil returned, he threw me the keys to his Land Rover. "If you're so interested in gold, kid, why don't we drive out to my friend's claim?"

Thirty minutes later, I was at the wheel of the Land Rover, bouncing down a gravel road with Cecil and another young guy named Jeff. Cecil motioned for me to turn onto a small bridge that wasn't much wider than his vehicle. "Take it easy," Cecil cautioned. "This is not one you want to miss." I clenched my teeth and carefully inched us across, half expecting to pitch sideways into the creek at any moment. From there, the gravel road turned into an old cart track, complete with huge divots and massive chunks of broken rock scattered everywhere. Driving up the hillside, I felt like one of those bronc busters at the Calgary Stampede, holding on for life and limb.

After a half-kilometre, I pulled into a muddy clearing. A few hundred metres below we could see a small crew hard at work, excavating a pile of old mine tailings. A teenage boy sat inside a backhoe, scooping earth into a large metal bucket, while a short, firmly built woman stood on a metal platform above the bucket, spraying it down with a hose. Meanwhile, a middle-aged man was crawling around under the platform, apparently trying to fix something. "After they dump the tailings into the bucket, they spray it down to separate the gold from everything else," Cecil told me. "C'mon, let's take a closer look."

The deafening clatter of mining equipment pierced the air as we got closer, and we could soon see what Dave, Cecil's friend, was trying to fix. The conveyor belt, which was supposed to be whisking the rubble away from the separating machine, was starting and stopping with the precision of a Quebecer running traffic lights through Montreal. Every time it jerked to a halt, rocks started to jam up at the bottom, which meant that everybody had to stop what they were doing until it was fixed again. Dave looked exasperated. "All this trouble for fool's gold," he laughed when we got closer. "But in my opinion, all gold is fool's gold."

A few minutes of tinkering later and the conveyor belt was working again. Dave walked over to the sluice box and pointed at some thin gold flakes that, curiously, looked more like silver. The key to making money from old mine tailings, Dave explained, was to take advantage of the latest technology. Modern equipment can extract even the smallest gold particles, stuff that was missed by early stampeders, as well as by the large dredges that came later. Dave and I continued chatting while Cecil and Jeff went off to poke around the site, which gave him the chance to explain how government reclamation costs were making it increasingly difficult to stay in business. "Not that I don't enjoy mining," he told me. "But if I had something else to do, I'd be doing it. There's no future or money in this industry."

Eventually, our conversation led us on to the topic of gold fever, possibly because Dave's cynical approach to mining seemed so far removed from the mentality of the gold rush. "Does it still exist?" I asked him.

"Sure," he said, levelling a sly, lopsided grin at me. "I know a guy who, when he sees a flake of gold, goes wild over it. And I have friends who would sooner protect an ounce of gold than a thousand dollars."

"It sounds like you could care less about the stuff."

Dave laughed. "Truer words were never spoke," he said. "Personally, I don't care what falls into the box, so long as somebody pays me for it."

Twenty minutes passed before I started glancing around to find Cecil, but he wasn't anywhere in sight. I walked to where his Land Rover had been parked and found it missing. Had he taken off without me? That's when I remembered: my backpack was still in the rear of Cecil's truck. And my journals, wallet and credit cards were stuffed into the backpack's top pouch. Damn it! Was this guy trying to rob me? Or was this some sort of practical joke?

Without consulting Dave, I ran down the cart track to the gravel road, a large lump lodged in my throat. I already knew that the back roads weren't well travelled. Would I have to slog the ten or fifteen kilometres back into town on foot?

Thankfully, as soon as I had reached the road I saw a Ford Explorer driving by. When the driver saw me waving frantically, he pulled over. "Ahoy fellow! What leaves you stranded all the way out here?" He was a clean-cut man in his mid-fifties.

"I came out here with a man from town," I said, trying not to sound panicked. "And when I wasn't paying attention he took off with all my stuff."

The man shook his head. "What was the fellow's name?"

"Cecil."

The man grimaced. "Are you serious? I'm sorry to hear that, because Cecil's not the kind of guy you want to get tangled up with."

This was not what I wanted to be hear, of course, yet all the way back to town, the man felt inclined to tell me all about Cecil. "He's a crook, a liar and a drunk," he told me sharply. "The kind of guy who regularly gets kicked out of every bar in town." Oh great! Gold fever had probably driven poor Cecil off the deep end, and like so many stampeders from a century before, I was now the victim of a Klondike scam-artist. Why was this town still filled with so many bad feelings? First I had lost my jacket, now everything else.

The man dropped me at The Eldorado, where to my surprise, I found Cecil's Land Rover parked. I walked to the back window and saw that my pack was still inside. The door was unlocked, so I opened it, lifted the pack out and quickly scanned to make sure everything was still there. It was, to my relief. "You're lucky," the man said. "He probably thought you'd be stranded out there for a while."

When I walked into the pub to confront Cecil about deserting me, I found him sitting at the bar with a pint in one hand, a cigarette in the other. When he saw me, his eyes widened and he nervously threw an outstretched arm around my shoulder. "Hey, buddy," he said, "You looked like you were having so much fun that I thought I'd leave you out there for a while. I was going to come back and get you later."

Likely story. "Well, why didn't you tell me that before leaving?"

"Hey, have a beer on me," Cecil said, trying to change the subject. "Bartender, get this man a drink."

And so it went for the next few minutes: me politely asking questions, Cecil dodging them with off-topic answers. Finally, one of Cecil's friends—a tall black man—wandered over to see what the commotion was about.

"Hey, have you met my friend Barney?" Cecil asked me, still trying to change the subject. "He's not black. He's just been out fighting forest fires."

The two men started talking with one another, and I decided to let things slide. I had all my belongings, and Cecil was obviously not about to give me an answer anyway. So I sat down on a barstool and ordered a coffee.

Perhaps five minutes had passed—the two men bantering back and forth, me drinking my coffee while breathing in revolting clouds of cigarette smoke—when in an oddly detached instant, I realized something. I looked up at Barney and saw that he was wearing my Gore-Tex jacket.

"Hey, that's my jacket!" I exclaimed.

"Excuse me?"

"My jacket!" I repeated. "You're wearing my jacket!" I reached over to the lower left pocket and put my finger through a hole to confirm it. "See, there's a hole right here."

Barney was clearly caught off guard, but rather than immediately deny my claim, he stood there with a rather dumbfounded look on his face. "Some drunk Native lady gave it to me a couple of days ago," he finally stammered.

"Certainly," I replied. "And if that's the case, you won't mind giving it back."

Barney rolled his eyes, then muttered, "All right." He started taking my jacket off, only to stop an instant later. "So how do I know this is really your jacket?"

"Because there's a hole on the inside pocket too," I replied. I reached inside the left breast pocket and poked my finger through another hole.

Barney was caught and he knew it.

By the time I left The Eldorado later that afternoon, you can probably imagine that I was starting to feel a little disillusioned with Dawson City. Still, things could have been worse. While I had been the unwitting target of Klondike scam-artists, I could at least say that I had recouped everything I lost. And that, dear readers, is better than most stampeders fared a century ago.

Chapter 21

The Road to Nowhere

August 20, 1998 - Dempster Highway Junction,
Yukon Territory

The Dempster Highway is a road unlike any other in the world. Starting innocently enough at a nondescript service centre a few dozen kilometres east of Dawson City, it strikes out along a gravel track festooned with potholes, dust, shards of razor-sharp rock and millions of trees no taller or thicker than a broomstick. For more than seven hundred kilometres the highway defies engineering sensibilities, slicing through two mountain ranges, jumping an imaginary line called the Arctic Circle, and pausing, but briefly, at the Peel and Mackenzie Rivers to cross them by car ferry. It eventually terminates at Inuvik, a small Inuvialuit village at the edge of the Mackenzie River Delta, no more than two hundred kilometres south of the Arctic Ocean.

For motorists and hitchhikers alike, the Dempster is not to be taken lightly. While the Liard Highway is desolate, the Dempster is almost impossibly so, primarily because it is a dead-end road with no through traffic. Even before I set foot on this road, I was having nightmares that involved getting stranded for days, or even weeks, until winter caught me posing with my thumb out. In such a circumstance, I could very well get buried under ice and snow until the following spring, when, if I were lucky, some well-meaning trucker would stop and chisel me free with a tire iron.

Things were quickly off to a bad start, for when I arrived at the junction where the Dempster meets the Klondike Highway, there was already a hitchhiking traffic jam. Walking over to canvas for information, I met two French girls who had thumbed all the way from Quebec. They were now standing on the Klondike Highway headed south toward Whitehorse. Behind them was a thickset German fellow named Ralph, who was either very constipated or had just polished off an entire bag of sour soothers.

He scowled at me as I talked with the French girls, perhaps annoyed that I was cutting in on his territory.

Two other German men were standing across the road on the Dempster (they were my real competition), complaining that they had already been standing there for three hours. "We want to go to Inuvik for a beer," said one. Clearly, these men were not in their right mind, for there was perfectly good beer inside the roadhouse, a mere two hundred yards from where they were standing.

As hitchhiking etiquette dictates, being first in line these guys had dibs on the first ride, so it seemed a bit pointless standing on the road behind them. For that reason I headed inside for some lunch and to work on my journal. The only problem was that when I glanced outside three hours later, at around three in the afternoon, they were still there. It was the same at five and after dinner at eight. When I eventually went outside to set up camp, they were gone. I breathed a sigh of relief ... until I glanced across the road and saw their tent pitched in the grass. Poor sods. An entire day of thumbing and they hadn't even managed a mile—much less a beer.

Regrettably, the next morning delivered more of the same for the Germans, and it wasn't until after eleven that they finally gave up. Just as I finished my fourth meal at the restaurant (the food was good, at least) I saw them kick their backpacks, pick them up like two sacks of potatoes and retreat to where Ralph was still standing. Only the French duet had managed a lift, which, quite frankly, made me wonder if I would ever get to Inuvik. But with no desire to head back toward Dawson, and with three people already waiting in line for Whitehorse, I was left with few options. So I settled my tab, hoisted my backpack onto my shoulders and strolled out onto the highway.

Imagine my surprise when just twenty minutes after I had settled in for a good, long kip in the sun, a van full of Austrians pulled up beside me and rolled down a window. "Where are you going?" asked the driver in near-perfect English.

"I'm going all the way to Inuvik," I replied.

"We're only going an hour up the road," he said, "but there's a campground in case you get stuck. Do you want a ride?"

I thought about it for a moment, weighing the consequences of being stuck in the middle of nowhere versus getting stuck a hundred kilometres from the middle of nowhere. I was itching to get on with it—and I've never had a penchant for making intelligent decisions along these lines anyway—so I said "What the hell," and shoved my backpack through the side door of their van. Thirty seconds later I had clambered into the back seat and we were on our way.

As the van pulled back onto the highway, I looked into the rearview mirror and saw one of the Germans who had been hitchhiking yank off his baseball cap, throw it into the ditch and start kicking the side of his backpack. I felt terrible, of course, but what can you do? Sometimes you're lucky and sometimes you're not. I promised myself that when I reached Inuvik, I would drink a beer on their behalf.

August 21, 1998 - The Dempster Highway, Yukon Territory

The Austrians dropped me in the middle of the Tombstone Mountains, a name, I must admit, that didn't leave me with a particularly warm and cheery feeling. The lady at the campground just shook her head when I told her that I was hitchhiking up the Dempster. She at least reassured me that the "Tombstones" were named after a range of snaggletooth spires rising to the west, rather than a hitchhiker who had been stranded and found dead at the roadside.

Much to the detriment of my story, though, the rides kept coming. Against all odds, fifteen minutes of thumbing delivered a curvaceous, fair-haired princess riding bareback on a white stallion (translation: a dirty white van with a working engine). Inside were another German-speaking couple, Christian and Birgit, as well as a middle-aged French fellow with his teenage son; the father and son were spending a month thumbing around Canada on their summer vacation. They motioned for me to get inside, and despite a thick haze of cigarette smoke billowing out the windows, I decided that any ride on the Dempster was a good one. I climbed in without a second thought.

When I asked Christian if he was from Germany, he replied, "Actually, I'm from Switzerland. And my parents are from Austria."

"Zee country is not important," said the Frenchman, precariously balanced on his small backpack as the van bounced down the highway. "Only zee people matter ... you get good ones and bad ones everywhere."

Christian used the opportunity to comment on people from northern Canada. "Yes, sometimes you meet people up here who seem very, very strange." He laughed. "But when you get talking in the bar with them, they're alright." He paused for a moment before adding thoughtfully: "But I think they're staying a very long time in their cabin during the winter."

I asked the Frenchman if he was from Quebec, but he shook his head. "No, I'm from France. We come over 'ere on vacation for one month."

"Hmmmm, I haven't met too many French people travelling around Canada."

"No, probably not," he replied. "For zee French, I think it's easier to go in Québec. I mean, why speak Engleesh when you don't 'ave to? I'm a little bit different."

Ten minutes later, zee Frenchman motioned for Christian to pull over, because he had found a place to go hiking for zee day. I nearly balked, realizing that he and his son were hiking out into the middle of nowhere with nothing more than a daypack between the two of them. For shelter, there wasn't a tree in sight. What if they got stranded out there in a storm? Or weren't able to get a ride back to the campground before dark? "It's very hard for him," said Christian once we started driving again. "I think he tries to spend his holidays very cheaply."

The Tombstones proved to be one of the most stunning sights I had yet seen, and Christian and Birgit could only concur. The colours of autumn arrive early this far north, and the alpine meadows seemed to roll on forever, a plush carpet specked with rich hues of auburn, red and yellow. What a sight! The absence of trees in the Tombstone Range also thwarts any natural sense of scale, and we found ourselves playing a curious game, guessing and second-guessing how far away the distant features on the landscape might be. What seemed to be only a few kilometres away would often prove to be thirty or forty. So it was with the large transport trucks, which appeared as miniature plumes of dust billowing across the horizon, only to tear past us twenty minutes later with a terrible rumble, hurling sharp stones at our windshield. But then the silence would return, and we would be alone on the road for miles.

"Perhaps this place is a little bit like the moon," Christian finally said. "It's very pretty, but you would have a hard time living here, I think." He and Birgit had themselves experienced such hardship recently, during a nine-day canoe trip down the Big Salmon River. On only the second day, their canoe had capsized and they had lost nearly everything: food, clothing, maps and two out of three paddles. For a week they had survived on almost nothing.

"So what did you do?" I asked.

"We found some bread floating on the water and dried it over a campfire," said Birgit. "And we dove down into the river and fished out a bag of spaghetti noodles." Christian also found some fishing line tangled in a tree, and with a little red spinner from his survival kit, he caught a few grayling. Most important, their cigarettes had stayed dry, so while everything else was in short supply, they had plenty of nicotine.

The Dempster hammered north unabated, tilting and weaving mercilessly. In places, the highway squeezed between mountains that seemed to shoulder together, impossibly blocking its progress. Yet somehow the Dempster made it through. By the time we reached Indian Creek, we had covered only half the distance to the Eagle Plains service centre, and Birgit was starting to get restless. With so many ruts and potholes along the route, Christian had kept his speed below seventy in order to save his tires.

"So what did you expect before coming to Canada?" I asked them at one point, knowing there was plenty of time to kill. I had met a few Germans during my travels, and had always found them gracious and insightful travelling companions. (Constipated Ralph had been an exception.)

They thought about my question for a minute, and finally Birgit said, "I think Germans see Canada with nothing but big trees, cold weather and people wearing flannel." And from that standpoint, Canada had been a big disappointment. In the Yukon, they hadn't seen a single big tree, the weather had mostly been hot, and even the flannel mackinaws were scarce. "It's like this picture we painted for ourselves is a fantasy," she said. "It doesn't even exist."

I could see Birgit's point. For the next few minutes, I told them about how Canada has an image and identity problem, how we can't even seem to figure ourselves out. "It's funny how most of my university friends, first thing after graduating, flew over to Europe to spend a summer travelling," I told them. "Yet I've met but a handful of Canadians in the Yukon this summer. Why are there so many Europeans up here?"

"We come over to experience nature," replied Christian. "We have very little wilderness left in Europe."

"And I guess Canadians go to Europe to find history and culture," I said. It was a simple concept, but it made sense. "We're searching for two different things. Europeans need nature; Canadians need history."

"Ah yes, but history is not always a good thing," Christian reminded me. "Perhaps you don't have much history over here, but at least you don't have a history like the Germans. History is not always a good thing."

"Maybe that's another reason why Germans travel," continued Birgit. "We don't like our history, so we're trying to find a new one."

Christian nodded, smiling across the cab at his sweetheart. "We are very lucky in Europe," he said, "but to be Canadian, I think, would be the luckiest of all."

August 22, 1998 - Eagle Plains, Yukon Territory

While eating breakfast at the Eagle Plains Hotel, we heard that a huge forest fire near Fox Lake had flared across the Klondike Highway, effectively halting traffic between Dawson City and Whitehorse. I couldn't help but think of poor constipated Ralph and the other Germans, and I wondered if they were still stuck at the crossing. Christian and Birgit, meanwhile, had told me that they were driving to Fort McPherson that day—a tiny Gwich'in village three quarters of the way to Inuvik—before returning to Eagle Plains. "Would you like to come along?" Christian asked.

No question about it. There was no place to go but Inuvik.

We crossed the Arctic Circle later that morning, although it didn't exactly jump up and trip us. Rather, we relied on an official-looking highway marker to locate it for us, then got out and took the requisite tourist photos. It was a crisp day, and we were travelling in plain view of the Richardson Mountains, which were erupting through slate-grey clouds to the east. The rest of the countryside was far less inspiring: primarily weed-like conifers, bent double from the wind and struggling to keep themselves rooted in permafrost. Shortly thereafter, we passed a sign stating that the Dempster was sometimes used as an emergency airstrip, implying that motorists should keep their eyes on the sky. Looking up, we saw nothing.

Christian continued to talk as he drove, about everything from travelling to politics to Yukon history. As we passed Glacier Creek, he suddenly jammed on the brakes. The van crashed through a huge trough in the road, causing my head to ricochet off the side of the van. Birgit, who had been leaning under the dashboard trying to dry her hair using one of the heat vents, came up rubbing her head. She gave Christian a piercing look.

"Whoa, maybe I talk a little bit too much," Christian said, obviously shaken.

"You want me to drive?" Birgit replied coolly. "*Then* you can talk."

With an extra-vigilant Christian at the wheel, we dropped down the far side of the Richardsons into the Mackenzie River Delta, and a couple of hours later reached Fort McPherson. It's the only thing that even closely resembles a town along the Dempster. After picking up a few groceries at a small convenience store, we came out and passed several pre-teen Native kids sitting on the wooden steps smoking cigarettes and eating junk food. They stared at us, but didn't so much as mumble a hello after we had greeted them. That's when we spotted two white girls in about their mid-twenties, walking down a dirt road toward the highway and looking very confused.

"You're not from around here, are you?" I asked as they got closer.

"Heavens no," said the one, her hair tied back into a ponytail. "My name is Tanya. I'm from Australia, and this is my friend Liz from France." They were looking for mechanical help because their van had stalled and they couldn't get it started again.

Christian, Birgit and I followed them back to a service centre near the edge of the highway where two Native men—one of them so drunk that he could barely stand up—were jimmying some wires under the hood. The drunk guy had the look of somebody who had just crawled out of bed: ruffled hair, dishevelled clothes and one of those grins that suggested he was well pleased with his surroundings whether he was fully aware of them or not. A tall Aussie bloke named Brian stood beside them, gently explaining that there might be a problem with the power connection. But when Christian got down on his knees and started poking at the engine from underneath, he disagreed. "I don't think it's the power connection," he said.

"Why not?" asked Brian.

"It wouldn't have just died like that."

The two debated the issue for some time, and in the end Christian gave up because Brian wouldn't listen to him. He shrugged his shoulders, wished me luck and departed for Eagle Plains with Birgit. Brian, meanwhile, continued milking assistance from the two Native fellows, and when he found out that I was headed for Inuvik, offered me a ride. "I just hope you're not in any hurry, mate," he said, "cause it may be a while before we're back on the road."

A few minutes later, an old camper truck pulled into the parking lot, this one piloted by a Dutch fellow named Robert and two girls from Liechtenstein. Brian waved Robert over so that he could give the van a boost; apparently, the two vehicles had been travelling together for the last few days, and the camper had already performed its fair share of support. The trick, Brian told me, was to get the van started and then take off at a reckless speed, which wasn't always easy. The van sputtered to a start, then abruptly stalled again. It started, then stalled. Started. Stalled. The group carried on in vain for several minutes until, miraculously, the engine roared to life and kept running. "Everybody jump in!" shouted Brian. We did, and he tore off down the street, barely stopping at the highway to make sure it was clear of oncoming traffic.

Inside the van, Brian worked feverishly at prying off the engine cover between the driver and passenger's seats. He wanted access to the motor while steering, although the rest of us weren't convinced that this was such a good idea. "Here, shove this into the back," he shouted, trying to steer while wrestling the large, greasy engine cover between the two armrests. Tanya and I quickly obeyed, finding a place for it near the back. With the cover removed a thick cloud of exhaust fumes and dust started billowing into the van, choking all of us. Brian fiddled, and every now and again the motor would backfire with a loud *crack!*, spraying a plume of sparks from under the dashboard into the back seat. Poor Liz clung miserably to the front passenger door while Brian continued tinkering. She was leaning so hard that if the door had somehow opened, I'm certain she would have landed in the ditch without bouncing once.

The noise, dust and fumes soon became unbearable, and as if on cue, the van died as suddenly as it had started. "Can I sit in the back seat now?" Liz asked feebly.

Brian looked over at her, a sardonic yet gentle smile crossing his face. "Oh, it won't hurt you," he said. "It's just a little fire to keep us warm." I'm not sure Liz entirely agreed with his assessment, but she decided to stay put.

After the camper had pulled up alongside us again, an idea flashed into Brian's head. "Rather than boosting the van a hundred times between here and Inuvik, why not simply switch the batteries?" he suggested to Robert. Brian's reasoning was that the van would stand a better chance of reaching Inuvik with a fully charged battery, while Robert's camper would probably make it regardless of which battery he used. Robert liked the idea, and within ten minutes the van was once again thundering down the road, this time with no exhaust fumes or sparks spraying into the back seat.

We arrived in Inuvik shortly after eight that evening, rolling in along a paved strip past clapboard homes, restaurants and motels, all standing on wooden pilings staked into the permafrost. There was a huge Inukshuk standing across from a domed Catholic church built in the shape of an igloo. Further along, we passed a massive log building—perhaps a community centre—built with trees that were obviously not from the area. I would later learn that it was built from more than a thousand logs, which had been tied together and rafted 1,400 kilometres down the Mackenzie River.

After the challenge of simply getting to Inuvik, we suddenly found ourselves debating what to do now that we had arrived. Some voted for dinner, others for a shower at the local campground. The one point everybody agreed on was that we should find a pub later that evening, which we did. I won't go into great detail on this account, only to say that we attended an event billed as "Party on the Permafrost," a title that sounded rather exotic and otherworldly to our southern ears. Little did we know that this world was actually quite like other worlds we were already familiar with. It was just fancy billing for a dark, earthy pub packed to the gills with beer-swilling locals, dancing and drinking and fighting over women.

Not that it mattered. My companions were quite content, and all of them took their participation very seriously. So much so that most of them eagerly lapped up the attention—if not the privileges—that our novelty earned us from the local crowd. The girls were turning down invitations for romance at least once every ten minutes, and on more than one occasion I was approached by a Native lady several decades my senior, requesting a dance. Perhaps they simply wanted to make us feel welcome, but I drew the line when one woman (who could well have been my grandmother) approached with a decadent smile and proceeded to slap me across the backside. I was suddenly feeling a little too welcome.

It wasn't until three in the morning that we retired to Brian's van. I must admit to a vague feeling of disquiet, mostly because of the local people I had met. I had always envisioned the Inuvialuit as proud people—hunters and whalers, skilled craftspeople and elders—not as groping grannies violating my personal goodies at a permafrost party. In one evening, my picture of these resourceful Northerners had become horribly distorted. Who were these people? Could I admire them after all? Over the next few days I would find out.

Chapter 22

Arctic Mercedes

August 23, 1998 - Inuvik, Northwest Territories

Everybody woke the following morning a little worse for wear, having taken their drinking a trifle too seriously the previous night. Tanya and I had somehow crammed ourselves into the narrow bunk fastened just below the roof of the van, and it took all the coordination we could muster to untangle ourselves and squirm our way into the morning light. It was not yet ten on Sunday morning so there was still plenty of time to get to church at the giant igloo. Brian, however, had other ideas. "I'm going for a beer," he announced. "Is anyone up for a drink before church?" His idea was greeted with a surprising level of cheer, considering that the group had only stopped drinking seven hours earlier. While I declined, everyone else set off in eager anticipation of some cold suds. We agreed to meet for mass just before eleven.

It wasn't until five minutes after eleven that Brian and the others stumbled into church looking road-weary and tattered, doing their best not to create a commotion. The congregation was actually quite large, comprised of a surprisingly diverse mix of black, white, and Native people. Most of them turned to stare as my ragtag friends came stumbling in, giggling, then slid down a long pew to where I was sitting.

The deacon, a distinguished middle-aged man with a few silver highlights in his hair, led the service with singing and a sermon that, to my surprise, had very little to do with fire and brimstone. Instead, he talked about the importance of being patient with young people who might not be interested in church. He referred to everyone as "brother." When it came time to take communion, Tanya—presumably the only Catholic in our group—walked up to the front to partake. Brian leaned over to me and said in a pained voice, "Lucky girl. That's probably the closest we'll get to liquor today. All the pubs are closed up."

My loose-knit band of travelling companions departed the following day, leaving me to walk around Inuvik and take in the sights by myself.

I strolled down to the banks of the Mackenzie River and watched hunters motoring in on aluminum skiffs loaded with geese and, at one point, a very large moose. At a restaurant called Togo's I feasted on caribou and musk ox burgers, and everywhere I went there were little Inuvialuit sprites, most of them bright-eyed and curious, always ready with twenty questions. Some of them called me "white guy."

Everywhere I went, people were also talking about Nunavut. Even though the creation of the new Canadian territory wouldn't directly affect the Inuvialuit—western cousins of the Inuit—it seemed to be on everyone's mind. Its official inauguration was a mere seven months away, and it was thus featured on T-shirts, coffee mugs and other knick-knacks in a variety of souvenir shops. Nunavut was also the favoured topic of conversation in restaurants, or outside on the streets, and I heard my fill of Nunavut jokes. One Native RCMP officer so cleverly disguised his joke as a self-deprecating comment that I stood there in horror for several seconds, not knowing what to say. It went something like this: "With all these land claims, sometimes it seems like the goddamn Natives want all of it." I glanced at him uneasily. "Even the goddamn Metis want some of it," he spat. Then a broad grin lit across his face. "But you've gotta hand it to those Inuit for getting Nunavut."

Most of the debates seemed to focus on whether Nunavut was a good idea or not. "I think it's too much, too fast," one man told me. He was a white fellow from Montreal who had been living in Inuvik for five years. "The Inuit have a lot of problems, and you don't solve those in one or two years—you solve them over a generation."

"At least their mistakes will be their own," claimed an Inuvialuit elder named Frank. "It won't be imposed mistakes coming from the south anymore." And he was speaking from experience. As an Inuvialuit child born into a family with a white father, he had been brought up an Anglican before getting shipped off to a Catholic school. There, he had been forced to learn French because his teachers were nuns from Quebec. Like all Inuvialuit children of that era, Frank had learned nothing about his own language, culture and traditions while attending the white man's school. It's no wonder that as a young man he had faced an identity crisis.

As for the modern Inuvialuit lifestyle—which to me appeared somewhat fractured in these northern communities—I wanted some insight into why these people were having such a difficult time adjusting to the modern world. And I didn't find answers until I strolled out to the edge of town one evening, past a diminutive carving shack. That's where I met Martin, a heavyset, happy-go-lucky white import from England, and Mike, a quiet Native fellow who seemed to exude the best qualities of his people. They were hard at work when I showed up, Martin making Inuktitut earrings out of mammoth ivory and Mike polishing a soapstone carving of some Inuit mermaid hottie with breasts like coconuts. They pointed at a crock-pot full of caribou stew and told me to grab some before sitting down.

"I never even took art in school," Martin chortled gleefully, as if reading my mind. "And now I get to make money sitting on a stool and playing with little toys."

"How did you get into carving?" I asked, spooning some stew into a bowl.

"Well, I went to Northern Images and said 'I'm not paying that bloody price,' so I had to teach myself—and that was about it." Martin told me that his first ring had been square and that his first eagle looked like an airplane. But over time, his artistic skills had improved. "It helps to have guys like Mike around," he told me. "This guy was born with a knife in one hand and a piece of wood for whittling in the other."

To my surprise, the two of them were quite candid, and for my benefit they explained a lot about modern life in the North. Martin described how he had flown up to Banks Island in 1979 and met a "red-headed Eskimo girl."

"She was the only red-headed Eskimo I'd ever met," he said, "so I had to marry her of course." For the next ten years they had lived on Banks Island, where he worked as a cook for the oil companies. "When you're living in an isolated community like Sachs Harbour, you really learn to take care of the land," he explained. With sixty to seventy thousand musk ox roaming the island, wild meat became a staple of their diet, and from the Native people he had learned to take real pride in butchering and cooking it. The downside, Martin continued, was that a lot of people on Banks Island tended to get caught up in petty competitions: "My wife is prettier," or "My truck is newer," or "My snowmobile is faster." That sort of thing.

"We eventually left Banks Island because of enormous jealousy and animosity," he said. "My wife and I had jobs, and it got to the point where our children were being called 'white niggers.'"

"Jealousy, animosity, drinking—whatever you want to call it," Mike said flatly. "People see somebody else getting ahead and they can't control their own lives, so they get jealous and take it out on those people."

I asked Mike about the peaceful traditions of the Inuvialuit and about their ties to the land. His answer was honest, though he looked sad, as if he were betraying his own people. "A lot of Inuvialuit don't know about tradition anymore," he admitted. He considered his statement for several seconds before continuing. "When things get a little too carried away, I go out hunting. I've learned to get away from it all."

"You have to understand," Martin continued, "before the Europeans arrived, these people had been living on the land for thousands of years. Hunting was how they survived. There was no such thing as accumulating wealth. Now the government is handing them cash or credit cards and they're thinking, 'What the hell do I do with this?'"

Mike further explained that although the older generation was still comfortable on the land, the younger generations seemed rudderless. "It's like they have one foot in the modern world, one foot in the traditional world, and they don't feel comfortable in either," he told me. It doesn't help that in this "white man's world," jobs are currently next to nonexistent above the Arctic Circle. During the 1980s, Inuvik went through an economic boom when fur prices were healthy, the military base was functioning, government jobs were plentiful and oil companies were spending money on exploration. All four of those industries have since collapsed, and the fallout has been brutal. Many Inuvialuit still have their hopes pinned on oil and natural gas exploration, but there's no guarantee that plans for a pipeline to the energy-hungry United States will be finalized anytime soon. There's nothing to do but wait.

"So what does an Inuvialuit teenager do?" Mike asked rhetorically. "Many who don't fall into heavy drinking ship themselves south and assimilate into the white man's world." Either way, he told me, the Inuvialuit seem destined to lose their roots.

"Then again," said Martin hopefully, "there are some Inuvialuit who have one foot in the modern world, one foot in the traditional world, and they feel comfortable in both. The Inuvialuit are incredibly adaptable people. In less than fifty years they've gone from living off the land to coping with the pace of modern trade and change."

August 29, 1998 - Tuktoyaktuk, Northwest Territories

Joe Nasogaluak is an Inuvialuit carver who once lived in southern Canada—that part of the country where, as a child with starry-eyed dreams of making it big, he had always planned to live and work. Fortunately for Joe, his father taught him the importance of hanging onto his roots. He advised Joe to first spend time on Banks Island learning how to trap, run with a dog team, hunt polar bears and live off the land. That way, if he eventually moved to southern Canada, he would remember who he was and where he had come from.

Six years after Joe moved to Banks Island, fur prices dropped and Joe had his excuse to jump ship. So he went to flight school, became a pilot, and eventually made his way south to Vancouver, where he learned to fly a helicopter. To pay his way through school he got back into carving, which quickly became his passion. He travelled across Canada, landed some major commissioned pieces, and was soon being featured in shows across North America and Europe. He ended up in Calgary, overworked and miserable, even though by the white man's standards he had achieved great success.

So he did what any successful Inuvialuit artist living in Calgary would do. He finished a couple of carvings, traded them straight up for two Mercedes Benzes, gave one of the cars to his girlfriend, then set off with a trunk full of groceries for Tuktoyaktuk. It was December, so he was able to follow an ice road clear across the frozen Mackenzie Delta right to the edge of his parents' doorstep. And for the next two years, he continued driving his Mercedes along dirt roads at the edge of the Arctic Ocean, using it as a fish truck to haul food to his dog team.

When I first heard about Joe Nasogaluak, I knew that I had to meet him.

I initially flew into Tuktoyaktuk at the invitation of another Inuvialuit man by the name of Roger Gruben, an ex-CBC radio broadcaster who has travelled widely, runs a successful tour company out of Tuk and has pretty much succeeded in every sense of the word. My primary reason for flying to Tuk was to see the Arctic Ocean. The highway (during the summer months, at least) ends abruptly at Inuvik, a couple of hundred kilometres shy of Canada's northern coastline. Long before setting out on my hitchhiking trip, I had vowed to dip a toe in all three oceans. I planned to keep that promise, so I was happy to accept an invitation to stay with Roger and his wife Winnie. After a few days in Inuvik, I hopped aboard an airplane bound for the ice-choked Beaufort Sea.

My first impression of Tuktoyaktuk was not—how shall we say—glowing. Crammed with weathered shacks poised at the brink of a storm-tossed sea, the town had the feel of a prairie ghost town. Most dwellings were box-style, cookie-cutter homes, shipped up on barges and slapped together in about two weeks during the very short summer season. One fellow, tired of his dwelling, had simply pushed it over on its side to make room for a new and larger home. Sled dogs lay everywhere, most of them chained to iron stakes in the ground, barking and howling and creating a deafening ruckus. There were also dozens of small fishing shanties at the edge of the Beaufort Sea, most of them with caribou antlers, musk ox skulls and whale bones tied to their roofs. This is done to bleach them in the sun for carving, I would later learn, but it only added to the sense of disquiet I felt shortly after landing in Tuk.

When I walked into Roger's home, however, that feeling disappeared entirely. Finely furnished and carpeted, his home was both spacious and cozy. On the wall in his living room was a framed *Financial Post* magazine cover from March 1993, with Roger's name and photo on it. *This Land is My Land*, the caption read. *Roger Gruben and other native leaders measure their financial clout in billions*. It was obvious that Roger was among those who had successfully jumped from the traditional into the modern world. When he saw me staring at the cover, he puffed out his chest and proudly announced: "Our leaders were once called chiefs, but now that we're in the business and corporate world, they're called chairmen of the board."

For lunch, Winnie prepared an enticing spread of traditional Inuvialuit food. There was caribou stew, smoked whitefish, bannock and what she called "Eskimo donuts," which looked like puffy wagon wheels with spokes in the middle. "I always say Tim Horton's should have my recipe," Winnie chuckled. "They'd definitely make a mint." We spread the Eskimo donuts liberally with homemade cranberry jam, from berries that Winnie had harvested off the land. She also gathered blueberries, blackberries and yellow salmonberries for jam, which to my surprise all flourish on the exposed and hostile tundra, thirty kilometres north of treeline.

It wasn't until later that evening that I finally met Joe. I found him sitting at a small table in his kitchen playing with his infant son Larsen. The inside of Joe's home was simple, yet warm and cheerful, and on the wall I noticed a picture of a young man standing on the pack ice with a rifle, beside a dead polar bear. Joe's wife Diane smiled at me, brought me a cup of coffee, then gathered up wee Larsen so that Joe and I could talk. "You know, I grew up dreaming of places like Toronto," laughed Joe. "But when I was living there a few years ago in the middle of a hot, stuffy summer, I couldn't wait to get back up here. I found myself dreaming about the cold wind off the Arctic Ocean, and summer days with twenty-four hours of sunlight. After that, I felt so gifted, like 'Why did I ever dream about those cities down south?'"

"I think a lot of people who grow up in small towns feel like lost children when they go to a city like Toronto," I told him. "I certainly did."

"That's exactly it!" Joe said, pointing a finger at me. "I was like a lost child. For me, that place was like Alcatraz. It's funny you should mention that, because when I was there I did a carving about a lost child."

"Well, Toronto and Tuktoyaktuk are pretty different worlds."

"You can say that again," chuckled Joe, leaning back in his chair. "It's like nobody down south knows where they're going. They just run around in circles looking busy all the time."

I asked Joe what he thought about Nunavut.

"There's both good and bad in it," he replied, initially taking a noncommittal stance. Then he thought for a few moments, as if remembering something important. He described how the Nunavut issue had inspired him to carve a piece with two Inuit hunters standing on an ice floe, the ice cracking and splitting apart.

"What does the carving mean?" I asked

"Well, these two hunters are trying to reach each other, but will they be able to do it?" he asked rhetorically. "As Inuit brothers, do we split apart or come back together? I think it's true of both Canada and Nunavut. Too many people are saying 'me' rather than 'we' these days. There's too much separation, too many little groups, too many people trying to govern themselves without thinking of the whole. Will the Inuit really know how to govern their own nation? I think we're all going to end up in little groups everywhere."

He poured himself another cup of coffee, pausing to collect his thoughts. Then he continued, "Everyone thinks it's going to be this big blast, all this money in their pockets. Well, it's probably not going to happen. Life goes on, and we're still going to be struggling from day to day. We're too eager for power. I think we're going to end up running ourselves over."

"Is there a way to get around that?" I asked, quite enjoying his point of view.

"Sure," he said. "When Nunavut comes into being, we shouldn't just think about what we want and what we can get, but about what we should be." He shook his head sadly. "You know, too many teenagers are ashamed to be Native these days, and I think it's because we don't have the things people down south have."

"But maybe those things aren't all that important," I suggested. I thought about Joe's Arctic Mercedes, and how he treated it like any other tool, not like a status symbol to spit and polish and show off to his neighbours.

"That's true," he said. "Even up here, I'm at a point where I don't need a fox, so why go out and trap it? I don't need the money. If people really want it, let them go and trap it. It's like exchanging this animal's life for a game of Nintendo. I don't really need it, and I'm learning more and more to live without the things I don't need."

Talking with Joe, I got the sense that he had picked up much of this logic while living down south, or rather by looking at the lifestyles of Canadians in southern cities and seeing that we have an awful lot of stuff that we don't actually need. This was true of me (even in my impoverished state), and I knew it to be true of others.

"Sometimes it hurts me to be Canadian because there are an awful lot of people in this world who don't have what we have," Joe added. "We already have so much, and when we want more, more, more all the time, we become a poor country because of this chronic sense of lack."

We eventually stopped talking philosophy, about the time Diane came into the kitchen and handed wee Larsen back to Joe. Larsen made little baby sounds when I reached over to tickle him under the chin. "We named him Larsen after Henry Larsen," Joe told me, "the RCMP officer who sailed around North America in the St. Roch during the 1940s." Joe described Larsen (the RCMP officer) as a great man who had helped many starving and suffering people. "But he never credited himself by naming the land," added Joe. "He was very unselfish." Joe also told me how his father—one of the last great hunters of his people—had been hired by Henry Larsen to provide food for his ship.

It wasn't until after one in the morning that I finally said goodbye to Joe and his family, stepping outside into a cold wind pitching off the Arctic ice cap. Winter was definitely on the move again. As I strolled past Joe's

Mercedes, which sat on a patch of dirt at the front of his house, I looked up at the sky and saw at once the most dazzling display of northern lights that I have ever seen—the aurora borealis slashing across the heavens with brilliant streaks of green, blue, red and yellow. They glittered and danced for me in sparkling waves, and for those precious few moments Nunavut seemed like a grand idea, perhaps the greatest idea of the century. I breathed deeply and thought of Mike and Joe, Roger and Winnie. They were not part of Nunavut, it's true, but I felt certain there would be others like them to build future greatness for the eastern Arctic. And if that were the case, maybe everything would be all right.

Chapter 23

The Lonesome Jubilee

September 1, 1998 - Inuvik, Northwest Territories

If hitchhiking north on the Dempster Highway had been a surprisingly simple affair, travelling south again proved to be far from it. For more than four hours I stood at the edge of Inuvik, thinking of Joe and his Mercedes—and in that four hours, only one vehicle passed. These odds were not comforting, and neither was the sign hammered into the marshy permafrost beside the highway, advertising the likelihood of my getting perma-stranded: EAGLE PLAINS 356; DAWSON CITY 767; WHITEHORSE 1,220. Even more discouraging was knowing that beyond Whitehorse it was another 2,300 kilometres to Calgary. And for anyone taking notes, this adds up to more than 3,500 kilometres, roughly the same distance separating Calgary from Toronto, only on roads that ... well, that are not really roads. On my entire trip, I don't think I ever felt further from home than I did that day in Inuvik, thumbing south.

By mid-afternoon I was getting desperate, and I realized that the situation called for one of those serendipitous little miracles that hitchhikers learn to depend on. That's when a pickup truck crammed with passengers rounded the corner and stopped. It was Winnie and her Gwich'in relatives, bless them, heading down to Fort McPherson for a feast. By this time I probably would have accepted a ride from Brian Mulroney, so without hesitation I jumped into the back and for the next two hours watched as a thick plume of smoke trailed off behind. A few times, I bounced into the air after the truck smashed through a large rut, my chattering teeth only magnifying the road's angry temperament. But it didn't matter. Without the distraction of people inside the truck, it was a marvellously surreal way to ride the northernmost public highway in the world. Three hours later, Winnie and her family dropped me at the Peel River ferry crossing just west of Fort McPherson, and after waving farewell, doubled back towards town.

The Peel River is not such a bad place to get stranded if one has to get stranded on the Dempster, because at least there are things going on. Native fish camps line the riverbanks in both directions, and there is a fine view of the Richardson Mountains rising to the west. It is also a good strategic location for hitchhikers. Vehicles are forced to stop and turn off their engines while crossing on the ferry, which (in theory) gives them ample opportunity to feel sorry for the poor stranded hitchhiker on the far side. And who could refuse some poor, destitute traveller on a hard northern route many miles from home?

Actually, quite a few people, as it turned out. I stood there for the remainder of the afternoon and into the evening, and by the time the ferry stopped running I had collected little sympathy and fewer rides to show for my efforts.

I rose early the next morning to continue thumbing, and in the first three hours almost a dozen cars passed my lonely post, shattering the silence every so often as they thundered by on gravel. Unfortunately, all but one were headed in the wrong direction. So I continued to sit there and listen to nothing, contemplating life as a polar bear adrift on an Arctic ice floe. If a polar bear eats a tourist and nobody is there to hear him scream, does he actually make a sound? Such is the result of spending too many hours sitting in a ditch, contemplating random philosophical questions.

The fellow operating the ferry, a good-natured Gwich'in chap named Abe, must have put a good word in for me. At around 2:30 a young guy driving a large five-ton cargo truck pulled over and said: "Aww hell, insurance says I'm not supposed to pick up hitchhikers, but you'll be here forever if I don't give you a ride."

The man's name was Shawn, and he had just started a 4,000-kilometre one-way ticket down to Moose Jaw, Saskatchewan. It was a one-way ticket in that he was a newlywed; he had been married just three weeks earlier, and if he didn't get his no-good carcass down to see his honeymoon-starved wife right pronto, he would be getting a one-way ticket to stay at a friend's house. Or maybe the doghouse. In fact, he had been married less than a week before coming up to Inuvik to finish a contract for his construction company. "I'm not in my wife's good books right now," he admitted sheepishly. "We told the kids I was going up north to repair Santa's house." The kids, not wanting to miss an opportunity, had apparently given him a detailed list of desired Christmas goodies to hand-deliver.

Shawn and I had no trouble finding things to talk about, having both grown up on the prairies: myself on an acreage north of Saskatoon, he on a farm near Winnipeg. We discussed fishing and hockey tournaments, firepit barbecues and country music. It was part of our shared history, even though we hadn't shared any of it together. One thing that made me laugh was his tried-and-true method for fetching dinner off his back patio, something right out of *This Hour Has 22 Minutes*. "There are so many geese where we live that you can sit on our back porch, drink beer and shoot supper," he told me. "My city friends find it pretty entertaining."

By the time Shawn and I reached the Klondike highway just east of Dawson, it was after ten. I could tell that he was starting to get tired, so in a moment of ludicrous bravado, I offered to drive. Shawn's company would not be happy if they knew he had picked up a hitchhiker, and I could only imagine what they would say if I were to slide behind the wheel.

"Sounds good," he said, tossing me the keys.

"Wait a second," I sputtered. "I was only joking. I've never driven one of these things."

"Can you drive a standard?"

"Yeah."

"Well, you don't need a special license to drive a five-ton," he told me. "You'll figure it out." Very reassuring, I thought, for somebody who had never been behind the wheel of anything larger than a station wagon.

Learning to drive the truck actually was quite easy ... once I got past an embarrassing entrance onto the highway. The hardest part was figuring out the nine or eleven or thirteen gears, or whatever it was. I can't remember. All I remember is lurching out of the parking lot like Bucky the Wonder Horse, certain that the truck was about to stall. "You have it in seventh," Shawn told me dryly.

"Seventh? You've got to be kidding." I stomped on the clutch, pulled back on the stick, yanked it sideways and tried to re-engage at a lower gear. Shawn's head nearly bounced off the glove compartment as Bucky shuddered and stalled.

"Okay, try this," said Shawn. He pulled back on the stick and put it in gear for me.

"Alright ... here goes."

This time I managed to make it onto the highway, and although the truck pitched back and forth a few times, I got some speed up, and then suddenly everything was fine. Shawn turned up the country music, leaned his head against the window and tried to get some sleep. The couple of times I had to stop between Dawson and Whitehorse, I even managed to get it started again without shaking too much chrome off the truck. And while I'm not sure that Shawn managed much sleep, he certainly didn't complain about it. He was probably just happy to lay back and relax for a few hours without having to stare at the road.

We arrived in Whitehorse shortly after four in the morning and pulled over at a motel, where Shawn invited me to crash for the night. To my surprise, he turned on the tube for a few minutes before flopping over and going to sleep; two hours later he got up, jumped in the shower and was soon back on the road. As he left, all I remember hearing was the door latch clicking shut behind him.

Three months later, while driving west from southern Ontario to do a story for *Equinox* magazine, I stopped in Regina to pick up a hitchhiker of my own. We pulled over for dinner at a service centre in Moose Jaw, and when we walked inside, there was Shawn sitting at a booth with his wife, having dinner with another couple. For a few seconds we just stared at each other, until we realized what had happened. Without missing a beat, I turned and pointed at the hitchhiker I had picked up. "It's not often you get to see goodwill being passed along," I said to Shawn. "You should know that this is my hitchhiker and I'm going to buy him dinner."

Canadian Heartland

*"The real act of discovery consists not in finding
new lands, but in seeing with new eyes."*
- Marcel Proust

Chapter 24

Ride the Wind

June 15, 1999 - Calgary, Alberta

For those who have never been to southern Alberta on a windy day, well, chances are good you have never been to southern Alberta period. Sweeping down off the great eastern slopes of the Canadian Rockies is a wind tunnel several hundred kilometres wide (to suggest a simple metaphor), and unless you count a few cows standing sideways or oil wells milking the bone-dry earth, there isn't much of anything to stand in its way. The wind is omnipresent here. It is no exaggeration to suggest that anyone and everyone—locals and visitors, humans and animals, ranchers and oilmen alike—whoever tries to work, play, jog, saunter, smile or frown on the prairies is affected by this wind. The same goes for hitchhikers, I soon discovered, standing at the edge of the Trans-Canada Highway thumbing east.

Violent gusts ripped at my bare legs and face as I gazed across fields of freshly planted wheat to the high-rise towers of downtown Calgary, my home and the city I had left behind two hours earlier. I was escaping Calgary a couple of weeks prior to the Stampede, something, I must admit, that I had mixed feelings about. Although I have always enjoyed the world-famous cowboy festival—bronc riders, chuckwagon races, cowboys getting gored and trampled by temperamental bulls—for some reason I wasn't in the mood for all the fanfare this year. Calgary may be the biggest small town in Canada, but these days it's a small town with crushing hordes that can top a cool million during Stampede week. So rather than stick around, I devised another plan: hit the road running and try to make Newfoundland by October.

Hitchhiking along the Trans-Canada is usually a cakewalk, and so it was for me that blustery day in mid-June. A postal worker named Bob, whose son had just returned from a peacekeeping mission to Kosovo, gave me a brief respite from the flagging wind in his delivery car before dropping me in Strathmore. Bob lived in a hamlet just north of the Trans-Canada with a population of twenty—counting children—where one of his friends used to run the post office and grocery store, act as a grain buyer and drive a school bus until, according to Bob, "he died from boredom." In his town, he explained, stress was an unknown condition.

After a greasy snack at a cafe in Strathmore my luck continued, for within thirty minutes an eighteen-wheeler with two trucks in tow screeched to a halt. Inside was a French-Canadian fellow named Luc, on a long-haul to Kentucky with three Westin Star truck cabs, brand-new and worth about $150,000 each. "That wind is pretty fierce out there," he remarked matter-of-factly as he pulled back onto the highway. "That's one thing I never got used to after moving here from Quebec." I could understand why. In his rearview mirror, I could see flecks of grit stuck between my teeth, one hazard of smiling at passing motorists in a wind storm.

Luc was on his way to Medicine Hat for the night, and we soon found ourselves chatting about a variety of things. Like many easterners, he had originally come to western Canada to work on Alberta's oil patch. As an engineer, he had worked all over the province until he could no longer abide the dust blowing in his eyes. "It drove me crazy having to work in that stuff," he grumbled. So he moved with his family to Kelowna, where he got into the construction business. When that died, he was forced to start trucking, even though he hated the crazy schedule. In particular, he disliked driving his rig across the States. "As soon as you cross that border there's a change," he lamented. "Driving through the States is hard on the nerves." It was clear to me that if Luc wanted to get rid of his stress, he should quit his job, move to small-town Alberta and start working four jobs.

At Brooks we passed a massive slaughterhouse with a billboard that proudly advertised: 700 JOBS. On the south side of the highway we could see several large cattle pens, where hundreds of beefy bovines are kept for their last supper, before they become supper. Luc told me that most of the jobs have gone to Asian immigrants or Newfoundlanders, people who are really desperate for work. "If you went in there I bet you'd never eat Alberta beef again," he laughed bitterly. "You can usually smell it long before you get here."

It wasn't until we reached Medicine Hat that we stopped at a Husky gas station for dinner, and even though it was after nine by the time we had finished, I decided to try for one more ride. As I walked across the parking lot, wondering how I was going to reach the far side of town before nightfall, one of several dozen transport trucks parked nearby blasted its horn at me. A blonde man wearing a red bandana leaned out the window and shouted, "Where ya headed, slick?" When I pointed east, he waved at me to jump in. "I'm only going to Swift Current tonight, but that'll at least get you into Saskatchewan."

After he had filled his coffee mug at the truck stop, we were back on the highway, the sun sinking fast in his rearview mirror. "My name is Lloyd," he said, reaching over to shake my hand. "But everyone since grade one has called me Smiley." Unlike Luc, Smiley was a homegrown Saskatchewan farm boy. He had farmed cash crops, worked on Alberta's oil pipeline and hauled fertilizer for the Saskatchewan Wheat Pool during the spring. He had also lived in Saskatoon for several years, where he used money he had earned off the oil patch to buy a restaurant and a biker bar. And although the restaurant business had been good to him, when he heard that the Hell's Angels were moving into town, everything changed. "The Rebels were manageable, but with the Angels—well, you're either for them or against them," he said. "I heard they were coming, so I was outta there long before they arrived."

Behind us, the last vestiges of sunlight made some cumulus quiver as the sun prepared to drop from sight. The fiery orb glinted like a shower of sparks off the oncoming traffic, half blinding us such was its peculiar angle. We passed a weigh station soon after that, one of many along the Trans-Canada where truckers stop to have their loads checked. "I like to avoid those places," Smiley commented dryly. "All the guys who work there know me by name, and they always tell me to take a break."

"Oh yeah?"

He nodded glumly. "Do you want to know what happens when you don't take a break?"

I wasn't sure what he meant.

Smiley rummaged through a map sorter at the side of his seat and pulled out a picture of a transport truck in the ditch, its cab crumpled beyond recognition. "That's what happens."

The empty miles passed, and about thirty minutes down the road it suddenly dawned on me that two truckers had offered me rides in the same day. Even with thousands of road miles under my belt, I could literally count on one hand the number of times a transport truck had stopped for me in five years. I had always assumed that insurance was the primary reason most truckers are not allowed to pick up riders, but I decided to ask Smiley about it.

"Every company is different," he explained. "I run my own outfit, which means picking up hitchhikers is my decision. I like to help people out, so I try to do it whenever I can." Smiley told me about a guy from Quebec he had picked up in Maple Creek a few weeks back. The man had thumbed all the way from Montreal, sleeping in ditches along the way. "A couple of mornings in northern Ontario he woke up covered from head to toe in ice," Smiley told me. "All he had was five bucks in his pocket, so I took him to a grocery store in Medicine Hat and bought him some sandwiches, milk and fruit. Well, the guy just inhaled them. And he was obviously an educated guy. He was probably just down on his luck."

I thought Smiley's story was a great example of the charity Canadians so often show for one another when the chips are down. This kindness can be rather amazing, especially when one considers the inter-provincial mudslinging that frequently ricochets back and forth across the country. When floods ripped through Quebec's Saguenay region in 1996, for example, money poured in from across Canada to help families who had lost their homes. Canadians were just as quick to offer help during the 1997 Red River flood in Manitoba, not to mention the ice storm of 1998, the one that froze a vast swath of eastern Ontario, Quebec and the Maritimes.

I only bring this up because it has often perplexed me how Canada—a country with so many regional differences—can seem so fractured, then suddenly and miraculously pull together when the going gets tough. Perhaps grassroots Canada is not unlike hockey. In the NHL, teams fight a battle of attrition for playoff rankings, yet when the playoffs arrive, Canadians from across the country will almost always cheer for the remaining Canadian teams if their own has already been eliminated. It doesn't seem to matter which teams. Flames fans will cheer for the Oilers and Habs fans will cheer for the Maple Leafs. Occasionally people will even cheer for the Vancouver Canucks, although that might be pushing it.

I wanted to hitchhike south to the Cypress Hills the next day, so I had Smiley drop me at a lonely one-horse town called Irvine a few kilometres west of the Saskatchewan border. Across the road was a dimly lit gas station and restaurant called the 20 Mile Post Cafe, and behind that, a dirt road that led into some scrub brush toward a small cluster of homes. Quite truthfully, I've seen graveyards with more festive cheer, and as I got out of Smiley's truck, I half expected to find myself standing in a field littered with tombstones. With a shiver running down my spine, I set out in search of a suitable place to pitch my tent.

I walked a few hundred metres along a spooky dirt road awash in inky blackness, and after finding nothing, opted instead to walk back toward the Trans-Canada. Beside the highway, I found a shallow depression in a ditch where the grass had been cut for cattle feed, so I laid my tent across some prickly two-inch stubble, pitched it and climbed inside with great eagerness. As I tried to fall asleep, transport trucks continued blasting along the highway, and every couple of hours the whistle from a passing freight train pierced the night air, loud enough to wake the dead. Sleep did not come easily, but at least I was on the road again.

June 16, 1999 - Irvine, Alberta

Irvine was the first of about a dozen small towns that I visited while travelling in a sweeping northeasterly arc from Alberta to Manitoba, through the heart of Canada's fertile breadbasket. Many of the places I planned to visit on my trip were places I had never seen, but the same cannot be said for Saskatchewan. I spent thirteen of my most formative years there, and even after moving to southern Ontario for high school and university, I had traversed the province no less than a dozen times between Toronto and Banff, primarily by Greyhound bus. Still, what I hadn't done for several years was travel off the four-lane superhighways, exploring Saskatchewan beyond the "Trans-Canada belt." On this trip, I planned to rectify that.

It might sound strange coming from somebody who loves the mountains as much as I do, but after all those years I still felt a strong kinship toward the Prairies and her people. This was especially true when people from Toronto made rude comments about my home province—describing a road trip across the plains as "a voyage of unspeakable tedium" or something like that. It has always been enough to make the hackles on my neck stand on end. "What's there to see on the prairies?" ask those not versed in the subtle beauty of the place. Once a prairie boy, always a prairie boy, I say, and I have grown to resent that old joke about watching my dog run away for three days. Give me a break. What kind of dog can run for three days?

A word of advice: the trick to appreciating Saskatchewan is to accept it on its own terms. This is big sky country, and to fully appreciate it, you have to develop a "fifty-mile stare." Trust me, there is freedom to be found along the biting edge of a remorseless wind, across this wide-open rangeland devoid of trees. In fact, I have always felt a strange sort of pity for those easterners so fixated on seeing the Rockies that they blast west, bypassing Saskatchewan almost entirely. A poem written by Saskatchewan author Cathy Jewison, for me, sums up these sentiments perfectly. Appropriately, it's called *God Lives In Saskatchewan*:

God lives in Saskatchewan
In a four house town
with a gas station
and a grain elevator

Saskatchewan is God's own land.
He cleared away all the mountains
and the trees
so He could see forever.

He sits on his porch
and keeps an eye on the cosmos
and listens to the music
of the spheres.

And He watches the Ontario drivers
zip through to Banff
as fast as they can
without even looking around.

Then He carefully jots down
their license numbers
in a book
for future reference.

Yes, Saskatchewan is about freedom. And it's about boundlessness. But I could have made do with a little less of those things while packing up camp that morning. By the time I crawled from my sleeping bag, the wind was belting in harder than it had been the previous day, thudding against the side of my tent with the authority of artillery. Clasping the tent firmly with one hand, I duck-walked around its perimeter, gingerly plucking pegs from the ground while at the same time removing collapsible poles from their nylon sheaths. Worse yet was trying to fold the tent so that it would fit inside its tiny stuff sack again; it was only by using a frenzy of hands, feet and chin that I eventually managed to brace the corners and fold it down. What to me was a nightmare, was probably the world's most entertaining game of solo Twister to your average bystander. If I had lost my grip for an instant, I would have been picking my tent up in Winnipeg four weeks later.

With my gear safely stowed, I walked toward the restaurant, waving cheerfully at school buses full of children as they rumbled past me on the dirt road. A young girl wearing a hockey helmet coasted over on her bicycle, having watched my novel technique for disassembling a tent from a nearby yard. "If you want to camp you have to do it over there," she scolded, pointing toward the far side of town. I apologized and explained that it had been late when I arrived and that I hadn't seen the campground. Perhaps the young hockey sprite had been expecting me to say something different, because when I spoke she suddenly clammed up, turned around and pedaled away as fast as her short little legs would carry her.

Five minutes later, I strolled into the 20 Mile Post Cafe, fielding suspicious stares from a few chain-smoking patrons wearing John Deere hats and sun-bleached Wheat Pool jackets. In fact, when people saw my backpack, they stopped talking entirely until I had walked across the restaurant and seated myself in a booth near the front window. I'm sure they weren't trying to be unfriendly—they just weren't used to seeing hitchhikers. I felt about as complementary to the scene as garden shears are to a hairdresser.

A tall woman wearing a green jacket and blue jeans entered the restaurant shortly after I did, her curly brown hair a beehive of tangles. "Did you order this wind?" she asked, looking at an old duffer seated halfway across the restaurant.

"Sure did," he said, winking mischievously and sweeping his hand across the table in a wide arc. "It's comin' in just how I like it."

After a tasty trucker's breakfast, I was back on the road, this time thumbing south along Route 41 toward Elkwater. Within five minutes an elderly couple had stopped: a man named Bozo and his wife Goenka, both with thick Slavic accents. They were on their way to a dentist's appointment in Medicine Hat, and stopping for a hitchhiker was a perfect excuse to be late. Moreover, it was a perfect opportunity for Bozo to tell me about emigrating from Bosnia in the late 1960s.

When they came to Canada, Bozo explained, he had worked on a farm for nothing more than room and board. Later, he had found steady work at a shoe factory before gravitating toward heavy construction and the oil patch. It had been a life of hard work, but he never complained because he was happy just to have a job. "We were very poor in Europe," Bozo told me. "Moving to Canada inspired us to change many things." Not surprisingly, the first thing to go was his Bosnian name. He exchanged it for Bozo, which he thought was a popular and widely accepted Canadian moniker. This is what happens, I suppose, when your first stop after arriving in Canada is the Shrine Circus.

Bozo and his wife dropped me at Elkwater half an hour later, and after stocking up on food at a small grocery store, I set out along a boardwalk running the length of Elkwater Lake. I spent the next two days walking and thumbing my leisurely way across the Cypress Hills, utilizing a spider-web of hiking trails and dirt roads. The days were hot and dry, the evenings cool and comfortable. Even surrounded by dense forests of poplar, birch and lodgepole pine, I could feel the sky dominating every vista whenever I climbed high enough to see it. I also encountered plenty of wildlife along the way: a pair of yellow-headed blackbirds perched on bulrushes, a white-tailed deer fawn drinking from a small lake and a cow moose that surprised me one morning when she loped through my campsite less than five metres from my tent.

I crossed the border from Alberta into Saskatchewan on my second day. It was hot and dry, and just about the time I ran out of water, a friendly Ojibwa conservation officer pulled up beside me on the dirt road. His name was George, and he was on his way to help restock Battle Creek with several thousand rainbow trout. He handed me a jug of water, and after I had told him about my trip, he invited me to tag along. Ten minutes later, we were standing at the edge of the creek helping a white-haired fisheries officer named Ron net trout fry and dump them into a large plastic barrel. In three or four eddies along the creek, Ron and George waded into the current, easing the juvenile fish into the water. "You have to do it slowly," Ron cautioned me. "They find it hard going from warm to cold too quickly."

After we had finished the job, George invited me back to his home at the ranger station for dinner. It was his birthday, he told me proudly, and his wife Tracey and step-daughter Alexis were cooking burgers and baking a cake. "Are you sure that will be okay?" I asked him. "I don't want to intrude on your special occasion."

"Don't give it a second thought," he replied. "We enjoy having company."

George was certainly not exaggerating. Tracey welcomed me with great enthusiasm, as did Alexis, Tracey's cute little toddler who was wearing a white flannel dress and red slippers. The peaceful simplicity in George's home was quickly evident, and we were soon seated around a big wooden table with burgers in hand, so thick we could hardly take a bite out of them. And so the evening passed, with eating, drinking and plenty of good conversation.

"A few years ago I was in Saskatoon, not doing much of anything but getting into trouble," George confided. "That's when I started having dreams about future events, which is what led me back into my Native spirituality."

George brought out photos of a teepee presentation that he does for people visiting the Cypress Hills. He also showed me several charcoal drawings, explaining that when he dreams, he often wakes up in the middle of the night and feels compelled to record them. He pointed to the first drawing of a turtle's back, which to him symbolized the Cypress Hills. A buffalo skull in the same picture represented a spiritual helper, guiding him to pursue a career in resource management.

"What's that in the upper left corner?" I asked him, pointing at a drawing of what looked like a teepee.

"That's a Sundance lodge," he replied. "Tribal elders have them every year. You enter a ceremonial teepee where you pray to the spirits for help, guidance and protection."

"What kinds of things do you ask for?"

I expected George to hesitate at such a pointed question, but he didn't. Instead, he asked me, "Do you remember last year when we had that big drought in southern Alberta?"

I nodded.

"Well, I had a dream that the Cypress Hills were going to burn, so I prayed for their protection. And at the same time I was at the Sundance ceremony, the Cypress Hills were getting eleven inches of rain." He paused for a moment, looking over at me to see if I was following his story. "Of course, I can't say my prayers saved the Cypress Hills, but I *can* say that my prayers were answered."

After we had polished off two gargantuan slices of birthday cake, George and I ventured outside again, this time to search for one of the park's elk herds. In his 4X4 pickup, we eased up a steep, rubble-strewn dirt track that sliced through tangled thickets onto a grassy plateau. We drove slowly across the meadow scanning for elk, but all we saw were several mule deer bounding along. At the far side of the plateau we climbed out of the truck.

"This is what you do to bring an elk in during the hunt," George said. He cupped his hands together and let loose with a high-pitched whistle, mimicking the call of a bugling elk. We stopped and listened. Nothing. For fifteen minutes, George whistled in intervals, but in the end there was only a faint echo drifting on the wind.

"You know, when I first left the city I came down here to take a walk with a Peigan medicine man," George told me, leaning back against his truck. "While we were walking, his spiritual helpers were swooping all around us, and he told me that if I wanted to find true happiness, I should look for a golden flower."

"Oh yeah? What kind of flower?" I asked.

He smiled, clasping a broad hand across his chin. "Well, for a long time I scoured the Cypress Hills looking for it," he said. "Then a few months ago I was giving a presentation to some students at one of the local schools. That's when I glanced down and noticed the golden flower on my park's insignia patch." He laughed loudly and heartily. "All this time and it was right under my nose," he chuckled. "That's when I knew I had finally come home."

I pitched my tent at a campsite not far from the ranger station and sat for some time watching billions of stars sparkle across the vast canopy of sky. I was pondering what George had shared. What gnawed at me was a simple question. Why wasn't I happy to stay in one place as George was? Or satisfied like Bozo to have a paying job? Why did I have this itch to travel, this desire to see what was around the next bend in the road? I had already met a lot of people on my trip, many happy ones, though I had also met my fair share of unhappy ones. Were the happy ones the people who had found home in a person, a place, a lifestyle or a job? Were the unhappy ones the people who hadn't?

Home. I would have to give that concept some thought. Fortunately, I still had more than ten thousand kilometres and eight provinces over which to do it.

Chapter 25

Thunder Breeding Hills

June 19, 1999 - Maple Creek, Saskatchewan

The green 4X4 came squealing around a corner at the outskirts of Maple Creek, pistons firing and rubber burning. As it whistled past me, I caught a glimpse of two dark-skinned Native men sitting in the open rear, smiling broadly, their backs propped up against the sliding window. Without warning, the driver slammed on the brakes and pushed the truck hard into reverse, coming to rest at a point where I could see several more Natives crammed hodge-podge inside the truck's extended cab. "Jump in!" shouted the younger of the two men sitting in the rear. "We're on our way to join the March West, and we're already running late!"

What he meant by the "March West" I wasn't entirely certain, but it sounded like an adventure, and where adventures are concerned I generally need little prodding. Even before I was seated, the truck lurched forward and we were soon screaming along a narrow strip of black pavement, bouncing and dipping over green hills, doing what must have been at least one-twenty in an eighty zone. Before long I started to feel nauseous; every time the truck crested the top of a rise, my stomach parted from the rest of my body, continuing in a straight line until it rejoined me at the top of the next hill.

To distract myself from thoughts of being tossed fifty metres into the air if the truck should roll, I started talking with the fellow who had told me to jump in. His name was Josh, and he was a young guy with long, stringy black hair drooping past his shoulders. He explained that he and his friends had joined the March West at an Assiniboine reservation near Regina a couple of weeks before. The March West was a group of horsemen riding across the prairies dressed in the traditional garb of Canada's North West Mounted Police. They were retracing the route taken by the original police force that crossed western Canada in 1874.

Ah yes, the North West Mounted Police. They and their modern descendants, the Royal Canadian Mounted Police, have long been a source of national pride. Dispatched to a land of outlaws and whiskey traders, the NWMP were forced into a complex variety of roles in their efforts to tame the western half of our vast country. They had to be effective soldiers, policemen and peacekeepers, just as surely as they had to be diplomats, trade intermediaries and skilled woodsmen.

When I pressed Josh for more information, he told me that the March West had set out from Manitoba more than a month earlier. The modern contingent of men, women, horses and covered wagons was thus scheduled to arrive at the old Fort Walsh police post later that day. Josh and his friends were there to provide a First Nations perspective.

"Do you want to come with us?" Josh asked, jolting me back to the present.

"Excuse me?" The wind was whistling so loudly that I wasn't sure that I had heard him right.

"Do you want to ride with us?" he repeated. He explained that they had left their horses grazing with a local rancher at the edge of the Cypress Hills, and that they had set an extra horse aside, say, for a hitchhiker.

"Actually, one of our friends is sick today," the other fellow told me, gingerly running his fingers along a staff decorated with eagle-feather ornaments.

My jaw must have dropped a metre. Over the years, I had hitched rides aboard airplanes and on boats, in cars and in trucks, in sickness and in health, in wealth and in poverty ... yet in all those years, I had never thumbed a ride on a horse. This only made sense. Apart from small communities of old-order Mennonites, Hutterites and Amish folk (who tend not to pick up hitchhikers anyway), there aren't many places in Canada where horses regularly travel the highways and thruways of our vast nation.

"You want *me* to ride with *you?*" I asked. "On *horseback?*" I wanted to clarify their invitation beyond a shadow of a doubt. "You have to realize that I haven't been on a horse for years." I was from Calgary, and my confession sounded ridiculous even to me.

"No problem," Josh promised, yet somehow I didn't believe him.

Thirty minutes later, we parked beside a fenced-in pasture, tucked between two rows of cone-shaped hills. Several horses were lolling in the afternoon heat near a red barn, and in the distance, a dirt road snaked through some trees toward the top of the Cypress Hills plateau. Two of the guys in the truck—a tall, muscular guy named Bronson and a stout fellow named Conrad—walked into the field and came back with several horses in tow. Bronson handed me the reins to a frosty grey mare that seemed rather unimpressed that she would have to put up with me for the next few hours. They haltered the horse, fit her with a saddle and adjusted the stirrups.

"Remember to let her know who's boss," Bronson coached, gripping the reins while I stepped my left foot into the stirrup and mounted. "If she senses that you don't know what you're doing, you'll end up kissing the ground."

"Know what I'm doing? You've got to be kidding!" I replied in a shaky voice. "If that's the case, I'll be spending all my time on the ground."

But Bronson didn't have time for petty, wimpish concerns. Two minutes later, he was leading us along a rough dirt road toward the plateau, bouncing along at a steady trot. And as I quickly learned, there are few things as decidedly painful for a novice horseman as sitting on a trotting horse. It's like riding an old lawn tractor while sitting on a tenpin bowling ball. It starts with sharp jabs of pain to the groin and tailbone areas, which mercifully, after about an hour, fades into a numb, all-encompassing sort of hell that spreads through your entire body. If I had known before, it became abundantly clear over the next few hours: a cowboy I am not!

"How are you doing?" asked Conrad. We had just stopped to water our horses at a small mudhole, and he must have seen me walking like an Egyptian. With hemorrhoids.

"I'll survive," I grimaced. "I just haven't done this for a while." I did, in fact, feel terrible, but my pride was at stake. Not only did I live in Calgary, but one of my uncles owned a ranch in the Alberta foothills. To admit that I couldn't ride a few kilometres on a horse would be like a Banff resident admitting they had never tried skiing.

"Are you sure?"

"Yeah."

I don't think Conrad believed me, because after we had remounted, he came riding over to check my stirrups. "Geez, that looks uncomfortable," he winced. "You'll want to let those *waaaay* down! Hey Bronson, lower the stirrups on Matt's horse, willya?"

Bronson walked over to check them. "Geez," he said. "Were you riding like that all the way up here?"

I nodded.

"Sorry about that," he said. "Here, let's try this." He reached over and brought the thick leather straps down by several centimetres, which allowed me to straighten my legs and weight the stirrups with my feet. "How's that?"

"Much better," I replied. "Thanks."

We caught sight of a massive line of horsemen a few minutes later: a sea of red, rippling in a long column across the upper plateau. Three riders rode in front, one with a Union Jack hoisted into the stiff prairie wind, and at the tail end of the column were three covered wagons. Although several riders wore blue jeans and cowboy hats, most participants were dressed in traditional police garb. If it weren't for the trucks and minivans lining a nearby access road, it could have been a scene plucked straight from the old Canadian West.

The convoy was moving slowly and precisely, which made it easy for our small group to overtake the riders out front. As he rode past, Bronson waved at the three trimly dressed officers near the front of the column, as did the rest of us when it was our turn. When the officers saw me, however, they were clearly taken off guard. Was it my red Gore-Tex jacket? The Mountain Equipment Co-op backpack hanging from my shoulders? Or was it the way I was riding my horse that gave me away? Whatever the cause, these police officers were eyeing me like they had seen my mug shot on a "most wanted" poster.

"Who are you?" asked one of the men—rather pointedly, I thought.

"I'm just a hitchhiker they picked up in Maple Creek," I said innocently, shrugging.

If he had any protests, I never heard them, for within seconds I was out of earshot. When I looked back, though, I could see his mouth gaping wide open.

THE NORTH WEST Mounted Police faced nearly insurmountable odds from the very start, so it's really no wonder that they have gained a reputation for bravery, efficiency and fairness. According to the history books, Prime Minister John A. Macdonald created the police force to pave the way for settlement across Canada's western half, to protect Canada's sovereignty and to bring law and order to a land dominated by lawless whiskey traders. The fact that a band of whiskey traders had in 1873 massacred some Assiniboine Indians at the "Thunder Breeding Hills" only gave Canada's fledgling government added incentive to act. So it was that our Dominion government recruited a force of three hundred police officers; they departed on horseback from Fort Dufferin, Manitoba on July 8, 1874.

Under the leadership of Commissioner George French, these men did their best to fight their way across Canada's southern prairies, but conditions were stacked against them from the very start. The days were long, their maps were poor, there was little potable water along the way and many horses died for lack of decent pasture. The situation grew so grim that men were stopping at mud holes to lie on their bellies and suck what moisture they could from the ground. In addition, as they marched westward, they left the trees behind as they crossed onto the open plains. This meant that cooking a hot meal required burning dried "buffalo chips," which actually worked fine—except when the dung was so wet that it wouldn't burn.

Considering these deplorable conditions, it should come as no surprise that riders from the March West of 1999 had to endure hardships too, even though crews were sent ahead to cook and set up camp for participants. There were blisters and saddle sores to contend with, as well as driving rain and blistering sun—all very real hardships. And there was the ever-present danger (particularly for those officers wearing nifty white helmets with the pointy spikes on top) that they might accidentally skewer a pair of underpants from a makeshift clothesline as they ducked out the door of their mobile trailer in the morning. One officer came face to face with this danger, and spent several minutes strolling primly around in the pre-dawn light, saluting fellow officers with underwear dangling from his helmet. The March West comics dubbed it "fruit of the plume," one legend that will surely make its way into the noble archives of the RCMP. The danger for that officer, of course, is that his story will never be forgotten.

Later that afternoon, a wide assortment of individuals and equipment arrived at Fort Walsh: police officers and teepees, cowboys and video cameras ... not to mention one badly limping hitchhiker. For a short time, I parted with my new friends to hobble around and take pictures. Everywhere I looked there were scenes straight out of Canada's Wild West. There were men wearing scarlet tunics, tan trousers, gauntlet gloves, black riding boots, and of course, pillbox hats or white pith helmets (sans underwear). Already assembled were the canvas tents of the police camp, plus a makeshift stable for the horses and a teepee circle erected by the

Nikaneet Plains Cree. The commanding officer bellowed "ATTEN-SHUN!" and his troops obeyed, saluting and whumping their feet together. Beneath a fluttering Union Jack, they performed flawless rifle drills and fired volleys from a nine-pound Gatling gun high over the hills.

"Pretty impressive, isn't it?" said a lean, rangy cowpoke standing next to me.

I had to agree.

"We rode part of this trail for the centennial back in ninety-two," he told me, talking through his bristly moustache. His name was Evan—a wrangler of no fixed address—and for several minutes he told me about the old settlers' trails that he and some local ranch hands had followed on horseback from BC all the way to Saskatchewan. From there, several friends had continued on to Ottawa, where they presented the expedition saddle bags to the Queen.

"What was your favourite part of the trip?" I asked him. People had asked me the same question about my own travels, and I had never been able to come up with a satisfactory answer.

"Y'know, everywhere you go in this country you got somethin' amazing," said Evan, a youthful gleam in his eye. "We got beauty, we got majesty, we got the openness of the prairies and the confines of the mountains. I guarantee it. You do one of those trail rides and you'll go home and plant a Canadian flag in the middle of your yard."

He sounded like an advertisement for Canada's immigration department, but his sentiments were heartfelt. We chatted for a while longer, and just before we parted, he reached into his wallet and, to my surprise, plucked out his business card. It described him as a "trail rider" by profession, as well as a "cowgirl chaser, pretty girl watcher and campfire storyteller." In bold letters emblazoned across the bottom, the card announced: "Have horse, will travel."

I rejoined Josh, Bronson, Conrad and a large gathering of their Native kin later that afternoon, just as everybody was sitting down at a teepee circle for a feast. "When the Creator first gave us life, we were sitting in a circle," Cree elder Gordon Oakes told the assembled crowd. "So the circle exists from the beginning of time." He invited everyone—Natives and non-Natives alike—to sit in their circle and partake in the feast, and soon we were gorging ourselves on baskets overflowing with sandwiches, fruit, cookies and fresh Saskatoon berries that quickly turned our tongues purple.

While we ate, I sat between Conrad and Bronson making small talk about the day, laughing at the discomfort of the long ride and how I had been hobbling around like a drunk ever since. They could have made fun of me, but they didn't. Instead, Bronson pointed to a colourful crest sewn into one of the teepees, which displayed four symbols of their native homeland. "The sun shines, the rivers flow, the grass grows and the buffalo roam," he told me proudly. "Our ancestors survived on the simple things."

Simple things indeed. His quiet confidence reminded me of Joe, the carver I had met in Tuktoyaktuk the previous summer. I remembered Joe telling me that many young Natives are ashamed of their heritage, and for that reason, I wished he could be at this gathering. These guys were not timid or ashamed of their traditions, and they obviously took great pride in sharing their roots, even with a stranger they had picked up at the side of the road.

Once the feast was over, I even joined them for a dance around the teepee circle. Although I felt out of place, Bronson and Conrad insisted that as a rider, I be part of their group. Before I knew what had happened, the lure of chanting and thudding of animal-skin drums had lured me into the circle. I shuffled and slowly pigeon-toed in time to the music, following the lead of those dressed in beaded costumes decorated with eagle feathers. I'm no cowboy and this wasn't *Dances with Wolves*, but it is probably the closest I will ever come to living out a Wild West fantasy. For a hitchhiker who can barely ride a horse, I guess I wasn't doing too badly.

Chapter 26

Romancing the Road

June 27, 1999 - Saskatoon, Saskatchewan

She was a farm girl with attitude driving a battered silver pickup, and when she stopped for me just north of Saskatoon, I stood agog for what must have been several seconds, trying desperately to catch my breath. She was a vision, all right: long silky hair, tattered blue jeans, a navy blue pull-on sweatshirt and dusty ball cap. She coyly tugged at the edge of her butterfly sunglasses in a way that made my heart start to flutter. It was like I had stepped into a Shania Twain video.

"Jump in," she said, breaking the spell. "My ex-boyfriend made me promise never to pick up hitchhikers, but you looked too interesting to pass up."

Renee was only a couple of years younger than me, as it turned out, which was surely why our banter felt more like flirting than normal conversation. But there was more to it than that. Like me, she had grown up attending a small country school with only a dozen or so classmates. She had also been forced to invent games with her siblings under the sweeping prairie sky—in her case, working and playing on her parents' buffalo and elk ranch. She was definitely one-hundred-percent prairie farm girl, yet her itch to see the world had also taken her to places like China, Africa and Central America after she graduated from high school. Overseas, she had taught English and taken part in humanitarian projects. Considering our shared roots and her serious case of wanderlust, is it any wonder that I liked her straight off?

"Some of the countries where I travelled feel a bit strange at first," she admitted. "In China, people are constantly yelling things at you, crowding around and wanting to touch you."

"Really?" A woman I once dated had worked in China for several months, and she had similar stories. "What did they shout at you?"

"Oh, I don't know," she replied. "Things like 'You're very tall,' or

'You're a very beautiful lady.' It's disconcerting. You feel like you're living in a movie."

"What did people say when they found out you were from Canada?"

She thought about it for a moment. "We're not looked down upon, that's for sure. I think people see us as peacekeepers, as willing to go into other countries and help."

"Well, that *is* what you were doing."

She smiled at that. "Yeah, but it always feels like there's so much more to do."

Over the years, many people (especially my mother) have grilled me about romantic interludes during my travels, and my answer has always been that mixing road trips and romance is seldom a good idea. There had been Jennifer from Yellowknife, of course (and there would be others), but apart from some superficial flirting and a moonlight kiss or two, I've always managed to avoid getting seriously involved. You see, romance tends to be the death of road trips. Just when you've caught your rhythm and are moving along at a good clip ... BOOM! ... you meet some smart, sassy woman who stops you dead in your tracks. The next thing you know, you've caught the dreaded "white picket fence disease" in a charmless little place called Spittletown or Redneckery, and are working at a hardware store selling welding parts and tractor tires. Never mind the mortgage and seven kids.

Yet somehow Renee made all of my fears and inhibitions disappear. Perhaps it was her sense of humour, her obvious spunk or the confidence with which she stated her strong opinions that made her attractive. All I know is that when she invited me back to her parents' ranch for lunch, I couldn't refuse.

"You'll love it," she said. "We live right on the South Saskatchewan River." Little did I know that I would end up staying for more than a week.

LIKE MOST PRAIRIE farm families, the Rabuts are used to living with a healthy dose of adversity and the unexpected. Even so, this adversity seemed particularly poignant at the time of my trip. As I travelled across the prairie provinces, newspaper headlines everywhere bemoaned the plight of farmers. A combination of low commodity prices, foreign competition and unpredictable weather had dropped farm incomes to levels not seen since the Great Depression, a situation that had caused monumental heartbreak, scores of bankruptcies and at least one feisty farmer from Alberta to embark on a cross-country adventure of his own. Scandalized by federal politicians and their agricultural policies, he drove his combine more than 3,500 kilometres to Ottawa and parked it on Parliament Hill, vowing not to leave until he was granted a meeting with big Jean himself.

Of course, unpredictable commodity prices aren't the only hardship that farmers face. If it's not spring flooding or summer drought, it might be a sick calf that needs tending at three in the morning. Or it might be a 500-pound elk mother stomping up and down on you when you get too close to her calf—the very misfortune that befell Renee's father Florent just before I arrived. "A couple weeks ago, we found him walking down the road all covered in dust and sporting a big bruise behind his ear," Renee chuckled. For Florent it was nothing more than a bruise, but for Renee it was a damn fine story. As we walked across the farmyard toward an elk paddock, I scanned the pasture for calves and ornery elk mothers.

Renee's brother Ryan was already prepping the necessary equipment for "cutting elk horn" when we arrived at the barn. At nineteen years old, Ryan was lean and wiry, but strong like a bull elk. I shook his callused hand, then followed him and Renee to a pasture where half a dozen elk bulls were grazing, their antlers at various stages of development. Although the Rabuts occasionally butchered elk for meat, they raised them primarily for their valuable antler velvet. After weighing the velvet, freezing it, grinding it into powder and inserting it into small capsules, they ship the velvet to Asian countries where it's used for homeopathic and medicinal purposes. With the influx of Asian people to the west coast of Canada and the United States, there was even a growing market for antler velvet in some parts of North America.

"We want that one and that one," Ryan told Renee, pointing each hand at an animal. He explained that one was an older male that had been "trimmed" many times before, while the other was a so-called "antler virgin."

"They usually put up a big fuss the first go around," Renee told me. "They have no idea what's going on."

"Poor things," I sympathized. "I don't think I would want to be trimmed either."

It was a good half-hour before we had separated the two bulls and chased them through a chute into a small holding pen. Once they were in,

Renee pushed the veteran into a large, cushioned clamp that held him in place, then climbed onto a small metal platform where she locked clamps around his shoulders with a motorized throttle. The bull was not happy, but his struggling was minimal; he had learned that resistance was futile. Meanwhile, Ryan brushed anesthetic at the base of the elk's antlers, padded them with cloth and attached small electric pincers that would dull the nerves. The pincers looked like booster cables for a miniature car battery. With a few quick swipes of the saw, the antlers were in Ryan's hands and the elk was released back to pasture.

"See? There's nothing to it," said Renee.

The second bull, as predicted, kicked up quite a fuss when it was his turn. As soon as he was lodged inside the padded stall he panicked, and despite Renee's best efforts to hold him in place, the young bull sputtered, swayed back and forth and kicked at boards a few inches from Ryan's legs. All the while, Ryan struggled to anesthetize the horns and cut them. After a few long minutes, the elk's eyes bulged and he suddenly went limp. When Renee released him, he slumped to the ground in a quivering mass.

"Oh my God!" cried Renee. "I think he's dead!"

"Get the butcher's knife!" Ryan shouted. If the bull were dead, they would have to hang, bleed and butcher the animal before blood clots formed in the meat.

Renee and I ran out the barn door at a frantic pace and jumped onto a motorized quad. "Hang on!" she shouted. Before I could grab anything, we were gunning toward the farmhouse at top speed.

Less than five minutes later we were back with a butcher's knife, ready to cut some elk steaks. But the elk had other ideas: as we rushed through the barn door he was staggering to his feet, and a few seconds later he trotted into the paddock, turning to glare at his tormentors once he had reached a safe distance.

"Do you get the feeling he's a little pissed at us?" said Ryan.

June 30, 1999 - Rabut Game Ranch, Saskatchewan

To me, the Rabuts' game ranch seemed the spitting image of what modern agriculture should be. They moved there in 1984, cleared brush from the land and built a road in to their property. By the time I visited, it was a large and diversified operation with roughly 130 bison and 130 elk.

The Rabuts were true pioneers. They had handled their farm in a proactive way that had helped them avoid many of the tribulations faced by farmers harvesting more traditional crops. This is not to suggest that farmers who grow wheat and run cattle are not proactive—merely that many farmers, faced with foreign competitors and the dismal state of commodity prices, are starting to look elsewhere to make ends meet. Some, like the Rabuts, have turned to non-traditional game like elk, bison and emu. Others grow garden-fresh vegetables and sell them at local farm markets, earning more on a square metre than some farmers do on an entire acre.

Even for a progressive thinker like Renee's father, however, desperate times have called for desperate measures. Florent laboured as an iron worker during the day, then came home to work on the farm in the evening. His wife Valerie delivered meat and tended to rabbits, emus, pot-bellied pigs and a plethora of exotic birds, which brought in money from farm tours. Renee and Ryan pitched in wherever they could. "The problem with a lot of farmers," Florent told me over dinner one night, "is that they don't want to change. They want to grow wheat and that's it." This was probably because their fathers and grandfathers had grown wheat, he explained, so change was more of an emotional issue than an economic one. "But if they're going to survive, they'll have to accept that things will probably never be the same."

While I stayed with the family, I gladly pitched in. I helped Valerie deliver bison meat to clients, and one afternoon I helped Renee stretch and salt a buffalo hide that smelled so putrid it made our eyes and nostrils sting. We could barely stand it. It was like being locked in a room with Preston Manning during a French lesson. Late in the week, I also helped Renee and Ryan set markers for a new fence, then pound some posts. The sweat and toil, the dust in my eyes and ears, actually felt good. Working beside Renee helped. We laughed and joked our way through all of it, and everywhere we went I rode piggyback on the quad with her, snuggled in behind with my fingers wrapped around her slender, curvaceous waist.

If that weren't enough, on most nights we were rewarded with repast fit for a king. We gorged ourselves on elk and bison steaks grilled on the patio barbecue, accompanied by fresh garden vegetables. "Beef is a four-letter word around here," Renee liked to joke. The meals were so incredible that I usually ended up doing the dishes to show my appreciation (as was my custom everywhere), a habit that quickly endeared me to Renee's mother.

Valerie had also noticed that Renee and I were taking more than a casual interest in one another. "As far as I'm concerned," she laughed. "You can stay as long as you want."

One sunny afternoon, the day's work all but finished, Renee and I decided to play hooky. We snuck off to a small lake where we launched a canoe, and after paddling around the lake for a short while, we snuggled up in the bottom of the boat for a long siesta. The dappled sunlight warmed us through, and we watched tiny oarsmen and tadpoles swimming through the water while dragonflies flitted about our heads. "What do you think they're doing?" Renee asked. To me, it looked like the neon-blue males were mounting the brown females in some sort of mating ritual.

"I would assume they're making baby dragonflies," I said, as stoically as I could muster.

She squeezed my hand, then turned to me with a funny grin.

"What?" I asked.

She giggled, then patted my hand. "Nothing," she replied. "I just think it's kind of nice that there's all this romance in the air."

"Yeah, I guess you're right," I laughed.

"It's too bad you're leaving in a few days."

July 1, 1999 - Batoche, Saskatchewan

The next day, Renee, Valerie and I drove to the nineteenth-century village of Batoche. It was at Batoche that Louis Riel, spiritual and political leader of the 1885 Rebellion, made his last stand with three hundred Metis. They faced off against Major General Middleton and an army of eight hundred troops known as the Northwest Fighting Force. You see, Riel had routed a company of the North West Mounted Police and declared a provisional government in opposition to the feds—a tactic some westerners might appreciate today—voicing a long list of grievances against Ottawa. Four days later, Riel's small band of militia had been crushed, though Riel himself escaped. He eventually turned himself in, was taken to Regina, tried, convicted of treason and "hanged by the neck until dead." He died a hero not only to the Metis, but to white homesteaders scattered across the plains.

There were no battles or public hangings scheduled on the day of our visit, despite a long list of grievances that still exist between Ottawa and the West. Instead, there was a bridal show, and Renee was one of forty women modelling wedding gowns dating from the late nineteenth century. The gown she wore was the same one her grandmother had worn at her wedding in 1937.

After what seemed like an eternity of primping, the brides were called out one after another in front of an old church, passing under a decorative arch before strolling along a sidewalk in front of the large crowd. When I saw Renee, I just about fell over. She looked absolutely stunning—and I swear her mother was giving me a gentle telepathic nudge from behind.

At the close of the ceremonies, all brides were presented with a single long-stemmed rose, which they cradled in arms of satin for the requisite photographs. True to form, Renee took great pleasure introducing me as "the hitchhiking photographer" she had picked up. One older lady gave me a suspicious sidelong glance, then turned back to Renee. "You've got to be more careful dear," the old lady counselled. "Haven't you seen *The Bridges of Madison County?*"

After dinner, Renee and I ignored the old lady's advice and drove back to Batoche to photograph the sunset near the old church. Rustling through knee-high wheatgrass, we talked, laughed and held hands as we watched the evening light play across the Saskatchewan River valley. When we returned to the farm after dark, everybody was in bed, so we poured some iced tea and sat on a pair of wooden stools to continue our friendly chatter. About two dozen bobby pins were still in Renee's hair from the bridal show, and I watched as she reached back to fiddle uncomfortably with them. I took my cue and slid around behind her, gently brushing her cheek with the back of my hand. One by one, I pulled the bobby pins out, letting them rattle softly as I dropped them on the counter. Renee's hair smelled of honey and I ran my fingers through it several times to straighten the tangles.

Neither of us said a word, happily drunk on silence. I pressed my cheek against hers, then moved to the back of her head and softly kissed it. For a few lingering moments, my hands caressed her shoulders, running down the length of her arms, then back up to the nape of her neck. Finally, I returned to my seat beside her.

"Thank you," Renee said. I could see her green eyes glowing in the dim light. She walked over and flicked the light switch, and suddenly, everything was dark. The only visible light seeped in through the front window from the farmyard lamp, and for a long time we stood close to one another, saying nothing, our fingers alternately entwined or gently stroking one another. "You're leaving soon," she said finally.

"I know."

"Will you write?"

"Of course," I said. "As long as you write back."

She laughed. "It's been great getting to know you." It was almost posed as a question, as though she were waiting for confirmation that it had been the same for me.

"Likewise," I replied. "Let's not be strangers, okay?"

I kissed the top of her head one last time, then turned and walked up the spiral staircase to the guest bedroom, watching her disappear into the shadows. Then I pulled the covers back, crawled into bed and lay there for a very long time, staring at the ceiling. How easily white picket fence disease creeps up on the weak-minded.

Chapter 27

This Ain't no Prairie Hick Town

July 6, 1999 - Highway 3 near Hudson Bay, Saskatchewan

"Those are the Porcupine Hills," chimed Valerie, pointing past the windshield of her minivan. At first I couldn't see anything—then faintly, in the distance, I picked out a blue-green smudge on the horizon. We were nearing the Manitoba border.

"They're not very high," I commented. "They don't even look as high as the Cypress Hills in southern Saskatchewan."

"The Duck Mountains to the south are higher," Val offered hopefully.

Mountains in Manitoba? It sounded like an oxymoron. Perhaps I was turning into a mountain snob, but to me the Duck Mountains sounded like some sort of gaffe made by a prairie geographer, perpetrated on a whim after drinking too much Ukrainian vodka. Manitoba might have a few hills, but the very notion that mountains exist anywhere between the Rockies and Quebec's Laurentians sounded like false advertising.

Of course, every province is guilty of geographical fraudulence to some degree. With so much geography to identify, I guess a little creative license has to be expected from time to time. I've heard ads gushing over a few hundred vertical feet of terrifying ski terrain in southern Ontario—typically anthills with ski lifts, at least when compared to the Whistlers and Blackcombs of our country. And I've seen Albertans go wild over swimming holes and a piece of muddy shoreline along the Red Deer, a river shared by hundreds of grazing cattle. But then, we all have to do the best we can. Alberta has no ocean, nor even a semi-great lake for that matter. So if Manitoba wants mountains that badly, I suppose she can have them.

The previous evening, Renee and I had said our heartfelt goodbyes. Then she had loaded her truck and disappeared down the lane on her way to an English-as-a-Second-Language course in Saskatoon. She planned to upgrade her skills so that she could teach overseas again. The next morning, I left with her mother Valerie to deliver bison meat on our way to Manitoba, where Val planned to spend a few days visiting her parents in Swan River. Driving together had given us the opportunity to chat about everything from farming to religion to politics.

We talked so much that it wasn't until we had passed the small town of Hudson Bay that I realized the scenery had changed. Gone were the livestock paddocks, the fertile black soil belt; gone were the fields of wheat, barley and lemon-coloured canola. It had all disappeared, replaced by a few bee farms and bush country that had never tasted a plow. This was the edge of the great Canadian Shield, that rugged landscape of trees, rivers, lakes and metamorphic rock that covers fully half of Canada. On the first summer of my journey, I had seen the northern edge of the shield rising up from Great Slave Lake near Yellowknife, but that was only the tiniest fraction of it. The shield also dominates northern Saskatchewan, most of Manitoba and almost all of Ontario and Quebec. For the next few days I planned to skirt along the edge of rock and prairie, following highways south until I reached civilization again.

It was time to go to Winnipeg.

July 12, 1999 - Winnipeg, Manitoba

A week later I coasted into The Peg, transportation hub and the largest city in central Canada. Roughly a month had passed since I had left Calgary, the only centre of comparable size I had seen for some time. Thus, walking through Winnipeg among sirens, blasting car horns and throngs of summer pedestrians was initially a shock. I had experienced this feeling before—an initial sensation of disconnect upon entering a big city—and in fact, it was a feeling that would repeat itself in large urban centres across the country. With the bustle of large cities came a dollop of sensory overload—but cities also meant hot showers, laundry facilities and the opportunity to park my piano in a corner for several days. And who could complain about that?

I didn't have to worry about finding a place to stay in Winnipeg either; most of my mother's relatives—a potpourri of uncles, aunts and cousins— had been living there for decades, and were more than happy to put me up for a few nights. I stayed with my cousin Bonnie, her husband Rex and their two-year-old son Zachary in a house under the shade of giant elm trees, just off Portage Avenue. "You couldn't have arrived at a better time,"

Rex told me when he picked me up downtown. "The city is in the middle of its annual Folklorama festival."

Now when most Canadians think of Winnipeg, perhaps a couple of things come leaping to mind. First of all, most Canadians know that Winnipeg is not a place for a beach vacation in January. This is obvious if one considers the phrase "Portage and Main"—Canada's coldest and windiest intersection—and how the mere mention of it has struck terror into the hearts of pedestrians for decades. This intersection symbolizes the ruggedness that is Canadian winter. It is a landmark that typifies the myth of resilience exuded by Canadians, but particularly Manitobans. Mind you, could we expect anything less from a province of French Canadians and Ukrainians, a province that is home to the largest population of Icelandic people outside of Iceland—not to mention a capital city that has been lovingly dubbed "Winterpeg"?

I suspect that many Canadians also envision a certain type of culture (or perhaps a lack thereof) when they think of Winnipeg. Is it not widely known that Winnipeg's fall fashion consists of four different patterns of camouflage pants, modelled by gun-toting, ball-scratching guys named Butch and Cody? I had already psyched myself up for farm supply stores, bait-and-tackle shops and redneck arm-wrestling tournaments ... not ballets, symphonies and multicultural festivals. It is possible, of course, that other Canadians are better informed than I am, but I can only relate what I had envisioned for myself. Really, this is just a roundabout way of explaining that Winnipeg surprised me. The Folklorama festival, the Winnipeg ballet and the Winnipeg symphony orchestra—all of which are renowned internationally—served to remind me that one should never pass judgement on places one knows little about.

Folklorama was a good example of how far my expectations had been from the reality. Before I arrived, I had no idea that it's the largest and longest-running multicultural festival of its kind in the world. For two weeks every summer, Winnipeg comes alive as various groups proudly flaunt their ethnic colours. There are typically more than forty ethnic pavilions, each with a different theme. It's a mini-Expo of sorts. At the beginning of the two-week event, festivalgoers can buy a passport that allows them to travel through a different country every evening; at many of these pavilions, there are people who barely speak a word of English.

Flipping through a copy of the festival guide, I quickly realized how many options there were and how impossible it would be to see it all.

In India, I could get a henna tattoo and learn meditation techniques (useful for a hitchhiker); in Haiti, watch fire-eating contests and limbo to the beat of steel drums (sexy); in Spain, do the Gypsy *rumba* with flamenco dancers (hip); and in Greece, take Greek language lessons and watch *kefi* dancers (intellectual). Less appealing to me were pavilions from East Asia. According to the guide, I could receive acupuncture while visiting China (hah!) or volunteer at a Japanese martial arts demonstration (yeah, right!). And the Korean pavilion sounded downright fishy. "Visit a *sarang bang*," it said—something that sounded like a skimpy piece of underwear, but is apparently a traditional Korean family room. And did I really want to sample Korean food like *kim chee, yak gua* or *man doo?*

Quite honestly, most of the cuisine looked tantalizing—a multicultural buffet of epic proportions. There were Hungarian *langos* (deep-fried sweet bread), *sopas para guaya* (cornbread with cheese and onion) from Paraguay, *tandoori* chicken from India, African *samosas*, and best of all, *casteleyn*, a type of rich Belgian chocolate. It was even heartening to know—if I were prone to excessive drinking, which I'm not—that I could get drunk in forty different countries, all within the same city. I loved the sound of *Slijivovica* (Croatian plum brandy) and *Borgona* (sweet strawberry wine from Chile), not to mention Zorba's Kiss from Greece, which I was certain had something to do with a naughty blonde goddess with a mermaid's tail. I might have even tried slowly dulling my senses on *sabra*, chocolate and orange liqueurs from Israel.

But none of this was to be. On my first night at Folklorama, I rendezvoused with a few family members to watch my uncle Dave's brass band perform with a bunch of beer-swilling *Herrs* and fleet-footed *Fraus* in the Rhineland of Germany. We gorged ourselves on Oktoberfest sausage, *sauerbraten* and *schnitzel* while young German dancers yelped and stomped their feet to a blitzkrieg of fiery polka numbers. Throughout the evening, a pair of wandering yodellers routinely appeared with backpacks, walking sticks, Bavarian felt hats and suspenders. They hoisted large mugs of dark ale into the air and shouted "Ouy! Ouy! Ouy!" encouraging the crowd to follow suit.

At one point, Rex leaned toward me with a thoughtful insight. "You know," he chuckled, "the German pavilion sits beside the Polish pavilion, which sits beside a Jewish Credit Union. It's nice to know that everyone gets along in multicultural Winnipeg."

After dark, we stopped at the Irish pavilion where we watched a group of young women dancing in the fashion of Riverdance, wearing muffin hats and aprons. Not long after, a three-man band took to the stage and soon had the audience singing along, clapping and making the requisite gestures for the Unicorn song. Yet it was the banter between the singer and the guitarist that proved most comical.

"I've got a terrible confession to make," the singer said at one point, quite apologetically. "Our guitarist is actually half Irish and half Scottish." He nodded his head, drawled "Oh yessss!" and waited for his comment to sink in. "That makes this a perfect gig," he continued, "because he loves to drink but he hates to pay for it." The guitarist cheered happily, raising his mug of beer high in the air.

For more than an hour we sat back and listened to this banter, toasting the lead singer's comments whenever he encouraged us to do so. He obviously wore the pants in that relationship. The evening eventually drew to a close, and to my delight, it did so in a way that quite summed up Winnipeg, Folklorama and a different version of Canadian patriotism that well suited our surroundings.

"This song is our way of saying thanks to everyone who makes Canada the greatest country in the world to live in!" shouted the singer. The audience roared, whistled and thudded the tables with their hands.

"It's a little piece written by Oscar Brand of Winnipeg," added the guitarist.

"It's called *Something to Sing About!*"

The guitarist gingerly strummed a few chords, then continued: "If we had it our way, this would be Canada's national anthem."

The chorus went something like this:

From Vancouver Island to the Alberta Highlands,
'Cross the prairies and lakes to Ontario's towers;
From the sound of Mount Royal's chimes, out to the Maritimes,
Something to sing about, this land of ours

Perhaps the song *should* be Canada's national anthem, for there were few occasions during my travels that I felt happier to be a part of it all.

Chapter 28

Lake of the Stars

July 21, 1999 - Kenora, Ontario

Dawn's first rays had just started filtering through the tiny cube-like window beside my bed when the morning's calm was violently—and with great fanfare—cut in half. Down a narrow hallway I heard the *thud, thud, thud* of heavy work boots echoing on floorboards, the stretching of springs on a hinged door, a crash as the door bounced back and hit the doorjamb, and finally, a peppering of swear words delivered with the vigour of Shakespearean poetry into the sticky morning air. A few seconds later, a buzz saw screamed to life outside the window. Welcome to northern Ontario, I thought to myself, land of opportunity and promise.

For the last three nights I had been crashing in a portable trailer near Kenora, a small cottage town nestled against the granite shores of Ontario's Lake of the Woods. My accommodation was compliments of a bushy-haired, middle-aged guy named Dean who had picked me up outside Winnipeg a few days earlier. The trailer sat beside his warehouse, where he manufactured everything from marble sinks and countertops to small fibreglass fishing dories and canoes.

It should be noted that Kenora was the perfect place to meet a canoe builder. The town lies on an old Canadian fur-trade route once used by the voyageurs and independent traders known as the *coureurs de bois*, all of whom plied the waterways of New France using birchbark canoes. Pierre Gaultier de La Vérendyre was first ordered by the French monarchy to explore the area to the west of the Great Lakes in 1731, and it wasn't long before thousands of beaver, fox, mink and muskrat pelts were being shipped from across Rupert's Land through Kenora, then down the Rainy River system to Montreal. During the late 1700s and early 1800s, the rival Hudson's Bay Company and North West Company battled for control of this key route.

Kenora was also the location of one of Canada's most bizarre border disputes. In 1870, when the town was known as Rat Portage, both Ontario and Manitoba claimed the outpost as part of their territory. Both provinces had jails in Rat Portage—on opposite sides of the same street—and both provinces issued mining claims and timber licenses for the same land. Confusion ensued, including a number of cases where prominent men from both sides were arrested and jailed for "liquor offenses" in the opposing province, only to be released by friends from the opposite side of the street. Manitoba even went so far as to incorporate the town in 1882, but had to give it back two years later when the Privy Council in London awarded Rat Portage to Ontario.

"This is cottage country now," Dean had told me, romanticizing a local lifestyle that revolves around outdoor pursuits such as fishing derbies, waterskiing, houseboating and Sea-Dooing. Apparently, the town hosts a fishing derby every summer with a grand prize of $100,000—one of several high-profile events designed to lure bigwigs from across southern Ontario and the United States. Typically, these bigwigs arrive in northern Ontario, buy property and build "rustic summer homes" somewhere among the labyrinth of fifteen thousand islands on Lake of the Woods.

When I arrived in Kenora with Dean, he had invited me to crash in his trailer for a couple of days while I explored the town. The cubbyhole-sized room was certainly big enough for me, but I hadn't expected Dean's employees to start work at the ungodly hour of six every morning. Normally this wouldn't have bothered me, but for the terrible grip of heat holding sway over Ontario. Extreme temperatures are not uncommon in southern Ontario, but even the cool northern forests around Kenora were topping 35 degrees most days, accompanied by humidity that would have killed a camel. It was bad enough to melt during the afternoon, but lingering heat that lasted through the night was a complete shock to my system. I had grown accustomed to dry prairie heat, Arctic breezes and the icy breath of mountain winds blowing off glaciers. At night I slept fitfully, if at all, sometimes for no more than two or three hours. It was a horrible, permanently debilitating condition of excessive perspiration that I dubbed *sticky squaloritis.*

Regardless, during the day I walked around Kenora, exploring the last vestiges of an industry town trying desperately to transition into a resort community. I walked past dirty brick buildings stacked between sidewalks of cracked concrete, wondering if such a transition was possible—only to arrive at the waterfront and find a town bustling with new wealth. Perhaps it is this strange duality, or maybe just a quirk of edging onto Lake of the

Woods that has resulted in Kenora's twisted network of roads etched along a convoluted shoreline. Whatever the case, I found that it was much easier to get lost here than it should be in a town of ten thousand people.

"I'm looking for the Bank of Montreal," I explained to a cashier while standing in line to buy some groceries. "Somebody told me that there's one in town, but I can't seem to find it." The cashier started to explain in all-too-complicated fashion how to get there—an explanation that surely would have gotten me lost again—when a friendly woman standing behind me intervened. She was shopping with a younger woman, a tall, attractive blonde who looked to be about my age.

As it turned out, giving directions was easier said than done. After five minutes of trying to explain the most direct route, I was still lost. "Come with us," the younger woman finally said. "It'll be faster if we just drive you there."

And it was. What would have surely taken me half an hour to find on foot took less than five minutes in their car. Not only did it save me time, on the way the younger woman introduced herself as Kelly and explained that she worked for Kenora's local newspaper, the *Daily Miner.* "You should come by and talk to one of our reporters," she told me after I had shared a few stories about my hitchhiking trip.

"Do you think so?"

"I don't see why not," she replied. "You've got an interesting story. We could probably use it for one of our weekend editions."

For the last few months, I had been writing a regular column about my trip for *Photo Life* magazine, and had even been interviewed for CBC radio after meeting a reporter in Prince Rupert during my first summer. Seeking out media coverage on a consistent basis, however, had never been my first priority, probably because it seemed to go against the spirit of spontaneity that is so integral to hitchhiking. Still, it would be a great way to see my scruffy mug in print before my book was published. "Sure, why not," I said. "I'll come by tomorrow."

"Oh, and my team is playing beach volleyball at the beer gardens tonight," Kelly added as I climbed from the car. "Would you like to join us?"

"Sure, I'd love to," I said, surprised and delighted. What a perfect way to spend an evening in cottage country! "How do I get to the beer gardens?"

She started to explain, then thought better of it. "Why don't I pick you up here at five?"

"That sounds great."

In the end, it was Kelly's friend Violet who drove me to the beer gardens, where it quickly became evident that volleyball was a mere cover for the real competition: beer drinking. These gatherings kept priorities straight. Competitors formed loosely knit groups of perfectly tanned twentysomethings who looked like they had stepped out of a *Friends* episode, and most seemed interested in socializing more than in playing ball. When teams weren't playing, they crowded under the shaded patio, talking loudly and hoping the next game would never come.

Actually, I would be lying to say that playing wasn't also fun. We lost our first game, our second game ended in a draw, and by then it was too dark to see the volleyball streaking through the air. So with handshakes and promises to meet again the following week, everybody dispersed.

At that point I was faced with a choice. I was just about to start walking back toward Dean's trailer when Kelly and Violet invited me to join them for a swim in Rabbit Lake, one of many prime swimming holes near Kenora.

It was not a difficult decision to make.

"Do you know that Kurt Russell and Goldie Hawn own cottages on Lake of the Woods?" Violet asked me, slipping into the cool, dark water. The only light still visible was a faint band of tangerine lingering to the west.

I stripped down to my boxers and took a running leap off the dock. The water felt unbearably soothing, and only then did I realize what I had been missing. "I've heard rumours that several celebrities own vacation homes up here."

"More than a few," corrected Kelly. "This place is a magnet for the rich and famous."

John Wayne, Arnold Schwarzenegger, Teemu Selanne ... some of it was probably hearsay, but almost everybody I met in Kenora had a story about a famous actor with property on Lake of the Woods, a sports figure they saw buying fishing tackle, or some multi-millionaire they heard about who owned a cottage with a helipad on the roof. One US billionaire had reputedly built a six-boat garage attached to a cottage the size of Buckingham Palace—and visited but once every summer.

As the last vestiges of light faded from the sky, I treaded water and wondered how the world's most famous action hero fares in this town. Turning to Kelly and Violet, I asked, "Do you think Arnold Schwarzenegger gets lost in Kenora?"

July 23, 1999 - Dryden, Ontario

The highways in northern Ontario have always had a bad reputation among hitchhikers. And as I stood in Dryden with dozens of cars whizzing past me, I finally understood why. Despite the perpetual flow of traffic, I spent three hours standing there choking on exhaust fumes before a weathered grey van eased onto the road shoulder and coasted to a stop a few metres in front of me. The driver had obviously recognized me as a hitchhiker long before passing. Through the windshield, I could see a bare-chested man with nut-brown skin and a baseball cap.

"*Parlez-vous Français?*" he asked when I walked up to the driver's window. He had the wild hair and slightly insane look of a man who has a secret fetish for sticking cutlery into electrical sockets.

"No, I speak English."

He gestured toward the back of the van, where I could see two hitchhikers already sitting. "I'm taking these guys as far as Thunder Bay, and if you give me ten bucks for gas I'll do the same for you." My first instinct was to decline his offer, but after we chatted for another minute I decided that he was kind of interesting. So I accepted his invitation, retrieved my backpack and shoved it through the side door behind the other two passengers.

The driver's name was Joel, and he was on his way from Vancouver to visit his parents in Timmins, Ontario. The two hitchhikers he had already picked up were from Quebec, returning from a summer of picking fruit in the Okanagan valley. There was an academic-looking fellow with short hair and glasses named Yannick, and a wiry guy named Pierre who was shirtless and wearing army surplus pants. Pierre also sported a barbed-wire tattoo around his right arm, in which he was cradling a small orange kitten. "I really like your cat," I said, reaching over to rub it under the chin. The kitten purred, but Pierre just stared at me blankly, not saying a word.

"He doesn't speak English," said Joel.

I looked over at Yannick. "Do you speak English?"

"A little bit," he said. "Where are you going from?"

"I'm from Calgary."

"Ahhhh ... Calgary!" said Yannick. "I like people in Calgary. People are very gentleman." He explained that he had just visited a friend there.

Although nothing was said about it, I sensed that Joel and the two Quebecers had been engaged in a fairly heated discussion before he had stopped to pick me up. A sort of nervous energy was hanging in the air. As it turned out, Joel was perfectly bilingual, and he eventually explained that when the topic of Quebec's possible separation from Canada had come up, the conversation had quickly degenerated into mudslinging. And now that there was fresh blood in the van, the argument threatened to boil over again. "I've almost left these guys at the side of the road a couple of times," laughed Joel. "The discussion got pretty intense." Then more seriously: "It just hurts so much to have Quebec want to leave this beautiful country. I grew up in Timmins, and the French culture is very much a part of my own identity."

"Why can't there be both?" said Yannick, trying to be diplomatic.

"What do you mean?" I asked.

In scattershot English he explained how he wanted a sovereign Quebec, but one that was closely linked to Canada's economy.

"Aren't you afraid you're going to lose those choices if you leave Canada?" I asked. "A lot of Canadians think separation should be all or none." Yannick nodded, and I continued, "But what if you could protect French culture within Canada? Don't you think Quebec could have it all?"

"It's impossible to explain in English," he finally said, a response that sounded rehearsed for his trip to western Canada. "I'm so vast because I'm Canadian. For now Québec is part of Canada, but in my heart I am a Québecer first and a Canadian second."

We carried on in broken circles like this for quite some time, Joel translating from the Quebecers to me and back again. A couple of times, Joel exploded in a tirade of French, obviously frustrated, and eventually we all grew tired of talking about a subject for which no resolution existed. "Before you got into the van," said Joel, "we had already agreed not to talk about three things: religion, politics and what kind of Kellogg's you eat in the morning."

So it was that we continued driving in silence, through an endless ocean of trees and rocks passing into shadow, twilight christening the rearview mirror. Joel found an oldies station on the AM dial, which he hoped would keep him awake and alert. "With all the moose crossing the highway, one distraction can mean disaster," he told me bluntly. By the time we had reached the junction of Highway 11 at Shabaqua, Joel could drive no further. We were still forty-five minutes from Thunder Bay, but it was past one in the morning and he desperately needed some sleep. So he pulled the van into a gravel clearing where Yannick and I could set up our tents. Joel bunked down inside the van while Pierre opened a tin of cat food, then lay contentedly on the ground with nothing more than a small blanket and his cat curled up on his belly.

Morning arrived early, and with no shade anywhere in sight, it wasn't long before the sun had chased us from our sleeping bags. We arrived in Thunder Bay about an hour later, and the first thing we saw as we coasted into town was a towering wall of decrepit-looking grain elevators rising above Lake Superior like a lost city of ruins. In the distance was the Sleeping Giant, a cliff formation that vaguely resembles a man sleeping on his back. "Just drop me at the nearest pay phone," I told Joel. Before continuing east, I needed to fix one of my backpack's shoulder straps, which had slowly been tearing loose for the last couple of weeks.

To my delight, when Joel stopped to drop me in town, Yannick offered me a warm handshake. "Good travels in Québec," he said. Even though we disagreed on political issues, it was nice to know we could part as friends.

As I flipped through a Thunder Bay phone book ten minutes later, I was also delighted to find a seamstress located only a few blocks from where Joel had dropped me. I walked over and found a plucky little woman named Pirkko standing behind the counter. She looked to be in her mid-fifties and had a thick accent that I couldn't quite place. "Where are you from?" I asked, unloading my backpack and spilling an assortment of stale oatmeal packets, camp fuel and sand-covered clothes onto her clean floor.

"I'm from Finland," she said. "Don't you know there are fifteen thousand Finnish immigrants living in Thunder Bay?" I did not, but she carried on to tell me about the Hoito restaurant (which serves traditional Finnish food), the Kangas Finn sauna and Bay street, a district in downtown Thunder Bay where you can still hear old-timers speaking the mother tongue.

"By the way, did you hear that Mel Gibson and his family are in town with their yacht?" she chirped, changing the subject to a more important topic. "One of my friends was hired to do his laundry, but she didn't find out whose clothes they were until later." Pirkko stood behind the counter, a dreamy look in her eyes. "I was so jealous," she giggled. "What I wouldn't give to wash Mel Gibson's underwear."

Chapter 29

Road Apples

I WANT TO tell you a story about hitchhiking across northern Ontario. I heard it from a fellow named Jimmy Robbins, a veteran traveller I met in the Yukon during the summer of 1998. During his early twenties, Jimmy was a student at Ontario's Lakehead University, so he used to thumb his way between school in Thunder Bay and his parents' home in Newfoundland, even during the winter months. At Christmastime, he would make the trip to save money for presents, traversing five provinces and more than four thousand kilometres of frozen bitumen with little more than pocket change. In 1998, he even thumbed his way back through the ice storm that had ravaged much of New Brunswick, Quebec and eastern Ontario, getting picked up and invited into the homes of strangers who had been living without electricity for days.

Ice storms aside, traversing northern Ontario was typically the most difficult leg of Jimmy's trip. That's because there are only two roads that cross this part of the province, and both of them are equally surly. There is the Trans-Canada Highway, a flagellating rollercoaster that runs wildly over granite hills and along the ragged crest of the Great Lakes; or there is Highway 11, a flat and desolate road slashing north through vast, empty tracts of boreal forest. Experience quickly taught Jimmy that Highway 11 was his best bet, primarily because truckers prefer this route for its light traffic and lack of icy hills. With this in mind, he developed a plan to cope with the often sub-zero temperatures. Rather than stand at the side of the road turning blue and hypothermic, Jimmy would sit inside a truck stop at the Nipigon highway junction, drinking coffee and waiting for somebody to offer him a ride.

That was how, one bitterly cold December afternoon, he met a trucker named Percy. When Percy saw the lonely hitchhiker sitting at a table drinking coffee, he mumbled gruffly at him and motioned for Jimmy to grab his backpack and hop on board. Jimmy couldn't have been more relieved. It was -35 degrees Celsius outside, and he had already been waiting for several hours. His cheer soon faded, however, when down the road the effects of excessive coffee-drinking started building an undeniable and increasingly urgent pressure in his bladder.

"I'm sorry to tell you this," Jimmy admitted sheepishly. "But I've really gotta go to the bathroom. Can you pull the truck over?"

Percy gave him a perturbed look, mumbled something about ice on the road, and told Jimmy that he would have to wait until Longlac.

How far they were from Longlac, Jimmy couldn't remember, but after another few minutes he realized that it was further than he could wait. "Look man," he finally said, desperation creeping into his voice. "I know it was really irresponsible of me to drink so much coffee back there, but the facts are, I GOTTA GO!"

"We can't stop 'til Longlac," Percy said flatly.

Jimmy could hardly believe his ears. But what was he going to do?

So it was that another ten minutes of the most unspeakable agony passed, every jarring bump on the road forcing Jimmy closer to the edge. It wasn't long before he had reached the point of no return. "Listen man," he finally pleaded. "I can't hold it any longer! Either you stop the truck or it's going on the floor!"

Percy looked at him coolly—not a wrinkle on his poker face—then repeated his mantra one last time. "I'm not stopping 'til Longlac, kid. If you've gotta go that badly, here's what you've gotta do."

A minute later, Jimmy opened his door, wrapped one arm around the truck's running bar and stepped precariously onto a six-inch steel grate. Blasting along at 120 kilometres per hour in the middle of a northern Ontario deep-freeze, he gingerly unzipped his fly, pulled out his equipment and aimed for the ditch. When he clambered back into the truck a couple of minutes later—red-faced and shivering, ice crystals hanging from his hair—he found Percy doubled over laughing. "You know, I've told a hundred hitchhikers to do that," Percy wheezed, trying desperately to catch his breath. "But you're the first guy who's actually ever done it."

July 26, 1999 - Thunder Bay, Ontario

On the afternoon I hitchhiked out of Thunder Bay, Jimmy's story sounded like a sweet wish. The asphalt steamed like a skillet as I sat on my backpack half-heartedly thumbing, penning a few notes in my journal and irritably pulling at a T-shirt that was clinging to me like a damp rag. At least the scenery on the road ahead promised to improve. Unlike the previous six hundred kilometres—where there had been little to see but trees, rocks and the occasional marsh hedging in against the highway's steel guardrails—the road from Thunder Bay to Sault Ste. Marie has some personality. No longer would I suffer the monotony of charmless mining and pulp mill towns belching fumes into the sticky air. Rather, I would be treated to towering mesas, green mountains and jaw-dropping views of Lake Superior ... interspersed with charmless mining and pulp mill towns belching fumes into the sticky air.

Many drivers curse the Trans-Canada through northern Ontario for its lack of scenic variety, much as they do the prairies. That is, until they catch their first glimpse of Superior. The northern Ontario section may be the most desolate and unpopulated section of our national highway, passing through a hinterland that is only surpassed by the roads of our far northern territories, but seeing Superior's vast silvery calm has an effect that seems to transcend the surrounding emptiness.

As I would later learn, of course, Superior is not always flowers and fairy dust. In size and in depth she has no equal, and so massive is she that you could pour Huron, Michigan, Erie and Ontario into her gut and still have room for three more Eries. She is "masculine and remorseless," as Pierre Berton notes in his book *The Great Lakes*, and, not infrequently, can produce storms that whip swells to the height of nine-storey buildings, raking spray across the tallest trees that cling desperately to the shoreline.

In the gloomy depths of these five lakes are the bones of an astonishing 10,000 shipwrecks, a good many of which have gone down on Superior. Over a single decade, from 1863 to 1873, nearly 1,200 sailors were lost on the Great Lakes, even as millions of dollars worth of valuables sank into the depths, never to be seen again. Berton hypothesizes that 800 million dollars' worth of salvageable goods lie untouched at the bottom of these lakes. In particular, Erie's shallow waters and shifting sandbars have swallowed many a king's ransom. A 6,500-square-kilometre quadrangle surrounding Long Point has swallowed nearly four times as many ships as the 28,000-square-kilometre Bermuda Triangle.

Advances in technology have prevented frequent sinkings in modern times, of course, but ships still sink occasionally. The most infamous modern disaster involved the 729-foot Edmund Fitzgerald, a goliath of a ship that was considered the largest and safest vessel operating on the Great Lakes when she was launched in 1958. She sank while travelling in the lee of Superior's north shore in 1975, during a terrible storm that swallowed her whole. Not a single crew member survived.

But enough about shipwrecks. As a hitchhiking landlubber, I had no plans to travel on the lakes, but rather along their stunning perimeter, and after nearly two hours of waiting in Thunder Bay I finally snagged a ride that took me all the way to a gas station in Nipigon. After getting dropped there, I figured that I might be in for another long wait, so I walked inside and bought a cold drink. That's when a truck driver, a short fellow with long hair and a Lanny MacDonald moustache, approached and asked where I was going.

"Is your name Percy?" I asked, cracking the tab on my can of Coke.

He gave me a sidelong glance. "My name is Dale. What does that have to do with anything?"

"Just curious."

Nevertheless, before climbing into Dale's rig, I paid a quick visit to the men's restroom just to be on the safe side. Trying to stem nature's tide while driving beside the world's largest body of fresh water would be something close to everlasting punishment. And to be quite honest, I think I would rather take my chances on a nineteenth-century schooner plying a dishevelled Superior than hanging from the running bar of a transport truck with my privates hanging out.

We were soon cruising east along the Trans-Canada, Dale shifting gears to either climb or descend the errant topography along Superior's north shore. For nearly two hundred kilometres between Nipigon and Marathon, the Trans-Canada rises and falls like a ribbon in the wind, the view from each subsequent hill crest more stunning only than the last. I had driven this road before, and what I remembered most was crawling like an ant over the tops of these ancient mountains, trying desperately not to swerve into oncoming traffic as fetching vistas sprawled before me. Now I was the passenger, and I could take full advantage of the view: shafts of gold and crimson streaming down through the clouds, silvery tentacles roaming between rocky islets. That evening, Superior seemed almost incapable of the mayhem that she has caused over the centuries.

"You should see this highway in October," Dale remarked. "When the lake starts cooling, the fog can get so thick it's like driving through whipping cream."

Not unlike Superior itself, the Trans-Canada through northern Ontario is no laughing matter. In fact, Dale claimed that it was one of the most dangerous highways in the country. "Believe you me, it was a bad-ass adventure when I first started driving it twenty years ago," he said. "Fortunately they've cut most of the corners out, widened the shoulders and added three lanes in a lot of places. Before the passing lanes were in, some people were taking foolish risks. They would pass around blind corners, pulling stupid stunts that caused a lot of accidents."

There are also plenty of wildlife encounters, inevitable when a road cuts through a sparsely-populated wilderness like northern Ontario. "Thick fog and thousand-pound moose don't really complement one another," Dale told me grimly. Having hit a moose just outside of Marathon a few years back, he could speak from experience. "One minute I was staring at the moose crossing the road; the next minute I was staring into the eyes of a paramedic. Those moose can sure put a dent in a guy's character. I quit trucking for five years after that."

Dale's story reminded me of an article I had read in a Kenora newspaper the previous week. Black flies had been driving moose onto the highway in droves, and over a single weekend there had been nine moose/car collisions between Kenora and Ignace. With the exception of Newfoundland, there are few places in Canada where moose and motorists battle for the roads as they do in northern Ontario.

Despite the risks, Dale loved seeing wildlife on his cross-country road trips. One of his most memorable encounters had happened during a trip through southern BC with his son. They were snoring soundly in the truck's sleeper when they were suddenly jolted awake, the cab rocking violently back and forth. Outside they found a black bear scratching his furry butt on the metal staircase. "We got a good laugh out of that one," chuckled Dale. "Most bears are nice from far, but far from nice."

Twilight was still lingering when Dale dropped me at a service centre just outside Marathon, which thankfully came equipped with a pizzeria for the road-weary and starving (moi). I ordered a ten-inch pizza, then found a pay phone so that I could call Renee. It had been three weeks since I left her parents' ranch in Saskatchewan, and I was starting to feel some pangs of loneliness—a sure sign that white picket fence disease was closing in again. Unfortunately, she wasn't home, so I left a message with her sister and dragged my sorry butt back to the restaurant, exhausted from hours of standing under the merciless sun in Thunder Bay that morning. I consoled myself with the pizza and a slice of apple pie, and sat there feeling sorry for myself.

The good news is that halfway through dinner I somehow talked my waitress, a shy French-Canadian girl named Natacha, into giving me a ride to Pukaskwa National Park the following day. She had come to Marathon from Montreal to spend time with her boyfriend (who worked for the Ontario Provincial Police) and she worked not only as a waitress, but as an interpreter at the national park. At closing time, she dropped me at a schoolyard in Marathon so that I could pitch my tent.

Natacha made good on her promise, picking me up at the schoolyard shortly after twelve. Less than an hour later, I was floating gleefully in Superior's cool, clear water near Hattie Cove, thumbing my nose at Ontario's oppressive heat wave. It was such an improvement from standing on steaming asphalt that I decided to stay for the night. I spent the next several hours swimming and lounging on a perfect swath of beach littered with driftwood, then walked inland late in the afternoon to find a peaceful stand of pine trees under which to pitch my tent.

I actually spent the next three days in Pukaskwa, on a hitchhiker's vacation of sorts. In the mornings, before the heat became too oppressive, I hiked along forested trails beside the White River; in the evenings, I sat on rocky cliffs watching the sun sink into Superior's spacious bosom. Mostly, though, I practiced doing battle with the heat. To accomplish this I would wade into the water and plop down onto the lake's sandy bottom, up to my neck in the world's largest bathtub. It was incredible! If only I could hitchhike while swimming, I thought, that would be the ultimate luxury.

I smiled at my daydream, then pushed it aside. That's when I realized with a certain degree of incredulity that stranger things have probably happened.

Chapter 30

Sailing Along

August 4, 1999 - Little Current, Ontario

"How's the water?" said a voice from out of nowhere. I looked up from my morning swim to see an elderly gentleman wearing a navy blue sailor's cap, leaning off the back of a yacht.

"Does 'tonic for the soul' mean anything to you?" I replied.

The man eyed me with amusement. "With this crazy heat wave, the water is exactly where everyone *should* be."

"I'll toast to that." I did a little backflip, circled and swam toward a ladder bolted to the waterfront pier. As I climbed out, I could see the man's gaze turn toward the North Channel, where a crush of sloops, schooners, powerboats and sailboats churned through the roiling blue. The drone of distant engines mingled with the snapping of spinnaker sails as muscular swells washed against concrete pilings. A group of school-aged kids stood on those pilings fishing for perch and rock bass, passing the long summer hours as they should be passed: outside. Mind you, this wasn't necessarily the healthiest thing for tourists. Some of the tykes were a tad wild with their casting, and more than once I saw them zing a fishhook past the ear of a startled pedestrian on the pier. It was a small miracle, really, that no blood had yet been shed.

This was my first day in Little Current—summer resort town, sailor's paradise and the largest village on Manitoulin Island. It is one of those idyllic places that surely act as a buffer zone between heaven and earth. The man seemed to be thinking the same thing, so I wandered over to continue our conversation.

"You've got a beautiful boat," I remarked, drying myself off with a dirty T-shirt and running a wrinkled palm along the back rail of his schooner. I was trying to sound like I knew more about sailing than jack squat, which can be difficult if, like me, you think a sailor yelling "PORT!" is asking for a stiff drink, or that "starboard" is NASA space-talk for a map used to pinpoint happenings in distant solar systems.

"She's been good to me," the man replied, patting his boat affectionately. "We're just on our way to Lake Superior for two weeks."

"Superior? You don't say. I was just in Pukaskwa a few days ago."

"No kidding. We're planning to sail right by there," he said. "How's the temperature? Superior is usually a lot colder than Georgian Bay."

"Great, compared to this heat. But what isn't?" That's when it dawned on me that this man and his boat would be passing a park where I had camped recently. Was my idea of thumbing a ride on a boat such a ludicrous idea after all? "Say," I asked, "what do you think the odds would be of hitching a ride on one of these sailboats? I mean, is it common for boaters to offer lifts to people between ports?"

"Not that I'm aware of," he replied. "I guess it would depend on where you're going and how big the boat is." It didn't sound promising. Nevertheless, for several minutes I grilled him about sailing etiquette, how best to approach a skipper and how far sailboats typically travel in a day, which, not surprisingly, depends on the make and model of the boat. The man told me that Tobermory, the nearest port on the south side of Georgian Bay (and a likely destination for a sailboat leaving Little Current) could generally be reached in a day or two. This would be perfect for me because I could then hitchhike down the Bruce Peninsula and into southern Ontario, a mere hop, skip and thumb from my next destination: Toronto.

"It can't be that hard to reach Tobermory," the sailor remarked as I gathered my belongings. "Why don't you tack a sign on the door at Wally's? That way you're not putting people on the spot." It sounded like good advice, so after thanking him, I stopped at the local boat supply store to do just that. With the dock attendant's permission, I taped a note to the front door that said something like this:

Alberta writer seeks passage to Tobermory in the next two or three days, preferably on a sailboat. Is not related to Preston Manning. Can cook and do dishes. Please leave a message with dock attendant.

With that finished, I tramped off to do some laundry, find a shower and dispose of any stray stubble. If I was to get a ride on one of these pristine cream-coloured yachts, the least I could do was look moderately presentable.

TO UNDERSTAND MANITOULIN, one must understand Ontario. More important, one must understand that Ontario is not what most Canadians think it is. It seems that when many Canadians think of Ontario, they tend to think of the southern part of the province and all that it stands for—bright lights, big city, yuppies, Bay Street, Liberal politicians. And some Canadians, particularly those living in western Canada, consider this version of Ontario to be the sole reason why Pepto-Bismol was created.

I bring this up only to draw attention to the peculiar line of demarcation that exists in Ontario like in no other province, handily separating north and south, running invisibly somewhere between Toronto and Thunder Bay. This line is difficult to pinpoint, of course, largely because it exists in people's imaginations, and imaginations tend to change with demographics. Nevertheless, it is safe to say that many Torontonians consider Barrie to be north, Perry Sound to be *really* far north, and Sudbury—well, Sudbury may as well be in the Arctic.

At least Torontonians are fairly consistent. As one moves north, definitions begin to blur. For example, on which side of the fence does Barrie fall? Is somebody from Sudbury a northerner or a southerner? Everywhere I went, I found that these distinctions were remarkably important to Ontarians. Not that people would fail to offer pleasantries should someone from the other side venture onto their turf—this is merely my way of pointing out that, contrary to popular belief, Ontario is far from unified. There are two very distinct cultures here that occasionally mix, but never blend. Depending on where you hail from, southerners are either modern, cultured urbanites or stuck-up yuppies. Northerners are either hardy, conservative pragmatists or gasoline-addicted backwoods bubbleheads. But that's what you get in a country the size of Canada. Geography is not static, but rather varies depending on who is observing it.

Knowing this, one begins to see that Manitoulin is both southern and northern in attitude—and that strangely, its northern half is generally more southern than its southern half. (And to think Ontarians find Quebecers irrational.) What I mean by this is that Manitoulin is more populated and developed on its northern half than on its southern half, and that, particularly during the summer months, it is invaded by a gaggle of southern Ontarians who attempt to mold it into an image after their own bustling, wealthy and flamboyant likeness. With the mass arrivals of wealthy city folks every June, money starts flowing through town and doesn't stop until the maple leaves start falling. Thus the northern half of Manitoulin takes on a southern persona during the summer, reverting back to its northern personality in the winter. The southern half of this northern island, not surprisingly, stays northern mostly all year round.

Regardless, everyone still votes Liberal.

I was in the midst of freshening my clothes at the local laundromat when such complicated musings were interrupted by an inquisitive woman in her fifties. After spotting my large backpack, she asked where I was travelling from.

"I'm from Calgary," I replied, then went on to tell her a bit about my hitchhiking journey and the book I planned to write. She and a friend of hers seemed intrigued and started asking the usual questions: "Is hitchhiking safe? Have you ever been robbed or raped? What's your favourite part of Canada?" But it was the reaction of a short, red-haired lady amidst the whirring and tumbling of clothes that rather caught me off guard.

"You're not that guy who writes for *Photo Life* magazine, are you?" she asked.

I was completely floored. "Uh, yeah ... actually, that is me." I'm not sure why it felt odd to have somebody recognize me, but it did.

"What a fantastic trip," she beamed. "I've been reading your column and imagining what it would be like to do what you're doing." She introduced herself as Sarah, and after chatting with me for perhaps fifteen minutes, she handed me her phone number and told me to call if I wanted to spend some time with her family at their cottage. "I'm not usually home during the evenings," she said, "but my husband Stephen and our children will be there."

I called the next day, after a tantalizing fisherman's platter of rainbow trout, whitefish and walleye at the Ship & Anchor Pub. An evening at a family cottage wasn't exactly the sailboat ride to Tobermory I had been hoping for (and I was quite in the mood to just sit in the restaurant, drink coffee and work on my journal), but for a number of reasons, Sarah's warm response to my project had, in turn, piqued my interest in her and her family. Even so, as I dialed the number, part of me expected to hear reticence or downright hostility in the voice of her husband if he were to answer. Even though Sarah had been reading about my travels in *Photo Life*, I suspected that Stephen might not be so enamoured with the prospect of inviting a celebrity hitchhiker into their home with two small children. Why should he be? I had never met the guy.

"Hello?" said a deep voice at the other end of the line.

"Hi, is this Stephen?" I asked.

"Yes."

"My name is Matt Jackson. I met your wife Sarah at the laundromat yester..."

"Yes, Matt," replied Stephen. "We've been hoping that you'd call. Would you like to come out here and stay with us?"

I could tell immediately that he was as enthusiastic and down-to-earth as Sarah. "Thanks," I said. "I would love to come out for a visit. I guess I just need some directions."

"It's a few kilometres out of town, so it'll be too far to walk," he said. "Why don't you call a taxi and I'll pay for it when you get out here."

That hardly seemed fair, but when I told Stephen that paying for my cab wouldn't be necessary, he insisted. So it was that fifteen minutes later, a taxi dropped me at the end of a long gravel laneway just off of Rocky Mountain Way. At the end of the lane was a cozy grey-shingled cottage hemmed in by stands of pine and cedar trees. There were magnificent views onto the North Channel, and beyond that, to the La Cloche Mountains. Before I could unload my backpack, a young, dark-haired man wearing leather sandals appeared from the cottage and handed the driver his fare. "You must be Matt," said Stephen, shaking my hand as though I were a long lost friend. "C'mon inside and I'll fix you something to drink."

After dumping my backpack at the door, Stephen introduced me to their children: a two-year-old boy named Kieran with fiery red hair just like his mom, and a seven-month-old baby girl named Bronwyn, still undecided about hair colour. Both were playing contentedly on the living room floor, in plain view of the steely grey waters of the North Channel heaving against their rocky beach.

Stephen and I were just starting to talk about travels—and about Stephen's time living in Calgary as a medical student—when a sharp rap sounded at the front door. It was two men he and Sarah had contracted to build a new home, arriving unannounced, eager to walk around the property with Stephen so that they could go over plans for the house. Stephen at first seemed torn, but when he came back into the living room and saw how well Kieran had taken to me, he asked if I would babysit for half an hour while he took the builders on a tour and answered some questions. "No problem," I said. "I like children. Go do your thing and I'll read Kieran a story."

The sun was dropping fast behind the distant hills when Sarah finally arrived home, shortly after Stephen and I had wrestled the kids into bed. "How did your night go?" Stephen asked Sarah, walking over and giving her a kiss.

"It was fine," she replied. "Everyone was really cooperative tonight." An avid photographer, Sarah had started arranging portrait sessions to provide an outlet for her creative energy, a side of herself that she had been developing ever since working at Outward Bound during her twenties. As a new mother with countless demands on her time, she found that photography helped to keep her sane.

"How about your night?" she asked Stephen.

"Great," he replied. "Matt saved the day when the builders arrived unexpectedly. He took care of the kids while I walked around with them."

Sarah looked at me, a bit shocked, then started laughing. "I'll bet you didn't expect your visit to involve babysitting two toddlers," she said.

"Canada's hitchhiking babysitter at your service," I replied. "And don't worry, I didn't read to your kids from any of my journals, so there's no need to worry about them hitchhiking home from playschool or anything."

"I'm glad to hear that," laughed Sarah.

The three of us grabbed drinks and settled down for the next couple of hours in lawn chairs stretched across their front patio, basking in the cool breeze blowing off the water. With a frosty Coke nestled in my hand, I felt more refreshed than I had in days—possibly weeks—and I could almost taste the spray as the surf flung itself a dozen feet in the air before turning turtle and rushing back into the lake.

"Our house is pretty exposed here," said Stephen, pouring himself a glass of dark ale. "That's one reason we want to build a new house a little further inland." Then he added, "You know, anybody who's tried to build a dock along this shoreline has seen it utterly destroyed."

"I guess these lakes are as hard on piers as they are on ships," I said.

Stephen nodded. "You learn to be pretty conservative when you make decisions, especially when you're out on a boat. I've been in some pretty crazy situations."

"Oh yeah? Like what?"

Stephen had a number of stories, but the story that stood out most involved both him and Sarah. On a dead calm evening, they had anchored in a shallow harbour with little protection from the elements. Without warning, a storm had crept in from nowhere, and for the next few hours their boat was tossed around like a cork, lightning bolts forking across the sky above the mast. After the telling, he turned to me with an expectant grin. "My friend Steve and I are sailing onto the North Channel tomorrow," he said. "There's plenty of room on the boat. If you want to try sailing so badly, why don't you come with us?"

"Really? I would love to!" I said, as though I hadn't heard a word about storms and waves and lightning. "Where are you going?"

"I think we're cruising up towards Killarney," he replied. "There's a long fjord east of here, along the north shore of Georgian Bay."

Anywhere on Georgian Bay's sparkling blue-green immensity would have appealed, but the country bordering Killarney was supposed to be some of the finest in Ontario: wispy pines dancing along a jagged shoreline, pink granite outcroppings, white quartzite mountains textured by rain and wind. By the time the three of us were ready for bed, Stephen and I had hatched our plan. If there was no boat waiting to take me to Tobermory the following morning, I would join him and his friend Steve for two days of Channel cruising. "You'll love it," Stephen chimed. "And it looks like we're going to have perfect weather."

Perfect weather, of course, can be a difficult thing to predict on the Great Lakes, as I learned first-hand later that night. Rather than have me wakened by crying toddlers, Stephen graciously pitched a tent in a small clearing beside their house. That way I could sleep outside and enjoy the fresh air whisking off the water. It was a fine idea, but at three in the morning I was suddenly and brutishly wakened by the sound of the sky falling down around my ears, and shortly thereafter, by a banshee wind that started shaking my tent like a South Carolina kitchen during hurricane season.

Before long, I realized with a detached sort of awe that this was no ordinary storm. It felt like the North Channel was preparing to surf inland, swallow my tent and disappear back into the lake, leaving no trace of me or my belongings. A few seconds later I heard a loud *snap!* as one of the tent poles broke, and the next thing I knew, I was fumbling through endless folds of wet nylon trying to find my glasses. Once I had found them, I jumped outside in my underwear and tried valiantly to re-erect the collapsed tent as the storm swirled around me.

That's when I saw Stephen running across the lawn, also in his underwear. "LET'S GET THIS THING IN THE GARAGE!" he yelled over the pitched wind as it tore past our ears. I followed his lead and in a matter of two minutes we had pulled all the pegs from the ground, folded the tent in two and dumped it inside the garage. We then retreated toward the cottage with singular purpose, my sleeping bag in tow and the rain biting at our heels. Not much was said when Sarah greeted us at the door with a pair of towels. We were still in something of a daze, and in the background we could hear a baby crying, no doubt wakened by the rattling of glass and shingles.

"Well, so much for perfect weather," Stephen said sardonically on his way up the stairs. "Let's hope for something better tomorrow."

August 6, 1999 - Little Current, Ontario

The next morning dawned blue and blustery, but other than the demise of Stephen and Sarah's tent, it appeared the worst of the storm had passed without causing too much damage. This was good news for us, and by late morning Stephen and I had rendezvoused with his friend Steve in Little Current. We bought groceries, did a routine maintenance check on his 24-foot sloop, then cast off our bowline (I've always wanted to say that). We left at noon, just in time to catch the opening of Manitoulin's bridge, and quickly slipped through the North Channel's bottleneck and onto the open, windswept expanse of Georgian Bay.

The open water—not to mention a stiff wind at our back—soon meant that it was time to raise the mainsail and jib, which Stephen did while Steve continued steering the boat due east. Before long, the waves had started heaving whitecaps across the water's surface, causing the boat to heel precariously over on its side. As the wind picked up, I noticed that Steve was taking increasingly fiendish pleasure in skipping the boat off the crests of oncoming waves—a little too much pleasure for my taste. Every couple of minutes the boat would launch itself off a wave crest, then toss restlessly to one side on its way down.

"Are these boats stable?" I finally asked, not wanting to sound like a total wimp. "I mean, how easy would it be to flip one of them?"

"Oh, it would take quite a lot to swamp this boat," replied Stephen. "And even if we were to tip sideways, it would eventually roll back up.

That's how these things are designed." I wasn't sure if that was good news, but I said thanks anyway and loosened my Vulcan death grip on the boat's chrome railing.

Within an hour I was feeling considerably more at ease, by this time accustomed to the boat's movements across the water, and even enjoying it. This was fortunate because several cups of morning coffee had by this time caught up with me, and I found myself leaning over the edge trying to pee as the boat pitched ruthlessly over the chop. When Stephen saw what I was trying to do, he chuckled and uttered a stiff warning: "Just so you know, the Coast Guard says ninety percent of men who drown in boating accidents have their flies undone." I thanked him for his advice, tightened my grip and finished with business. Needless to say, from that day on Jimmy Robbins' peeing adventure in northern Ontario seemed far less outrageous than it once had.

We dropped anchor off a small, rocky islet later that afternoon, not far from McGregor Point. We were in a perfectly sheltered bay in the middle of the long, narrow fjord called Baie Fine, and we practically had it to ourselves. On both sides we were hemmed in by outcroppings of white quartzite, ruffled green hills and rows of scented pine trees marching along the shoreline. The water had a brilliant aquamarine blush, and in a sheltered cove behind the island, its calm surface reflected the cobalt sky like a dewdrop. Even the small islet had a few token conifers, all of them erupting from the dome-shaped rock like something in a Group of Seven painting.

Before long, the three of us had slipped into our swimsuits and started flinging ourselves repeatedly off the back of the boat—an exercise that I won't describe further for fear of underrating the experience. "Now this is what I call hitchhiking," I enthused, climbing onto the chrome railing to prepare for another dive.

"And you didn't even have to stick your thumb out," said Steve. He was floating belly-up in the water a few metres away.

And that's pretty much how we passed the afternoon: basking in slothful exuberance and taunting the oppressive heat for its inability to affect us. Mostly we were content to swim in big, lazy circles off the stern, listening as Steve related stories of his childhood and how his family had travelled around the world for his father's job. He had lived in Peru for six years, Spain for two, Africa for four and on the Canary Islands for several months. "I've lived on Manitoulin for nine years now," he told us happily.

By this time, we were laying on sun-warmed rocks on the small islet. "It's the first time I've ever had a real hometown, and I love it!"

As the waning light of late afternoon fell upon us, Stephen fired up his barbecue and out came a stack of Polish pepper sausages, which slid down perfectly with ginger ale and a bottle of red wine. The sausages, like everything that day, were like a dream. The evening ended around a campfire on the small island, where we talked about everything from sailing to raising children to our good fortune at being born in Canada. We eventually let the embers die so that we could lie on our backs and gaze at the Milky Way, bright and sparkling and completely unaffected by the artificial glow of city lights. We tried to pick out constellations, but none of us were very good at it, so beyond the Big Dipper and Cassiopeia, we had to make up a few of our own. There was one we named the Big Donut because it kind of looked like, well, a big donut (dinner obviously hadn't been enough), and another that resembled the maple leaf on Canada's flag, which we craftily called the Big Leaf. There was also one grouping of stars that looked vaguely like Joe Clark doing yoga. We named this one Big Flipper.

As it turned out, getting back to the boat under the night's peaceful hush proved to be a more challenging affair than we would have liked. Imagine: all those grim tales about shipwrecks on the Great Lakes, and here we were, tested to the limit of our abilities by the simple matter of finding our way back to Stephen's boat—half-cut, wearing sandals and without a flashlight. Fortunately, despite some impressively steep slopes dropping down to the water's edge, we managed to reach the boat without breaking any limbs or skewering ourselves on any wayward pine branches. Our reward was falling asleep to the gentle rise and fall of Georgian Bay's star-specked surface.

Chapter 31

Bay Street Shuffle

August 24, 1999 - Orangeville, Ontario

Not unlike Rome at the height of the Roman Empire, all roads in southern Ontario eventually lead to Toronto. Indeed, when one studies a map of the south, it seems like some small engineering miracle how easily and freely these roads flow toward this urban behemoth. Of course anyone who has sat for hours in traffic—drumming restless fingers on their steering wheel, listening to bouncy, pre-teen girls on the radio, exchanging rude gestures with other drivers—might dispute this claim. What does seem clear (economically and culturally, at least) is that Hogtown is the centre of the known universe in Ontario. Some people like that fact, others don't.

Whatever the case, dozens (if not hundreds) of kilometres before reaching Toronto, a certain nervous energy starts to manifest. Speed picks up dramatically, every second car has a smug driver with a cell phone attached to his or her ear and, as you near the city centre, people start changing lanes as if they were self-appointed Mario Andretti stunt doubles. I've been told that even the Old Order Mennonites of Waterloo County—gracious, peace-loving people to the last—are affected by this "road rage" mentality, so close to Toronto's gravitational pull are they. This goes double on Sunday mornings when dozens of men, women and children dressed in the plainest black can be seen steering their horse-drawn buggies toward church, jostling for position along the roadsides. If you listen closely, you can sometimes hear bearded guys named Cleo and Amos exchanging words as they haul on their reins: "Cuttest thou me off, unholy cad?" or "Thou clod, place thy words up thy butter churn."

And so it was that I came to Toronto late in August, following country roads along the serpentine Niagara Escarpment from Tobermory, dipping into the fertile, misty croplands of Waterloo County and eventually back up to Highway 10 at a little town called Orangeville. Hitchhiking had not been nearly so hard in the south as I had imagined it would be, though considering the crush of traffic that grew in volume the closer I got to the city, perhaps I should have expected no less. It was a simple matter of doing the math: more cars meant more potential rides.

Despite all these potentials, the ride that stopped for me just south of Orangeville was the last ride I would have expected. In fact, when the Greyhound bus came swerving onto the road shoulder fifty metres from where I was standing, I figured that it had to be a mistake. An open door and a sharp *toot! toot!* on the horn suggested otherwise, so I hoisted my backpack onto a shoulder and hobbled toward the bus as fast as my legs would carry me. When I reached the door, I addressed the driver suspiciously: "You do realize that I'm hitchhiking, don't you?"

"Yes, I know," said the middle-aged driver. "But I've got plenty of room today, so hop on board."

There were only about eight passengers on the bus, and when I climbed inside, I saw that most of them were glaring at me. Still, it was hard to tell what, if anything, these people thought about the driver stopping for a hitchhiker. Were they angry I didn't have to pay a fare? Or were they worried I was going to hijack the bus and force the driver to go to Sudbury? I ignored their stares and dropped my pack across a pair of empty seats three rows from the front, directly behind a Mennonite gentleman with leathery skin and a long, dusky grey beard. He smiled at me from beneath his felt hat, and of all the passengers, seemed the least perturbed by the driver's unexpected prank. I slid into another pair of empty seats across the aisle so that I could talk to the driver.

"So where are you coming from?" I asked.

"Owen Sound," he replied, introducing himself as Jeff as he shifted up through the gears. "I drive this route about three times a week."

"I have to say, I'm a little surprised that you picked me up."

"Aww, I sometimes stop for hitchhikers if I have room," he told me. "Or I'll stop if I think they're in a poor location."

Jeff was a veteran "Hound driver" of thirteen years—though judging by his eagerness to talk, he was obviously a storyteller, too. His best story involved a girl he had met in Vancouver two decades earlier, then followed to Europe.

"She had a father in the bus and trucking industry," Jeff explained. "So that's how I ended up driving tour buses in Europe." It was also in Europe that he developed the rather peculiar habit of picking up hitchhikers while driving tourists on paid vacations. Cheerfully, he described how whenever he saw backpackers with Canadian flags stitched to their packs, he would pull over and let them on the bus. Like me, most of the travellers were at first disbelieving and suspicious. Yet they would often end up riding the bus for several days. "They would eat and stay at all the same places the tourists were staying," laughed Jeff, "and it was great for me because I had people to speak English with, rather than German or Italian."

The traffic had been picking up considerably ever since Orangeville, and as we neared Toronto's outskirts, traffic lanes doubled, then tripled and quadrupled as the smog grew thicker and greasier by the minute. On every side, slowly and in degrees, the urban tangle that is Toronto took shape. By the time we had hit the multi-lane super-freeways of the inner city, traffic pressed in at 130 km/hour around us ... and that was the bare minimum. Some vehicles blasted by us as though we were standing still, clocking what must have been 150 km/hour or more. Transport trucks, travelling in convoys of half a dozen, loomed like gigantic steel walls on wheels, blocking important signage and exits, road trains hammering along on multi-lane asphalt tracks.

Once we reached the Gardiner Expressway, I knew that we weren't far from downtown. We whizzed by Ontario Place (an amusement park and provincial exhibition ground), past row after row of flashing neon billboards and into plain view of Lake Ontario. Through the stifling smog I picked out the 553-metre CN Tower—arguably the world's largest knitting needle—rising above the Skydome and a cluster of less impressive skyscrapers that rose to its knees. "I was born right over there at St. James hospital," Jeff announced, pointing out the windshield at a diminutive building hiding in the shadows. "And to think all of this along the waterfront used to be industry." Then, as though an idea had just occurred to him, "Can you believe that until 1967 the Royal York Hotel was the tallest building in the city?"

Navigating through the congested streets, Jeff stopped first at the Royal York to let some passengers off, then continued through the mayhem of rush-hour traffic toward the main bus terminal. We passed Bay Street, where a mob of pedestrians in suits and ties hurried home with briefcases, or perhaps to another meeting. For a few moments I was lost in silent contemplation of the Bay Street shuffle. I wondered whether any of those people were classmates of mine from Wilfrid Laurier and tried desperately to conjure up images of working in one of the office buildings at the corner of King and Bay. I tried to imagine crunching numbers, buying and selling stocks, marketing products or writing memos. But I couldn't. I might as well have been living on another planet. Would it be different had I followed another road? Would I be wealthier? Most assuredly. Happier? Hard to say. Have more freedom? Not a chance. My Bay Street dream was as dead as Ben Johnson's athletic career—and the sweet thought of it still made me smile.

Once we arrived at the downtown bus depot, I helped Jeff unload some baggage, then sat for a few minutes to exchange more travel stories. We eventually shook hands and bid one another *adieu*. But as I loped off to find a pay phone, toward the maze of office towers, traffic and congestion, Jeff called out one last request: "When you write your book, don't forget to put a good word in for Greyhound."

August 25, 1999 - Toronto, Ontario

I spent several days in Toronto catching up with old friends, walking the downtown circuit and getting hopelessly lost on the city's transit system. More than once I jumped on the subway travelling in a direction opposite to what I had planned, which meant, invariably, that I had to spend a great deal of time backtracking and getting un-lost. Everywhere I went there was the perpetual crush of people, confusing and often irritating, along with cars and emergency vehicles in the process of creating yet another traffic jam. As I suffered through the sticky summer heat and watched the tawdry burlesque of city life, even the occasional afternoon shower brought faint relief. The rain did nothing to dispel the oppression of heat and humidity; nor did it cure the urban claustrophobia I was suffering from. On the other hand, it did bring to street level an overpowering aroma wafting up from the city's sewers.

But Toronto is not all despondency, lest I give that impression. Like any world-class urban centre, Toronto pulsates with twenty-four hours of insomnia-induced bustle, which means there's always something going on. Wanting to understand it better, I arranged to meet with an old university friend of mine, Jana, and her boyfriend Tom at a Thai restaurant a few blocks from Yonge Street. They had both spent their lives in the greater Toronto area, so if anybody could set me straight on this city and the role it plays in Canada, it would be them.

I even managed to find my way to the restaurant without getting hopelessly lost, proof that I *could* survive in Toronto, given more time (and a great deal more inclination). But any welling up of pride was cut short, for Tom's mind was already on food. "You can't name a culture that doesn't have a restaurant somewhere in this city," Tom said happily as we sat down. He clasped his menu with stubby fingers, browsing hungrily through a list of exotic choices. Tom's hair was thinning and he seemed shorter than I remembered, but he had a youthful vigour and a vibrant sense of humour about him. He came across as being smart, optimistic and thoughtful.

Jana looked as I remembered her: tall and slender with long, dark hair. Reaching over to rub Tom's back, she said, "Instead of one Greek family living in town with a restaurant, we have a whole section with Greek restaurants." In Toronto's case, it's appropriately called Greektown (imagine that), which, according to Tom, was no Big Fat Greek exaggeration. There's also Little Italy, two distinct Chinatowns, and in the corner of the city where Tom lives, a massive Portuguese and Brazilian population.

"Whenever Brazil wins a soccer game during the World Cup," Tom chuckled, "the city has to close down the streets. It gets so loud that you can hardly talk in your apartment." The Brazilian-induced mayhem, of course, pales in comparison with Italy's World Cup victory celebration a few years back. Toronto is home to one of the largest populations of Italians outside of Italy, and after Italy won the Cup, a million people flooded the streets.

"It sounds like Toronto goes crazy no matter who wins," I laughed.

"Oh, I'm sure some people have a trunk full of flags," agreed Tom. "It wasn't all Italians on the street, so they must pull out whatever's appropriate for the occasion."

It was all a bit overwhelming when I opened my menu to items that I couldn't pronounce, much less recognize. But it was a brilliant change from the burger-and-fries, burger-and-fries monotony of highway food, so I cast off my inhibitions and followed Tom and Jana's lead when they ordered a hot and sour broth with tofu, bamboo shoots and mushrooms. For the main course I ordered *gai phad khing*, some sort of fiery chicken dish served with shredded ginger that soon had me gasping for air.

After catching up on basics about families and jobs (Tom was still working his way through medical school; Jana was finishing her training as a radiation therapist), discussion turned back to life in Canada's largest centre. "Did you know that Toronto is the most ethnically diverse city in the world?" Tom asked me.

"Really? I had no idea."

"It's kind of surprising, isn't it?" Tom chuckled. "When you live here, you tend to think Toronto is Canada, and you see Canada as this multicultural country where absolutely everyone gets along. It's not until you get away that you realize this isn't always the case."

"What do you mean?"

"Well, when I was a teenager," he continued, "I lived in a small community in northern Ontario for Canada World Youth Exchange. I was surprised to find so few ethnic people living in those rural areas. Almost everyone was white—either English or French." Tom was also surprised to find resentment coming from some of the local people, angered that some Torontonian—probably "some rich bastard from Bay Street"—had closed down their mine.

Of course, Tom had many good memories too, and one of his fondest was the day he sat down with a group of teens from across Canada to discuss what Canadians had in common. "I was stunned when this kid from Saskatchewan whipped out a piece of paper and drew a detailed map of his town, labelling the thing almost down to the metre." He laughed at the thought. "Spending time in a town with less than four thousand people was as exotic as spending time in Indonesia. The way the community functions is just so completely different."

"We live in the same province, but we're so different," agreed Jana.

Tom flexed a funny little grin across his face, suggesting that he hadn't thought about these memories for quite some time. "All those pickup trucks ... geez ... driving around with dogs in the back." He laughed and took a bite of my *gai phad khing*. "The fire and ambulance services were completely staffed by volunteers. People gathered at the post office to sling gossip. Everyone knew everyone. The rural culture was fascinating!"

"So would you live there again?" I asked him.

Tom chuckled faintly, took a swig from his beer and pondered for a short moment. "It's nice to know that small towns exist," he admitted, as democratically as he could muster, "but as for me living in one? Not a chance!"

Chapter 32

"Why are you at our Wedding?"

August 30, 1999 - Peterborough, Ontario

By the time I left Toronto, August was edging hard against September. It made me ponder where my summer had gone. In some ways, it felt like a mere two weeks had passed since leaving Calgary, yet when I opened my journal and counted the weeks, it was clear that it had been more than ten. Checking my dwindling bank account also assured me that the latter figure was correct, for I was down to my last five hundred dollars. And although I was still expecting money for a couple of magazine articles I had penned before leaving Calgary, if some funds didn't arrive soon, I would once again find myself in that familiar and precarious position that had signalled the end of my two previous summers: utter destitution.

Despite this disquieting realization, I unfolded my map and set my sights on the Haliburton Highlands, that charming slice of eastern Ontario littered with lakes and cottages, sandwiched between Highway 7 and Algonquin Provincial Park. The very way "Haliburton" christens the tongue—not unlike a ripe strawberry—was enough to make it appealing in and of itself. This was accompanied by an immeasurable desire to avoid the hysterical drivers and dispiriting scenery of Highway 401, which cuts with mind-numbing monotony along the southern edge of the province. These facts considered, there was really no question which route I would travel. The 401 is a highway for double- and triple-trailered transport trucks trying to meet deadlines—not for hitchhikers prone to dawdling.

As it turned out, hitchhiking east to Peterborough and then turning north proved to be the right decision. Rather than travel two superhighways in a single day, it took me six days, twelve highways and a dozen rides to cover the same distance through postcard-perfect villages like Bancroft, Barry's Bay, Wilno and Eganville. Most of these towns looked remarkably vibrant for their size, yet the townsfolk seemed neither hurried nor particular about schedules. I discovered charming Mom-and-Pop general stores and saw pinnacled church steeples rising above leafy town centres, hedged in by rows of old brick buildings: banks, clothing stores and family restaurants. The suburban shopping mall—North America's most unforgivable crime against small city centres—had not yet infiltrated these parts. I noted gratefully that this had also kept alive the outer fringes of these villages, where loon-song echoed thick and shivering across the water on misty mornings, and where ranchers tended livestock in the rolling green hill country that dropped enticingly toward the Ottawa River valley.

My rides over this stretch of road proved to be as varied and interesting as the countryside I passed through. Near a town called Lakefield I was picked up by Nancy, a woman driving a cream-coloured Volkswagen convertible. She invited me back to her small trailer in the forest, where over a cup of tea she told me about running a steakhouse and pub for several years in Bancroft. She and her husband had also built the first luge run in northern Ontario, where she had competed in several competitions—including the Canada Cup and North American championship—winning several medals in the process.

Further along the road, I met a pair of middle-aged guys—Mark, a laundromat owner, and Jeff, an accountant from Toronto with an office at Yonge and Eglinton. Jeff was on vacation and Mark had recently split with his wife, so they invited me to crash with them at a motel, where we spent an evening watching Clint Eastwood movies. It was male bonding at its finest. The next day I joined Jeff for a round of golf at a nearby course, then promptly forgot my wallet in his golf bag before pressing on. I was fifty kilometres down the road before I realized my error, and it was no small feat trying to contact them. Without complaint, they drove an hour out of their way just to bring it to me.

The most interesting ride began when a friendly middle-aged man picked me up just outside of Pembroke. Steve Lawson was from Ottawa, and he sold fibre optic systems and switching equipment for a high-tech firm based in Kanata. What interested me most was not Steve's job, but his bilingual family: his wife spoke French fluently and his children attended a French immersion school. Steve himself had been raised in a bilingual family, though he claimed to have lost most of his French long ago. "Living on any border where there's a transition zone," he explained, "you're going to pick up pieces of both languages and cultures. I have what you'd call a strong functionality in French, even though I do butcher the language. My kids love to make fun of me."

"Do you ever run into problems, living next to Quebec?" I asked.

"Not really," he replied. "People who live in Quebec work through English when they come to Ottawa, and we work through French whenever we go there. No one really minds. In Canada, we're basically all immigrants anyway."

If only everyone saw things from Steve's perspective.

When Steve dropped me at a bustling Ottawa suburb called Carleton Place, he handed me a card with his phone number. "My sister Kathryn is getting married to a French guy later this week," he said. "Once you get to Ottawa, give me a call. Maybe you can come to the wedding."

His invitation startled me. "Are you sure that will be okay with your sister?" I asked.

"Just call me and I'll let you know," he said.

There was a lot going on when I finally made it to Ottawa, not least of which involved meeting my parents and sister, Jennifer, to help her move into a new apartment. She was starting her freshman year at the University of Ottawa, and my arrival coincided perfectly with frosh week. My mother arranged for me to stay with the same friends that they were staying with, where we enjoyed a brief reunion of sorts. It was during these two days that I took a hard look at my budget and the distance I had yet to travel—and decided that it would be impossible to continue. It was depressing to realize that I would need a fourth summer to complete my trip, but the decision was inevitable considering that I'm one of those inflexible people who insist on eating every day. If food were not a necessity, I surely could have continued for several weeks longer.

I was cheered marginally when my father prodded me awake at five one morning, eager to visit the annual hot-air balloon festival in Gatineau, a small French-Canadian city just across the river from Ottawa. Although my father is a staunch supporter of Quebec's French language rights in principle, his only firsthand experience with those French language rights came a few years before while he was driving our family through Montreal on vacation. It was there that he made the perennial mistake made by every Ontario driver visiting Quebec: he turned right on a red light. As a result, he was forced to exchange pleasantries with a short-tempered francophone police officer, who refused to hear his explanation in English. At the same time, countless cars bearing Quebec license plates were running a red light directly behind the cop.

To make a long story short, the cop handed my father a fat ticket and gave him a look that said, "Screw you, Ontario man." My father was not happy. In fact, he felt like an idiot. And one thing common to all fathers— including mine—is that you never make them feel like idiots, particularly in front of their wives and children. Not surprisingly, my father never paid the ticket, and as a result has never returned to *la belle province* for fear of being arrested under warrant.

So it was that I drove my father's car across the Alexandra Bridge to Hull that morning. My father was in top form, really, considering all the Quebec cops on the prowl. In a gravelly, purposely-exaggerated French accent, he said things like: "My wife told me to go to Hull, so I said okay." Once I had parked the car, we joined the throng of pedestrians swarming along a sidewalk beside the Ottawa River, all chattering away in French. We gave each other a knowing grin, not understanding a word, yet quite enjoying the fact that nobody knew my father was a fugitive on the loose. It was our little secret.

We were yanked from our reverie when a loud, thickset woman suddenly appeared in front of us, blocking our path with the authority of a CFL linebacker. She was demanding money for what we quickly surmised were two tickets. At first we had no idea what she was asking, but the fact that she was clutching a mitt-full of tickets and holding out her hand seemed to eliminate most other possibilities. In good fun, I considered ordering a coffee and bagel from her, but her sour expression inspired me to save my humour for somebody who might appreciate it more. We fumbled for our wallets and, after a few seconds, produced several crisp bills, which did much to appease her. She smiled and directed us through the gates with a wave of her hand, then moved on to the next person.

Inside the fairgrounds were dozens of hot air balloons at various stages of being inflated. Some, like the Michelin Man, were already standing erect, while many others were still stretched across the dew-laden grass, flat and lifeless. My favourites were a large rectangular balloon in the shape of a Canadian flag and, beside that, another shaped like a Mountie riding a cartoonish black steed. Crews were busy filling both of them with hot air, and after I had spent several minutes taking pictures, my father walked over and said: "I wonder how hard it would be to hitchhike on one of these things? You could probably make some pretty good time."

It wasn't long before the balloons started lifting into the crisp autumn sky, one after the other. Up to a hundred hot air balloons participate in the

Gatineau festival every year, which—as one might imagine—is a spectacular sight when dozens of them float over Parliament Hill at the same time. Indeed, it was a fine morning to stand there nursing a hot cup of java, watching the balloons jockey for position over Canada's capital and the misty Ottawa River.

September 4, 1999 - Ottawa, Ontario

"Are you sure they won't mind?" I asked Steve. All I had to wear were jean shorts, hiking boots and a navy blue T-shirt that had seen its fair share of abuse.

"Don't worry, you'll fit right in," Steve assured me. "My sister is English and her fiancé is French, so it'll be a real convergence of French and English culture. You'll love it!" Somehow I didn't believe him, but he seemed so warm and genuine that I decided to take a chance. With heartfelt gratitude, I accepted the invitation to attend his sister's wedding.

Hopping aboard a city bus, I followed Steve's directions into downtown Ottawa, where, not far from the Rideau Canal, I found a swanky ballroom packed with people wearing tuxedos, bridal gowns and flowery corsages. I was pretty sure Steve hadn't heard me when I explained my wardrobe situation, because I felt completely out of place. Nevertheless, when Steve saw me at the entrance, he walked over with a broad grin—perhaps sensing my discomfort—and grabbed my shoulder like I was a long lost relative.

"Are you sure this is all right?" I asked him again. "People are going to wonder what side of the family I'm from. We'll start rumours."

"Relax," he said. He reached into his pocket and pulled out a twenty-dollar bill. "Here, this is for you. Get yourself something to drink." He then pointed at a group of his French relatives sitting in one corner— uncles and aunts from his mother's side—then nudged me with his elbow. "Wait for a few more beers," he said, winking. "When they're sober they're federalists, but after a few beers they all become separatists."

My own drink helped marginally (though it didn't particularly incline me toward separation) and for a few minutes it gave me something to do other than stand there and feel self-conscious. To be fair, nobody gave me any reason to believe that Steve's invitation had been anything less than genuine. They were all incredibly cordial, either ignoring my beggar's clothes or failing to see them, and it wasn't long before Steve had wandered back across the room with his wife Joanne in tow, an exotic-looking woman with jet-black hair and an olive complexion. She was dressed in a slinky black dress. I think that's when I finally started to relax, because like Steve, she had a pleasing glow about her that was immediately disarming. "We're so glad you could make it," she said, shaking my hand warmly. "Just pretend that you're one of us."

Everybody was soon organized, and before I could find a seat, the ceremony had started. First the flower girl, then the bridesmaids, then Steve's sister Kathryn stepped down the aisle toward Marc, the groom in waiting. Kathryn was short and firmly built, and had a pretty face that reminded me somewhat of Shania Twain; Marc was a slim, handsome man with grey hair and a gentle smile. Kathryn stopped in front of the Catholic father, where Marc took her side. They exchanged vows and rings while the father talked about the usual wedding stuff: the importance of commitment, the family unit, that sort of thing. There were, of course, verses in both official languages.

After the ceremony ended, Steve invited me to get in line for the buffet. It was there that I met several of Steve's siblings, including two sisters named Debra and Shannon, as well as a tall, good-natured fellow named Kerry. I commented on how the convergence of French and English tradition at the ceremony was so apparent, and how it had been accomplished so seamlessly.

"Yes, everyone likes to think French and English are two entirely separate cultures," Kerry chuckled. "But that's not true. Our mother was the lynchpin of a family that was half English and half French, so we all grew up with both languages and cultures."

"We call it the *pamplemousse* factor—that is, the grapefruit factor," Debra added, spooning some fruit salad onto her plate. "Although we mostly spoke English around the house, it wasn't unusual to have French words mixed in for good measure."

As we proceeded down the line, Kerry grabbed a napkin and drew a rough sketch of his family tree. At the top were his father Clifton (who was English, but spoke French fluently) and his mother Carmen (who was French, but spoke English fluently). Of seven children four were fully bilingual, including Bridgette, a francophone. Only Steve, Kerry and Kathryn did not speak French fluently, although they could get by with the language when they needed to. "This is what happens when you grow up on the boundary of two cultures," Kerry explained. "It happens a lot in a place like Ottawa."

There were speeches and games after dinner, and by that time I was feeling quite at ease among my hosts. The final event before the dancing started was the cutting of the cake, where I took more photographs and finally had a chance to walk up and congratulate Kathryn and Marc on their marriage. They stared at me with a befuddled expression.

"Who are you?" asked Kathryn.

"We've been wondering all night why you're at our wedding," Marc added.

"Well..." I began, not entirely sure what to say. "I'm a hitchhiker that Steve picked up outside of Pembroke a couple of days ago. I'm writing a book abou..."

And that's exactly when Steve appeared at my side, handily defusing the situation. "He's travelling across Canada to write a book," Steve explained. "I figured that it would be a great opportunity for him to take part in a bilingual wedding ceremony."

I was half expecting the newlyweds to be annoyed, but they weren't. Instead, they asked me a few questions about my journey and, after we had chatted for a few minutes, Kathryn turned to me and said: "It's wonderful that you could join us. We hope you'll stay for some dancing."

"I wouldn't miss it."

The festive atmosphere continued into the wee hours of the morning, and although I was underdressed, I felt obliged to prove my worth on the dance floor. Steve and Joanne whisked across the hardwood hand in hand, while Marc, his new wife and his daughters took turns cutting the floor to pieces. Although I felt a bit like the subject of one of those "What person doesn't belong" cartoons, I soon discovered that where Bob Seger and Shania Twain were concerned, I fit right in. So with great satisfaction, I joined my finely-dressed friends as they danced the night away, celebrating the marriage of two people I barely knew. Can you think of any better way for a summer to end?

Journalist Voyageur

"I hold that a writer who does not passionately believe in the perfectability of man has no dedication nor any membership in literature."
- John Steinbeck

Chapter 33

Hooligan's Holiday

July 1, 2000 - Ottawa, Ontario

When I rounded the corner onto Rideau Street, a few blocks from Ottawa's Parliament buildings, I saw before me what could fairly be termed an unusual sight. A dozen pedestrians were running amok through the streets in red and white underwear, chanting loudly and bouncing up and down on the bumpers of passing vehicles, including a taxi that just happened to be in the right place at the wrong time. As the mob swarmed his car I could see a black man at the wheel flash a look of surprise, then roll down his window and start pumping his fist in the air. The revellers seemed quite satisfied by his response, and after a minute or two moved on to their next victim, leaving the vehicle intact and the driver with a bewildered grin stretched across his face. If this were any other occasion he would surely have been livid, but for the fact that it was Dominion Day in Canada's capital city.

Every year on the first of July, tens of thousands of hooligans flood Ottawa from across the country. The visitors call themselves tourists, of course, disguising their unruly intent to disturb the peace and make a general nuisance of themselves. They come equipped with markers, vials of red and white paint and fake tattoos of every size and variety, which they apply liberally to exposed body parts. They slot miniature flags into tangled hairdos, tie Canadian flags around their necks (as a superhero wears a cape) and fling gigantic flags the size of small parking lots into the air. Some of these flags are so big that they could be used in a pinch, say, to safely catch some poor Member of Parliament (MP) forced to jump from a burning tenth-story office window. Mind you, on Canada Day there aren't many MPs in these buildings. That's because they're all outside, running up and down the streets in red and white underwear, yelling, screaming and bouncing up and down on the bumpers of passing taxi cabs.

Since ending my trip in Ottawa the previous summer, I had been carefully plotting my return to coincide with Canada Day—an event, I dare say, that every Canadian should experience at least once. After a hooligan's holiday in the capital, Ottawa would be the jumping-off point for my fourth and final summer on the road, leading me through Quebec and then to the Maritimes and Newfoundland. In preparation for my travels, I spent the day walking around the city, listening to the national anthem resounding through the streets and admiring how typically mild-mannered Canadians can get so pissed up and obnoxious when national pride is on the line. It was all quite remarkable, really.

Amid the flag-waving pandemonium, bands played in the streets and beers were drained shotgun-style, even as patriotic T-shirts were hawked from sidewalk stands. One shirt had a hockey-stick-wielding beaver on the front that boasted, DAM COOL COUNTRY EH! Another featured an American flag with a caption that read THE RIGHT TO BEAR ARMS, below it a Canadian flag with the caption THE RIGHT TO BARE BREASTS, followed by a rather pointed question: WHERE WOULD YOU RATHER LIVE?

But it wasn't relations between Canadians and Americans that concerned me in Ottawa early that July, but rather relations between anglophones and francophones. More specifically, relations between a certain anglophone hitchhiker who spoke about seven words of French (most of them unsuitable for polite company) and a province full of francophones that he would soon be travelling across with little more than a pocket-sized French-English dictionary.

I would like to say straight up that it's not my fault that I speak no French. Unlike most Canadians my age, I never had the chance to take French in school because I spent eight years living in a small German community in Saskatchewan. I learned *sprechen sie Deutsch*, not *parlez-vous Français,* and the one occasion that I did visit Montreal as a teenager is pretty much a blur. In fact, the only memory I have from that trip is meeting several Quebecers who had very little patience for a young kid from Ontario who didn't speak their language. With this in mind, I convinced my bilingual sister Jennifer to join me for *crêpes* the morning before my departure, hoping to learn French over breakfast.

We started with a review of the basics, things like *bonjour* (hello), *merci beaucoup* (thanks for the bouquet of flowers) and *s'il vous plait* (don't play with the silverware). As a hitchhiker, I figured it would also be important to learn about navigation and how to ask for directions, for I was sure to get lost in a province that outlaws English signs. Jennifer taught me that *droite* means "right," *gauche* means "left," *toute droite* means "straight ahead" and *vas faire futre* means "piss off, jerk."

I figured that I should also familiarize myself with road hazards, such as *gros camions* (big trucks) that can run you over when they see you're wearing a red CANADA T-shirt that you bought in Ottawa on Canada Day. In the cities, buses and taxis are more of a threat—apparently some drivers refer to anglophone pedestrians as *cahos de vitesse* (speed bumps) in their sick little circles.

"How would you say 'I don't speak French very well?'" I asked Jennifer, taking out a pen so that I could write down her answer.

"Oh, that's an easy one," she replied. "Je ne parle pas beaucoup de Français. 'Parle' is the verb 'to speak' and 'ne pas' indicates the negative."

"And how would I tell somebody that I'm a journalist travelling across Canada?"

She had to think about that one for a moment. "You would probably say something like 'Je suis un journaliste qui voyage à travers le Canada.'"

"Good, good." I had her spell the words out and indicate pronunciations so that I could practice while standing at the side of the road.

"Here's another one you might want to know," she suggested. "'Je n'ai pas voté pour Preston Manning.'"

"Does that mean 'I didn't vote for Preston Manning?'"

"Yes."

"Perfect. I'm sure that one will come in handy."

My private French lesson carried on for the next hour. I learned all about colours, how to find a washroom, how to comment on beautiful scenery beside the road and how to ask people about their families and jobs. Basically, I wanted to know enough French to fill the empty air should I get picked up by somebody who didn't speak English—which was sure to happen at some point during my travels, particularly in rural Quebec. These phrases and words would also act as a foundation for me to build on as I travelled.

"And how would I order a hamburger?" I asked.

A playful grin crossed my sister's face. "Voulez-vous couchez avec moi."

"Hmmm, I think I've heard that one before. Isn't there a song that talks about hamburgers?" I wrote the phrase in my notebook. "So to order a cheeseburger, I would say 'Voulez-vous couchez avec moi avec fromage, s'il vous plait?'"

Jennifer burst out laughing. "I dare you to say that to some kid at McDonald's."

"Huh?"

"Loosely translated, what you just said means, 'Would you like to sleep with me with cheese, please!'"

"Alrighty then. I guess I'm ready for Quebec."

THUMBING EAST FROM Ottawa, a hitchhiker can reach Montreal by following one of two routes. The first traverses the north side of the Ottawa River through Quebec, while the second cuts cross-country through rural Ontario. As it was early in the summer, I decided to take the highway through Ontario—after all, I had several weeks of travelling through francophone territory ahead of me. Why rush the inevitable? This made better logistical sense anyway, for I was planning to stay with *Equinox* magazine editor Martin Silverstone for a few days. He lived in Ste-Anne-de-Bellevue, a small French-Canadian village at the west end of Montreal Island, and after consulting my map I could see that the route through Ontario would drop me right at his doorstep.

On my way out of Ottawa, I stood at an off-ramp near Blair Road for nearly three hours before a black Camaro pulled over, rescuing me from the dizzying effects of dehydration under a relentless sun. The driver was a middle-aged fellow with a shag of dirty blonde hair, dressed from head to toe in black. When I climbed into the passenger's seat, I noticed that his left leg had been amputated just above the knee.

"Where are you going?" I asked.

"Down the road about thirty minutes," he replied, "but that should get you out of town, at least. It's hard to get a ride standing at these off-ramps."

No kidding.

The man's name was Bryan, and for the next half-hour we enjoyed lively conversation about many things. Like Steve Lawson, Bryan worked in Kanata's high-tech sector, and he explained how California's Silicon Valley had been luring a lot of Canadians south. More importantly, he shared with me the three rules for successfully navigating Quebec as an anglophone. "First, try to speak French whenever you can," he advised. "They'll appreciate it, and if they're in a good mood, they'll give you a break. Second, smile and walk away if they talk down to you." He saw that

I was scribbling his advice down, so he paused to let me catch up.

"What's the third rule?" I finally asked.

He levelled his gaze. "Never, never, NEVER get in a car with a drunk Frenchman, because you'll probably wind up dead." This wasn't much of a surprise. Quebec's traffic laws are some of the most stringent in Canada, yet the province is infamous for its wild drivers. Indeed, their penchant for ignoring traffic lights borders on fetishism—a bad habit at best, a provincial duty at worst.

Conversation eventually turned to Bryan's leg (or lack thereof) and the reason for his amputation. In May of 1993, he and his girlfriend had been gunning down the Gatineau Parkway on his motorcycle when he hit a rock, lost control and wrapped himself around a tree backwards. His girlfriend lost her foot in the accident, yet she still managed to crawl three metres to his side, then another three metres up the embankment to flag down a passing vehicle. "We married each other, even after that," he proclaimed proudly. "We're still together after nine years and I love her all to hell."

"What happened after you were rescued?" I asked.

"Once I was at the hospital, they put me in a coma beyond the legal limit of narcotics," he explained, telling his story as calmly as if it were fiction. "Over the next month I died twice, woke up Sunday to wish my mom a happy Mother's Day, then went right back under. You know, back then I didn't understand that it was an accident. I only saw that I'd caused my girlfriend to lose her foot, and it was tearing me up inside. But she's stuck with me through it all, and a guy couldn't ask for more from a woman."

When it was time to get out of Bryan's car, he opened his door and hopped around to the back to help me unload my gear, a gesture I found rather ironic. "Thanks for sharing your story with me," I said as he climbed back in. "You've inspired me."

After another couple of rides, I crossed Canal Sainte-Anne onto the west end of Montreal Island, where my driver—an American traveller named Gideon—dropped me. My map was in French and not very detailed, so my walk into Ste-Anne-de-Bellevue proved to be my first test in a month of tests-to-be.

After spending thirty minutes searching fruitlessly for Martin's condo, I finally decided that asking directions using poor French was better than walking aimlessly around town for several more hours—even if trying to understand directions in French might result in the same. So I sucked up my pride and approached two men chatting outside a fire station. "Excusez-moi, monsieurs," I squeaked in the most pumped-up, gladiatorial voice I could muster. "J'aimerais trouver rue Ste-Pierre?"

If the men noticed my poor language skills, they gave no indication. Rather, they launched into a complex barrage of French, using a flurry of hand signals to help illustrate. I couldn't have been more at a loss. As a visual learner, I've always found hand signals altogether useless when it comes to understanding directions, even in English—so you can well imagine how I fared in a language I barely knew. I didn't understand a single word. Still, I was too embarrassed to ask him to repeat, so I smiled, told him *merci*, and headed off in the general direction he had been pointing.

Thirty minutes later, after following a confusing jumble of intersecting rues, I began to rue my decision to accept Martin's invitation. This town was more confusing than Kenora, and my frustration was only heightened when I passed the same fire station again. Thankfully, the guy who had given me directions was no longer standing outside. A couple of blocks south, I stopped to take out my map again, hoping that staring at it for the umpteenth time would somehow demystify everything and miraculously deliver me onto Martin's doorstep. Just when I was about to give up, a white van pulled over and a man in a paint-splattered T-shirt leaned out the window.

"Where are you going?" he asked in perfect English.

Thank God, somebody I could communicate with. "I'm trying to find Ste-Pierre Street," I replied. "I've been wandering around for the last hour trying to find it."

"I know," the man laughed. "I've passed you a couple of times and somehow figured you were lost. Get in and I'll drive you over there."

When the man finally dropped me at Ste-Pierre—a narrow corridor seemingly designed to thwart detection by anglos—Martin had just arrived home from work. So it was that my dismal sense of direction, combined with a less-than-satisfactory map, actually helped me time my arrival perfectly.

"Come in, come in," said a bare-chested Martin. He opened the door, shook my hand and then wandered off into the next room to finish changing. I had worked with Martin on a couple of *Equinox* stories, but this was the first time I had met him in person. Strangely, he looked much as I had envisioned him: short and muscular, with greying hair and an intensity about him that was neither comforting nor disconcerting. He seemed both athletic and academic, but in a pleasingly simple sort of way. Ideas came at him from every direction, and as we walked around town buying groceries and inviting people to his housewarming party that evening, our conversation probably changed direction a dozen times. More than once, Martin even stopped strangers on the street to invite them to his bash. The fact that Ste-Anne was a close-knit community seemed to induce this sort of thing, though part of it was certainly attributable to Martin's outgoing nature.

People started rolling in shortly after eight, and Martin was soon occupied with baking cookies, barbecuing chicken breasts and visiting guests with scattershot efficiency. Young, old, tall, short ... Martin seemed to know the entire town, and as the evening progressed, it seemed as if the entire community was trying to squeeze into his modest living room, like one of those university pranks where everybody jams into the back of an Austin Mini. For my part I offered a few times to help Martin with his hosting duties, but each time, before my assistance could be comprehended and/or accepted, Martin was two rooms away. I eventually gave up, sat down and began socializing with his guests as warm evening air wafted in through the open windows.

Martin's party should have ended quite innocently, and probably would have had a tall, gregarious fellow from Martin's rugby team not been present. Mackintosh was originally from New Brunswick, which should explain a lot. Liquored up and feeling quite cat-burglar-like, he somehow convinced Martin and me to join him for a paddle at the community swimming pool, even though it was one in the morning and the pool had officially closed several hours before. If we wanted the privilege of a swim during the wee hours of the morning, we would have to do it illegally, stealthing our way in over the chain-link fence.

The first part of our midnight raid went strictly according to plan—or so it seemed as we dropped one by one over the metallic gate. That's why we were so surprised when, less than five minutes later, a pair of police officers appeared at the scene and indicated rather sharply that we had better get out. I was the last one back over the fence, and like Martin and Mackintosh before me, I was hauled off by my arm and thrown into the back of a police van. Martin and I exchanged stone-faced expressions, but Mackintosh didn't seem the least bit fazed. He just sat there and grinned.

"Where are you from?" demanded one of the officers, looking squarely at Martin. The other officer was talking loudly in French into his CB radio, no doubt announcing our detainment to other police units scattered across the immediate vicinity.

"I live just across the street," answered Martin.

"What about you?" He was looking at me now.

"I'm from Calgary," I replied sheepishly, grateful that he was at least interrogating us in English. "I'm just out here visiting for a few weeks."

"I'm from New Brunswick," Mackintosh offered happily. The officer glared at him, visibly annoyed that he looked so chipper. Then he passed a notepad back to Martin. "I'll need to see your identification," he announced, "and while we're checking that, write your full name and address down here."

"I don't have my identification with me," Martin replied, trying to stay calm. "I mean, c'mon guys—we just went for a little swim."

That seemed to annoy the officer even more. By this time, his partner had finished talking on the CB, so we were treated to two pairs of glaring eyes. "Do you know that the fine for disturbing the peace is a hundred and thirty-five dollars?" the second officer asked, openly irritated.

"I'm sorry, I'm sorry," Martin apologized, raising his arms in self-defense. "We don't want to cause you guys trouble. My friend Matt is writing a book about travelling across Quebec and we just wanted to show him a good time."

The officer's stern expression seemed to soften a little. He looked over at me to see if what Martin said was true. I nodded dutifully.

In the end, the police officers grudgingly let us off the hook, although as we climbed from their van I got the impression that they thought we were a bunch of hooligans who deserved to be ticketed. Maybe we were hooligans, and perhaps we did deserve to be fined, but none of that really mattered. We weren't—which made me want to call my father in the wee hours of the morning just to rub it in.

Chapter 34

On a Thumb and a Prayer

July 17, 2000 - Montreal, Quebec

The proprietor of the cafe stared passively across the counter at me, face half-hidden behind the folds of his morning newspaper. Then, as if in the presence of somebody famous, he suddenly snapped to attention. "Hey, you're that hitchhiker guy from Calgary. You were in the *Gazette* this morning!" He leafed through a cluttered stack of newspapers on the counter, trying to find the story.

Was it the large backpack that had given me away? My red CANADA T-shirt? Or my poor French, which had run roughshod over morning tranquility as I tried to order a muffin and coffee?

I actually hadn't seen the story myself, because the reporter who interviewed me hadn't been sure when they were going to run it. The proprietor presented the article, which was perhaps five or six paragraphs long and accompanied by a picture of me. The headline read: HE'S ON A THUMB AND A PRAYER: HITCHHIKER'S OUT TO 'DO' QUEBEC. I chuckled and let my eyes wander down to the first line. "Matt Jackson is a rare kind of traveller," it said. "The kind that would send shivers down the corporate spines of Greyhound, Air Canada and VIA. He hitchhikes." Now that was amusing. I could only hope that my travels *would* send shivers down a few corporate spines: if I had executives worried about me encouraging hitchhiking alternatives to the masses, perhaps they would offer a juicy financial package for me to keep my big mouth shut.

"Do you mind if I borrow this for a few minutes?" I asked the muffin man.

"No problem," he said, with what sounded like an Italian accent. "Would you like some breakfast, too? It's on the house."

It's a personal policy of mine to never turn down free food, so after showering the man with plenty of *mercis*, I retreated to a table with his newspaper tucked under my arm, eager to read all about my trip.

MONTREAL IS WITHOUT question one of Canada's most fetching cities, with its bilingual charm and European ambiance. I spent several days walking its narrow cobblestone streets in the old part of town, always on guard, for they are the kinds of streets designed to accommodate sauntering horses pulling carts to market, not high-speed contraptions of steel and glass driven by Frenchmen. Snaking between exquisite stone buildings, my favourite street was rue Saint-Paul, with its charming cafes and restaurants spilling onto sidewalks. The street is also home to the old Catholic Chapelle Notre-Dame-de-Bon-Secours, which has been converted into a museum. With the younger generation turning away from religion, I guess the old church has been forced to convert buildings rather than souls. On this account, they have done a fine job.

The more I wandered around Montreal, the more acutely I had to face my own ignorance about the province, an ignorance that most Albertans exude in abundance when it comes to appreciating the distinctness of Quebec. Despite French instruction that starts in primary school, your average Albertan couldn't fart in French, and our understanding of Quebec's culture is arrestingly simplistic. The prevailing attitude is basically that learning French at school is a chore rather than an opportunity, and that Quebec is merely one of ten equal provinces, a province that just happens to be full of people who drive fast, talk funny and eat lots of poutine.

For example, most Albertans have no clue why Bill 101—a law that outlaws English signage in Quebec—would even be considered by the provincial government. To an anglophone, such a law would be tantamount to killing individual rights and freedom of expression. Part of this attitude, no doubt, has to do with the severity with which these sign laws are enforced at times, but part of it certainly has to do with ignorance about the Québécois. As Taras Grescoe notes in his book *Sacré Blues*, the collective good of society is far more important to Quebecers than it is to English-speaking Canadians. It means that protection of the French language and culture as a whole should, and does, eclipse individual rights to place English signs in front of your store, or the right to send your child to an English school.

For my part, I found wandering around trying to read the French signage an exotic and oddly pleasurable pastime. It was during these wanderings that I heard about the language police, those much-feared enforcement officers who roam at large making sure that provincial sign laws are obeyed. One disgruntled shopkeeper I talked to had been ticketed for a button on his photocopier that said PRINT, while another man was fined for a trash can with the word PUSH on the front. While riding the Metro, I also noticed a picture of a large creature busting some kung-fu moves, with the added sound effects *VLAN! BOUM! PAF!* scrawled beneath. I had no idea that punching noises sounded any different in French than they do in English, but then again, I'm not bilingual. I tried punching the seat in front of me, but to be perfectly frank, it sounded the same as it would have sounded had I punched a padded subway seat in Calgary. Whether this is because I have an untrained ear, or because the language police simply haven't discovered the seat yet, I will never know. When they do, I expect the transit company will be heavily fined.

Having said all this, the tension between French and English in Montreal was not nearly as severe as I had anticipated. Most people I came in contact with were more than willing to speak English, particularly if I tried speaking French first, and on more than one occasion I met francophones who bent over backwards to be helpful. Take Yannick, a fellow who approached me in Montreal's old town while I was searching hopelessly for a bank machine. I must have looked confused, because he stopped and asked me something in French. I replied in broken French that I couldn't speak very much French, and that I was actually from Calgary.

"WOW!" he exclaimed. "From Calgary?"

I nodded.

"WOW! Calgary Stampede!" he exclaimed again. He made a strange gyrating motion with his hips as though he were making love to a bubblegum dispenser, but was probably intended to look like he was riding a horse. "I like Calgary Stampede!"

And that was it. Yannick and I were thereafter bonded, and he led me several blocks out of his way to a bank machine, apologizing over and over again in broken English for his poor English, while I apologized over and over again in broken French for my poor French. When he got me to the bank machine, he embraced me like a long lost friend, said "WOW! Calgary Stampede!" one last time, then turned and walked away.

Getting out of Montreal was an entirely different matter. I relied heavily on goodwill of a very different sort: the kind that happens when you travel in a given direction until somebody tells you that you're travelling in the wrong direction. The general plan was to ride the Metro over to Longueuil on the east side of the St. Lawrence, then catch a bus south to Brossard where I would be able to access Autoroute 10 toward Sherbrooke. To be sure, another comedy of errors ensued, the first of which involved me wandering onto the tarmac of the Longueuil bus terminal, despite plentiful French signage indicating that under no circumstances were pedestrians allowed to wander onto the tarmac of the Longueuil bus terminal. I was hauled away by a security guard, but spared another ticket thanks to a hurried explanation that I was from Calgary, didn't speak French very well and was thus not really accountable for my actions.

"WOW! Calgary Stampede!" exclaimed the security guard, who started making a strange gyrating motion with his hips.

"Yes, the Calgary Stampede," I replied. I was just glad I wasn't from Vancouver, lest he be forced to pretend he was picking the lock on somebody's car.

After talking in broken sentences about the Stampede for a couple of minutes (with apologies for poor French and English peppered throughout), the security guard led me to the correct bus stop and told me to wait inside until the bus arrived. This I managed to do with great efficiency, and without making so much as one wrong turn.

The next challenge developed shortly after I reached Brossard, where I realized that the exit onto Autoroute 10 near the bus terminal had nowhere for a hitchhiker to stand, much less for a vehicle to pull over and stop. On previous occasions, these sorts of conditions had not kept me from trying, but under the circumstances (the fact that it was starting to rain, that cars were whizzing by at speeds not unlike a NASA space shuttle, and that there were all too many Frenchmen behind the wheels of those vehicles) another option seemed like a wise choice. After studying a selection of bus routes at the Brossard bus terminal map, I decided to walk to another bus stop several blocks away. This would presumably take me further out of town to where the highway was more inclined to produce a shoulder.

I waited patiently for perhaps twenty-five minutes with no bus in sight, until a bus servicing a different route stopped to inform me that my ride wouldn't be along until rush hour. Must have been in the fine print. At least the driver, no doubt feeling sympathy for the poor dumb anglophone, told me to get on board so that he could drop me a few blocks closer to the edge of town. A few minutes later, he let me out near a highway exit that looked much more promising.

It was there that I staked my claim, and within thirty minutes, an exotic-looking fellow with long, flowing black hair squealed to a halt in a small grey sports car. He addressed me in English, but with an accent that I couldn't quite place. I waited patiently while he rearranged several boxes of Café Bravo coffee in the back seat to make room for my backpack. "This is the first time I've ever picked up a hitchhiker," he told me, sounding rather proud of himself.

"Welcome to the club," I replied. "Now that you've done it once, you'll never go back."

The fellow's name was Norton, and he had been a Canadian resident for seven years since leaving India at the age of seventeen. Prior to that, Norton and his family had lived in Afghanistan, but his parents sent him to India for schooling shortly after the war broke out with the Russians. "Let's just say the situation was no longer very comfortable in Afghanistan," he told me. "So when I had the chance to come to Canada in 1993, my family jumped at the opportunity."

Norton was in the mood to talk, so I let him. His story proved to be one of the more interesting tales I had heard in a while, a shining example of what a young immigrant with no money and fewer language skills can do when he has backbone, enterprise and a healthy dose of determination. When he arrived he was by himself in a country halfway around the world, had less than three hundred dollars in his pocket and didn't speak a word of either French or English. He worked at three factory jobs and enrolled in a six-month crash course in French.

"Why did you pick French instead of English?" I asked.

"I've always liked the sound of French," he told me candidly. Then, as though he was divulging some sort of well-kept secret, he confided, "When I found out that French was a romance language, I knew that I had to come to Montreal."

Not that Norton had much time for romance those first few years. Between his schooling and three jobs, he typically worked twenty to twenty-one hours every day, and for the first six months he ate nothing more than hot dogs, bread and water. "I weighed two hundred and fifteen pounds when I left India," he laughed. "And after two and a half years in Canada I weighed only a hundred and fifty-five pounds. All my coworkers used to say 'Norton, you're going to die a young man.'"

"So why did you do it?"

"After finishing my French course, I had an opportunity to prove that I could sponsor my brother and his family." Which he did, and after his brother arrived with a wife and three children, he and Norton continued to work reproachable hours to save money so that their sister and parents could come to Canada as well. Norton must have seen my jaw drop, stunned as I was by his accomplishments at such a young age, because he started laughing out loud. "Human beings are very adaptable," he told me. "In our tradition, family counts for a lot. I really didn't have a choice."

"Well, you always have a choice Norton," I said. "Your story is remarkable." I couldn't imagine myself, or any other Canadian for that matter, doing what he did.

"My father always used to say 'Help yourself and God will help you,'" he continued. We all worked together to make it happen. It was crazy at first, but now it's beautiful. Now I have a car, five restaurants and a comfortable life."

Perhaps the most surreal moment in my conversation with Norton happened just before he dropped me off near Granby. When he had finished with his story, I took it upon myself to tell him a bit about my own life and my reasons for hitchhiking across the country. I told him some of the funny stories, about my trip up to the Arctic Ocean and when I looked over at him, I saw that he was equally as stunned by my life.

"Let me get this straight," he said with an incredulous tone. "You've spent the last four summers hitchhiking all over Canada?"

"That's right."

"I can't believe you've done that," he stammered. "You're crazy!"

I suppose it takes one to know one.

July 19, 2000 - Saint-Gerard, Quebec

Quebec's Eastern Townships came as something of a surprise to me, considering that I had been expecting nothing but plucky *habitants* engaged in farm chores, gossip and endless games of cribbage while sitting around a wood-burning stove. But that is the rural Quebec of myth—the one I learned about in school, and one that bears little resemblance to the Eastern Townships of modern times. Not surprisingly, it's also a myth quite detested by the modern Québécois for implying that they are dull-witted bumpkins, when in fact, most Quebecers have not one bumpkinesque quality about them.

The Eastern Townships are not French anyway, at least not originally. Settled by British Loyalists fleeing north after the American Revolution, the Townships were primarily anglophone for more than a century, until the railroad and the forest industry brought French woodsmen into the area. It was only then that sleepy little English hamlets started blending with the *joie de vivre* of the French, and *voila!* the Townships were magically transformed into something of a bilingual potpourri, aided further by generations of mixed marriages.

For my part, I couldn't have been happier, and on my journey through the rolling forests and farmland I saw plentiful evidence of this mixing. I met a francophone man with the last name Robert, married to an anglophone woman with the last name Garneau. I caught glimpses of round barns (built in that shape so the Devil couldn't hide in the corners) and multi-storied Victorian homes complete with dormer windows and ornate gables. I was also pleased when ride after ride produced drivers who were dexterous in both languages, a fortunate situation that lulled me into a false sense of security until somewhere outside Saint-Gerard (a quaint little French villa northeast of Sherbrooke). It was there that I met Michel, an amiable French-Canadian man in his mid-fifties.

"Où vas-tu?" asked Michel, inquiring as to my destination.

I understood him! I understood him! I did a happy little jig at the roadside. "Québec City," I replied.

Michel nodded and motioned for me to throw my belongings in his trunk, and soon we were barrelling down the road toward destiny, listening to the mutterings of a French radio host juxtaposed with English-language songs.

It became painfully evident soon thereafter that Michel, from Lévis (a town across the river from Quebec City), knew about as much English as I did French. It didn't take us long to exhaust our repertoires of bilingual words and phrases, which had been assembled mainly for pleasantries during short and unavoidable confrontations. But this ride was no brief interlude. Rather than give up and settle for sitting there with a dumbfounded look on my face, I decided to test my creativity. This primarily involved using the words *beaucoup* and *petit* in a dazzling medley of arrangements for which I surely would have been ticketed had I been within earshot of any self-respecting Québécois police officer.

For example, by the time we passed Coleraine I had looked up the word "barn" in my French-English dictionary and pointed out the window at a large red barn. "Le beaucoup grange," I said, pointing excitedly at the barn in a way that I had never pointed at a barn before.

Michel nodded politely, smiling at my effort. He pointed a few hundred metres up the road to a small white house. "La petite maison," he said.

"Ahh yes, la petite maison," I had to agree. The house was small. "Très petite," I added, scrunching my thumb and index finger close together.

I looked across the road and saw a paddy with some cows grazing. "Beaucoup vaches," I suggested, then decided that there probably weren't enough cows to be *beaucoup* quite yet. Unfortunately, the herd wasn't quite *petit* either. I settled for middle ground: "Beaucoup-petit?" Or was that "Petit-beaucoup?"

And so it was that our time passed. I spotted things at the roadside, looked them up in my dictionary and then described them using various combinations of these two delightful words. In fact, I was having so much fun that down the road I felt compelled to point out another barn, this one *beaucoup beaucoup*, and not long after passing Thetford Mines, a *beaucoup beaucoup beaucoup* barn. Michel was probably regretting ever having picked me up, but I was having the time of my life.

At Vallée-Jonction, we dipped into a beautiful valley with a picturesque little town scattered across its green flanks. "Il y a beaucoup agriculture ici?" I asked Michel, pointing out the window at the bounty of fertile cropland. I wanted to know if there was a lot of agriculture around these parts.

"Maïs," replied Michel, shrugging. Corn it was. Still, I couldn't help but feel cheated that my beautifully contrived question had fetched but a one-word answer.

Eventually Michel, a man of obvious fortitude, turned the radio to an English station, evidently with the intention of appeasing me. Was he tiring so soon of the intellectual stimulation that our exchange offered? That was hard for me to believe. "Voulez-vous Français radio?" I asked.

"For you," was all he said, in a tone that suggested I sit back, listen and shut up. I took the hint and did just that, quietly tucking my dictionary into the top pocket of my backpack.

We reached Lévis shortly after dinner, and Michel was kind enough to drive me across the St. Lawrence River to Quebec City. This was either because he wanted to save me a ride on the ferry or because he didn't want me to see where he lived for fear that I would invite myself in for dinner. He motioned at me, indicating that he needed to know where to drop me.

I searched my memory for words that proved stubbornly uncooperative, then reached for my dictionary again. After a minute of frantic flipping,

I finally decided on "J'aimerais autobus arrêt," a sentence that really means nothing in French, but would have to do. A sentence like that only makes sense if the person you're addressing realizes that you're an anglophone imbecile who is cutting and pasting words together, trying to make a whiff of sense. Realizing this, Michel did just what I had asked him to do. He dropped me at a city bus stop.

And that was how I arrived in Quebec City. As Michel turned to drive away, I could see him grinning from ear to ear, no doubt grateful that this short but painful chapter in his life was finally over.

Chapter 35

Two Heroes

July 25, 2000 - Quebec City, Quebec

At the crest of a hill beside Quebec City's regal Chateau Frontenac, overlooking the St. Lawrence River's impressive girth, stand two bronzed statues of men who played an important role in making Canada the creative, bilingual, mud-slinging place that it is today. For this, Canadians are eternally grateful. Ironically, General James Wolfe, leader of the British forces who attacked and laid siege to Quebec City during the summer of 1759, now stands shoulder to shoulder with the Marquis de Montcalm, commander of the French militia who were crushed while defending Quebec against the British onslaught. What makes this memorial truly unique is that it proffers hero status to both men: the victor and the defeated. And while it may seem strange that two mortal enemies are now standing amiably side by side like old school chums, one never knows the obscene gestures they exchange when people aren't looking.

Some people claim that the French and English have never gotten along, so it's pointless trying to make them now. A lot of the people who share this view live in Quebec City, of course—the beating heart of the province's separatist movement—and are affiliated with the Parti Québécois, some of the finest rabble-rousers our country has ever known. More than two hundred and forty years after what French Canadians call "the Conquest" (when Wolfe kicked Montcalm's French *derrière* all over the Plains of Abraham), they still recall with great pangs of remorse their ancestor's failure to defend New France against the hostile invaders. The decisive battle only lasted a few minutes, but as historian Daniel Francis relates in his book *National Dreams*, "the significance of those minutes has echoed down through Canadian history ever since, creating a broad and enduring gulf between French and English understandings of the country."

Yet the English, condescending as we can be at times, can't seem to figure out why a battle that was fought more than two centuries ago is still causing such anxiety and diatribe. Some Englishmen, most notably Governor-General Earl Grey in 1908, have even suggested that the Plains of Abraham should be considered the birthplace of Canada as a cohesive entity. Men like Grey have obviously never seen what happens when you pour Alberta oil into St. Lawrence sea water. "Can the French not see the English have their best interests at heart?" men like Grey repeat in exasperated tones. "Will they never understand that living under British rule has been a blessing? Why must they continue to whine? Sheesh. They lost. Get over it already."

Still, by world standards any tension that exists between the two cultures today manifests itself mainly in petty bickering rather than outright hostility. Canada and Quebec are no Israel and Palestine, India and Pakistan, north and south Ireland. Some have even speculated that Canada and Quebec need each other as they need their squabbles, whether or not they want to admit it. Canada is there to listen patiently to Quebec's endless complaints while helping the persnickety hen guard her eggs against assimilation by any and all foreign interests, especially English ones. Quebec, on the other hand, lends differentiation and identity to Canada, a country desperately in need of differentiating itself from its big brother to the south.

When I first arrived in Quebec City, my journey through the province had so far been *beaucoup beaucoup* successful, so I figured it was time to stop for a few days and immerse myself in the history and nostalgia of the place. Quebec City is arguably the choicest, most stunning, most European city in all of North America, and seeing it for the first time only served to reinforce how vital French culture is for enhancing our country's self-image. The city's turreted fortification wall, artsy cafes, stone buildings and cobbled streets offered me *un buffet très tentant* of distractions. *Les belles filles*, attractive French girls who seemed to be everywhere, had my neck swivelling madly in circles. On many evenings I simply walked around town, blissful and exuberant, until the sun disappeared, soaking in the sights, sounds and romance: the sweet fragrance of food and fine wine blending with music. It was like old Montreal, only on a grander scale.

One sunny afternoon, I even signed up for a tour of the old fortification wall. Although I've never been one for official tours, I wanted a refresher course on the events of September 13th, 1759, the day Montcalm and his militia swept down rue Saint-Jean, past McDonald's where they ordered lunch to go, through the gates of the fortification wall before Montcalm realized they had given him a goddamn Quarter Pounder with cheese instead of a Big Mac, back through the walled gates to rectify matters, and finally, up onto the Plains of Abraham to face off with Wolfe's troops.

Our interpretive guide was a happy-go-lucky fellow named Martin, who was also a student of history and political science at Laval University. He was gregarious and knowledgeable, and didn't even seem to mind that I was English. After I signed in and paid the requisite five dollars, he led me and a half-dozen other English-speaking tourists toward the ramparts, bastions and powder magazines of the old fortification wall.

"Québec City was a strategic military settlement," Martin began as we walked past the statues of Wolfe and Montcalm, where a pigeon had recently marked its territory on the *monsieur*. "It sits on 'igh ground and is located where da river narrows, so it was much easier to control da boat traffic." We all eyed the statues of the two heroes, guarding a reluctant peace between English and French Canadians. To me, they looked rather unstressed about it all.

"If the British won the war, why are there statues for both leaders?" asked a man from Ontario, obviously the token troublemaker.

"I know it's strange to 'ave monuments for both generals," explained Martin in a conciliatory tone. "But you 'ave to understand dat Québec was still mostly French at da time of da Seven Years' War. Da British wanted to maintain peace even dough da city was under dere control."

I had learned while in Montreal that the phrase *"Je me Souviens"*—as written on the Quebec license plate—is from a poem by Quebec poet Eugene Taché. Ironically, the phrase means "I remember," though few people today remember that it comes from a line in Taché's poem that says (and I paraphrase): "I remember that I was born under the lily, but I have flourished under the British rose." Not surprisingly, the words evoke a variety of deeper meanings depending on who is doing the remembering. Some remember their roots and how they have flourished in a bilingual, multicultural Canada. Others remember the British bastards who, for centuries, have been trying to control everything to do with their province.

And here's the rub. For nearly two centuries following the conquest, the British ruling class controlled much of Quebec's economy and culture, so it should come as no surprise to English Canadians that *la belle province* has felt the need to defend its interests aggressively. If my time in Quebec had taught me one thing, it was that most anglophones—myself included—could try a little harder to appreciate the differences between the two solitudes. "English Canada has a significant other, and its lifelong dialogue with Quebec has made it a richer place," writes Taras Grescoe in his book *Sacré Blues*. He further states that it is our continuing dialogue with francophone Quebecers and First Nations people that "makes English Canadians more than just unarmed Americans with health cards."

As we walked beside the Citadelle, Martin continued his narrative. He explained how all of Quebec City had been designed with defense in mind, all streets converging to a single point near the river so that soldiers could be deployed quickly to any part of the fortification wall. Apparently, these streets now serve to deploy tourists in quite the same way, bringing them all to a centrally located tourist booth so Martin can charge them five bucks and explain why they arrived there in the first place.

Unfortunately for the French, the wall was not yet complete when the British arrived in Canada during the spring of 1759 with nearly 200 ships and 8,000 troops. For the entire summer, Wolfe and his men terrorized the surrounding countryside, destroying crops, torching homes, and slaughtering farm animals and their owners in a savage spree that was clearly not heroic in any way. Then, after several months of bombarding the city and blocking resupply from France, Wolfe's army moved in for the kill. Under cover of darkness, he and his troops scaled the brooding cliffs at *L'Anse au Foulon* up onto the Plains of Abraham, a maneuver that caught the French completely by surprise. "Already tired from fighting, Montcalm's men 'ad to regroup to da far side of da city," said Martin, in a tone that expressed a certain degree of sympathy for the French troops. "And although da French were effective militia fighters, da British were well trained in classical European warfare. Dey didn't stand a chance."

"You can tell he's biased towards the French by making excuses for them," griped the man from Ontario. "He should just face facts. They got their butts kicked."

Thirteen hundred men died that morning on the Plains, even though the battle was only a few minutes long. Wolfe himself was killed, and Montcalm died several days later from wounds suffered. The French returned in 1760 with reinforcements, but not before England had already arrived with three reinforcement ships of their own. The takeover became official in 1763 after the French signed the Treaty of Paris, officially ending the Seven Years' War. Quebec City became Canada's capital until that role was relinquished to Ottawa after Canadian Confederation in 1867.

As we neared the fortification tower at rue Saint-Jean and, with it, the end of our tour, I asked Martin a question that I had been itching to ask since the beginning. "What do you think would have happened if France had won the Seven Years' War? Do you think people in western Canada would be speaking French?"

"Probably not," Martin said flatly. "Da anglicizing of North America would 'ave taken place eventually. Even if da British 'adn't done it, da Americans probably would 'ave settled western Canada."

So the French didn't stand a chance. When considered in this light, it's really quite remarkable that a province of six million francophones adrift on a continent with a quarter of a billion anglos—a culture that is infamous for trying to assimilate other cultures unto their own likeness— has not only survived, but prospered. For that fact alone, Quebec has my admiration and respect.

Chapter 36

Sacred Blues

July 27, 2000 - Autoroute 175 north of Quebec City

When I left Ottawa at the beginning of the summer, the one area of Quebec that had given me the greatest cause for both excitement and concern was the Lac-Saint-Jean region, home of the *bleuet* (blueberry)—not merely a small, delectable fruit, but an affectionate nickname levelled at the region's largely rural inhabitants. I had heard rumours that the people of Lac-Saint-Jean were renowned for their charisma, tall tales and a unique brand of the Québécois tongue that some say borders on singing. Others, French-language snobs no doubt, liken a *bleuet's* accent to fingernails grating against a chalkboard. Not that this had any bearing on my trip ... good French or bad French, it was still unfathomable to me.

The things that excited me about Lac-Saint-Jean were the same things that worried me about it. Here was a remote corner of the province, tucked two hours north of Quebec City, that promised a taste of the exotic: a distinct and spontaneous people hemmed in by a colourful tapestry of orchards and villages, alternatively dropping to the edge of a magnificent lake or rising to meet cliff-top vistas overlooking the Saguenay fjord. Lac-Saint-Jean's relative isolation from other parts of Quebec—not to mention Canada—has surely contributed to its firmly separatist constitution. It is a fact: seventy percent of the people living in the Lac-Saint-Jean region voted for separation during the 1995 Quebec referendum, and the vast majority of those who live there are francophone with little connection to the English-speaking world. And here I was, a Calgary man sporting a red CANADA T-shirt, jauntily wandering into the heart of it all.

It was nearing the end of July when I finally left Quebec City, and I will forever be grateful that it was a thickset man by the name of Gino who squealed his minivan to a halt along Highway 175. Although he looked to be in his thirties, his hair was thinning and he sported a dark shadow of stubble on his broad cheekbones. After plunking my backpack into his van, I climbed in and started speaking to him using broken French.

We carried on like this for some time, until it was clear we weren't getting very far. It was only then that Gino switched to broken English, telling me about the Alcan aluminum plant that he worked at near Jonquiére, which, next to Chicoutimi, is the most heavily populated city in Lac-Saint-Jean. Although he lived in the heart of *bleuet* country, it quickly became obvious that Gino had learned a good deal of English.

"I like to watch English television sometimes," he admitted. "And I 'ave a sister who works as an Engleesh teacher." This was good news for me. In fact, it turned out that Gino spoke enough English to communicate just fine with somebody whose French was improving with each day, and between the two of us, we were able to discuss all topics of shared relevance on the national scene.

"You know Shania Twain?" asked Gino.

"Yes."

"Elle est belle!" he exclaimed, raising his thumb into the air.

I couldn't argue with that assessment.

As we drove north, Gino and I broached pretty much every politically charged topic relating to Quebec, and our discussion gave me new hope for the rest of my trip through Lac-Saint-Jean. "It's a 'andicap when you can't speak Engleesh," he told me frankly. Like many of his friends, Gino was angered by the provincial government's policy to restrict English education to children whose parents had attended English school in Quebec. "Why can't I go with my girls to Engleesh school?" he said, exasperated. "It's good to speak two languages, and my girls will be disadvantaged if dey can't speak both Engleesh and French."

Of course, Gino was no great lover of anglophones who don't recognize French as Quebec's mother tongue, particularly anglos from Montreal who make no attempt to learn French while living there. What burned Gino most was when "Americans and Ontarians"—as he referred to them—show no patience for Quebecers who struggle with English while travelling abroad ... especially when many "Americans and Ontarians" expect Quebecers to address them in English when they come to Quebec. "Is it not true dat in Rome you do as da Romans do?" he asked me with a shrug.

I nodded. He was right, of course.

"I mean, even you are speaking French and you are living in Calgary," he continued. This was a strong assessment of my feeble language skills, but it made me feel appreciated for my modest efforts.

Eventually separation came up. "What do you think about it?" I inquired, coming just short of asking how he had voted in the 1995 referendum.

"It might 'ave been a fresh idea when René Lévesque was 'ere, but now da idea is old and stale," Gino told me bluntly. "Everyone just wants to work and 'ave a 'ealthy family." Then shrugging, as if addressing Quebec politicians: "Do you 'ave another question please?"

Next under Gino's guillotine was the Catholic Church. Gino was raised in a family with fourteen children, and for my benefit he described in painful detail a time when the church was more powerful than the government, a time when Catholic priests travelled around Quebec actively "promoting" childbirth. The only problem, according to Gino, was that "promoting" all too often meant "coercing." This philosophy has created its fair share of rifts in the province, and the Catholic Church is now struggling to regain the trust of younger generations.

"'You do more babies for Jesus!'" ranted Gino, shaking his finger like a high and mighty priest. "Tabernack!" The sudden vocalization of a French swear word caused him to reflexively duck his head beneath the dashboard, perhaps fearing lightning bolts that would singe the last of his hair into nothingness. In English, the word "tabernacle" is hardly obscene, of course, yet so much as whispering it in front of a nun would probably warrant a week of scribbling Hail Marys on a chalkboard.

Gino dropped me at a parking lot in Chicoutimi, and as I climbed out he handed me his phone number. "Call me when you get stuck," he said.

"Thanks Gino," I replied. "After I hitchhike around Lac-Saint-Jean I'll come back and visit your family."

"Don't be..." He searched for the right word. "...shy!"

"I won't be."

Beside the parking lot where Gino dropped me was a strip of unsightly fast food restaurants: Tim Horton's, Harvey's, and across the road from that, a Wal-Mart—the great Satan of American culture. So much for the exotic flavour of Lac-Saint-Jean, I thought to myself, marching into Harvey's to order some dinner. Mind you, once inside I quickly became entranced with the prospect of dazzling a pretty French girl behind the counter with my encyclopedic knowledge of French vegetables, so it wasn't long before the deplorable ugliness of the Wal-Mart had faded from memory.

"Qu'est-ce que tu veut dessous," the pretty French girl asked, smiling warmly while inquiring about hamburger fixings. Her smile was the kind that said, "You're kind of cute," which put extra pressure on me for a tactful response.

"Moutarde, oignon, mayonnaise, laitue, trois tomates et cinq cornichons, s'il vous plait," I said, rather pleased with myself. All that practice in Quebec City had paid off handsomely. Still, despite my deft display (and even though French, I suspect, was originally designed to induce amorous feelings in women), my prowess with it wasn't enough to inspire the kind of deep, unbridled passion that I had been hoping for. Once I found a table, she turned to the next customer and promptly forgot about me.

But that's okay. If garnishing my hamburger in French wasn't enough to leave a distinct impression, my next feat most certainly did. Walking into Tim Horton's, I found myself the focus of great attention among its coffee-drinking patrons, and the buzz of conversation came to an abrupt halt when I entered. The restaurant was packed, and the confused stares I was fielding made wading through the fray with my backpack rather disconcerting. It was like being in small town Saskatchewan.

CRRAAASSHH!!!

That was the sound of a heavy, wooden box full of suggestions getting knocked off the counter. I had swung my backpack sideways to avoid body-checking an elderly woman with a cane into a napkin dispenser.

"SACRÉ BLEU!"

That was the first thing that came out of my mouth, confirmation to all present that I was, indeed, an anglophone. Had there been any doubt?

To my relief, the restaurant erupted with laughter, a tension-breaker if there ever was one. Clumsily, I kneeled down to pick up the box and the scattering of suggestions that were now littering the floor, grateful that the language police were nowhere near. If they had been, I would surely have been ticketed for causing a suggestion box in the heart of separatist country to make a sound like "CRRAAASSHH!!!" That's the sound a falling suggestion box makes in Calgary.

At the counter, a girl of about fifteen with short, dark hair and a round face sized me up as I rattled off my order. As I was having great difficulty marrying the desired number of creams and sugars to my coffee in French, she eventually interrupted: "You know, it would probably be easier if you just ordered in English." Normally her response would have pleased me greatly, but I was in Lac-Saint-Jean, damn it, and I didn't want to be let off the hook so easily.

"Okay, I'll have a coffee with one cream and four sugars," I relented. "And one of those chocolate dip donuts over there." I thought for a moment as she assembled my order. "Say, where did you learn to speak English, anyway? I thought people up here speak only French."

"For the most part," she replied, then went on to explain how she and her family had lived in Ontario for several years.

Collecting my goodies, I quietly found a seat to work on my journal, hoping to avoid further carnival antics. I didn't yet know where I was going to sleep, but I was confident that once midnight rolled around, a suitable park, church or hidden plot of grass would present itself as it always did. In Quebec, I had been taking advantage of the many grand cathedrals of the Catholic Church, easy to spot and often surrounded with plenty of grass to pitch my tent. So I tugged at my coffee, lost in thoughts about my journey thus far, and let my pen saunter through the pages, recording fond memories of people I had already met. Perhaps an hour had passed when my perfect, silent reverie was shattered by a firmly built woman shouting "Monsieur! Monsieur!" from behind the counter. I looked over to see her waving frantically at me, a telephone receiver in her outstretched hand. "La telephone!" she exclaimed. "Pour vous!"

The telephone? How could it be for me? Nobody knew I was here. I glanced over my shoulder just to be sure she wasn't talking to somebody else. "Pour vous!" she said again, pointing at me and then at the telephone.

I walked over and gingerly plucked the phone from her fingers. "Hello?"

"This is Valerie," said a voice at the other end of the line.

Valerie? I consulted my memory for recent acquaintances and came up blank. I didn't even know a Valerie in Calgary, much less in Quebec. "Valerie who?"

"I served you coffee and a donut earlier this evening," the voice replied. "Remember? From behind the counter?"

Of course I remembered. "Sorry, I didn't know your name was Valerie."

"That's okay," she said. "Listen, I've been talking to my parents about you, and they want to know if you'd like to come over and stay with us tonight."

I was floored. "Why would they want to do that?" I asked.

"Well, with all your stumbling around I kinda felt sorry for you," she giggled. "I figured you could use some help."

What a thoughtful gesture—even if it was based on a presumption that I was completely incompetent. "That's awfully nice of you," I said. "How would I get over to your place?"

"We'll be over to pick you up in ten minutes."

July 28, 2000 - Saint-Nazaire, Quebec

Something snapped the next morning on my way to Lac-Saint-Jean, and quite truthfully, I lay the blame on nobody but myself. You see, a person reaches a point while learning another language when he becomes so supremely tired of apologizing for poor grammar, and so utterly sick to death of asking people to repeat themselves that he will do just about anything to blend in. When people address him, he will smile and nod, use liberal applications of *Oui! Oui!* and pretend that he knows what they are talking about, even if he has no clue. He will also make no effort to slow the speed of people's banter. Rather, he will seek guidance using a blend of his own intuition and the vague meanings he deduces from facial expressions.

There are times, of course, when these sorts of questionable tactics backfire. This is especially true at that critical juncture when a person knows enough of a language to make it sound like they know more than they actually do. There's no doubt that blending strategies, at times, may draw puzzled looks from those soliciting a response, or may lead you to respond in a way that is completely unrelated to the conversation. In a worst-case scenario, such strategies may even result in a piece of triple-layered chocolate fudge cake being delivered to your table that you had no intention of ordering.

Hitchhiking through lakeside towns such as Péribonka and Saint-Félicien gave me ample opportunity to practice these sorts of strategies. One such occasion came shortly after I was picked up by a kind, respectable-looking gentleman in his mid-fifties just outside of Saint-Nazaire. He wore a loose-fitting navy blue golf shirt and wire-rimmed glasses, and had a dusting of silver hair on his head. René didn't speak a word of English, so rather than apologize for my poor French, I decided to blend by way of nodding and smiling a lot, and generally *not* letting on that my expertise in French became marginal after an impressive listing of fruits and vegetables.

And my tactic worked. Sort of. At least until I made the mistake of asking him what he did for a living.

At first, he seemed pleased by my inquiry and erupted with a long and heartfelt explanation of what, presumably, his profession was. Most of what he said I didn't understand, yet somewhere in the telling I managed to pick out the words *Professeur* and *Université de Chicoutimi*, which, not surprisingly, led me to conclude that René must be a professor at the University of Chicoutimi. No need to worry about the details. All I wanted was enough information to keep the conversation rolling along.

"Est-ce que vous avez de la famille?" I asked next, inquiring about his family.

René glanced sideways, giving me a slightly puzzled look before starting to talk again. Along the way I heard definite references to a *mère* (mother), a *père* (father) and lots of *mes amis* (friends); to assure René that I understood him, I continued peppering him with nods, smiles and plenty of *Oui! Ouis!* as he talked. I didn't, however, catch anything about children, so after he had finished I decided to ask him again, this time more specifically.

"Est-ce que vous avez des enfants?" Children were always a popular topic of discussion, and I figured that this question would keep him busy until well after we had reached our destination.

To my surprise, the question had the opposite effect. René stopped talking entirely and became noticeably fraught with suspicion. For several minutes we both sat with stunned expressions, contemplating what to say next.

Eventually, René cleared his throat and, after finding his voice, managed in slow and very pained English: "I ... am ... a ... Catholic ... priest."

July 29, 2000 – Ste-Monique, Quebec

My leisurely dawdle around Lac-Saint-Jean was cut short the day after René dropped me in Sainte-Monique, a picturesque little village on the north shore. This is where I first heard about *La Traversée Internationale du Lac-Saint-Jean*, an annual thirty-two-kilometre swimming race across the deep, cold swells of the lake. It was a much-heralded event that every year attracted crazed contestants from around the globe, eager to swim through water that, even during the summer months, can most generously be described as an ice floe. I was told that the swimmers had left earlier that morning and that if I hurried, I might catch them as they reached the finish line in Roberval at the far side of the lake.

For more than an hour I stood in despair, watching vehicles pass that didn't seem to appreciate my tight timeline. Even when a battered pickup truck finally did stop, it turned out that the driver was going a mere ten minutes down the road. I would have to do better than that if I was going to beat the swimmers to Roberval.

My next ride—this one with a young Québécois couple who preferred listening to Eric Clapton on the radio as opposed to conversing in French hiccups with me—drove beside the pastoral scenes of Rivière Mistassini to Saint-Félicien, which sits on the even more scenic, though unpronounceable, Rivière Ashuapmushuan. Unpronounceable as it was, it still held great appeal, primarily because it put me within striking distance of Roberval. What I hadn't counted on was the long slog to get out of Saint-Félicien. With no shoulder on the road, I eventually had to stop at a short strip of pavement that was marked for delivery trucks, hoping that one would mistake me for cargo.

After thirty minutes I was almost ready to start walking again when a small hatchback pulled over with three people crammed inside, smoking cigarettes and blaring their stereo. Somehow they found room, and with me squashed against the door, we sped off in the direction of Saint-Prime, a village halfway between Saint-Félicien and Roberval. Along the way, I struck up conversation with the two girls and the driver, whose name was Dave Blackburn. Dave was shirtless and sported a long, angular goatee, and although he had an English name, he didn't speak a word of the language. Nevertheless, we chatted amiably in French for a few minutes, and before I knew what had happened, we were traversing the marina along Roberval's waterfront. Perhaps Dave had felt sorry for me as Valerie had two nights before, or perhaps he simply had nothing better to do. Whatever the case, his kind gesture got me to Roberval just in time to see the last of the swimmers stroking through the gates at the marina.

It was utter pandemonium along the waterfront. Through a boisterous crowd crammed along the edge of a pier, I could see a water corridor marked off by buoys and patrolled by police boats. More spectators sat aboard a fleet of sailboats and power boats lined along each side of the corridor for a couple of hundred metres, many of them swimming in the water to stay cool. An announcer shouted in French through a loudspeaker, chanting "Go! Go! Go!" as each swimmer approached from the lake and started down the final corridor toward the finish line. Stephane Lecat of France had already captured the trophy for first place, while Liam Weseloh was Canada's best showing at eighth. Other countries that had participated were surprisingly diverse, including Australia, Egypt, Argentina and Bulgaria. The announcer broke into English only briefly to interview one of the Australians, who explained that although he was happy to finish, he was disappointed with his overall showing.

It wasn't long before Quebecer Marc André Girard came in at position number seventeen. The crowd went wild after he touched the marker, a sentiment that only surged in decibels when Quebecer Julie Robert swam in at Girard's heels. I fumbled my way to the small dock where officials were helping the two swimmers out of the water, and by feigning a speech impediment somehow managed to talk my way into a press pass.

As they climbed from the water, the swimmers were briefly embraced by friends, family and well-wishers before getting whisked off to the front of a podium. Julie Robert in particular—tired and worn down—received deafening applause. She looked completely overwhelmed, but humbly raised her hand and waved at the crowd. After a few words with the announcer they were once again swarmed by friends and family at the sidelines, getting kissed on both cheeks repeatedly.

The evening proved to be as loud and festive as the race itself, with Montreal singer Michel Louvain whipping an impressive audience into song and dance. He reminded me of a French Neil Diamond, such was his elegance. I sat and watched the show for some time before slipping off for a quieter moment along the pier, the glitter of celebratory lights dancing along the waterfront. Just as I was getting ready to take some pictures, however, a gruff female security guard approached and said something in French that I couldn't understand.

"Pardon?" I asked.

She pointed at the yellow security tape cordoning off the pier. It seemed rather petty to deny me a few simple photographs, so I tried explaining that the pier was the only place I could get some decent pictures of lights reflecting off the water.

"Il y a des feux d'artifice ici," she repeated.

I still had no idea what she was talking about, but my blending instincts took over and I found myself pleading with her in French to let me take some photos. "Je suis un journaliste!" I told her, pointing happily at my camera. But she would hear nothing of my plans, and so I was forced to retreat with my tail between my legs and no valid reason why this had all happened.

Later that evening, feeling slightly rebellious, I tried sneaking onto the pier twice more from different points along the waterfront. I stealthily ducked under the yellow security tape, yet twice more was I apprehended by Brunhilda, then promptly escorted off before I could get any pictures. It was like being in high school all over again.

So much for blending.

A few minutes later, while I nursed some iced tea and fries at a nearby picnic table, a wave of multi-coloured flames suddenly erupted beside the pier, right about where I would have been standing with my camera and tripod. Fireworks burst across the night sky in volleys of brilliant light while the crowd stopped whatever they were doing to *ooooooh!* and *aaaaaah!* and be generally amazed. I was amazed too, partly by the marvellous spectacle that was the fireworks show, and partly by the calm persistence of the security guard who had prevented me from wilfully barbecuing myself.

I looked up *feux d'artifice* in my French-English dictionary the next day. It did indeed mean "fireworks." If I was going to practice blending in the future, I guess that's one word I might want to remember.

Chapter 37

Gino

July 31, 2000 - Chicoutimi, Quebec

It's always heartening to watch transformation at a laundromat—to stuff one's dirty, foul, sweat-riddled travel clothes into a pair of machines, and *voila!* an hour later watch them reappear as clean garments of forest freshness. It's one of those miracles of the road—something travellers obsess about on those hot, deplorably sticky days when there's no lake to run screaming toward and hurl yourself into. You know the weather is becoming unbearable when signing up for the *Traversée Internationale du Lac-Saint-Jean* starts to sound appealing, because drowning in the middle of a lake as deep and unbearably blue as that sure beats thirty-five-degree heat and humidity.

It was in this oppressed state of mind—my clothes saturated, my brain like Crisco shortening—that I returned to Chicoutimi. It was five days after Gino had dropped me there. I called him from the laundromat expecting a half-hearted response, but when he answered the phone and heard it was me, his voice raised with pitched excitement. He wasted no time inviting me over. "I will make you a feast to be proud of," he announced, a response that made me feel far more important than I was ... like royalty, or some western diplomat on a peacekeeping mission.

"That's all right Gino, just make what you normally would," I replied. A short visit would be nice, but I didn't want to disturb his family's routine.

"No, no," he insisted. "I must show you some Québec 'ospitality."

Thirty minutes later, Gino and his two young daughters picked me up, my backpack full of fresh-scented clothes. On the way home he told me that he had put my name on his softball team's roster for a game that evening, which evidently meant that I was going to play some ball. "I told everybody dat Reggie Jackson's brother was playing for us tonight," he laughed, "so dere might be a little bit of pressure on you." Gino obviously thought he had a pinch-hitter, but he was getting nothing of the sort.

"Sorry to break this to you *mon ami*, but I'm from Michael's side of the family." I was clearly white, and I was surprised that Gino hadn't noticed.

Gino's home was nestled on a plot of prime pastureland surrounded by acreages at the southern edge of Jonquiére. An aging barn sat directly behind his large white-washed home, in plain view of a field dappled with lemon-coloured canola. It was a scene that could have been plucked from Lac-Saint-Jean and dropped into Alberta's Peace River country with little disruption, and for a fleeting moment it reminded me of my uncle's farm near Spirit River.

After we entered his house, Gino led me upstairs to a guest bedroom that obviously doubled as a play area if the bounty of toys were anything to go by. While Gino continued with dinner preparations, I had the opportunity to explore this bounty with his two daughters, four-year-old Rose and one-and-a-half-year-old Blanche.

It quickly became clear that Gino's daughters were no dummies, which turned out to be a great disadvantage for me. While Blanche happily accepted me without hesitation, Rose grilled me with an endless stream of four-year-old questions designed to probe who I was and where exactly I had come from. The fact that I sat there with a dumb look on my face—rather than responding intelligibly to her inquiries—really began to frustrate her, to the point where she started shouting at me. No doubt she figured that added decibels would facilitate understanding on my part. It didn't help in the slightest, of course, and none of the French I knew seemed adequate to appease an agitated toddler. What was I going to ask her? *Que faites vous comme travaille?* "I go to playschool, thank you very much," would have been her response, and my reputation as a capable adult would have forever been tarnished in her mind.

That's when a clever idea came out of nowhere. "Est-ce que vous le monstre du biscuits?" I asked, poking her in the tummy with my index finger.

She started giggling, looking at me with buoyant blue eyes.

"Est-ce que vous le monstre du biscuits?" I repeated. I was asking her, I'm pretty sure, whether or not she was a cookie monster.

She continued giggling, then started smacking her lips. Obviously she was a cookie monster, and I lamented not having any cookies to appease her further.

Then came another bright idea. On my travels around Lac-Saint-Jean, I had met a professional clown named Jacko, and for five dollars he had sold me a red clown nose. Not just any red clown nose, but one with a battery-powered light that made it glow cherry red. I rooted around inside my backpack, found it, then produced it on my generous snout for an honest four-year-old assessment.

That was it. Rose cracked up. "Monsieur clown! Monsieur clown!" she repeated over and over, her chest heaving with deep belly laughs that soon had Blanche giggling too. The medley of distorted expressions that crossed my face would leave my face sore for a week, but Rose remained suitably entertained until Gino had finished preparing dinner. My diplomacy skills with French toddlers had passed the ultimate test.

A teammate of Gino's named Serge was waiting for us at the dinner table downstairs. Gino had cooked some filet mignon sandwiches, and as he finished tossing a salad it became apparent that Serge's English was even better than Gino's. "'ow do you say 'filet mignon' in English?" Gino asked of nobody in particular.

"It's da same, Gino," Serge replied. "The French 'ave such good food dat it's da same in both languages."

The food *was* good, no question about it, and it bolstered our energy for the game that evening. This was important, considering that Gino's team was defending a stellar season with nine wins and only one loss. On top of my masquerading as Reggie Jackson's brother, this near flawless record heaped a great deal of pressure on me, a reality that was only heightened when I considered my general incompetence at the plate. Using a large stick to whack a palm-sized ball as it soars through the air has always been, for me, like trying to dispose of houseflies with a chainsaw. Furthermore, I was worried that a dismal performance on my part might serve to fray delicate ties between Quebec and English Canada even further. Was the fate of a unified Canada riding squarely on my shoulders?

The blokes on Gino's softball team welcomed me openly despite my lack of appropriate clothing (they hadn't seen me play yet). All of them wore uniforms, but all I had was the usual: khaki pants, a blue T-shirt and hiking boots. Serge passed me his glove and I ran into left field to practice catching pop flies. At least several of the players spoke English to varying degrees. One of the friendliest was a broad-shouldered fellow named Big Pete who had glasses, a stringy goatee and a slight paunch.

"Why do they call you Big Pete?" I asked.

"I guess it's easier to say dan 'Gros Pierre,'" was his reply.

The game started slowly. My first time at bat I hit a pop fly; the second time around, I dribbled a feeble grounder past the pitcher's mound. On both occasions I was thrown out at first. But my game did improve, and despite leading Gino's team to its second loss, I'm pleased to announce that I didn't completely disgrace Alberta. I caught a couple of pop-ups in the outfield, and in the seventh inning I hammered one over the shortstop's head that earned me a double. Gino was up to bat soon after, and before I knew what had happened, he had smashed the ball over the fence. It was the only home run of the game, and we celebrated by rounding into home, fists pumping the air, then laying a flurry of high fives onto our cheering teammates.

Darkness had fallen by the time our game finished, but with a babysitter at home Gino felt no need to go anywhere quickly, so a group of us gathered round the bleachers with a cooler full of beer to laugh and tell stories. It was only then that Gino told everyone how he had met me (surprisingly, nobody had asked that question during the game), and I was thus committed to giving a full verbal rendition of my travels. Even though the bulk of my story had to be related in English, most of the players seemed to understand, or at least nodded their heads and made appreciative comments at intervals. It was a surreal experience: an Alberta hitchhiker captivating a team of francophone ball players in the heart of separatist country.

One by one the players dispersed, until there were only six of us left. Our conversation was casual, yet somehow we got talking about the Montreal Canadiens, about the overwhelming response to the recent death of Maurice "Rocket" Richard, and about what the Canadiens as a hockey team symbolized for Quebecers. "It's da dream of every Québec boy to play for da Canadiens," Gino said proudly. "When I was young, I was always Jacques Lemaire." He made a couple of crafty moves with an imaginary hockey stick before firing an imaginary puck into the top corner of an imaginary net. "And in my dreams, I always stood tall and proud at da national anthem."

"At games dese days 'ardly anybody even stands up," laughed Big Pete.

That was the opening I needed. I had wanted to bring up the topic of Quebec separation all evening, but hadn't known how. "So what would happen if Quebec separates?" I asked. "What would you call the Montreal Canadiens then?"

The players looked at one another, then laughed and kicked at the dirt. "Dat's a good question," admitted Gino. The others nodded their heads, agreeing that this odd dilemma had never occurred to them.

"I know this is a taboo subject for some Quebecers," I continued, treading into uncharted waters, "but who here voted 'Yes' during the 1995 referendum?" Three of the five raised their hands, including Gino and Big

Pete, a majority that made me grateful this was merely an informal tally. The fact that Gino raised his hand surprised me a bit, though he did qualify his answer.

"Most Quebecers are actually very proud to be Canadian," he said. "Dey don't want to live elsewhere, and dey are 'appy to be well-received around da world."

"Then why did so many vote 'Yes' in the referendum?"

Everyone sat quietly for a moment, the question hanging in the air. "More dan half da people don't know why dey voted 'Yes,'" Gino finally said. "But we must be proud of Canada because we call da cheese in our poutine 'Canadian cheese' and we're proud of it."

When I asked the others why they had voted "Yes," Big Pete, the most self-assured guy on the team, said that he knew Quebec's history, was proud of it and thought the province could do better on its own. Gino wanted to see Quebec's natural resources, things like hydroelectricity and forestry products, stay in Quebec. The third fellow must have felt shy, or perhaps liked the other answers better, because he deferred his opinion to Gino and Pete.

The two players who had voted 'No' also had valid reasons. "I think Québec gets more from Canada dan we give," said one of them. "Why leave such a profitable arrangement?"

The other guy who had voted 'No' agreed, but Big Pete wasn't convinced. "I don't know if dat's true," he said with a guarded voice.

Of course, nobody wanted to push a pleasant discussion into a heated debate—especially one that involved a guy named Big Pete who was standing there with a baseball bat in his hand. We agreed to end the conversation and go home.

As Gino and I drove through the city and out into the countryside, he told me something that pretty much summed up his feelings about separation, something that probably summed up the feelings of many Quebecers. "You know, I don't tink I would vote 'Yes' again," he said, "if dere was another referendum, dat is."

"Really? Why not?"

"I think dere's more opportunities for my daughters if we stay in Canada," he said. He turned south toward the edge of town, a canopy of stars in the sky appearing like bright points of promise.

"Den again," he conceded, "you never know."

Chapter 38

Good Times in the Maritimes

August 13, 2000 - Campbellton, New Brunswick

All the way across Canada, people had been preparing me for the Maritimes. It was to be a sort of hitchhiker's Nirvana—a place where the air is fresh, the seafood orgasmic, the people friendly and the rides long and plentiful. A place where people aren't just hi-how-are-you friendly, but c'mon-inside-young-feller-and-sink-your-teeth-into-this-here-lobster friendly. Not that the Maritimes have a monopoly on hitchhiker hospitality—as I had discovered many times during my trip—it's just that I had heard over and over again that as far as unabashed acceptance of strangers goes, the Maritimes are in a class of their own.

It wasn't until I had crossed the New Brunswick border at Campbellton that I was finally able to put this theory to a test. After waiting for thirty minutes at the roadside—on a spacious, hitchhiker-friendly roadside, I might add—a French couple named Robert and Micheline pulled over in a small hatchback. I barely had time to click my seatbelt buckle before they had invited me to stay with them at their cottage on Baie des Chaleurs, a strip of beachfront just north of Bathurst. Their skin was deeply tanned, and when I explained that I had just travelled through Quebec, they told me they had been there recently themselves, traversing the Gaspésie on their Harleys. It was either sunburn or windburn that had turned their skin the colour of chocolate.

Micheline, who worked as a secretary, was a slender woman with stringy auburn hair that draped down the length of her back. Robert, an amiable fellow with a bristly charcoal moustache, managed a scrapyard. Although the pair had day jobs, they were also part of the motorcycle crowd that live by the rule, "Work hard, play hard"—a fact that became apparent when we arrived at their home. The view out the front was nothing short of stunning, but their home was clearly functional more than decorative, and came equipped with plywood floors and bits of furniture that had obviously seen their fair share of beer-swilling action. "We want to put in 'ardwood flooring," Micheline told me, "but for now, plywood is easier to clean up after a party."

But that didn't matter to me. Robert and Micheline, if not polished, gave new definition to the word "hospitable." For starters, they were so certain I would join them for dinner that they didn't even bother to ask me. After I had been sitting there for five minutes watching them feast on pizza fingers, garlic bread and Coke, the couple said in a sort of bewildered tone, "Aren't you going to 'ave any food?" In other parts of Canada it's considered good form to refrain from eating until you are formally invited to dinner, but that's not how things seem to work in the Maritimes.

While we ate, they brought me up to date on world events, because I was as starved for news as I was for food. It had been weeks since I had read an English-language newspaper. At the top of the list was a blockade at the small New Brunswick Native community called Burnt Church, where Canadian fisheries officers had been squaring off with aboriginal fishermen over the illegal harvesting of lobster. The season had officially ended many weeks before, but the First Nations group continued to set their traps, claiming that their aboriginal status gave them the right to harvest lobster year-round. The confusion over the lobster fishery had started the previous fall after the Supreme Court of Canada waived a conviction against a Native eel fisherman named Donald Marshall. In the same breath they had pronounced that a treaty from the 1760s gave Mi'kmaq fishermen the right to earn a moderate livelihood from the Atlantic's bounty. The media had broadly positioned the debate as Natives versus non-Native fishermen, and tempers had been flaring ever since.

On the lighter side, the couple also told me about the upcoming Acadian national holiday, an event of great fanfare that takes place across Acadian lands every August 15th. This was news to me. I didn't even know what Acadians *were*, much less anything about a national holiday. "Acadians are people of French ancestry who were deported from Nova Scotia by da British," Micheline explained. (There go the British again, carting people around on a whim.) "But beyond dat, I don't know much."

"Caraquet is da place to be right now," enthused Robert, referring to a small village on the peninsula just east of Bathurst. "Dere's a big party brewing."

"What sort of party?"

"Lots of drinking and dancing and making noise," said Micheline, a dreamy look in her eyes. "It's a time for all Acadian people to celebrate deir roots."

"You should check it out," said Robert.

Although they weren't sure of specifics, their description of Caraquet was enough to pique my interest. And my interest was only heightened further when later that evening, we heard the roar of booming mufflers as two of their friends rolled in on their hogs. There was Claude, a bad-ass biker wearing chain boots and a leather Harley Davidson vest, his wavy black hair peeling out from under a bandana. Lean, muscular and with forearms as thick as a maple tree, Claude was definitely the kind of guy one preferred to be friends with rather than enemies. At his side was a beautiful blonde girl named Solange; I made great efforts not to look at her for fear of going from the former to the latter in less than sixty seconds. The last thing I wanted to learn about was how to make Acadian pretzels out of hitchhikers.

Claude and Solange had stopped by for a short visit, but I soon lost sight of them behind the blue haze of cigarette smoke. Everyone roared hysterically, sloshed back beer and whiskey and started celebrating Acadia's national holiday a little early. Actually, I got the impression that pretty much any day would have been worthy of celebration. As I fetched a drink, I noticed a white T-shirt under Claude's vest with two flags side by side. One was the Canadian flag; the other looked like a French flag with a gold star.

"What's that?" I asked, pointing at Claude's chest.

"Dat's da Acadian flag," replied Robert.

"You guys have a flag too?"

"Of course," he said. "And we also 'ave our own constitution."

"You're kidding."

Geez. Here was a culture with its own holiday, constitution and flag— one that had apparently been part of Canada for more than three centuries—and I knew next to nothing about it. That sounded like reason enough for a detour.

August 14, 2000 - Highway 11 on the Acadian Peninsula, New Brunswick

Lobster, lobster, lobster. Everywhere in the Maritimes there is talk of lobster, a sort of seafood-induced hysteria that holds sway over Maritime minds during the summer months. Not that you can really blame people, because lobster brings in a lot of tourist dollars and is pretty damn tasty to boot. There's boiled lobster, baked lobster, barbecued lobster, lobster rolls, lobster sandwiches, lobster pot pies and probably lobster slurpees at 7-11. Even McDonald's gets in on the lobster action; every so often along the side of the highway you'll see a billboard the size of a parking lot advertising the much-vaunted McLobster. I even heard that New Brunswick elected a lobster as Premier once—Mr. Clawed C. Bottom, I think—though that could very well be a tall tale.

It was with lobster on my brain that Micheline dropped me at a highway exit around noon the following day. I had made up my mind to visit Caraquet before continuing south toward Nova Scotia, which would require an hour-long detour along a sparsely populated peninsula where Maritime goodwill would be put to its first real test. And I'm happy to report that Maritime goodwill passed the test, but for one unfortunate and sour turn of events at a roadside diner. After getting picked up by an Acadian man named Guy for a short ride between seaside villages, we decided to stop for a bite, and invariably our conversation drifted to Burnt Church and the conflict over the Native fishery. It was the biggest story in New Brunswick that summer and it seemed to be on everybody's mind.

One thing I hadn't realized, until Guy offered a bit of background, was that there has been a tradition of unrest in the Miramichi Bay area. For years, disputes have led to shouting matches, vandalism and the occasional brandishing of firearms—even between factions of non-Native fishermen. This is because many of the small communities along this coast depend almost solely on the lobster fishery for income, and fishers tend to get a wee bit territorial when it comes to protecting their livelihoods.

As you might imagine, when thousands of unregulated Native traps started plunging into east coast waters after the Marshall decision, there was a swift backlash from non-Native factions, who saw their lives put into jeopardy. As a result, the Supreme Court's decision (which was supposed to ensure that the Mi'kmaq people retained some of the freedom they had enjoyed before colonization) backfired in a big way. In October of 1999, angry mobs of non-Natives had run amok through the Burnt Church reserve, destroying lobster traps, vandalizing fish plants, issuing threats and setting trucks alight on the Burnt Church pier.

It was in the midst of discussing these events that Guy and I heard a gravelly voice drifting across the restaurant. "There's a war coming!" warned a grey-haired man with a lean and chiseled face, his words laced with venom. He had overheard us discussing the fishery from across the patio and decided to offer his two cents' worth. "White fishermen are just waitin' to see what the federal government is gonna do about those Injuns. We're waitin' to see if they're gonna make the right move." The man was obviously sour with fear and anger.

"I understand your frustration," I said, "but maybe Native treaty rights *should* allow for year-round fishing in some waters." I didn't know enough to comment intelligently, but I didn't want to dismiss outright the possibility that the Natives had a legitimate case. Maybe they did, maybe they didn't. Besides, I've always had the charming habit of jumping into the role of the devil's advocate, even when wisdom suggests that I should keep my big lobster-trap mouth shut. This was clearly one of those occasions.

"HOGWASH!" the man snarled. My comment, far from being received with the thoughtful acumen of a debate-loving man, only served to make him angrier. "HOW CAN YOU HAVE TWO SETS OF LAWS? THAT'S A GODDAMN RECIPE FOR DISASTER!" Tact was not this man's forte—and finding myself suddenly in the path of an Atlantic gale, all I wanted was to defuse the situation. Besides, if the man's blood pressure shot up another notch I was worried he would suffer cardiac arrest, collapse on somebody's table and ruin a perfectly good lunch.

"THOSE INJUNS ARE NOTHIN' BUT A BUNCH O' NO GOOD LAZY BUMS!" he shouted. "THEY JUS' WANT TO MAKE THEIR OWN LAWS AS THEY SEE FIT!"

Guy and I endured the man's ranting for a couple of minutes longer, until my shock and embarrassment started turning to anger. "LISTEN!" I finally barked, looking at the man with a piercing stare. "You should know that I'm part Native myself and I'd appreciate it if you didn't generalize! It's not fair to call any one group of people anything!" Yes indeed, I really said that.

The irate man looked dumbfounded. In fact, he didn't say another word, but stalked off with a dirty look.

"You certainly shut him up," said Guy, smiling from across the table.

The adrenaline buzz of conflict was still coursing through me, but I managed a faint smile. "Yeah," I said. "I just hope he's not going home to fetch his shotgun." And so it was that we finished our lunch with eyes glued to the door, ready to toss the table like they do in gangster movies if our hysterical friend reappeared with a loaded firearm. But he didn't, and we managed to leave the place in peace rather than in pieces.

"By the way, I'm not really Native," I admitted to Guy, once we had returned to his car. "I just wanted to give that guy some pause for thought."

"I know you're not," he said. "But it made for a damn fine story."

EVENING WAS CLOSING in fast by the time Pierre, an Acadian fellow on his way home to Caraquet, stopped to pick me up. Like Claude from Bathurst, he was another tall, firmly-built fellow, though a slightly softer centre and receding hairline hinted at middle age. Pierre was also up on his Acadian history, and during our drive along the north shore of the peninsula, he was able to shed much light about who the Acadians were and where they had come from.

"Basically, da Acadians are a French community dat survived deportation," he began. "I can trace my own ancestry from a long line of Acadians who fled Nova Scotia after da British demanded an oath of allegiance." That was in 1755, according to Pierre, a year when thousands of Acadians began migrating into northern New Brunswick and to remote island communities like Prince Edward Island. The Acadians who didn't flee were mostly shipped to colonies in the American South or back to Europe.

"Da British government was really just looking for farmland to cede to British settlers," Pierre explained, "and da Acadians 'ad already cultivated land for dat purpose. It was easy for da British to move in and simply take land dat 'ad already been cleared." In the meantime, Acadian refugees quietly established new communities; some of the largest and most important were in northern New Brunswick, where they managed to subsist for a century with very little equipment and few supplies to sustain them. They were experts at farming tidal areas, Pierre explained, so many of them built dikes to transform the rich, silt-laden marshes along the coast into arable land.

"So how did you end up with a flag and a national holiday?" I asked.

"Dat didn't 'appen until da late eighteen-'undreds," said Pierre. "A bunch of Acadian delegates got together to 'affirm' da Acadian identity." He used his fingers to trace quotation marks in the air. "That's when dey chose a national 'oliday, an Acadian song and a flag."

"That's incredible," I said, and meant it. I was from Alberta where "Roots" referred to a brand of clothing, not to one's lineage. In fact, most Albertans I knew were happily ambivalent about their ancestry. It was nice talking to someone who cared about who he was and where he had come from.

As we drove into Caraquet, it quickly became obvious that the community was preparing for a major brouhaha. There was electricity in the air, and the place had the feel of a town readying itself to celebrate the persevering spirit of its ancestors by getting drunk and dancing the night away. Red, white and blue bunting fluttered from buildings along the main drag, and pedestrians scurried in and out of the liquor store with bags of precious commodities. "Da liquor store is da only thing open tomorrow," smiled Pierre, "and it's gonna be real busy!" To my surprise, when it came time for Pierre to drop me at the centre of town, he instead invited me to stay with him and his family for a couple of nights. "You can pitch your tent in our backyard. If you're gonna experience Acadian Day, you should spend it with a real Acadian family."

The following afternoon, Pierre and I launched his Zodiac for a trip to Caraquet Island, a warm-up for the more dramatic festivities planned for later that evening. Pierre's wife Lisé and her friend Isabelle packed a picnic lunch, and we were soon cruising past the marina under a canopy of unblemished blue, heading toward a fleet of fishing boats offloading their catch amidst flocks of herring gulls. The pungent odour of a working harbour wafted on the ocean breeze, but we drifted by and were soon whisking across the open water. "A large sandbar in da bay blocks boat traffic at low tide," Pierre explained over the drone of the engine. "But it's 'igh tide right now, so we don't 'ave to worry about following dose markers."

After cruising around the bay for fifteen minutes, Pierre edged the boat up to a sandy spit where he let the ladies off to walk the beach. In the meantime, he and I continued around to the far side of the island to look for lobsters. We puttered along at low speed, peering through blankets of seaweed floating on the surface (the result of a recent big blow), but in the end we were quite unsuccessful.

"It doesn't really matter," said Pierre. "Da lobster are molting right now anyway. Dey aren't any good to eat."

"So why are the Natives at Burnt Church still harvesting them?" I asked.

Pierre shrugged. "Because dey're lazy?" he said. "It's easier to catch dem during da summer when da weather is good."

We made it back to Caraquet just in time for Lisé to go to work, and for Pierre, his son Patrick and me to join some fifteen thousand revellers marching festively up and down the streets shouting, singing, blowing through plastic trumpets and banging pots and pans together. The trumpets emitted the sort of mournful, agonizing blasts that only a very sick moose could make, but several times more annoying. Nobody seemed to mind, though. This was Acadia's national holiday, and even the sickest moose would have been welcome, so long as it was having a good time.

For a photographer, the march was a dazzling medley of Acadian colours flashing everywhere: parachute-sized flags, banners, painted faces. It reminded me of Canada Day in Ottawa. Costumes of red, white and blue were all topped decadently with the requisite gold star, and several industrious groups had even assembled theme-related costumes: frogs, potatoes, clowns, that sort of thing. Pierre told me that these groups were affiliated with a particular Acadian nickname or clan.

Some of the clan nicknames seemed odd to me—the potato clan, for instance. Why anybody would want to be a member of the potato clan is beyond me, yet I saw gigantic spuds swaggering gaily down the street with obvious pride. Why not a wolf clan, a whale clan or an eagle clan? Now *there* would be clans worthy of affiliation. Wolves stealthily stalk prey through the forest; whales dive to the depths of the ocean; eagles flash with beak and talon above the clouds. But potatoes are only good for one thing. They get cut up into French fries, dumped into a vat of hot vegetable oil and then get consumed by people like me who dribble ketchup down their shirts. Doesn't really fit with the legendary backbone and fortitude that Acadians are known for, does it? Still, the costumes were quite something.

For Pierre, Lisé and me the evening ended at the Caraquet arena, a concert for which tickets had long been sold out. Pierre, ever the resourceful chap, somehow managed to get me a ticket by loaning his truck to the event coordinators. So inside we went, where the best of Acadian music was soon whipping the crowd into a folk-rock frenzy. I watched from the sidelines as Pierre, wearing an Acadian headband, danced with Lisé like a giddy child on Christmas morning. They kicked up their heels and spun whirlwind circles through the crowd, jubilant to be Acadian at the start of a new millennium. The joyful simplicity of it all was impressive, and reminded me of something Pierre had told me that afternoon while we were skimming the water in search of lobsters: "People expect too much dese days. If dey focused on da simple tings, they would see dat 'appiness exists right in front of dem."

Such was Pierre's pearl of wisdom. I suspect it was the same attitude—practiced by his ancestors—that helped the Acadians survive nearly impossible odds.

Chapter 39

Burnt Offerings

August 17, 2000 - Highway 11 near Burnt Church,
New Brunswick

The man's name was Albert, and he was my one-way ticket down New Brunswick's Acadian coast all the way to Moncton.

Albert was a Newfie, and a good bloke at that. He was candid, comical and immediately disarming. Since reaching the Maritimes, I had met a lot of people who exuded these qualities: Robert and Micheline, Pierre and Lisé. It was to the point where I was starting to buy into that whole Maritime hospitality superiority thing, when I remembered that Newfoundland is technically not part of the Maritimes. I had been lumping them together for some time, mostly because I had heard that Newfoundland was the friendliest of all the eastern provinces, the kind of place where drivers literally fight over hitchhikers. "Just wait 'til ye get to the Rock, lad," one fellow had boasted. "They'll be foightin' over ye to give a roid." "Roid," of course, was Newfanese for "ride," and it was nice to hear that roids would be plentiful in one of Canada's most sparsely populated provinces. I could hardly wait to get there.

"Do ye want to stop for a boit?" Albert suddenly asked, a few minutes after picking me up. "Moi treat." We had only just met, but already the guy had invited me to stay at his home in Moncton, and now he was offering to buy me lunch. Funds were tight, and as it was already well past noon, I felt obligated to accept his invitation. Albert was probably as hungry as I was.

Albert turned off the highway and parked his car at a roadhouse-style diner; two minutes later we strolled into a dimly lit restaurant, eager to appease our grumbling tummies. Albert had only forgotten to mention one small detail, which came up shortly after we had seated ourselves, prodigiously studied the menus and were on the cusp of ordering what looked to be a most satisfactory lunch.

"I'm fasting," Albert told the waitress. "Just bring me a glass of water please."

"You're what?" I was taken completely off guard.

"I'm fasting," he said again, nonchalant as the ocean breeze. "I'm not going to order, but I thought you moight be hungry, so I wanted to boi you lunch."

This was a new one. I had never been picked up by someone who invited me to lunch, then announced as we were ordering that he had had no intention of eating from the very start. Still, Albert looked like the kind of warm-hearted guy who actually enjoyed watching other people eat on his nickel, so I did my duty (painful as it was) and ordered a burger, fries and a Coke. The meal was quite wonderful, though it was a bit disconcerting to watch monastic Albert sipping at his beverage while I stuffed my face. Fasting was something he did every year, for reasons of health and spirituality.

After lunch we pressed on towards Miramichi, and Albert began telling me stories about growing up on the Rock (otherwise known as Newfoundland). He had obviously grown from a long lineage of characters, down-to-earth but well equipped with a sense of humour. "Newfoundlanders, wherever they go, always remember where they're from," Albert explained. "Do you know how to recognoize a Newfoundlander in heaven?" He looked over at me, and when he saw that I didn't know, hit me with the punchline. "Because they're the only ones who want to go home," he chortled.

Albert also confided that most people would never leave the Rock if there was work for them. "And contrary to popular belief, Newfoundlanders are smart and versatoile people," he told me. He was referring to that nasty myth that Newfies are kind of dopey and backwards—the dullest pencils in our national box of pencils, if you will—and that they deserve their reputation as butt of our country's jokes. "A lot of communities are so isolated that you have no choice but to become a jack of all trades," he said. "A lot of toimes you have nothing to get boi on but wits and ingenuity."

I wasn't surprised to learn that Albert's father and seven brothers were cod fishermen. Or at least they had been fishermen, until all the cod disappeared. A combination of severe overfishing, scientific myopia and political mismanagement of the fishery had left precious few in the ocean around Newfoundland's Grand Banks. "Everyone has a bit of guilt over it," Albert admitted, "and now they're gonna do the same thing with shrimp. They say 'a little bit, a little bit,' and 'a little bit' eventually becomes 'a lot.' But it's difficult not to put pressure on the fishery because Newfoundland's economy, and some would say soul, depends on it."

It was while discussing these painful issues that, as if on cue, Albert and I were promptly flagged down by a pair of large Native men who were holding sticks and standing in the middle of the highway. They looked like backwoods thugs, though rather more serious and ill-tempered. On the road behind the men, a pile of smoldering tree branches billowed smoke into the afternoon sky. "Geez, I'd forgotten about this blockade," whispered Albert as one of the men approached. "I think we were supposed to take a detour several moiles back."

We had arrived at Burnt Church.

"Are you the journalist they're expecting?" asked the Native man, with an air of gruff reproach that clearly suggested one of us had better be.

"Yes he is," replied Albert, pointing across the car at me.

Before I could respond, the man had flagged us past the blockade, indicating that we were to follow a sombre and dispirited-looking fellow called "the war chief" to the far side of the reserve.

"What do you mean I'm the journalist they're expecting?" I exclaimed.

"Well, you're a journalist," Albert said. "Aren't you?"

"Yes, but I'm not the one they're expecting. We might be in for it now, because that war chief guy looked a little short on humour."

Albert shrugged. "I didn't know what else to say."

So with a certain sense of disquiet that you can well imagine, we followed the war chief for several kilometres along a narrow road through thick forest, emerging abruptly at a second blockade several minutes later. This one also featured several charred logs that had been clumped together and set alight, tended by two more sumo-sized Natives who looked equally as cheery as the first pair. Perhaps it was the blood-red Mi'kmaq flag snapping in the wind that made me feel uneasy, or maybe it was the large wooden sticks the men whapped against their palms, a perfect girth for beating imposters to a pulp. Whatever the case, the war chief gave us a sullen nod before turning around and driving back in the direction we had just come, leaving Albert and me to sit nervously in his car awaiting the consequences of our little deception.

"They're just standing there," noted Albert, after several uneasy seconds had passed.

"Maybe they're waiting for us to come and talk to them," I suggested.

"Do you think I should just droive away?"

"I don't know." We scanned them warily through the rearview mirror. "I think we should at least get out and ask them a few questions." I grabbed my notebook—in a manner not unlike that of a two-year-old grabbing his security blanket—then slipped my camera around my neck as I climbed from Albert's car. If either one of us were going to get beaten silly, I was at least going to capture it on film. One has to look at the bright side in these sorts of circumstances.

Walking toward the stone-faced duo, I couldn't help but notice that my stained khaki pants and grubby T-shirt contrasted rather sharply with Albert's cheery pin-striped golf shirt and white sneakers; the two of us must have looked an unlikely pair of journalists. Fortunately, neither of the men seemed to notice.

"Hiya guys, how are you today?" beamed Albert, greeting them as he might a pair of long-lost cousins. "Moi name is Albert and this is Matt." Perhaps he wanted to buy them lunch too, in which case I was going to suggest fresh lobster tails at a seafood restaurant in Miramichi.

As it turned out, the men weren't interested in long-lost cousins wearing golf shirts or in lobster-tail lunches. All they wanted was for me to record their plight so that the world would understand why they had set up the blockade, which I did in great detail, without letting on that the world would be none the wiser after talking to the likes of us. "I'm just a poor Native fellow who wants to feed his family," said the shorter man with army pants. "I don't think it's too much to ask for my constitutional right to fish year-round." They carried on to relate how for decades, in their opinion, the Natives from Burnt Church and other reserves had not been receiving a fair and equitable share of the East Coast fishery. And from the sound of things, they did have a point. While thousands of non-Native fishermen were pulling in millions of dollars a year from a government-sanctioned lobster harvest, Natives had been getting a pittance.

"Why can't we have a fair share of the resources?" asked the second man. "Is that too much to ask?"

After several minutes, I could see that the first guy was starting to get a little misty-eyed, but I felt that leaning forward and hugging him might be viewed as inappropriate under the circumstances. Besides, if there were any Canadian Press photographers lurking in the bushes, I would have some explaining to do when pictures of me hugging a barrel-chested Native man in military fatigues appeared on the front page of the *National Post*.

Fortunately, it never came to that. I penned some notes, took photos of the smoldering blockade and generally indicated my sympathy for their cause. Albert agreed heartily and (presumably because he couldn't buy them lunch) ran back to the car to fetch some cookies that his wife had recently baked. They accepted the food gratefully, though with somewhat startled expressions. Were journalists now bringing care packages from home?

Fifteen minutes later, Albert and I were back on the road, neither bloodied nor bruised, having just avoided a long detour. One thing was for certain: this particular Newfie was as sharp as any pencil in the country.

Chapter 40

Perfect Storms need not Apply

August 29, 2000 - Yarmouth, Nova Scotia

Blame it on George Clooney, his salty-dog heroics and that damn Hollywood flick, *The Perfect Storm*. They were my somewhat skewed inspiration to hitchhike along Nova Scotia's French shore, all the while exploring small fishing villages for an opportunity to jump aboard a sword boat and sail off into the liquid blaze of a setting sun.

And really, who wouldn't want to be George for a day, even if it meant wearing checkered flannel? Ever since I'd seen his movie in Ottawa and watched the *Andrea Gail's* dramatic fate on the silver screen, I had been dreaming about hitching the high seas ... on much calmer high seas, of course. Perhaps it was George's poetic ode to the fisherman's life, or maybe it was just leftover nostalgia from sailing the Great Lakes the previous summer. Whatever it was, it caused me to tramp from the highway clear down to the docks in Yarmouth to start combing the wharf for boats. Thumbing across Atlantic Canada without insight into the fishing life seemed not only a wasted opportunity, but a blatant denial of the region's heart and soul, historically speaking anyway. And I would toss my cookies before that happened (or perhaps while it happened). As a vagabond journalist I had grown accustomed to hardship, and if that meant gripping the starboard rail with white knuckles and hurling into a frothy sea, so be it.

Yarmouth is a quaint little seaport town, the kind of place you expect to see sleep-deprived guys tramping around in work boots and rubber hats, smelling like cod and smoking big pipes. It had a romantic feel to it, no question, and it wasn't long before my efforts unearthed a prospect: a young guy with bloodshot eyes, a stubbly face and a cigarette hanging from the corner of his lip. He was leaning from an open window in the wheelhouse of a large fishing boat, having a bad hair day. "Are you headed out to sea in the next couple of days?" I asked.

"Yup," he said. "Headin' out late dis afternoon." Was that an accent, or the result of squeezing the butt end of a cigarette between his lips?

"How long are you going for?"

"Just headin' out for da night," he replied. "We're comin' back sometime tomorrow mornin'."

"No kidding." This sounded promising. "What are you guys fishing for?"

He looked up at me as if it had just occurred to him that I might not be from Yarmouth. Was it my blatantly idiotic line of questioning? "Herring. Dat's all a seine boat is good for," he said. "You from around 'ere?"

"No, I'm from Calgary." I told him a bit about my hitchhiking trip and explained that I wanted to experience the melodrama of life on a fishing boat, just like George. Well, almost like George. Could he guarantee there would be no sharks, rogue waves, crazy storms or back-breaking labour?

"Yer in luck, cause tonight she looks fine," he told me. "Clear sailin'."

"I don't suppose you'd have room for me, then?"

"Sure, you kin come along."

"That's fantastic!" I enthused. "By the way, my name's Matt."

"Darren," he replied. "And dis 'ere's da *Eastern Fisher*."

And that's how I talked my way onto a Nova Scotia fishing boat. I was going to be George Clooney for a night, sans checkered flannel.

THE *EASTERN FISHER* had been using Yarmouth's harbour to offload catch, but Darren, his crew and the boat actually hailed from Pubnico, a small fishing village a few dozen kilometres south along Nova Scotia's French shore. Which Pubnico they were from was a matter of debate, however, because when I studied a map of the southwestern part of the province, I found more than one. There was Pubnico proper, located in the crease of a large bay; not far from there, along a peninsula to the southwest, sat West Pubnico, followed by Mid West Pubnico and, finally, Lower West Pubnico. To the southeast (go figure) lay East Pubnico, Mid East Pubnico and Lower East Pubnico, lined neatly in a row. Down the road still further was Pubnico Beach, probably used by all the tourists and bikini-clad Nova Scotians during the summer months. This was followed by Shag Harbour, which was either the hangout for naughty Pubnico teens or the secret headquarters of Austin Powers.

There was obviously more than enough Pubnico to go around. Whether this was because the town's founder felt he had stumbled onto a good thing, or whether he simply suffered from a chronic lack of imagination, I will never know. All I really learned about Pubnico was that it is the oldest Acadian settlement in Canada, founded in 1653, and that most fishermen hailing from there speak a quirky sort of "Franglais" that probably offends language purists from both camps. According to one man I met, their dialect consists of one third French, one third English and one third profanity.

Shortly after dinner I met the *Eastern Fisher's* crew down by the wharf. There were seven of us in total, including myself, Darren and a friendly, pear-shaped cousin of his named Philip, who was actually a cook. He was along for the ride just like me. The others were both young and old, rookies and veterans alike. One of the most experienced was Amos, a wiry fellow with glasses, a thick moustache and deeply calloused hands. Calvin was another veteran, and with his full grey beard, the most likely-looking fisherman on board. "You wouldn't have known it in dose early days," he told me. "When I first started fishin' I was sick like a dog." There were also Dwayne and Richard, both of them young, able-bodied and eager, though Richard was perhaps the better candidate for a Mark Wahlberg stunt double.

The crew spent the next hour preparing for the night ahead, checking nets and filling the boat with ice, and shortly thereafter we cast off the bow and stern lines and chugged from the harbour toward the open ocean. Our destination was the German Bank, located sixty kilometres off the Nova Scotia coastline; the crew assured me that it was one of the best places for herring. They also told me that seine boats fish at night because that's when the herring rise to the surface. The fish are so sensitive to light that even a full moon can force them to stay low, which meant that tonight really was the perfect night: no moon, clear skies and not a whisper of wind.

The sun set shortly after we passed the mouth of the harbour, casting ribbons of pink and crimson between rocky shoals. It wasn't long before several crew members had vanished below deck to grab some shut-eye. A long night of fishing lay ahead—just like the previous night, and the night before that, and the night before that—so it paid to sleep while they could. Only Darren, Dwayne and Philip stayed in the wheelhouse, where they kept me suitably entertained with stories.

"Pink sky at night, sailor's delight," chimed Dwayne. "You should know dat it doesn't get much better dan dis." I could only imagine. Even though Nova Scotia was rapidly shrinking from sight, the water was practically a mirror.

"Yup, it should be a good night, alright," sighed Darren.

"How long have you been doing this?" I asked him.

"Dis is my first year," he said. "I guess you could say I'm a captain in training. My father owns da boat." Darren looked to be about thirty, if that, which seemed kind of young to have this much responsibility. But what did I know?

"So how's the fishing these days?"

"Herring is a nice bonus," Darren explained. "But da price for it 'as been low for da last ten years." He told me that back in the 1970s, herring used to sell for two or three hundred dollars a tonne, climbing as high as four hundred dollars a tonne in the 1980s. "Now we're lucky to get one 'undred and twenty dollars."

"Yeah, it used to be dat we'd make six 'undred dollars every night," lamented Dwayne.

"And da first year I came aboard 'ere I made eight thousand dollars in my first week," said Darren. "Boy, dose were da 'eydays. Now you need a month to make dat much money."

During the winter, of course, it was a different story. The *Eastern Fisher* might be an eighty-foot boat rigged for herring during the summer, but as a lobster boat during the winter and spring, it made a whack o' cash. "Lobster is definitely da main source of income," Darren said, smiling. "Dis 'ere is a very good lobster area."

"How much can you make with lobster?"

Darren arched his eyebrow. "Dat depends if you 'ave yer boat paid for."

"Some guys make ten to fifteen thousand dollars in da first week alone," trumpeted Dwayne. "And a 'undred and fifty thousand for six months of work is not unheard of."

"Geez, that's a lot of money," I said. And to think Albertans feel sorry for these poor eastern fishermen.

"One thing you 'ave to understand about lobster fishin' is dat dere's 'uge risks involved," said Philip. "Da Atlantic during da winter can get pretty rough, and dat's when fishin' for lobster becomes a very serious occupation." Philip held his hand in the air, his thumb and index finger three centimetres apart. "I've seen dis much ice frozen on da front of my clothes during da winter."

Darren and Dwayne nodded.

The three of them also bristled at the mere mention of rope, which has a tendency to get tangled in things as it goes over the edge of the boat. This can result in any number of ugly scenarios, which might include getting a foot wound in rope that's attached to a rapidly descending lobster trap. Add to that frigid water, inky blackness and a heavily weighted boat that can swamp should the surf hit it from the wrong direction and you've got a recipe for a full-on lobster rodeo. "You've got more salt water goin' up yer nose, ears and mouth dan you know what to do with," laughed Dwayne. "It ain't child's play, dat's for sure."

"Yup, when all da other boats are tied up," says Darren, "da lobster fishermen are still out workin' dere tails off."

"Has anything ever happened to one of you?" I asked.

"I've lost friends lobster fishin'," said Philip, in a tone that suggested this was not a rare occurrence. He carried on to relate a harrowing experience that his father had at the tail end of a hurricane back in the 1960s. "He still has da rosary he made out of twine, because 'e didn't think 'e was gonna make it."

Dwayne carried on to tell a gruesome story about another lobster fisherman who nearly cut his hand off in a bait cutter. It happened when a large wave smashed into the boat, unexpectedly pitching it sideways. "Da poor guy 'ad to amputate da last tendon 'imself and stick it between two boxes of frozen bait to keep it cold," said Dwayne. "He was more in control dan da other crew members."

On that cheery note, I followed Philip and Dwayne below deck for a snack and some coffee, leaving Darren to man the wheel by himself. To my surprise, there was a robust lounge with benches, a large table and a full kitchen, including stove, refrigerator and microwave. It was the works. There was even a television, which Dwayne turned to a music station with black rappers from Los Angeles, a sight that felt oddly alien aboard an Acadian fishing boat chugging toward its destiny on the German Bank.

"How many boats are going to be out there?" I asked Dwayne, after a few minutes of watching the rappers dance like lobsters on steroids.

"Oh, I'd say 'bout twenty-five," he replied. "Dere are also a lot of draggers dat go after ground fish such as cod, flounder and 'alibut."

That's when it occurred to me that I still didn't know anything about how a seine boat actually works. "How big is a seine net?" I asked.

Dwayne, although conscious, was fading rapidly. Philip was wide awake, though, and he busied himself rooting around in the cupboards for something more substantial than a bag of stale Twizzlers. "It's two thousand feet long and 'angs about two 'undred feet deep," answered Dwayne with a yawn. "Can you believe dey cost two 'undred thousand dollars? And to tink dey're really only good for 'erring."

"Dat's why dey're always sewing patches in it," added Philip cheerfully. He had found something that looked like chocolate cupcakes, which he quickly devoured.

"It's all part of da job, even dough we don't get paid for it," sighed Dwayne. "But I guess if dere wasn't money in it, we wouldn't do dis foolishness."

After a few more minutes of television, Dwayne headed into the bunkroom for some sleep, while Philip returned to the wheelhouse. I checked my travel clock and, seeing that it was almost midnight, decided to take a catnap in preparation for the long night ahead. I stretched out on the bench between the wall and the kitchen table, and although it was narrow, somehow managed to get comfortable. I pulled my jacket over my chest and to my surprise, it wasn't long before I had drifted off to sleep, the soothing hum of the boat's diesel engine echoing in and out of my dreams.

I WAS WAKENED abruptly at quarter to three by a shrill voice crackling over the intercom, calling all hands to deck. The others were busily donning fleece sweaters, rain jackets and bib coveralls made of rubber, so I pulled on warmer clothes and hurried behind them to the wheelhouse. Philip and Darren were still there, as I had left them three hours earlier. The fluorescent glow from the depth chart, sonar and other instruments was the only visible light coming from the cabin. Darren steered his boat, watching the instruments like a hawk, while at the same time exchanging information with other fishing boats in French. For the last three hours, Philip explained, Darren had been searching for fish, and it finally looked like he had found some. "Right now it's a game of cat and mouse," Philip told me. "But first we 'ave to get into position."

The call, unfortunately, ended up being a false alarm, so everyone flopped onto padded benches to smoke cigarettes or to fetch coffee from the kitchen. Outside, the sea was like a small city of fishing boats, their lights festooned across the water in every direction, cutting through the obsidian cloak of a moonless night. Darren pointed at the depth sounder, which was showing little green and yellow squiggles moving across the screen. "Dose are fish," he explained. "When da screen turns red you know dey're packed tightly together. Mostly we're lookin' for schools of fish in less dan a 'undred and twenty feet of water."

Over the radio, reports from other boats started pouring in. One fisherman sounded completely distraught, announcing over and over in pained tones: "Wot a mess! Wot a mess!" He had tangled his net on the stern of his boat and torn a big chunk out of it. Another boat reported two whales in their net. "Minke whales like to feed on 'erring," said Dwayne, "which means we sometimes trap dem and 'ave to dump da entire load." A third boat crackled in with news of a record catch—too much for them to handle—and pleaded with another boat to come and take some of it off their hands.

As the minutes slowly turned to hours, there were three more false alarms, which sent everybody scrambling to positions on deck. On every occasion they stood dutifully at hand while Darren tried jockeying his boat into position, but each time the school of herring moved out of range before the men could drop the net.

It wasn't until quarter to five that we finally got the call—a sharp blast on the foghorn—which signalled Calvin to slide a small skiff off the rear of the boat, pulling the seine net with it. In only a few minutes we had looped a huge circle with the fishing boat back to the skiff, and shortly thereafter started closing the bottom of the net, which was dangling two hundred feet below the surface. In fifteen minutes, the net was sealed. Only then were massive floodlights turned on, meaning that it was time for Calvin, Dwayne and Richard to start the gruelling task of hauling the net back in. Had the floodlights been turned on sooner, the bright glow reflecting off the water would have caused the herring to dive beneath the net and escape.

Over the next hour, the net was slowly hauled in one metre at a time, the odour of fish hanging in the air like a Japanese sushi bar. Gulls pecked and fought with each other overhead while a lone seal made an appearance at the side of the net, looking for a free meal. By this time we could see the herring, thousands of silver bellies flashing across the water, a few of them dropping onto the deck as the net was reeled in and stacked. In the net we also found a small dogfish and a foot-long squid, the latter of which Darren fetched from the deck and threw at my feet.

Dawn was soon upon us, and the closer the herring got to the surface, the larger the catch seemed. According to Darren it was small, though, and even more disappointing was the terrible quality of roe, which was discovered after Amos and Darren had split several fish up the middle. Roe is the primary reason herring is valued at all and, sadly, it meant that their all-night effort was for naught. I felt terrible for them, but Amos just looked at me and shrugged. "Dat's fishing, my boy, it's all part of da game."

Just as we were about to head back towards Yarmouth, Darren answered a call from another boat. "Eastern Fisher, dis is da Tasha Marie, do you copy? Over. Eastern Fisher, dis is da Tasha Marie, do you copy? Over."

"Dis is da Eastern Fisher," replied Darren. "Over."

"Darren, good to 'ear from you lad. We've got too much to 'andle 'ere. Do you 'ave some room? Over."

"Copy dat, we've got room. Where's yer coordinates? Over."

After a brief explanation, we turned toward a boat silhouetted against the rising sun, and within a few minutes had pulled up and dipped our pump into their nets, even as friendly jeers were exchanged between crews. Darren and his men would only get about forty tonnes, but at least the boys wouldn't go home empty-handed. "Everyone knows one another," said Amos, pointing at several minke whales surfacing between the boats. "Today we didn't get anything, but next time it might be da other way around."

As we headed back to port, Darren handed the wheel to Calvin so that he and Philip could tuck downstairs for some well-earned shut-eye. Meanwhile, Dwayne, Amos and I chatted around the kitchen table while Richard cooked some bacon, eggs and French toast, a spread that soon disappeared without a trace. Amos explained that he had recently bought a lobster boat, something he now planned to put all his energy into. "Lobster licenses cost about three 'undred thousand dollars," he told me, "so if I can pay da bills, I'll be fine. Den in ten years I'll sell my outfit for retirement money." A good lobster outfit, apparently, goes for more than a half-million dollars these days.

After breakfast we turned on the television, and the first thing we saw were federal fisheries officers ramming Native boats with a Zodiac near Burnt Church. It was two weeks since I had passed through the blockade, but the issue had obviously not been resolved, and tensions were continuing to escalate. Looking across the table I could see Amos and Dwayne scowling, and after a few minutes Amos finally muttered, "They're a bunch o' lazy buggers who want to fish in da summer so dey don't freeze dere butts off. Dey don't want to play by da same rules we 'ave to."

When I asked Amos about Native treaty rights he wasn't fazed in the slightest, and explained why the Natives were misleading people with their rhetoric. "For one, lobsters molt during da summer so dey're no good to eat anyway," he explained. He also pointed out that white fishermen have to make huge payments, while the government simply hands Native fishermen licenses, boats and equipment for free. "Does dat sound fair to you?" he sputtered. "As far as I'm concerned, dey can fish da way dey used to fish two centuries ago if dey want complete control of da fishery."

Not for the first time, it occurred to me that the Canadian government had managed to create for itself a most unenviable dilemma: disarming an irresistible force moving against an unmovable object with hurricane-class magnitude. Perhaps *this* was the perfect storm. Whatever it was, it was threatening to wipe out everything in its path—Natives, non-Natives and lobsters alike—and I didn't envy any of them. Where were the salty-dog heroics of George Clooney when you really needed them?

Chapter 41

One Fair Isle

September 9, 2000 - Borden, Prince Edward Island

Hitchhiking on Prince Edward Island turned out to be a cinch, all things considered. Even my technique for fetching a ride was simple, and in three easy steps might successfully be employed by any other hitchhiker who visits Canada's fairest isle. Step one: sit down at a table in a greasy truck-stop diner. Step two: order a plate of scrambled eggs, bacon, hash browns and toast. Step three: strike up conversation with the guy sitting at the next table. If his name is Percy, remember to visit the bathroom before climbing into his truck. If his name is Al MacDonald, then sit back and smile my friend, because you've just hit the jackpot. He'll spend the next week driving you from one end of the island to the other.

This may sound like a hoax, but I assure you that I have not fabricated this story to qualify for a Cavendish bed and breakfast weekend. This really happened to me while I was sitting at a restaurant in Borden, the small island community sprawled at the base of the thirteen-kilometre Confederation Bridge. The previous evening, I had pitched camp under bridge spans on the New Brunswick side—a sorry mistake, to be sure—for I had been kept awake all night by the clatterings of trucks rumbling across Northumberland Strait, taking advantage of twenty-four-hour access to the mainland. Giving up in a state of sleep-deprived stupor, I packed my tent by six in the morning, flagged down a ride with two Ontario tourists, and arrived on the island shortly before seven. Once at the restaurant I opened my journal and settled myself down for some grub. Fifteen minutes later an amiable guy named Al MacDonald walked in palming his cell phone, and that was pretty much it. We started talking about potatoes, and somewhere between my first egg and second slice of bacon, he offered to be my official island tour guide.

It's not really surprising that Al was a MacDonald; every second person living on Prince Edward Island is. And if they're not a MacDonald, they're more than likely a MacLeod, MacLellan, MacDowell, MacKenzie,

McCuthcheon, McAvity (a family known for their bad teeth), McKay, McClure or perhaps even a McDonuts—a somewhat more Canadianized moniker, don't you think? For the benefit of all you foreigners, I might point out that McDonuts just happens to be the surname of Alexa, the highly respected ex-leader of Canada's New Democrat Party. At least that's what the Right Honourable Jean Chrétien, Canada's most fearless leader, used to call her during Question Period in our House of Commons.

If I couldn't have asked for a guide with a more suitable island surname, I also couldn't have asked for someone with a job that better represented PEI's economy. Al was a buyer and seller of potatoes, and after finishing breakfast and paying our respective tabs, we jumped into his truck and drove across town to check his fax machine for messages. He was gearing up for the harvest, that six-week period every autumn when everyone in the PEI potato business survives from dawn until dusk on caffeine and nicotine. "In another couple of weeks you won't be able to move on this island," Al told me. "There will be truckloads of spuds everywhere. During the fall, when that harvester is going full tilt, look out, cause it's like mining for gold."

Al's office was located inside an old brick home at the edge of town, and while I waited for him to finish with business, I snooped around his office. On the wall just above his desk I noticed a poster with about a dozen mug shots of PEI's premier spuds: Yukon Gold, Shepody, Goldrush and Russet Burbank. They sounded like a bunch of desperados. It was like one of those "Most Wanted" posters you see tacked to the message board of a post office in the old Wild West.

With business taken care of, and with no pressing concerns for the afternoon, Al decided to take me for a little jaunt around the countryside. Before leaving Borden, however, he abruptly turned west and detoured along a road near the base of the bridge, passing what looked to be the town's abandoned ferry terminal. In the distance, we could see the bridge snaking off toward New Brunswick like a giant eel, across the heaving strait of Northumberland.

"It must have been tough for Borden when that bridge opened," I offered in a deferential tone. From what I remembered, several hundred people had lost their jobs after the Borden ferry was decommissioned, and the lost jobs had added fuel to the fire of critics. Some people claimed the bridge was a curse, rather than a government-funded blessing that had cost the feds nearly a billion dollars.

"Yeah, a lot of people were completely upended," Al told me. "But most of them are settled again." He paused for a moment, lost in thought. "And that bridge has been great for the island."

"How so?" I asked. My gut told me that some might disagree, viewing the bridge with begrudging acceptance, if not downright hostility.

"Well, for one thing the bridge offers guaranteed access to off-island markets," Al replied. "With the ferries, you could never guarantee overnight service because even under ideal conditions it would take a couple hours longer to cross. And in the winter, forget it. If the ferry got stuck in the ice, a forty-five-minute crossing sometimes turned into ten or twelve hours. My mother knows. She worked on the ferries for sixteen years."

I asked Al why some people had opposed the bridge.

"Well, the pace of living has definitely changed," Al admitted. "Visitor traffic has nearly doubled, and the price of land has gone up a lot. But we all knew that was going to happen before it was built. It was pretty much guaranteed. Some of us wanted the bridge because it was progress and strictly economics. For others, I guess it interrupts their quality of life."

Al and I spent the next hour cruising along back roads on the island's interior, ending up near Victoria, a town fifteen minutes due east of Borden. It was here that we came upon a stunning vista overlooking Northumberland Strait, where the deep and vivid blue of the water was flecked by whitecaps. However stirring the view was from shore, it didn't look like the kind of place you would fancy being on a windy day, particularly in a small boat. And for those not in the know (as I was not before meeting Al), this windy patch of water that separates PEI from the mainland had much to do with Prince Edward Island's decision to join Canada in 1873, after refusing to do so six years earlier. Among other things, the federal government lured islanders into the Dominion by promising to pay for year-round mail service.

And how did they provide this service? Well, before the superferries and long before the bridge, the only tried and true method for navigating the ice-choked strait during the winter was by iceboat. These were seventeen-foot skiffs or dories that weighed upwards of four hundred pounds, curled up like a giant ski at one end. The boats were built with cedar and heavy oak, reinforced with aluminum runners along the bottom for scootering over the ice. They were powered by men who harnessed themselves to the gunnels with leather straps, and who were capable of pushing and pulling boats over nearly any obstacle: around ice blocks, over pressure ridges and through thick lolly (slushy ice floating on the water). Gallantly, through conditions that would make modern postal workers curl into the fetal position and start weeping, they ferried mail, medicine and passengers to and from the island. The harnesses these men used were designed not only for pulling the dories, but doubled as insurance in the event a crew member broke through the ice or slid off an ice pan into water so cold that it threatened to stop his heart. To say these guys were tough is an understatement.

Considering winter weather that had a nasty habit of blowing in from nowhere on Northumberland Strait, it's surprising there were not more iceboat disasters over the years. Only one person ever lost their life. Nevertheless, there were some close calls, including one in 1885 when a fleet of three iceboats set out for the island with twenty-two passengers and crew. Before nightfall, a blizzard had marooned them on the drifting pack ice, and all they could do was bank two of the boats together and crawl between them for shelter. They burned the third one to stay warm.

Their plan sounded like a good one until, deplorably, the fire had melted a hole in the ice. This meant they had to pull the boats apart, exposing their wet clothes to the raging storm. By the following day, the fuel was gone and they had drifted some thirty-five kilometres off route. That's when they spotted a church steeple through the blowing snow and pushed hard for shore. They made it—barely—but found themselves wading through neck-high snowdrifts in a swamp, the weakest among them giving up to die. Rescuers eventually found everybody, though one man had frostbite so bad that both feet and all his fingers had to be amputated. A second man was found in the swamp clinging to a frozen tree branch. His condition was so perilous that the branch had to be sawed off and the man carried into a farmhouse still attached.

An outcry echoed across the nation soon after the incident, forcing the Canadian government to consider less primitive methods for crossing during the winter months. Some islanders proposed a floating railway bridge anchored by cables to the sea floor, while others (including charismatic Senator George W. Howlan) were advocates of a tunnel under the strait. One local politician even suggested damming the Strait of Belle Isle between Newfoundland and Labrador, thereby reducing the large quantities of ice that float into the Gulf of St. Lawrence from the north Atlantic.

In the end, the federal purse could only afford a new steel-hulled ferry called the SS Stanley, primarily because they had just spent seventy million dollars on the CPR to appease British Columbia. Although the government hoped the ferry could handle winter crossings under any condition, within two years the vessel had proved desperately inadequate. It had a nasty habit of getting locked in ice and being dragged up and down the strait for days at a time, which meant that iceboats were once again called into service. It wasn't until 1917, when the 300-foot *Prince Edward Island* was christened, that larger vessels proved capable of safe year-round passage. The final iceboat crossed Northumberland Strait on April 28, 1917, and it was only then that the iceboat service and its courageous men passed happily into obsolescence.

September 11, 2000 – Trans-Canada Highway, P.E.I.

We were on our way to Charlottetown along the Trans-Canada when Al's cell phone rang. *Again*. He grabbed it from the map sorter, pressed a button and started talking into the mouthpiece. "Hello, what can I do ya for?" he said. The next five minutes involved business dealings that were none of my concern, so I contented myself with staring out the window at the picturesque farmland drifting past. Al had already warned me that his phone rang a lot at that time of year.

"It's hard to believe life was possible before cell phones," I commented after he had finished his conversation.

"Well, it wasn't impossible," he laughed, "but as soon as your competitors have a phone, you've gotta get one just to keep up. Internet, e-mail, cell phones ... geez, it's the whole damn works! It never ends."

I could relate to his deep-seated frustration. Checking my e-mail every few days on the road was not always easy either.

"In my business, information is crucial," Al continued as we blasted down the highway. "And I'm not just talking about local competition. I have to know what's happening with potatoes in Idaho, in Washington, in Delaware and in Wisconsin. We live in a global market now, and what you don't know can kill you."

This guy certainly didn't match the image of "lazy easterner" that some Albertans paint of the Maritimes, and when I mentioned this to Al it was obvious that I had struck a nerve. It was a particularly tender topic for the fact that Stockwell Day, the newly inaugurated leader of the Alberta-based

Canadian Alliance party, had recently been voted in during a by-election, the same one that saw Progressive Conservative leader and former prime minister Joe Clark elected in Nova Scotia.

"It makes me so angry when that Day fellow makes comments about lazy easterners," complained Al. "We're actually Canada's mobile work force, and the vast majority of people I know out here have worked hard all their lives." After a few moments, he added: "I wish we had the subsidies for big business that Ontario and Quebec receive."

He certainly had a point.

There was no doubt in my mind that Al was a hard worker, and beyond that an excellent tour guide, despite frequent distractions from his mobile phone. Being a potato buyer meant that he was obliged to drive all over the island with the thing surgically grafted to his ear, doing quality checks and cutting deals with farmers. I was along for the ride, and within a couple of days I had seen mechanical potato harvesters digging potatoes up and spitting them into trucks, sorters picking bad spuds out as they whisked past on conveyor belts, and warehouses stacked with huge crates full of freshly harvested crop. "Can you believe that PEI plants more than a hundred and ten thousand acres of spuds every year?" Al asked me. Even he found the statistics startling. "That's one third of Canada's potato crop! That's a helluva lotta spuds!" Indeed it was. Enough to keep Al's distant cousin Ronald smiling for a very long time.

Of course, the business of growing spuds is always a gamble, even on Prince Edward Island. Nothing is ever a sure bet when it comes to agriculture, as I had learned from my uncle in Alberta. "Every year these farmers throw a million bucks into the ground, then hope and pray they get something in return," Al explained. "Farmers are the biggest gamblers on earth. They have four to six weeks to get their money out, and with a change in weather the whole crop can end up staying in the ground."

In addition to seeing vignettes of the potato business, driving around the island with Al brought other unexpected bonuses. Backcountry roads that would have been impossible to hitchhike for lack of traffic, were now offering up their diverse and scenic treasures: little white farmhouses, hedgerows, rusty-red soil and fields of potatoes (which, incidentally, are pronounced "podadoes" by most islanders). One afternoon just outside Shamrock, we passed a striking medley of rusty-red soil, potato fields and hedgerows converging beside a little white farmhouse. Near Inkerman, it was instead a little white farmhouse sitting in front of hedgerows and rusty-red potato fields. Needless to say, I wasn't startled when, as we looped back toward Borden, we passed more rusty-red potato fields and hedgerows beside another little white farmhouse. The sheer variety of landscapes on the island's interior was mind-boggling.

Lest I give the wrong impression, Prince Edward Island *is* stunning. As Al told me with a healthy dose of pride, "There's not a piece of granite on the entire island," which surely accounts for the province's Edenesque quality. "Even Jacques Cartier thought so," continued Al. "He said 'Tis the fairest isle that is possible to be seen.'"

There's no question that PEI, not unlike southern Ontario, has a pastoral beauty about it. There's also no question that it is, and will always be, potato heaven. The rich, soft loam protects potatoes from bruising, while cool evenings in the fall help the spuds to bulk up. If the island lacks an element of scenic variety for that reason, so be it. The United States has to get its "Freedom Fries" from *somewhere*.

September 13, 2000 - Summerside, Prince Edward Island

Al pulled up in front of the McDonald's in Summerside, cell phone attached to his ear, and waved for me to throw my things in the back. I had spent the previous day walking around Tignish at the northwest corner of the island, and had pitched my tent in a small clearing near Cape Kildare. That morning I had woken at dawn and watched, very much in awe, as the sun set rusty-red sea cliffs alight. The contrast of red cliffs, blue ocean and green forest is something PEI is famous for, and something I had never seen firsthand. It was a photographer's dream come true!

Not surprisingly, my tour north was courtesy of Al, who had chauffeured me to the tip of the island the previous day. Like an old friend, he had handed me his cell phone number through the window and told me to call if I ran into trouble. Thankfully, I had managed to get back to Summerside on my own.

"Good news," said Al, after he hung up. "My mom's baked you an apple pie."

"Really?" Maritime goodwill never ceased to amaze me.

"Yeah," he said. "And she wants to know if you'd like to help her pickle this year's cucumber crop."

Hmmmm, that was interesting. Did I look like a cucumber expert? Were hitchhikers from PEI famous for their pickling skills? I explained to Al that hitchhiking and pickling cucumbers were quite different things, but he assured me that it wasn't rocket science. He also told me that he had arranged for us to go fishing that evening with his friend Joe, who knew a great spot for mackerel.

Al's mom was bubbly and warm when she greeted us at the door. Nancy had been retired for several years, and was enjoying every minute of it. With greying hair, a warm smile and the perky disposition of a grandmother, she looked like the kind of person who would be content anywhere, provided she could bake apple pie and invite people over to help her eat it. After hanging our coats at the door (this is what you do at a grandmother's house), we walked into the kitchen and saw several dozen cucumbers stacked neatly on the table beside a medley of red peppers, onions and a single head of cauliflower. Nancy was obviously organized, too.

Al went back to work soon thereafter, and it wasn't long before Nancy and I started peeling the cucumbers, slicing them in half and scooping the seeds out. The other vegetables were next and, while listening to television announcers banter about Tiger Woods at the Canadian Open, Nancy reminisced about working on the PEI ferries. "Boy, it was a good job," she said dreamily. "I don't think there was a day I went to work that I didn't want to go. It was a good paycheque every two weeks. And when you bring up four kids as a single mom like I did, you certainly appreciate the steady pay."

Nancy had retired in 1991 after a heart attack, so unlike six hundred fellow ferry employees, she was not uprooted when the bridge came into service. She had even invited two builders to stay with her during construction so that she could get updates and bake apple pie for them. Like me, I'm sure they were most grateful.

"Even though the bridge was good for business, you kind of felt sorry for the people who lost their jobs," Nancy told me. But, she added judiciously, at least employees got a nice severance package, a lump sum that many of them invested into Gateway Village, an island-themed mall with gift shops and historical attractions. This had been the tradeoff for lost jobs; without steady pay, former ferry employees were at least profiting from increased tourist traffic coming in via the bridge.

The afternoon passed quickly, and by the time Al called me at 4:30, Nancy and I had finished with the cucumber crop. In fact, we were just sitting back to drink some tea and eat our second piece of apple pie.

Al explained that his friend had just called to tell us the fish were biting. Twenty minutes later, he picked me up at Nancy's and we headed straight for the docks. And for the sake of keeping events brief, dear reader, here is an abbreviated synopsis of the evening's events:

5:18 pm. Arrive at marina. Meet Al's friend Joe.
5:28 pm. Head out in boat. Water choppy. Apple pie wants to come up for a look around, but I manage to keep it subdued.
5:41 pm. Reach protected inlet beside large wharf.
5:46 pm. Al catches first fish. It's a mackerel.
5:48 pm. Joe catches second mackerel.
5:51 pm. I struggle to cast line.
5:54 pm. Al catches two more mackerel. I wrap fishing line around ladder on wharf.
5:57 pm. I zing fish hook past Al's left ear.
5:58 pm. Al decides it would be smart to show me how to cast.
6:10 pm. Get in groove. Al very relieved.
6:35 pm. Fish really biting.
6:42 pm. Al shows first sign of worry. The mackerel seem to like me.
7:06 pm. I claim title in Prince Edward Island Open with 23 fish. Al shows disgust. Swears never to give prairie boy a fishing rod again. No more rides either.
7:07 pm. Al tells me he was kidding.
7:35 pm. Arrive at main harbour to gut fish.
8:05 pm. Back at Nancy's to eat more apple pie. Listen to more stories.
9:45 pm. Call it a night.

Chapter 42

Eastern Highlands

September 15, 2000 - Pictou, Nova Scotia

I first realized that I had landed in New Scotland when I heard the wail of bagpipes drifting across Pictou harbour, and when I saw grown men buying groceries and walking around fast food restaurants wearing kilts. I've always taken a keen interest in Scottish culture, possibly because my grandfather Bill Baird was himself a Scot, though he didn't really possess any of the more obstinately charming qualities Highlanders are renowned for. He was quiet and generous and didn't even drink malt whiskey. Still, he did appreciate things like the Highland fling and clan tartans and Scottish music, which is one reason, I'm certain, why my sister Jennifer ended up taking Highland dancing lessons for several years. This is also why, every so often, my brother Rick and I would be dragged off by our parents to some distant competition, where we were forced to watch six-year-old girls stumble around a stuffy auditorium to the wail of the bagpipes. My grandparents really, truly liked this music, and I was never sure why.

But I'm older now, and more mature, and have come to see that Highland culture is more than just cross-dressing men and instruments that sound like a potato sack full of angry cats. In fact, I now find bagpipe music rather compelling—in an eerie kind of way—and when I hear its nasal pitch, the music sends a sort of quiver down my spine. Mostly, though, I've learned to appreciate Scottish culture because I've seen that Highlanders are hardened and manly and don't mind spitting in their hands and can throw big logs in the air and don't take crap from anybody. Who wouldn't be proud to have a little Scottish blood coursing through their veins?

Take the *Hector*, an old cargo ship that in many ways exemplifies the ruggedness of the Highland spirit. In a hold that was less than thirty metres long and seven metres wide, 189 Scottish immigrants set sail from western Scotland in 1773, "united by a spirit of purpose" to establish new homes in Canada. They were fleeing the tyrannical rule of English lairds who had outlawed tartans and the playing of bagpipes.

Unfortunately, their voyage across the stormy Atlantic didn't go very well. Gale-force winds blew them hundreds of kilometres off course, eighteen children died from outbreaks of disease and for the last two days passengers survived on "moldy scraps of food that had previously been discarded." But on the fifteenth of September, their ship sailed triumphantly into Pictou harbour. Over the next two centuries, more than a million Scots would follow the *Hector* to a scattering of settlements along this coast. It was "the pioneer ship of a great movement," one that sparked a wave of Highland immigration to an area that Canadians now call "the birthplace of New Scotland."

So the Scots are survivors. They would have to be, considering the kind of weather they put up with in Scotland. Perhaps aware of this, Nova Scotia seemed eager to provide me with a little Highland authenticity when I first arrived in Pictou. The sky opened up with rain that was thick and mind-numbingly cold—accompanied by gale-force winds, the kind that make it nearly impossible for kilted gentlemen to keep their underwear hidden from the eyes of a scrutinizing public.

The rain was so dense, in fact, that it stopped me from hitchhiking for two full days, forcing me to look for accommodation instead. I feared waking in the night and having to bail my tent out with a coffee mug, as I had been forced to do in New Brunswick earlier that summer. Everything in town was booked, of course, as it always is when you *really* need a room, and it was only the goodwill of a young Subway manager that saved me from the deluge. He gave me permission to sleep on some cardboard boxes on his storage room floor. Talk about hardship, though. At seven in the morning I was wakened by one of his staff looking for more napkins.

The rain eventually lifted, and I pressed on toward the highlands of Cape Breton. Their distant summits beckoned me along twin-lane blacktop to Antigonish, home of the Scottish Highland games, and beyond that to Troy (home of Natalie MacMaster), Creignish (home of Ashley MacIsaac) and Mabou (home of the Rankin family). The roads of Cape Breton are somewhat mind-bending, careening along cliffs that drop with rather ominous resolve toward the Gulf of St. Lawrence. Yet I pressed on, holding any sense of vertigo at bay, and soon passed through Mabou, where Gaelic words are painted across several buildings along the town's main strip. *Tigh Litrichean*, which means "House of Letters," was printed across the top of the post office. The town hall featured the phrase *Ciad Mile Failte*, or "a thousand, million welcomes." And the town grocery store had a sign that read *Failte Thig Astigh*. I never did find out what that one means, but it's probably something like "Feed thy face, oh hungry one."

Most heartening was Cape Breton's apparent determination to fend off the great American marketing machine. A good many international fiddle stars have been born on the island in recent years, which is surely one of the reasons for the public's renewed interest not only in fiddling, but in the ancient Gaelic tongue, which tends to go hand in hand with traditional Highland music. Many of the schools on Cape Breton are once again teaching Gaelic, and during my travels across the island I attended a *Ceilidh* (pronounced *kay-lee*, which is Gaelic for "party") where I watched four teens between the ages of ten and sixteen light the crowd on fire. The hills were once again alive with the sound of fiddle music, no question about it, to the point where music was now the island's most successful export next to youth itself. So much for the days of coal and cod, both of which have all but disappeared.

Still, as many youth from Cape Breton leave for greener pastures in Ontario or western Canada, older individuals are arriving, bringing their skills and knowledge with them. These are people who have the ingenuity to shift the island's fortune away from spiralling dependency on government handouts. One such person was a Québécois fellow from Montreal, driving a car with Ontario plates. I'll call him Jacques. The reason for this pseudonym will soon become obvious.

Jacques picked me up just north of Inverness on his way to Cheticamp, a small Acadian village (of all things) located at the south end of the Cabot Trail near Cape Breton Highlands National Park. He was a large, stocky man in his early thirties, soft around the middle, balding prematurely, but as sharp as they come. "Some of the kids say there's nothing to do out here," he told me with a smirk, "but I tend to disagree." We were following the scenic coastal route north of Dunvegan, and with every bend in the road the view of forested hills and bare headlands dropping down to the ocean made us feel positively euphoric.

Jacques was a social worker who had lived in western Canada for a couple of years before accepting a job in Ontario. But he really, really, *really* wanted to move to Cape Breton Island within the next five years. "I have this clear vision of a dream home beside the ocean," he told me, "where I would walk out onto the porch one day and just die." He had an eloquent way of expressing himself.

"Why Cape Breton?" I asked. "Aren't there plenty of other places where you can buy a dream home beside the ocean? Places where the economy is more stable?"

Jacques smiled, then carried on to describe a trip he had taken many years before. Apparently, he and a friend were camped on a Nova Scotia beach near Inverness when a huge storm blew in off the Gulf of St. Lawrence, hurling eight-foot swells onto the beach near their camp. "That night, I swear I saw the face of God," he told me candidly. "I looked up and saw a glowing face in the clouds, two stars where the eyes should be, and ever since that night I've been dreaming about coming back."

"But do you think you'll be able to make a living here?"

"That's a good question," he admitted. "I've always been a believer in destiny, though. If you keep a positive outlook, things are bound to work out."

On our way to Cheticamp, Jacques and I pulled over on several occasions to breathe in the salt air, regard the spectacular views and bask under a flawless blue sky. The weather had improved dramatically since we left Pictou, and we were soaking it up. We also stopped at a small music store to browse for Celtic tunes. I purchased *The Ceilidh Collection*—a mix of Highland, Acadian and Newfie music—and we pushed on toward Cheticamp with the sound of dancing fiddles urging us down the road.

In Cheticamp, we stopped for a bite at a seaside cafe. Jacques told me that he wanted to spend the afternoon exploring the village and invited me to tag along. This sort of offer had occasioned itself numerous times on my journey—such as my time chasing buffalo with Nils in northern Alberta—so I accepted the invitation without hesitating. Plus, I really liked the hopeful perspective Jacques brought to life on Cape Breton. As we walked around town, he told me about his plans to start an island retreat. "I figure I might go back to school, get my master's, then come out here and open a bed and breakfast," he explained with a grin. "Once that's underway, I also want to open a centre for holistic healing."

The afternoon passed in easy company, walking around the streets of Cheticamp, poking our noses into tourist shops and admiring a splendid display of hooked rugs at the Elizabeth LeFort gallery. One rug covered an entire wall and featured, among other things, the faces of Canada's prime ministers up until the 1960s, as well as several scenes with Canadian explorers such as Jacques Cartier and Alexander Mackenzie. It is one of the most amazing things I have ever seen.

During all of this, I should have seen something coming, particularly when Jacques proposed splitting the cost of a room at a bed and breakfast for the night.

But I didn't.

If not then, alarm bells definitely should have gone off when we walked down to the beach that evening, and Jacques casually laid a blanket on the sand.

But they didn't.

I have known enough gay people—indeed, had many gay friends—that I can say with conviction that I have never been homophobic. And I have great empathy for the gay rights movement. But then, I've never been taken off guard quite like I was with Jacques. If anything, I was ignorant as bliss, going merrily about my business reserving a room, then happily plunking myself down on Jacques's beach blanket. I even went so far as to joke, when I saw a man and his dog walking along the beach toward us, that it would be quite funny if the man thought we were gay, not for one instant thinking that Jacques actually might be.

Jacques didn't look impressed by my comment.

And so it happened, as we were lying in our beds in Cheticamp that night, talking through the pitch blackness, that Jacques made a startling pronouncement. "I just want you to know that I'm gay," he blurted.

There was a long, pregnant pause in that inky void. Then, after what seemed like an eternity, the faint murmurings of a squeaky Rick Moranis voice coming from my side of the room. "I just want you to know that I'm not," I said.

Another long pause.

"I understand," Jacques finally said. "I just wanted you to know."

"Thanks."

But of course I didn't really mean thanks. I was feeling too much like a first-class idiot, and I really would have preferred not knowing. Perhaps it was the timing of his announcement, or maybe it was the comment he had made earlier about me being "an attractive man" (another signal, remarkably, that I hadn't picked up on). Whatever it was, I didn't know whether I should feel embarrassed or nervous or nothing at all. Was I blowing things out of proportion? There was even a subtle nagging that

I had offended Jacques with my off-handed remark at the beach. Even in these enlightened times, gay people have to contend with a great deal of discrimination, and I now felt all the worse for being a part of it.

"Have you ever been with a woman?" I heard myself ask. We had been lying in silence for several minutes, and I couldn't think of anything else to say.

"I've been with many women and many men," he replied. "Are you feeling nervous now that I've told you?"

"No, not really," I said. "Just surprised. You don't come across as being gay."

"What do you think of me now?"

"I could care less whether you're gay or not," I said, being quite honest. "I've had a lot of friends who are gay, and I've always believed each to their own."

"I'm glad," he said. "A lot of people freak out."

"Maybe telling me while we're lying in bed wasn't such a hot idea though."

"Good point."

September 22, 2000 - Breton Cove, Nova Scotia

Joan Kerr runs a bed and breakfast in Breton Cove, a tiny hamlet nestled in the wild hills along the Cabot Trail. She has lived there since 1979, after teaching for thirteen years in the ghettos of inner-city Boston. She prefers Cape Breton to Boston, even though for the first couple of years she and her husband didn't have a telephone and it was sixty-five kilometres to the nearest grocer in Baddeck. One winter they didn't even have a vehicle, which meant they pretty much lived off venison, rabbits and fish. But that didn't matter. When I met her, she had been on Cape Breton for twenty-one years, and never once has she wanted to go back to Boston.

For my part, I came to Breton Cove because I had seen a brochure in Pictou advertising the annual North Shore Gaelic Festival. I had dreams of stumbling onto a small, intimate gathering of Gaelic-speaking Scots at a seaside village—plus I wanted to see firsthand how these small Celtic communities keep their culture alive in a world ruled by CNN and the Internet. If there was such a dreamy little place, Breton Cove sounded promising.

As it turned out, Breton Cove is so small and so intimate that when I hitched a ride along the Cabot Trail from Cheticamp, my chauffeur almost drove right past it. A few rustic homes were scattered along the road, and a town hall the size of a shoebox sat beside a softball field. There were no signs advertising a festival, no decorations or fanfare. We didn't even see any people. In short, it didn't look like the kind of place to host a festival of any sort, much less one that sounded so grand and important. So I stopped at a bed and breakfast, where I met Joan, and she assured me that the festival was happening the next day.

The next morning, after waking in my tent a few hundred yards from Joan's bed and breakfast, I joined several guests in her home for eggs, bacon, fruit and freshly baked bread. There was a happily retired couple named Guy and Marilyn from Texas, to whom I took an immediate liking, and three college girls from Massachusetts who were up in Canada working for the Jehovah's Witnesses. For the most part I talked to the retired couple (for fear of being recruited by the girls), and learned that they had also come to Breton Cove with plans to attend the Gaelic festival.

Guy, Marilyn and I walked over to the Alexander Smith community hall an hour later, though we were somewhat disappointed to find but a handful of people already present. Still, the itinerary for *Feis Cladaich a Tuath* ("Festival of the Shore of the North") looked interesting, so the three of us paid our admission and decided to stick around to see what would happen. Over the next hour, people started trickling in—mostly locals, but a few tourists as well—and by eleven there were about two dozen of us seated around a long wooden table in the main meeting hall, psyching ourselves up for a beginner's class in Gaelic.

"Good morning," said our teacher, a bright-eyed and whiskery fellow named Angus MacLeod. He had a thick head of dark hair, a bushy black moustache and a deep voice that reminded me of Darth Vader, though Angus's disposition was not nearly so menacing. He was clearly younger than most of the Gaelic speakers I had already met. Before starting, he confirmed that even though Gaelic is making a comeback in schools, islanders from his generation never had the chance to learn Gaelic because for years schools tried to eradicate the language.

"So how did you learn it?" I asked.

"Mostly from tapes and books," he said. "And whenever I got stuck, I would ask one of the old-timers." He had worked to learn Gaelic primarily out of academic interest and nostalgia for his dying culture, and it was mainly the poetry and music that had inspired him. "What I really found helpful were the songs. I spent three years without listening to an English song, and when I started listening to them again I was amazed by how much repetition there was." He shrugged a heavy, forlorn shrug. "And to think I used to like that stuff. Anyone who learns enough Gaelic to understand songs and poetry will never go back to English."

Though all of us were initially doubtful of Angus' claim, the more we immersed ourselves in the language, the more doubtful we became. "If all you've ever spoken is English," he warned the group, "you're going to use parts of your nose and mouth that you've never used before." He further explained that Gaelic is an ancient language that—as far as academics can determine—came from pagan or prehistoric times. By the time our lesson had finished, French would seem easy by comparison.

The first thing Angus did was hand us a list of the Gaelic alphabet with the phonetic sounds of each letter. Missing from the list were *j*, *k*, *q*, *v*, *w*, *x*, *y*, and *z*. "And *h* isn't really a letter either," he told us, "even though it's one of the most used letters in the Gaelic tongue. It never starts words and doesn't have a sound of its own." He went on to point out that *h* does have a sound when it is combined with other letters; when combined with *b* or *m*, for example, it makes a *v* sound. And because there is no *k* in the Gaelic alphabet, the letter *c* has a hard sound.

Another interesting quirk of Gaelic, we soon discovered, is that there aren't any words that mean yes or no. "You always answer in the verb that's appropriate," said Angus. "For example, to the question 'Did you run?' you would answer 'I run,' or to the question 'Did you throw the ball?' you would answer 'I throw ball.'" It was kind of like talking to a factory worker from St. John, New Brunswick.

We soon graduated to a few basic greetings, which Angus urged us to write down in phonetic form until we got used to the rules of pronunciation. We learned *Ciamer a tha thu*, which is pronounced *kimmer-a-how* and means "How are you?" We learned *glé mhath* (pronounced *gla-va*), which means "Very well." And my favourite one for the road: *Tha mi à gluasad fhathast*, which is pronounced something like *Hammy-a-gloo-a-sad-hast*, and means "I'm still moving." Although it would likely confuse some drivers, I decided to memorize this last one so that I could answer in Gaelic whenever somebody asked me how my trip was going.

My mother: "How's the trip going, sweetie?"

Me: *Tha mi à gluasad fhathast.* C'mon mom, what do you expect?"

All of these strange spellings and pronunciations even had Guy and Marilyn quipping at each other, threatening to break their marriage against the rocks. "This could mean a whole new way of communicating for us," said Marilyn at one point, rather sharply I thought.

"Together fifty years and it all falls apart after two hours of Gaelic lessons," I laughed. "Will wonders never cease?"

"Well, it would make a good story to tell our friends," chuckled Guy.

That evening, after a tasty chicken dinner at the town hall, the room began to fill with people—most of them locals, but a few tourists as well—and a century-old milling table was whisked into the centre of the room. Milling tables, I learned, were traditionally used by Scottish women for two things: (1) to pre-shrink wool that would be used for clothing, and (2) for a bit of wholesome shagging when Scottish men returned from the forests, fields, mines or wherever they went with their big boots and axes. Because of a milling table's ribbed surface, I imagine it was probably preferred for the former activity, though use of the table during a "milling frolic" seems a more appropriate term for the latter. In actuality, a milling frolic involved a group of women beating wool repeatedly against the table's ribbed surface, and because it was so tedious, it became tradition for these groups to sing Gaelic folk songs while working.

For the last two hours of the festival, Angus led a group of perhaps two dozen locals at the milling table, chanting Gaelic songs while striking the wool back and forth against the surface—back and forth, back and forth—with an impressive sort of tedium. Although Guy and Marilyn had left, there was by this time a scruffy-looking computer programmer from Vancouver and a pleasant farm couple, George and Geraldine, visiting from Saskatchewan. Even the tourists—some of us Gaelic experts by this time—were invited to join in, and we all did our best to keep up with Angus during the choruses. As I sat beside George at the table, he leaned over to me and whispered, "It's nice to know these people can keep their language and culture alive in this day and age. Isn't it great to be a part of it?"

I smiled and continued beating the wool. I was quite enjoying the tedium, which seemed to fit quite perfectly with my off-key singing. I couldn't have agreed more heartily with George, or said it so succinctly.

Chapter 43

Humpback Rodeo

HERE'S A STORY for you. Imagine a highly placed business executive from New Jersey who has worked his way up through the ranks of a large US-based network marketing company. He's a young firecracker full of drive, respected by his peers—and he has just been assigned to visit Newfoundland (some obscure little rock in an obscure little country called Canada) to spend a week training new recruits. Not surprisingly, the guy from Jersey has never heard of Newfoundland. When a guy named Seamus calls to make travel arrangements, however, Jerseyman can't help but be impressed with the man's gregarious nature, his oddly lilting accent and his description of a land with ancient mountains, rushing rivers and forests that edge hard against a restless sea. Jerseyman is also fascinated by one of Newfoundland's most legendary sporting pastimes, something Seamus calls "the Humpback Rodeo."

Now if you were from New Jersey, stories about gutsy sailors cruising the open seas on the back of a humpback whale would probably sound either half-cracked or deliciously exotic. Either way, it's a pretty vivid mental image. If you're a Democrat, you probably hang up the phone on Seamus, organize a group called CAVAM (Citizens Against Violating Atlantic Mammals), and start advocating for humpback rights. If you're a Republican, like Jerseyman, you ask Seamus if you can bomb ... I mean, attempt to ride one of the whales during your visit to Newfoundland.

Perhaps, dear reader, you can already see where this story is going. Although Newfoundland has its fair share of whales—not to mention its fair share of gutsy sailors—none would be foolish enough to ride a humpback as it plunges from the tossed surface of the Atlantic down into its gloomy depths. Still, when a determined businessman from New Jersey seems quite willing to put aside any and all sensibilities to try one of Newfoundland's most legendary non-sports, there's nothing to do but saddle him up. And that is how, on a lavishly bright summer's day, several gently smirking Newfoundlanders and one excitable New Jersey executive came to be on a tour boat bouncing across the Atlantic's restless chop.

Of course, riding the seas on the back of a humpback whale (even an imaginary one) is not to be taken lightly. And for that reason, the captain and his crew had to take great care when outfitting Jerseyman with all the newest, coolest, highest-tech equipment that money had bought. This included, but was not limited to: (1) a rope tied around Jerseyman's ankle so that the crew could pull him off the whale if it started getting testy; (2) one of those big, floppy rubber fisherman's hats; (3) a toilet bowl plunger to pump the whale's blowhole should it dive too deep; and, of course, (4) a sharp knife to cut the rope if it got tangled in the whale's fins or barnacles. I am not kidding about any of these things. By the time they had finished suiting him up, Jerseyman was a sight to behold. And if the broad grin into his mates' cameras was anything to go by, he was ready to challenge one of the great creatures of the deep.

Predictably, it didn't take much for one of those exuberant "Look at me, honey" moments to degenerate into one of those "You guys are a bunch of idiots" moments when Jerseyman finally realized, with a feeling that could fairly be described as sinking, that the humpback rodeo was nothing more than a terrible Newfie farce. I personally like to think that, shortly after returning to the States, Jerseyman found a small souvenir from his buddies up north splashed across the pages of his company newsletter. The souvenir would be a picture of some bloke wearing a rubber fisherman's hat, clutching a sturdy-looking toilet bowl plunger in his hand like a fencing sword. Can you think of anything that would more easily earn him the respect of his peers?

September 28, 2000 - Corner Brook, Newfoundland

Newfoundland is a place where it can sometimes be hard to separate fact from fiction. I hadn't been there a week, yet most of the truths I had taken for granted about the province had already been dashed against the sea-swept rocks of my mind. It's a fact: the people of Canada's most easterly and sex-loving province are not just a bunch of unshaven guys with rubber hats and tobacco pipes standing on a dock looking for government handouts. While it is true that Newfoundland's economy once relied heavily on the fishing industry—and that some locals were forced to rely on government handouts when that industry collapsed in 1992—the natives here are really just a bunch of unshaven guys with rubber hats and tobacco pipes who are diligently rebuilding the economy one brick at a time. As for the ones who can't be bothered, they sell their rubber hats and pipes, move to Newfoundland's third largest city (Fort McMurray, Alberta) and are never heard from again.

Of course, this is an overly simplistic view of Newfoundland, a province that has been working hard to diversify its economy with forestry, oil and gas exploration and tourism. Nevertheless, the collapse of a half-billion-dollar industry would have been a tragedy anywhere, and with forty thousand jobs literally gone overnight, some of the people who relied on the fishery for generations have understandably found it difficult to adjust. With little in the way of secondary skills to fall back on, many have simply abandoned their homes and drifted off to find greener pastures in other provinces. They had to do this; the cod may never return. Fishermen from Newfoundland, Spain, the US and other countries spent years harvesting massive quantities of cod from the Grand Banks; they simply got too good at what they do, and government officials didn't have the political backbone to stop them until it was too late.

Another legend that died hard—and I do mean very hard—was the notion that Newfies fight over hitchhikers. I'm not sure who started this rumour, but whoever did has been quite successful, because the rumour has quietly spread across the whole of Canada. When I discovered firsthand that hitchhiking in Newfoundland is actually quite difficult, I was rather disappointed. I had been looking forward to causing some roadside fisticuffs. Of course, the person who started this rumour is probably the same guy who comes up with all those Newfie jokes—you know, the ones that portray Newfies as kind of dopey and backwards. All along it has merely been one hell of a self-deprecating smear campaign— Newfoundland's greatest gag on Canada. If Newfies are stupid, then hell froze over a long time ago, and the New Democrats will form a government sometime within the next century.

But back to thumbing, and how revoltingly impossible it is to hitchhike on the Rock. For two days after stepping off the ferry at Port-aux-Basques I stood at the side of the road, watching as car after godforsaken car drifted past, the drivers hardly bothering to give me a sideways glance. I eventually made progress in short, insubstantial hops to Corner Brook, but two out of the five drivers who picked me up were from southern Ontario. In my mind, this should be a fairly embarrassing statistic for the good people of Newfoundland, who pride themselves on being the pinnacle of Canadian hospitality. It probably wouldn't have been so bad for me had the autumn rain not copped a frosty disposition, threatening to send winter with all its unfurling fury across the land. Not that there was anything I could do about it. As the seconds turned to minutes and the minutes to hours, my teeth started chattering and my hands grew so cold that I could barely hold my thumb in the air. This was no way to end such an epic road trip.

On my third day, I decided to give hitchhiking another try, so I packed up my tent and walked to a highway exit at the edge of Corner Brook. Incredibly, after only a few minutes a vivacious older lady named Genevieve—her hair dyed jet-black—pulled over in a brand new Chevy Cavalier. When I thanked her for stopping, she replied almost matter-of-factly that she tries to pick up hitchhikers every day. And as we rolled past the high, green ridges of the Long Range Mountains, she handed me a notebook to prove it. "Write a few words in this, would you deary?" she clucked like a mother hen. "Every hitchhiker I pick up, I ask them to sign my journal."

Genevieve was a step-on tour guide for a bus company, and she loved to talk about Newfoundland. But it wasn't twenty minutes before she had to turn off toward Pasadena, leaving me stranded on yet another empty highway, trying desperately to think warm thoughts. This time I shivered for over an hour before a genial fellow driving a small red pickup pulled over. His name was Ron Burnett, a guy with the working-man look of an islander—faded blue jeans, thick beard and a soiled baseball cap—but without the edgy accent most Newfies are so renowned for. I asked him about this.

"My wife and I are transplants from southern Ontario," he admitted. "We moved here four years ago to start a dairy farm."

Ah yes, another ride courtesy of southern Ontario.

"Don't most people do things the other way around?" I chuckled. "Why would you come all the way to Newfoundland to start farming?"

"Well, part of it was because of this," he said, pointing out the front windshield at an ocean of rock and forest, scenery that was getting more spectacular with every passing kilometre. "And the price of quota was pretty much the cheapest anywhere in the country." By quota, Ron meant the license every dairy farmer needs to produce and sell milk. Were he and his wife starting to fit in? "Let's just say that I've been here long enough to not know what I am anymore," he told me with a wry grin. "As far as I can tell, I'm half Newfie, half mainlander, three quarters nuts."

Ron further explained that he and his wife Jane had moved to Newfoundland because they liked the friendly people and laid-back lifestyle. Before they began farming, they hardly saw one another; Ron had a high-paying job with Ontario Hydro, while Jane worked as a vet with large farm animals. "At least we work together now," he told me, "although that has its challenges, too. Sometimes we work side by side for eighteen hours and then go home together." He chuckled at the thought. "But what we've lost in money, we've more than made up for with quality of life."

As for the people of Newfoundland, Ron had plenty of stories about their kindness and integrity. Not long after arriving on the Rock, Ron had come down with kidney cancer, and there were guys they didn't even know coming over to work in the barn. "Sometimes they'd help us for half a day when they should've been at home doing their own stuff," he said with a tone of awe.

As we approached Deer Lake forty minutes later, I started preparing myself for another long wait at the side of the road. Instead, Ron invited me back to the farm. A frozen highway and empty stomach were one option; a warm farmhouse and free food were the other. It was not a difficult decision to make. Besides, it would be a perfect opportunity to spend some time with Newfoundland's younger generation, the people who are slowly but surely making the province self-sufficient.

Ron pulled off the highway to buy coffee at what looked like a brand-new Tim Horton's, and as we walked inside, he spotted a friend at the drive-through window. This meant stopping to exchange a few friendly barbs. "Now *he's* a true Newfie," Ron chuckled after we had walked inside. "He laughs from the time he wakes up 'til the time he closes his eyes at night—and maybe five minutes after."

Ron and I arrived at the farmhouse twenty minutes later, where we were greeted by tall, curly-haired Jane, dressed in sweat pants and a work shirt. I also met their dog Elsie and their eighteen-month-old son Noah, who Ron affectionately called "Buckaroo." Noah had wild auburn hair and a round face that lit up when he heard we were going to visit the cows. Jane handed me a pair of coveralls ("to keep the cow shit off") and soon we were at the barnyard preparing to feed the cattle, Ron fetching hay bales from a field behind the barn while Jane prepped the milking stalls. I was assigned the task of keeping an eye on wee Noah, who, I realized gratefully, wasn't difficult to entertain. He was so entranced by the animals that for several minutes he simply waddled back and forth between the barn and the barnyard, tiny red mittens dangling from his wrists, staring with fascination at several dazed-looking cows waiting patiently for lunch.

"I bet you never would have expected to find a dairy farm in Newfoundland," said Jane as she walked past. I hadn't really thought about it, but the thick forest and moonscape rock that make up so much of the province did seem an unlikely setting for a homestead. "Most of us are first-generation farmers," Jane admitted. "The milk marketing board is only seventeen years old in Newfoundland. That's why a lot of Newfoundlanders grew up without drinking milk. It simply wasn't available." This was also why dairy farmers from the Rock were currently selling milk to public schools at cost, providing cheap milk for kids so that they would pick up the habit of drinking it. Ironically, while dairy farming was relatively new to Newfoundland—certainly compared to fishing— many years before the milk board existed there was a private dairy farm operating near Signal Hill, within spitting distance of St. John's harbour.

Later that evening, as Ron tucked a yawning Noah into bed, Jane stood in their kitchen stirring a large crock-pot full of chili. It was half past nine and dinner was only just ready, another typical day for a woman working as both a dairy farmer and a new mother. It made me exhausted just hearing about her unholy schedule, a schedule that started at half past four in the morning and often didn't finish until ten at night. The previous day was the first day Jane had taken off in eighty days. It was, she said stoically, the closest thing she would get to a vacation that summer.

"And what if Noah wakes up in the middle of the night?" I asked.

"Well, it makes for a rather fractured state of mind," she said, laughing.

"Ahh, the joys of being a self-employed mother."

"You get to choose when you work," she grinned. "The only problem is that you're always working." Regardless, Jane's eyes sparkled. "I guess if you like what you do, then it's not really work, is it?"

With Noah tucked into bed, the three of us were finally free to sit down at the television, watch the Sydney Olympics, eat dinner and talk about life on the Rock. When Ron turned to the CBC, however, we were greeted instead with the shocking news that Pierre Elliot Trudeau had just died. At the anchor's desk, Peter Mansbridge led viewers through a memorable tribute to Trudeau's life: his charismatic public performances, the creation of the Charter of Rights and Freedoms, rare snippets of his private life.

For more than an hour the three of us were glued to the screen, quietly disbelieving.

What made the news particularly hard for me to swallow was that Trudeau was the first prime minister I had ever known. And even though my parents and grandparents (Albertans to the core) were less than fond of him, it hadn't stopped me from learning about and appreciating his contributions later in life. But it was more than just that. For many Canadians, including me, Trudeau somehow embodied modern Canada's potential as a bilingual, multicultural nation. He was a sophisticated, charismatic francophone Quebecer with Scottish roots—an intellectual who, as Taras Grescoe once wrote, "demanded vision and imagination from his citizens."

In addition, Trudeau was an avid traveller and outdoorsman, the kind of leader who publicly encouraged young people to get out and taste the freedom of the open road. Indirectly, he had inspired my own trip. Can you imagine Jean Chrétien telling college kids to hitchhike today? Or a single member of the Canadian Alliance party? I'm sure that curling would be considered daring by the likes of Stephen Harper and his right-wing entourage. Trudeau, on the other hand, is probably the only leader in world history to actually *encourage* hitchhiking as means for a younger generation to see their country. There was no question in my mind that as Canada's coolest prime minister, our country would dearly miss him.

September 30, 2000 - Gros Morne National Park, Newfoundland

The Long Range Mountains already had a dusting of snow by the time I arrived in Gros Morne. To reach the national park, I had endured another two-hour stint on the road, an icy wind biting at my face, only to learn that worse weather was expected within two days. Time was obviously of the essence. As a result, shortly after a Corner Brook city foreman named Todd dropped me at the seaside village of Rocky Harbour, I made plans to hike to the lofty heights of Gros Morne Mountain.

And so it was, first thing the next morning, that I set out along a winding trail through stands of birch and maple trees cloaked in riotous colours. The sides of the trail were equally brilliant, boasting ostrich ferns dabbed with autumn paint. I stopped often to watch for caribou and moose; the former because they were a pleasant curiosity, the latter because it was rutting season, and bull moose have a tendency to chase down and trample anything that is not a female moose at that time of year. I saw nothing but chipmunks.

It felt good to get my circulation going again, and as the trail turned to steep switchbacks, I watched my breath shoot wintry cloudbursts into the air. At higher altitudes, pincushions of trees marched up the sheer flanks of the Long Range as if defying gravity. Only Gros Morne, the highest mountain in the park, seemed devoid of anything except slate-coloured rock. These heights are where winter resides, and as I moved from boreal forest past scraggly tuckamore and finally onto the open slopes of the mountain, I could feel the temperature starting to plummet.

Despite the chill, after a glorious seven-hour ramble through the woods I found myself at a place called Ferry Gulch, where I happily pitched camp in an open meadow. It felt wonderful to be alone, quite truthfully, with no exhaust fumes or need to make conversation. It felt doubly good because in Gros Morne there are vistas to inspire awe in every direction. After a pleasing dinner of Irish stew, I walked back along the trail to a lookout above the Gulf of St. Lawrence. My efforts were rewarded with a view of the setting sun—a crimson ball of fire drifting between seams in the clouds—dipping into the ocean just west of the Tablelands. These Tablelands, according to a brochure I picked up in Rocky Harbour, are the oldest rocks on Earth.

In the presence of such timeless treasures, it was the perfect place for me to contemplate the end of a journey that had dominated my life for the last four years. In less than two weeks I would be on my way back to western Canada, eager to settle down and start writing about my travels. Yet a part of me would inevitably stay here in Newfoundland (the part of me that always itches to be somewhere else), just as it had in every other province and territory I had already passed through.

Had I learned anything from my trip? At this point it was hard to say. A wise man once said that you take a little piece of every person you meet with you, and if that's true, it would certainly explain why my road trip felt like a disjointed yet pleasing tangle of stories, memories and wisdom. It would likely take me months, if not years, to sort it all out. Time, the great leveller, is a master when it comes to pushing and prodding a journey into something cohesive and meaningful.

The bad weather arrived the following day, but not before I had packed up camp and slipped over the summit of Gros Morne Mountain, past a herd of skittish caribou, down a gully on the far side and past my token bull moose. He was dallying in a pond and looked quite serene, just like I felt. By the time the torrential rain started pelting down, I was already at the Fisherman's Landing restaurant in Rocky Harbour eating battered cod, and feeling quite proud of myself for having successfully avoided the tail end of a hurricane drifting up from the south. The contemplative questions were still tugging at my mind, though, threatening to turn me into a self-reflective basket case ... until I heard about a Newfie band playing at the Anchor pub next door. It seemed like the best way to drop-kick serious thoughts into oblivion, and on that account I was quite right.

The smoke-drenched air was loud and festive at the pub, and as I waded through the fray I could see blue-collar workers mixing with a few trimly dressed Parks Canada employees to the sound of Newfie classics like "Heave Away." I arrived just in time to see the band bring out something called "the Ugly Stick," which according to the lead singer was supposed to represent his mother-in-law. It was an old mop covered with rattles, which one of the guitarists held by the neck, deliberately and happily smacking it against the floor. One exuberant girl from the audience liked the number so much that she grabbed one of the band members and started dancing with him, even before the song had finished. Not that I could really blame her. The band was a lot of fun, and before I knew what had happened, I too found myself on the dance floor.

Later that night, I was even saved from having to pitch camp in the deluge. After dancing a few songs with a tall girl with short auburn hair, we struck up casual conversation. Her name was Mary, and after we had traded stories for a few minutes, she told me there was an extra bedroom at her house that I was welcome to use. So we ran together through the pelting rain, clear across town, me feeling bad for ever doubting the hospitality of Newfoundlanders. Although hitchhiking hadn't been easy, most of the people I had met on the Rock were friendly, disarming and full of cheer. In Mary's case, we stayed up for another hour with her roommate Claudia, drinking herbal tea and laughing like old friends. It was only as we headed off to our respective bedrooms that I learned something about Mary that greatly surprised me. She was actually not from Newfoundland at all. She was from southern Ontario.

Chapter 44

End of the Road

October 6, 2000 - St. John's, Newfoundland

So it was that I arrived in St. John's a few days later, in much the same way that I had started my epic journey three and a half years earlier: in the pouring rain. I still had a week before an airplane would fly me back across the country, a trip that would last but a few hours instead of the twenty-seven weeks it had taken me to reach Newfoundland from Calgary. And this didn't include the twenty-one weeks I had spent thumbing up the West Coast and across the northern Territories.

Air travel is travel reduced to its barest functionality. On the way back, I wouldn't meet another Renee and have the chance to shovel bison manure on a game ranch; I wouldn't meet a Stephen and Sarah and sail across the Great Lakes under an impossibly blue sky. Nor would I play ball with Gino and his teammates, or wear checkered flannel, yell "Ahoy, mates!" and be George Clooney for a night. Suddenly, flying across Canada on an airplane seemed a rather depressing notion. Would I see anything of value at thirty-five thousand feet?

With the rain pelting down around my ears, I made a wise decision and booked myself in at a youth hostel called—and this is the name, I kid you not—*Ben and Betty's Backpacker Bunk & Bagel.* It was owned and managed by a slightly eccentric couple, both of whom were around my age. Ben was a wiry fellow from Alberta with thick plastic-rimmed glasses—the kind that any self-respecting artist wears—and a dark shadow of stubble on his cheeks that never seemed to disappear, even after he shaved. Betty was from Ontario, and sported thick, bobbed hair and a bubbly personality. Both of them were involved with a local art gallery (though Betty was also a writer), and when they heard that I would be homeless in St. John's over the Thanksgiving weekend, they wasted no time inviting me for dinner.

"Thanks a lot guys!" I enthused. "I would hate to miss turkey dinner."

"Actually, we're not having turkey," Betty corrected. "We're having a surprise."

"What's the surprise?"

"You'll have to wait and see," she said. "If I told you, it wouldn't be a surprise now, would it?"

The surprise, it turned out, was a New Age feast that didn't at all resemble traditional Thanksgiving fare. Not that any of us homeless people—myself, a girl from France and another girl from Australia—were about to complain. In addition to pumpkin pie, there was a tossed spinach salad with slices of mandarin orange (tasty), sushi (which I thoroughly detest) and a chicken stir-fry dish (which I quite enjoyed). Overall, I have to report that it was a delectable spread.

Not surprisingly, it was the generosity of Ben and Betty that formed my strongest impression of the pair, as had been the case with so many other people I had stayed with across Canada. The serendipitous, almost karmic goodwill that I had benefited from in so many places had imprinted deeply on me, and I knew that I would miss these casual and spontaneous meetings with strangers in distant, far away places. The most gratifying thing about these chance encounters was that often (sometimes after a few short hours) it would start to feel like I had found a new home.

Home. I remembered contemplating that concept under a star-filled sky on the prairies so many months earlier. I was still in love with the Canadian Rockies—which is where I planned to return—but had I carved out a home there? It was a grandiose landscape, but would I be satisfied staying in one place for any length of time? It was hard to say. Perhaps home wasn't any single place anyway, but rather a state of mind, a feeling of belongingness that I could experience anywhere if I let myself appreciate the similarities I shared with others—and see beyond the differences. If that were the case, I had found many homes across Canada.

Still, reaching St. John's felt horribly anticlimactic in many ways, so long had it taken me to reach its frenzied, steeply pitched streets and its multicoloured clapboard homes. They stood shoulder to shoulder in long sweeping rows, dropping toward the city's tiny harbour like the brilliant arc of a rainbow. It was hard to believe that the quaint, serpentine throughways—streets with names like Flower Hill and Pleasant Street— had once been lined with pubs and brothels that serviced tough-as-nails sailors from Holland, Portugal, Spain and Britain.

Part of me had to suppress the urge to turn around and start thumbing west. Another part of me would have been content never to hitchhike again. But such, I suppose, are the consequences of any long road trip. Travelling would never begin if one didn't feel an undeniable itch to get out and see things that one has never seen before. And it might never end if the vagaries that accompany travel didn't require some measure of sacrifice: giving up creature comforts and the need to know the details of one's day (or week) before you actually got there.

The rain continued falling over the next few days, and I passed the hours in quiet reflection. I did laundry, read a book by an American writer named Tim Brookes who had hitchhiked across the United States, and wrote e-mails to friends and family to let them know I had arrived safely in St. John's. Ben also taught me how to play a Japanese board game called *Wei Chi* in the middle of his living room floor.

In the evenings, out came Ben's guitar and fiddle, and an Australian didgeridoo—a musical instrument made from a long, hollow wooden stick—which we all took turns trying to play while Ben strummed chords on the guitar. When it was my turn, about all I could muster were a few guttural blorts that sounded something like a cow farting. I passed it along quickly, and decided that I would leave the playing of music to those with a small measure of talent.

So that's pretty much my road trip. During the forty-eight weeks I spent thumbing, I travelled nearly thirty thousand kilometres, shot more than twenty-five thousand photographs, met hundreds of people from every walk of life, dipped my toes in three oceans, ate hundreds of greasy meals at roadside diners, washed countless piles of dirty dishes and met one former prime minister of Canada (Joe Clark), who I must say is a real gentleman. And no, he didn't pick me up at the side of the road. I met him and his daughter at Discovery Days in Dawson City, and despite my scruffy appearance, he happily talked to me for several minutes about Canada and the trials and tribulations of hitchhiking through politics.

What struck me most about the end of my trip was not so much what I had seen, but all the things I had missed. Every highway branching off in this direction or that had been an opportunity passed up; every place where those roads diverged had represented at least one road that I would never see. I felt kind of sad for having missed those roads, even though none of us can travel every road at the same time, all at once.

And perhaps we wouldn't want to anyway. I suspect that a road trip, like life, was never meant to be all-inclusive. After all, it's the very nature of making choices that gives life meaning, and ultimately defines who we are. Even with the most carefully laid plans, we can never be sure where the road will lead us next. All we can do is stand at the side of the road with the sun in our face, under the arc of a double rainbow, and watch as it disappears against the backdrop of rain clouds scudding in from the west.

Epilogue

The Road Home

"We are here to help one another along life's journey."

- William Bennett

THREE YEARS AFTER finishing my trip in Newfoundland, I sat down at my desk in Canmore, Alberta to write this epilogue.

It was October of 2003. The chill of autumn had returned to the Rockies and snow already cloaked the highest peaks, creating a perfect backdrop for me to reflect on the changes in my life and the lives of some of the people I met on my trip. I have been lucky enough to stay in touch with many of them, and in some cases have even gone back to visit. That several enduring friendships were forged as a result of my trip is, in my mind, the single greatest legacy the road has offered me.

Just two weeks before I wrote this, I joined Amos D'Entrement (one of the fishermen I met in Nova Scotia) and his family in Canmore for a feast. Amos had brought with him fresh lobster, scallops and haddock, and proceeded to make the best seafood chowder I have ever tasted. Amos has been fishing his lobster boat for the last three years, and with lobster prices up, has been doing extremely well. In the aftermath of the Burnt Church fishery fiasco, the federal government has been buying lobster licenses from non-Native fishermen so that Native groups can share in the wealth. Although the simmering dispute has been resolved, prices for lobster outfits have tripled. This is great news for guys like Amos who already own an outfit—but for young guys trying to break into the industry, the cost of owning a boat has skyrocketed out of their reach.

On the other side of the country, on Vancouver Island, Stephen and Heather McPhee are now the proud parents of two wonderful children. I met their oldest son Gabriel—now a precocious five—when I was out on the West Coast taking pictures for a magazine assignment three years earlier. Happily, Stephen is no longer washing dishes for Heather at a tree-planting camp, but rather practicing law in Nanaimo, at one of the largest firms on the island. For now, Heather has dedicated herself to staying at home with their children. They see Jim and Libby Connor often, and since my last visit, windsurfing has eclipsed mountain biking as their sport of choice.

Gino Gagnon also has a new child, a two-year-old named Jeanne who is named after the heroine in Jeanne of Arc, a popular Quebec theatre production. Gino has stopped playing softball during the summer months, but has been refereeing dozens of hockey matches every winter. Nevertheless, he still hasn't come up with an alternative name for the Montreal Canadiens in the event Quebec ever separates. When I talked to Gino over the phone shortly before writing this, he said something that touched me deeply. "Since this day I met you, I realize an English person can be good," he told me. "Both of us change and we can imagine each other in a different light. It's a beautiful thing when two strangers become friends."

Steve Lawson and his wife Joanne survived the dot-com meltdown in Kanata, and were pleased when the industry started growing again. They have moved into a new home surrounded by woods near Chelsea, Quebec. Their two boys, Andrew and Justin, are in French immersion, while their daughter Gracie attends English school. According to Steve, living on his street is like a window into Canada's two enduring solitudes. Nearly everybody on his side of the street receives an English-language newspaper, while nearly everyone on the far side gets a French-language newspaper.

Ron and Jane Burnett are still milking cows in Newfoundland and working obscene hours. They are currently building a new barn that will hold two hundred bovines, more than twice as many as they have now. In 2002, they took two days off in a row and went to Rocky Harbour near Gros Morne; in 2003, they managed a sixty-hour vacation to Prince Edward Island. Jane is hoping that in a few years they will be able to get away for at least three days. As for Noah, he's now four years old and can already drive the tractor and operate the front-end loader by himself.

Not unlike Ron and Jane, Stephen and Sarah Cooper were also in building mode for some time, but have since finished their new home, which sits a couple of hundred metres up from their cottage. I have been back on two occasions to enjoy it, and have to admit that it's much warmer and drier than their initial accommodation. Stephen is still working as a doctor, and for the last few years Sarah has been working as a Manitoulin wedding photographer. She has also been teaching photography courses for an outdoor company that guides sea kayaking trips on the North Channel. Their summers are spent sailing, kayaking and canoeing with their children.

In Tuktoyaktuk, Joe Nasogaluak's Mercedes is no longer running, but he is still carving for art galleries around the world. One of his latest pieces depicts an Inuvialuit hunter who has fallen asleep at the edge of a seal hole. Joe has also started his own Arctic tour company. He takes people out with his dog team during the winter months, under the dancing aurora borealis, and teaches them how to build igloos and make traditional Inuit food while crossing the tundra on wildlife viewing excursions. More impressive, he is currently planning a self-supported expedition to reach the North Pole with his dog team in 2009, as Robert Peary's team did a century earlier. He asked me if I wanted to come along for the ride, but that is one ride I will likely turn down.

Arno Botha has also been busy. Despite the premature end of his first bike trip across Canada in 1997, he trained hard and in 1998 managed to complete the journey in just twenty-eight days. Perhaps because their lives were going in separate directions, he and Cezanne got a divorce shortly after that. Cezanne moved to Grande Prairie with their children, where she currently works in a doctor's office; their daughter Natacha lives in Calgary and is taking journalism at the Southern Alberta Institute of Technology. As for Arno, in 2001 he spent 139 days cycling from Prudhoe Bay, Alaska to Tierra del Fuego in Argentina. More recently, he has fallen in love with climbing, and is currently planning to bike from Grimshaw through Alaska, Russia and China to Mount Everest, and then climb it.

As far as anyone knows, Robb Stemp is still wintering in Southeast Asia and travelling Canada's northern highways during the summer months. Jazz passed away in 1998.

More briefly, Al MacDonald has given up the potato business in favour of opening up a small East Coast music store in Borden. He hasn't shipped a potato in two years. My uncle Lawrence and aunt Dorothy have sold most of their farm, but are still farming rented land on a limited basis. Kelly was recently diagnosed with diabetes, and for that reason he and his family have also moved to Grande Prairie. Kelly decided that farming was too difficult to make a living at these days, and with his health issues, it didn't make sense to continue.

Pierre and Lisé Mourant are also battling illness, as their ten-year-old son Patrick was recently diagnosed with hip cancer. Ever the Acadian optimist, Pierre is currently taking time off work to spend with Patrick, and to shuttle him back and forth from Caraquet to a much better hospital in Halifax. Nils Giversen, the Danish traveller I met in Fort Smith, managed to track me down through one of the magazines I work for. He returned to Denmark shortly after I met him, enrolled in documentary filmmaking and has since won several awards for investigative journalism. Finally, Everett and Christa Vander Horst, the young minister and his wife that I met on the Chilkoot Trail in 1998, have moved from Smithers, BC to Grand Rapids, Michigan. They now live only a few blocks from where my brother Rick and his family live.

And what of Renee Rabut and her family? Well, I went back to visit the Rabut game ranch in the fall of 1999, and in February of 2000 Renee came out to the Rockies to see me. We spent a couple of days laughing and joking as we had at their ranch, skiing together through fresh powder snow. Shortly after that, Renee left for China, and while working as an English teacher, fell in love with a Chinese man named Chris Lan. They were married, and are now living near her parents' ranch. With the severe drought that has decimated western Canada over the last few years, she and Chris are working hard to help her father fend off bankruptcy. Renee and Chris are also the proud parents of a two-year-old boy named Daniel.

As for my own life, it has also seen its fair share of upheaval since the end of my journey. Just before Christmas in 2001, a month after I signed a deal with a Calgary-based media company to publish this book, my father suddenly and unexpectedly passed on. It was a shock for everyone, but certainly for me, considering that I had spent the previous few years pursuing personal ambitions with great fervour. Although my father had initially voiced some misgivings about my adventures in the mountains, he had come full circle to become one of my staunchest supporters. The realization that my father will never get to read this book has been a painful cross to bear.

I am grateful, at least, that I didn't have a lot of time to dwell on this fact. As the oldest in my family, many responsibilities suddenly fell to me, including the care of my grandmother Clara in Edmonton, who was diagnosed with Alzheimer's only a month after my father's passing. I spent much of the next year travelling back and forth between my home in Canmore, my grandmother's home in Edmonton and my mother's home in southern Ontario, helping everyone to adjust.

In many ways, the experiences with my own family since my father's passing have brought into sharper focus lessons that I learned along the road. There's no question that my trip changed me. It taught me flexibility and compassion—or rather, it reinforced those qualities in me—just as it taught me courage and persistence. The road also taught me that you can't make it through life on your own.

Life is not about every man for himself on the way to the summit, as I might have been tempted to believe a few years earlier. While there is certainly a place for individual achievement in this world, to ignore the needs of others for selfish pursuits would be to waste our greatest potential. If I have learned anything of lasting value from my journey, it is that in some small way we are all connected. We all need the assistance of others at times, just as sometimes we need to be willing and ready to help others. This timeless exchange is the way of the universe, and there is great joy in realizing that fact. Serendipity, it seems, often has a purpose.

More than anything, this road called life—its winding, serpentine, unpredictable course as ephemeral as the air we breathe—is something we must celebrate and appreciate every single day.

Acknowledgements

A SPECIAL THANKS to my partner Stacey for all of her support and for inspiring me with her own life.

Thanks to my parents Bud & Sandy Jackson for their unconditional love and support, and to my siblings Rick, Jennifer and Steve for their unflagging encouragement. Particular thanks to my mother for so selflessly acting as my anchor on the road, and to Jennifer for help with French translation.

Thanks to my grandparents Bill & Norma Baird who were the grandparents every kid wished they'd had. They both offered so much of everything, and it's a great regret of mine that both of them passed away just before this book made it to print. They never did get to see this project come to fruition. Also thanks to my grandmother Clara and my step-grandfather Bob Babb for being a part of the project more directly, and for offering their lives as glowing examples of kindness and generosity.

Thanks to my uncle and aunt, Ron & Toni Jackson, who provided moral and financial support during my journey. Without their belief in my dream it would not have happened.

Thanks to Jason Hoerle, Mark & Susan Picard, Mark Halpin, Frank Creasey, Brad Mitchell and Corina Rothlisberger for providing me with food and a roof over my head when I was in desperate need.

Thanks to Mark Halpin for the use of his shadow on the cover and to Mike Vincent for the loan of his thumb, necessary for the image on page nine.

Thanks to Anette Thingsted, Pat Anger, Mark & Susan Picard, Megan Lappi and Marilyn Lappi for constructive suggestions about the manuscript.

Thanks to Alan Morantz, Laurel Aziz and Yvonne Jeffery for help with the editing, and to Curtis Foreman for saving the book from getting bogged down. Thanks to Tracy Read for help with the book's dust jacket copy.

Thanks to Kyla Kowalchuk and Sam Wolde-Micheal from Vistek in Calgary, as well as Mark Sitler-Bates and Andrew Mills at Heers in Waterloo for their skills in the film lab. Andrew also took the picture that appears on the book's title page, which he generously donated for the cost of dinner.

Thanks to Paul Chesley, Patrice Halley, Carl Hiebert, Pat & Baiba Morrow and Bruce Kirkby for giving me advice on which photographs to choose and for inspiring me with their own. Thanks also to Pat for writing the book's Foreword. Since his example was in many ways what inspired me to undertake a career in photojournalism, it seems appropriate that he should be a part of this project.

Thanks to Steve, Chris and Martin at CSM Media for their creative energies, which included help with the book's layout and the design of my web site. A huge thanks to Kirk Seton for stepping in at the last minute and designing a fantastic book. Steve also contributed financially to my cause while I wrote the book, which helped to keep me fed during the countless manuscript revisions.

Thanks to Clive Ashworth, Ron Sargent and Ivadelle Coneybeare of the Listowel post office for keeping my care packages on track and finding a box of film that went astray.

Thanks to the gang from Mirimichi, New Brunswick: Jamie Wood (Francis), Shawn Wood (Bird), Mike Wood (Spider), David Hale (Butter) and John Pineo (Little Ralph) for indoctrinating me into the ways of nicknames (they named me Snapper), and for coming up with a title for this book during a night of carousing in Fredericton.

Thanks to the many magazine editors across Canada and the United States who were either directly or indirectly involved with this project. Of particular note are Marion Harrison, James Little, Suzie Ketene, Kendra Toby, Michelle & Lionel Hughes, Eugene Buchanan and Annalee Greenberg.

Also thanks to the many other individuals who have supported my dream to become a photojournalist, including Wayne Van Sickle, Adele Frizzell, Russ Osborne, John Krebs, Larry Hoskin, Cam Owens, Kristi Tibbitt, Matt Intihar, James Taylor, Jana Tavener, Carl & Peggy Ackerl and the gang at Banff Caribou Properties.

Most of all, thanks to everybody who picked me up and took me into their homes and hearts. I've taken a little piece of each of you with me. I wish the book were long enough to include all of you. Since it is not, I've singled out a few of you that deserve more than just a passing mention. Unfortunately, that's all I have room for.

Ture & Marjorie Christiansen from Vancouver, BC
Lynn & Ann Hauer from Carmanah Point, BC
David & Shelagh Pryke from Qualicum Beach, BC
Carlene Lowes from Quadra Island, BC
Beverley Loewen and Bruce Jordan from Quadra Island, BC

Captain Norm Thomas, Fourth Mate Sander Fraser and the crew from the *Sir Wilfrid Laurier*, Canadian Coast Guard vessel

Karen Perras & Gabriel Raven from Queen Charlotte City, BC
Glenn & Linda Davies from Queen Charlotte City, BC
Scott Arnott & Samantha Bennett from Prince George, BC
Dan Lower & Brennan McCaw from Yellowknife, NWT
Andrew Morton from Yellowknife, NWT
Laurie, Sheena & Andrew Dexter from Fort Smith, NWT

A special thanks to Neil Hartling of *Nahanni River Adventures* from Whitehorse, Yukon, as well as the folks from the Nahanni River raft trip: Ben Ware, Patty Chevalier, Katy Miller, Carell Walgrave and Ray Blackport.

Mitch & David LePage of Fort Nelson, BC
Tracy Aven from Dawson Creek, BC
Teresa Keenan from Maple Ridge, BC
Urs Tappolet & Claudia Durr from Horgen, Switzerland
Jim Robb from Whitehorse, Yukon
Hugh & Mary Minielly from Belleville, Ontario
Bruce & Jane Minielly from Aylmer, Ontario
Rosie Albert & Frank Stefansson from Inuvik, NWT

A very special thanks to Patrick Schmidt, Murray Arsenault & Lorna Sampson for taking me in during an extended stay in Inuvik, NWT. Also a very special thanks to Ian Brown of Parks Canada for organizing a ride on a twin otter to Banks Island with his parks staff. It would not have been possible without his support.

Robert Earle & Roni Mould from Watson Lake, Yukon
Kendall-Ann Sullivan & Jimmy Robbins from Whitehorse, Yukon

Ron and Alison Philips from Fort Qu'Appelle, Saskatchewan
Jim Carson from Maple Creek, Saskatchewan

The First Nations group from Carry-the-Kettle reserve near Regina: Josh
O'Watch, Elton Haywahe, Bronson Haywahe, Conrad Rope, Kevin
Haywahe, Wilfrid Haywahe, Georgina McKay and Bonnie Tomahsah.

Will Chabun from Regina, Saskatchewan
Brad & Elaine Forsyth from Swan River, Manitoba
John Wilson & Cindy Armstrong from Winnipeg, Manitoba
Bayne & Jennifer Balchen from Swan River, Manitoba

All of my family from Winnipeg, Manitoba: Dave & Kathy Baird, Bonnie,
Rex and Zachary FergusonBaird, Brian & Lisa Wilcox, Helen Mohan and
Peter & Marion Hoving. And all my family in Alberta's Peace River Country
who were not mentioned: Trevor, Chrissy and Mekayla Labrecque, Dallas
Labrecque, Dustin Labrecque, Pearl Holowaychuk and Duncan & Doreen
Finlayson.

Dean Pickell from Kenora, Ontario
Shauna DéGagné from Kenora, Ontario
Doug & Sharon Alkenbrack from Kagawong, Ontario
Jeff, Gloria & Stephanie Van Alstine from Ann Arbor, Michigan
Shannon Clohosey from Tobermory, Ontario

The gang from Port Perry, Ontario, some of whom include Mark Delaney,
Scott McCoshen, Grant McCoshen, Tyler Wootton and Mike Hamilton.

Ed Donald from Peterborough, Ontario
Nancy Scheurer from Peterborough, Ontario
Jeff Prince and Mark Bedore from Carleton Place, Ontario
David & Rosemary Spendlove from Ottawa, Ontario
Rowland & Cynthia Floyd from Ottawa, Ontario
Luc Robert & Suzanne Garneau from Bolton, Quebec
Christyne and Valerie Tremblay from Chicoutimi, Quebec
Patrick St. Georges & Edith Lemieux from Montreal, Quebec
Barbara 'Babz' Robinson from Calgary, Alberta

Alan Moore and Chris Martin from *Fresh Air Adventures* in Alma, New Brunswick

Bill Ralph of *Lord's Lobster Ltd.* for the salmon in Saint John, New Brunswick

Julie Cloutier & Stephane Cyr from Digby, Nova Scotia
Brad d'Entrement from Pubnico, Nova Scotia
Dorothy Taylor from Canning, Nova Scotia
Richard & Joanne Harvey from Canning, Nova Scotia
Juanita and Rachel Robinson from Wolfville, Nova Scotia
Nigel Armstrong from Charlottetown, P.E.I.
Lynn MacInnes from St. Peter's Bay, P.E.I.
Greg & Leanne Burrows from Pictou, Nova Scotia
Kevin & Nancy Andrews from Stephenville, Newfoundland
Machelle Curtis from Corner Brook, Newfoundland
Danielle Richard from Rocky Harbour, Newfoundland
Ray Williams from St. John's, Newfoundland
Merrill Francis & Janet Russell from Tors Cove, Newfoundland

Selected Readings

Berton, Pierre. *Klondike: The Last Great Gold Rush*. Toronto, Ontario: Anchor, 1972.

Ibid. *Seacoasts*. Toronto, Ontario: Stoddart, 1998.

Ibid. *The Great Lakes*. Toronto, Ontario: Stoddart, 1996.

Brookes, Tim. *A Hell of a Place to Lose a Cow: A Hitchhiking Odyssey*. Washington DC: National Geographic Adventure Press, 2000.

DeKay, William. *Down Home: A Journey into Rural Canada*. Toronto, Ontario: Stoddart, 1997.

Ferguson, Ian & Will. *How to be a Canadian: Even if you already are One*. Vancouver, British Columbia: Douglas and McIntyre, 2001.

Francis, Daniel. *National Dreams: Myth, Memory and Canadian History*. Vancouver, British Columbia: Arsenal Pulp Press, 1997.

Gordon, Charles. *The Canada Trip*. Toronto, Ontario: McClelland & Stewart, 1997.

Grescoe, Taras. *Sacré Blues: An Unsentimental Journey Through Quebec*. Toronto, Ontario: Macfarlane, Walter & Ross, 2001.

Hawks, Tony. *Round Ireland with a Fridge*. New York: Thomas Dunne, 1998.

Kerouac, Jack. *On the Road*. New York: Penguin, 1959.

McLean, Stuart. *Welcome Home: Travels in Smalltown Canada.* Toronto, Ontario: Penguin Canada, 1992.

Mintzberg, Henry. *The Canadian Condition: Reflections of a Pure Cotton.* Toronto, Ontario: Stoddart, 1995.

Morantz, Alan. *Where is Here? Canada's Maps and the Stories They Tell.* Toronto, Ontario: Penguin Canada, 2002.

Morrow, Patrick. *Beyond Everest: Quest for the Seven Summits.* Camden East, Ontario: Camden House Publishing, 1986.

Morrow, Pat & Baiba. *The Yukon.* Willowdale, Ontario: Firefly, 1997.

Pole, Graeme. *The Spiral Tunnels & The Big Hill.* Canmore, Alberta: Altitude, 1995.

Stackhouse, John. *Timbit Nation: A Hitchhiker's View of Canada.* Toronto, Ontario: Random House, 2003.

Steinbeck, John. *Travels with Charley: In Search of America.* New York: Viking, 1962.

Stenson, Fred. *RCMP: The March West.* Nepean, Ontario: GAPC Entertainment, 1999.

Woods, John G. *Snow War: An Illustrated History of Rogers Pass.* Toronto, Ontario: National and Provincial Parks Association of Canada, 1983.

Ordering Information

IF YOU'VE ENJOYED *The Canada Chronicles*, Why not Share the Adventure with your Friends, Family and Colleagues?

Check Your Local Bookstore, or Order Here using one of these Three Easy Methods.

1. Order online at www.mattjackson.ca

2. Order Directly from the Author by e-mailing him at matt@mattjackson.ca

   Please include your full Mailing Address, and a valid Visa or Mastercard number along with the expiration date. Books are $50.00 plus 7% GST (Or $40.00 US). Canadian orders will have $5.00 added for Shipping & Handling (for the first book), and $3.00 for every subsequent book. American orders will have $7.00 (US) added to the purchase price of the first book, and $5.00 (US) for every subsequent book.

3. Write your full Mailing Address on a piece of paper. Then send it with a Cheque, Money Order or valid Credit Card number (Visa and Mastercard only) to:

   SUMMIT STUDIOS
   #105, 2572 Birch St.
   Vancouver, BC
   V6H 2T4

Books are $50.00 plus 7% GST (or $40.00 US). Canadian orders please add $5.00 for Shipping & Handling (for the first book), and $3.00 for every subsequent book. American orders please add $7.00 (US) to the purchase price of the first book, and $5.00 (US) to the price of every subsequent book.

Author's Note

ALL OF THE characters in this book really exist, and all the events really happened. In a few cases, I have changed the names of individuals to protect their privacy. To all of you who picked me up, I extend my most heartfelt gratitude. Thanks for bringing me into your homes and for sharing a small part of your lives with me. For those of you who are in the book, I hope that I have done you justice.

About The Author

A GRADUATE OF Wilfrid Laurier's Business Administration program, Matt Jackson was lured away from the corporate world by the thrill of adventure journalism while still a university student. He is now a magazine writer, photojournalist and professional speaker specializing in travel, adventure, science, conservation and human interest stories.

Matt's work has been featured widely in more than two dozen popular magazines including *Equinox*, *Explore*, *Canadian Geographic* and *BBC Wildlife*. From 1998 until 2001 he was a regular columnist at *Photo Life*, Canada's national photography magazine, and he is now a contributing editor at *Canadian Wildlife* and *Saskatchewan Naturally* magazines. *The Canada Chronicles* is his first book.